W. Arthur Lewis and the Birth of Development Economics

W. Arthur Lewis during his Princeton years

W. Arthur Lewis and the Birth of Development Economics

Robert L. Tignor

PRINCETON UNIVERSITY PRESS
PRINCETON AND OXFORD

Copyright © 2006 by Princeton University Press
Published by Princeton University Press, 41 William Street,
Princeton, New Jersey 08540
In the United Kingdom: Princeton University Press,
3 Market Place, Woodstock, Oxfordshire OX20 1SY

All Rights Reserved

Library of Congress Cataloging-in-Publication Data

Tignor, Robert L.
W. Arthur Lewis and the birth of development economics / Robert L. Tignor.
p. cm.
Includes bibliographical references and index.
ISBN-13: 978-0-691-12141-3 (alk. paper)
ISBN-10: 0-691-12141-9 (alk. paper)
1. Lewis, W. Arthur (William Arthur), 1915– 2. African American economists—Biography. 3. Princeton University—Faculty—Biography. 4. Development economics. 5. Economic development. 6. Ghana—Economic conditions. 7. Africa—Economic conditions. I. Title.

HD82.T518 2005
330′.092—dc22
[B] 2005048819

British Library Cataloging-in-Publication Data is available

This book has been composed in Palatino

Printed on acid-free paper ∞

pup.princeton.edu

Printed in the United States of America

10 9 8 7 6 5 4 3 2 1

Contents

List of Illustrations   vii

Preface   ix

INTRODUCTION   1

CHAPTER 1
Getting Started: Education and Race   6

CHAPTER 2
The Colonial Office   42

CHAPTER 3
Unlimited Supplies of Labor   79

CHAPTER 4
The Gold Coast   109

CHAPTER 5
Ghana's Chief Economic Adviser, 1957–58   144

CHAPTER 6
Ghana: Part 2   179

CHAPTER 7
The West Indies, 1959–63   212

CHAPTER 8
The Princeton Years, 1963–91   240

CONCLUSION   268

Bibliography   279

Index   303

Illustrations

W. Arthur Lewis during his Princeton years *frontispiece*

FIGURE 1. Ida Barton Lewis, Lewis's mother and probably the most powerful influence in shaping his personality   139

FIGURE 2. Lewis, graduate of the London School of Economics, 1937   140

FIGURE 3. Lewis with the League of Coloured Peoples, 1937. Lewis is in the back row, and the founder of the League, Dr. Harold Moody, is sitting in the middle in the front row.   140

FIGURE 4. Wedding of W. Arthur Lewis and Gladys Jacobs in 1947. The wedding took place on the island of Grenada, and the other adult woman in the picture is Gladys Jacobs's sister.   141

FIGURE 5. Lewis on a canoe ride on the Volta River with Kwame Nkrumah, prime minister of the newly independent government of Ghana in 1957. With Lewis and Nkrumah are Lewis's two daughters, Elizabeth and Barbara.   142

FIGURE 6. Lewis at a cocktail party with the Ghanaian minister of finance, Komla Gbedemah, with whom Lewis worked closely during his stay in Ghana   142

FIGURE 7. Lewis, vice-chancellor of the University of the West Indies, meeting with students in 1962   142

FIGURE 8. Lewis meeting with Eric Williams, the Prime Minister of Trinidad and Tobago in 1962, when Lewis was traveling around the West Indies trying to save the political federation of the islands. This meeting occurred in Jamaica, and Lewis is pictured here with his wife, Gladys.   143

FIGURE 9. Lewis receiving the Nobel Prize in economics from King Carl Gustaf in Stockholm in 1979   143

Preface

I HAVE NEVER WRITTEN a biography and had never intended to do so. Indeed, in many ways I do not regard this as a standard biography, even though it focuses on the life of the Nobel laureate economist William Arthur Lewis. I decided to undertake this study when I learned that Gladys Lewis, his widow, had deposited her husband's papers with the Mudd Library at Princeton University. Not only did I know Arthur Lewis as a colleague at Princeton University and a friend, but I had also encountered numerous references to him in my researches at the British Public Record Office in London. Lewis had been involved in many of the topics that I had researched: colonialism; decolonization; race relations; and economic development. I could not pass up the opportunity to look at all of these questions through the eyes of a man who himself came from the colonial/decolonizing world, who wrote some of the most influential essays in the new field of development economics, and who had the opportunity to implement his ideas in Ghana and the West Indies.

The reader should be aware that this study has several agendas. It concentrates on the writings and the public service of an extraordinary life—W. Arthur Lewis's—and deals only in a single chapter with Lewis's life from the moment that he joined the Princeton faculty until his death in 1991. In part this is because Lewis had articulated the core of his ideas in the essays that he wrote in the 1950s and in part because he became much less involved in public activities once he was at Princeton. The book deals at much greater length with Lewis's African experiences, even though these did not occupy the greater part of his life. They did, however, offer him an opportunity, however brief and disillusioning, to test some of his theories on economic development.

I have also emphasized the African dimensions of Lewis's life because I am an Africanist myself and a historian of colonialism and decolonization in Africa. This study is intended to be a contribution to African history as much as an overview of a life of pioneering achievement: hence, my emphasis on Lewis's relations with African nationalists and governments and my assessment of his contribution to African decolonization and economic development.

Lewis dealt with Africa on many occasions. The first occasion arose during and then just after World War II when he advised the Colonial Office and the Colonial Development Corporation, while still an academic in Britain. The African country with which he was most closely associated was the Gold Coast, later Ghana. He wrote a report on Gold Coast industrialization in 1953 and then served as Ghana's and Nkrumah's chief economic adviser from 1957 to 1958. He returned to Ghana in 1963 to offer advice on the country's Seven-Year Plan, and he was a valued consultant on the Volta River project during the 1950s when the dam was first being planned. I have examined the Gold Coast, Ghana, and the Volta River project at some length so as to be able to assess Lewis's place in this aspect of Ghana's decolonization and economic change. Lewis cannot always be at the center of the story in these African chapters if one is to provide a valid assessment of what he was able to achieve and what he could not do. I felt it necessary to describe the larger setting in some detail.

Because I am not an expert on economic development, or Ghana, or British education, or the West Indies, or, for that matter, the general debates occurring in Britain over the pace of decolonization, I have sought the advice of people who are. They have been immensely helpful and generous with their time, and I want to thank them while assuring them that any mistakes that I have made in areas of their expertise, or elsewhere, are entirely my own doing. Readers with knowledge of the subject matter will recognize the names and know their fields of expertise. In every single case, however, they went beyond the task of reading and commenting on those portions of the manuscript in which they were expert. Many of them generously commented on the entire work. I thank them profusely. Jeremy Adelman, William Baumol, William Bowen, Lawrence Butler, Eric Davis, Angus Deaton, Mark Gersovitz, Gene Grossman, Jeffrey Herbst, Harold James, Shamil Jeppie, Arno Mayer, Nell Painter, Colin Palmer, Richard Quandt, Richard Rathbone, and Stanley Stein all made this study a labor of love and displayed the qualities of collegiality that make research and scholarship such an intensely rewarding experience.

There could have been no study of this kind without the assistance of Gladys Lewis. She deposited her husband's papers at the Mudd Library of Princeton University and gave permission for scholars to use these papers. She has been supportive of this study throughout and was kind enough to meet with me on several occasions to converse about her husband, her own life, and the issues that were central to his life and work. She also helped select the photographs that appear in this volume. I devoutly hope that this study pleases her and other members of the Lewis family, whose friendship it has been my pleasure to experience. But this work is obviously not an authorized biography. It represents my interpretation of Arthur Lewis.

I am also deeply indebted to numerous libraries and archives, all of which are mentioned in the bibliography. I thank the many staffs for their extraordinary professionalism. Historians take for granted access to the rich and diverse primary source materials, located, in many cases, all over the world. We should not, since so much goes into collecting materials, preserving them, and helping researchers use them. I wish to acknowledge here the indispensable work that archivists and research librarians do in making historical scholarship possible. Finally, this is the fifth book of mine that Princeton University Press has published. Their high publishing standards are universally recognized, but I would be remiss if I did not acknowledge the encouragement that I have received during the last decade from Brigitta van Rheinberg of Princeton University Press. She handles the diverse and difficult stages of getting outside readers, guiding the manuscript through the Press's editorial board, giving advice on how the manuscript can be made better, and then overseeing the details of the final production with such enthusiasm that what could be painful and tedious becomes joyful.

W. Arthur Lewis and the Birth
of Development Economics

INTRODUCTION

WORLD WAR II SET IN MOTION radical changes around the globe, many of which W. Arthur Lewis, the subject of this study, favored and sought to accelerate. Radiating outwards from the bloody battlefields of the Soviet Union and Western Europe, the war spread its social disruption, its maiming of civilian and military populations, and its waves of death and destruction into East and Southeast Asia. Although the war began in Europe, it quickly drew Asia, Africa, and the Americas into its orbit. Large contingents of Indian, African, and West Indian soldiers were ferried across the seas and fought alongside European and North American forces. Moreover, winning this modern war entailed more than having larger, better-equipped, and better-led military forces. Victory required well-educated and loyal civilian populations, lending their intellect and their belief in the allied cause to the bravery of their military colleagues. Here, too, the contributions of civilian populations from around the globe were desperately needed. Africans, West Indians, and Indians rose to the challenge, mostly enthusiastically, to repulse the destructive ideologies and war ambitions of German Nazism and Italian and Japanese Fascism.

By war's end, new configurations of power and new attitudes toward race and wealth had come to the fore. India was the first of the imperial territories to gain independence from Europe's mighty empires after the war. Race relations were being reexamined and altered. In South Africa a Nationalist Party, seeking to resist the wind of change blowing through the world's polities, erected a system of racial separation through apartheid. Elsewhere, partly because the peoples of the world had worked together to defeat the Axis powers, political leaders rewrote racial legislation and promoted racial mixing. President Harry Truman integrated the American armed services in this period. Concerns about wealth and poverty and the distribution of income within countries and between countries, which had not been addressed during the war years, now emerged as burning political issues in all of the world's countries.

Three considerations that surfaced so forcefully in the aftermath of the war—decolonization, race relations, and economic growth—were preeminent issues in the life of W. Arthur Lewis. As a person of color who grew up in an impoverished and largely ignored corner of the British Empire, he devoted much of his academic career and public life to elucidating these matters and promoting a vision of a decolonized, color-blind, and prosperous community of independent nations. From the moment he arrived to take up his studies in Great Britain, he sought out Fabian socialists in order to share with them his understanding of the oppressive colonial forces that had led West Indian populations to riot against their colonial rulers in the 1930s. Despite many disagreements with the British Colonial Office, he joined with its officials to combat fascism and to draw up plans for a changed relationship between Britain and its colonies once the war had concluded. Physically unable to serve in the British armed forces, a graduate of the prestigious London School of Economics, and one of that institution's most accomplished young economists, Lewis soon became a fixture at the British Colonial Office. Even as it seemed that military victory was still far removed, officials in the Colonial Office set about preparing for a world that they recognized would be radically different from the colonial world over which the British had held sway before 1939. Lewis threw himself into the task of advising the Colonial Office with an enthusiasm surely intensified by the fact that he expected the postwar world to be more egalitarian, less racist, and less imperialist than the prewar had been.

World War II brought W. Arthur Lewis to the attention of members of Britain's ruling class. Even before 1939, however, he had already impressed his teachers at the London School of Economics with the perspicacity of his economic reasoning and the elegance of his ideas, which he was able to express with uncommon clarity and irrefutable logic. Although the LSE had never had a faculty member who was of African descent, Lewis's performance in class and on his thesis persuaded them that he was just the person to break the color barrier at their institution. Such was to be the pattern throughout his life. The first person of African descent to hold a named chair at a British university (Manchester), he went on to become the chief economic adviser to Ghana, tropical Africa's first country to gain its independence from European rulers after World War II. He followed this stint in Ghana by becoming the first black principal of the University College of the West Indies, the first vice-chancellor of the University of the West Indies, and in 1963 the first black professor at Princeton University. Not surprisingly, he was also the first economist of African descent to win the Nobel Prize in economics, an award presented to him in 1979.

Lewis, then, was an extraordinary man in his own right, well deserving of an intellectual biography. His contributions to the field of development economics were significant and pioneering and made him the founding figure of a wholly new branch of economics in the 1950s. His 1954 article on economic development using unlimited supplies of labor, published in *Manchester School*, was arguably the single most influential essay in this field. It was certainly one of the most frequently cited essays of the late 1950s and early 1960s. His activities with the British Colonial Office, the United Nations, the World Bank, the government of Ghana, and the University of the West Indies gave him a public presence attained by few scholars. This combination of scholarly and public factors, so movingly encapsulated in his personal papers, makes his life a prism for viewing some of the preeminent preoccupations of the mid–twentieth century. The narrative of Lewis's life provides an observer with a privileged place from which to view people of color entering the imperial center as students and pursuing careers in professions like economics where specialized training provided access to power. Lewis experienced race relations during an era when civil rights were coming to the fore; he wrote on the methods for promoting economic development when economic growth was on everyone's lips; and he held important public positions in Africa's first decolonized state, Ghana, and in the West Indies as those colonial islands seemed on the pathway to an independent political federation.

According to the historian Daniel Halévy, war is a potent accelerator of historical trends.[1] Nothing could be more true of World War II. In its wake, and far more quickly than any of the principals anticipated, white and black, colonizer and colonized, rich and poor were caught up in debates and disputes over racial justice, political independence, economic growth, and the redistribution of wealth. Under pressure from peoples of color, colonial populations, and the better-organized segments of the less fortunate part of the world's populations, ruling groups bent to these demands by altering civil codes, amending racial laws, and taking an interest in global economic development. W. Arthur Lewis was deeply involved in all of these changes. In the early part of his career, as a student and young lecturer at the London School of Economics, he came face to face with British racial discrimination. As a young man still in his twenties, he fought to open Britain's leading government institutions, notably the armed forces and the Colonial Office, to nonwhite British subjects like himself. He led British-based, West Indian delegations of the League of Coloured Peoples to the Colonial Office, demanding that the British government make its institutions accessible to all qualified candidates, not just those born of European parents. As part of this campaign, Lewis devoted a full issue of the League's publication, *The Keys*, to exposing the racism and hypocrisy of the British ruling classes who were calling on the empire to rally behind the war against Fascism and were pointing up the vulgar rac-

---

[1] Daniel Halévy, *Essai sur l'acceleration de l'histoire* (Paris, 1948).

ism of the Fascist ideology, while at the same time refusing to enroll well-qualified persons of color in the officer corps of the armed forces or in high-level Colonial Office postings.

As the war drew to a close, Lewis turned his attention to the nationalist movements that were bursting forth around the world, especially in Africa and the Caribbean, and that were destined to culminate in decolonization settlements. Lewis worked with nationalists in the Gold Coast before independence, celebrated their triumphal moment of political independence in March 1957, and then left the comfort of his prestigious academic position as a chaired professor of political economy at the University of Manchester to become Ghana's chief economic adviser and the individual charged with the responsibility for guiding the country's economic programs. Ghana seemed an ideal setting to implement formulas for economic growth. Not only did the country have a sound infrastructure and a relatively high standard of living, but its charismatic leader, Kwame Nkrumah, whom Lewis knew and admired and of whose leadership he expected great things, seemed to embody just the right mix of idealism, talent, and savvy to lead his people to political and economic successes.

Ghana proved disappointing. Nkrumah frustrated Lewis by blocking the economic adviser's initiatives. Before long, Lewis found himself sidelined and believed that he had no alternative but to leave Ghana before being compelled to resign in a public dispute that he believed would endanger other decolonizing efforts in Africa.

Departing Ghana, he went back to his homeland, the West Indies, to which he had always intended to return. Here, too, as principal of the University College of the West Indies and then vice-chancellor of the University of the West Indies, he seemed to be ideally situated to blend academics and public involvement. In his writings on economic development, Lewis always underscored the importance of education for economic development. Human resource development was to his way of thinking the key to economic development. What better opportunity could he have to foster the economic growth of his home territory than to serve as the head of the area's leading institution of higher learning? In addition, the British West Indies seemed on the verge of becoming an independent political federation, a goal that Lewis had championed since his youthful days and that he knew would buttress the mission and strength of the University of the West Indies. Nonetheless, in the West Indies, as in Ghana, Lewis struggled mightily, but with disappointing results. He kept the university from disintegrating even while the West Indian political federation failed. The effort left him exhausted and ready to take up a more serene academic position in the United States.

Racial justice and economic progress were Lewis's passions. Yet he was, at heart, an intellectual and a scholar. He spoke often of his distaste of politics. The compromises that politicians had to make to achieve their goals dismayed him. He thrived at Princeton, publishing prolifically and receiving countless invitations to offer advice to important government agencies. Yet here, too, he was drawn into swirling controversies over the place of race in higher education. His critical comments about the black power movement and its influence on young minds left some intellectuals deeply dismayed, though, in truth, they stemmed from long-held and well-thought-out perspectives on the way forward for people of color in predominantly white societies.

Although Lewis was fond of saying that he became an economist by accident, because the occupations of engineering, colonial service, and business were closed to him, it is hard to imagine that he would not have gravitated to a field so well suited to his personality and way of thinking. His was a precise mind. He was truly a child of the Enlightenment, as he liked to say, for he believed that men and women through hard study could understand the universe in which they lived and divine the laws that would lead to human betterment. It was this energy that led him to the scholarly breakthroughs in the mid-1950s, notably the article on unlimited supplies of labor and the treatise on economic growth, and again in the 1980s when he wrote about the history of economic development. These were his most important scholarly achievements. They were foundational works in the emerging field of development economics and economic history, and they made their way into the curriculum of universities. And because they were written by a man of color from the colonial world, they catapulted Lewis to the top rank of consultants, in high demand from Western governments, like Britain and the United States, as well as decolonized territories, like Ghana.

CHAPTER 1

Getting Started: Education and Race

WILLIAM ARTHUR LEWIS WAS BORN in the city of Castries on the small West Indian windward island of St. Lucia on January 23, 1915, the fourth of five sons of George and Ida Lewis. Although he spent the greater part of his adult life in England, Africa, and the United States, and only a small proportion in the West Indies, his experiences growing up in the Caribbean left an indelible imprint on his life. They imbued him with a lifelong interest in elucidating questions of wealth and poverty, power and powerlessness, and racial identity and discrimination that were deeply embedded in West Indian history.[1]

PERSONALITY FORMATION

Lewis's parents had migrated to St. Lucia from Antigua twelve years before his birth.[2] They came to an island, that, despite being part of the British Empire for more than a century, still retained much of its early French influence. Most inhabitants spoke a French-influenced

---

[1] There are a number of accounts of Lewis's life, including several autobiographical notices. More revealing than most are William Breit and Roger W. Spencer, eds., *Lives of the Laureates: Seven Nobel Economists* (Cambridge, Mass., 1986), pp. 1–20; W. Arthur Lewis, "Autobiographical Note," *Social and Economic Studies*, vol. 29, no. 4, December 1980, pp. 1–4; "Sir Arthur Lewis," in Gerald Meier and Dudley Seers, eds., *Pioneers in Development: A World Bank Publication* (New York, 1984), pp. 119–37; and John P. Lewis, "William Arthur Lewis," in *Luminaries: Princeton Faculty Remembered*, ed. Patricia H. Marks (Princeton, 1996), pp. 157–65. Excellent general overviews and appreciations of Lewis's contributions to the field of development economics may be found in J. H. Frimpong-Ansah, *Professor Sir W. Arthur Lewis: A Patriarch of Development Economics: Paper Presented at the Annual Conference of the Development Studies Association* (University of Manchester, September 1987); and Mark Gersovitz, Carlos F. Diaz Alejandro, Gustav Ranis, and Mark R. Rosenzweig, eds., *The Theory and Experience of Economic Development: Essays in Honor of Sir W. Arthur Lewis* (London, 1982). Many obituary notices appeared at the time of his death on June 15, 1991. An especially useful collection of these exists at the London School of Economics Archives (hereafter LSE Archives): *Star*, June 22, 1991; *Times of London*, June 17, 1991; *Guardian*, June 24, 1991; *Annual Obituary*, 1991, pp. 351–53; and *Independent*, June 18, 1991.

[2] University of the West Indies, *Special Awards Ceremony, July 23, 1998* (Mona, Jamaica, 1998), pp. 14–15.

Creole language and were Roman Catholics. In contrast, the Lewises were Protestants, probably originally Moravians, but in St. Lucia they became Anglicans, with a strong cultural and ideological orientation toward England. Despite their preference for English culture, or perhaps because of it, they saw themselves as a part of a distinct minority community. For the parents of Arthur and his four brothers, St. Lucia was a place to raise a family and to set their sons on a socially upward path by acquiring a first-rate English education. It was not a place where their children expected to live out their lives. It is no surprise that all of the Lewis children moved on to other parts of the world, using their intellects and their success at school to stake out careers in larger settings.[3]

The young Lewis, whose parents were originally schoolteachers, was from his earliest days a gifted student. So quick was he in his studies that when an illness required him to remain at home, three months of his father's home schooling put him far ahead of his classmates. He was advanced two full grades over classmates. This promotion proved a mixed blessing. Associating with youngsters two years and three years older and physically more mature left Lewis with "a terrible sense of physical inferiority as well as an understanding . . . that high marks [were] not everything."[4]

Although his father died when he was seven, his mother, Ida Lewis, proved equal to the task of raising the five boys. Lewis called her "the most highly disciplined and hardest working person I have ever known, and this, combined with her love and gentleness, enabled her to make a success of each of her children."[5] She inspired her children to strive for high attainments by reminding them that "we are as good as they."[6] By this she meant that her children could perform as successfully as the privileged and powerful white elite. And achieve they did. One son became a psychiatrist, another a lawyer and judge, rising to become a Supreme Court justice for the Caribbean islands, and then later governor-general of St. Lucia; and yet another an important civil servant. Arthur owed more than he publicly acknowledged to his parents and his older brothers, but especially his mother, who was in charge of his rearing from age seven on. She instilled in her sons the

---

[3] I am indebted to Vaughan Lewis, W. Arthur Lewis's nephew, for these insights into the Lewis family. Interview, St. Lucia, February 2, 2002.

[4] Lewis, "Autobiographical Note," p. 1.

[5] Ibid.

[6] Interview with Professor John P. Lewis of Princeton University, December 17, 1997. W. Arthur Lewis echoed these sentiments in his brief memoir, *Lives of the Laureates*, p. 17, when he wrote that he was an optimistic economist, "taking it for granted that anything the Europeans could do we could do."

virtues of discipline and hard work, a responsibility for making their way in the world, however hard the challenges might be, and a respect for fellow human beings. The family expected the older boys to look out for their younger siblings and to help them up the ladder of educational and occupational success.

Yet another factor in Lewis's personality formation was religion convictions. Both parents were devout Anglicans, who were unafraid to ask for crucial financial and emotional support for their children from the St. Lucian clergy. Lewis imbibed a rigorous Church of England training at home and in his schooling to the extent that later in life, though no longer a practicing Christian, his mastery of biblical texts allowed him to debate the intricacies of Christianity with Protestant and Catholic clergy and Jewish rabbis. In lighthearted moments, he claimed to prefer Indian religions among all of the world religions because of their tenets of nonviolence. Yet there can be no denying that his youthful religious and moral upbringing suffused his research, teaching, and government work. He approached everything that he did with a spirituality and reverence for life.[7]

Of Lewis, it was said that he did not suffer fools easily. More to the point, however, was a determination to fashion his own fate and not to allow others to take advantage of him or to use his talents for their purposes. These traits, too, were part of the family ethos, which Lewis did not hesitate to characterize as being suffused with "the Protestant ethic."[8] They could make Lewis hard to deal with, "prickly" as several commentators, even good friends, noted. He would not allow himself to be placed in untenable political positions, as the officials of the Colonial Office and, after them, Kwame Nkrumah in Ghana learned to their dismay. Rather than compromise ideals, he resigned lucrative and prestigious positions.

Ida Lewis also equipped Arthur with a determination not to be defeated in the face of racial discrimination, and instilled in him a highly developed sense of self-worth. His family values gave him the courage to speak his mind when he knew that he was right and circumstances were wrong. This influence, coupled with the strength of his Christian religious conviction, gave him a set of unshakeable beliefs and a personal grounding that saw him through many hard times.

---

[7] Much of the material in this paragraph and throughout this section comes from an interview with Gladys Lewis and her daughter, Elizabeth, and Hilda and William Baumol that occurred on September 1, 2004. I am deeply indebted to them for the time that they took answering my questions and the interest that they displayed in this study.

[8] Norman Girvan, "Sir Arthur Lewis: A Personal Appreciation," in *Sir Arthur Lewis: The Simplicity of Genius* (Cave Hill, Barbados, 1989), pp. 19–26.

The Lewis upbringing had its lighthearted moments as well. Lewis was no driven and obsessive upwardly mobile person, determined to get ahead at all costs. He enjoyed the amusing side of life. He had a delightful sense of humor that kept him from taking himself or life too seriously. When William Baumol, one of his closest and oldest friends, sent him a note, partly in jest, addressed "Dear Sir Arthur," Lewis asked Baumol what he had done to offend his Princeton economics colleague. His most delightful photographs invariably show him relaxed and laughing. Nor could the many trying events that he experienced over his lifetime, often the result of racial slights, wear him down. He expected life to be full of ironies and disappointments. The history of human endeavors, he noted in a letter to one of his Princeton graduate students much later on, contained mainly a record of follies and mistakes, with occasional inspired successes.

Surely, Lewis also owed his determination to succeed academically and intellectually in the larger British world to his mother's encouragement. Not only was he a brilliant student, but like all true intellectuals he lived for the world of the mind. It is difficult to imagine Lewis making his mark in politics, even though he suffered the outrages of racial discrimination as sharply as the other members of his generation. Radical politics, an arena that was becoming available to the rising West Indian intelligentsia of his generation, attracted those of a more extroverted and populist bent. In Lewis's opinion, entry into the political arena compelled its practitioners to approach matters in partisan ways, even polemically. These methods did not suit Lewis's temperament. To him, politics meant subordinating one's passion for high intellectual achievement to political successes. It often entailed ignoring the understandings attainable in scholarly pursuits to improve the lot of others for immediate and highly personal political gains.

Lewis was acutely aware of the way that his upbringing and education led him to value intellect over emotion, even to hold his emotions on a tight rein. When confronted with personal dilemmas, say racial prejudice, or generalized problems, like the economic advance of colonized territories, he approached their resolution through reason. He sought to suppress emotional responses—and generally succeeded—a characteristic that renders a biographical study of him exceedingly difficult since he allowed few to penetrate behind the curtain of ratiocination that he drew around his persona. As he came into contact with politicians, first in Great Britain, and then much more intimately in Ghana and the West Indies, he came to have many reservations about the way that they allowed their political ambitions to warp their public policies. When asked in 1959 to compose a eulogy for George Padmore, one of the West Indies's most flamboyant politicians and pan-Africanists, he spoke as much about his own temperament as he did of his fallen comrade. "We were respectful, rather than intimate friends. George was an active man of affairs, warm, pulsating, moving history along whereas I am an academic, unsure, critical, and contemplative."[9]

The Influence of St. Lucia and the West Indies

The St. Lucian white population that surrounded the Lewis family and that was in many respects its model for success was a small one. It did not regularly come into contact with the majority black population. Here, the black majority was not subject to the daily humiliations that characterized the lives of, say, African Americans in the United States. This undoubtedly made it easier for Lewis to withstand the racial discrimination that he faced so overtly in the early years of his career and that he continued to deal with later on in more subtle forms. It also enabled him to embrace a nonracial liberalism and a strong sense of his common humanity with others. It did not shield him from the acute pain of racial discrimination, especially if it came at the hands of individuals, like educated Britons and later on Americans, whom he admired and who he thought should also accept a nonracial and humanitarian view of the world.

Though small, St. Lucia, like the rest of the Caribbean in the 1930s, was a colony marked by deep fissures. Like the other Crown Colony islands of the British West Indies it was rigidly controlled by its governor and the Colonial Office. Until universal adult suffrage finally arrived in 1950–51, a small white elite of landlords, merchants, and professional classes lorded it over "an oppressed peasant proprietary class fighting to maintain its precarious existence."[10] Poised awkwardly in between was a small group of educated blacks, including the Lewis family, who were able to take advantage of increased schooling opportunities and who were drawn to the education and values of the white elite but were subject to the same color discrimination that their poor and uneducated brethren experienced.

In his pamphlet *The Negro in the Caribbean*, Eric Williams, a future prime minister of Trinidad and a lifelong friend of Lewis, sensitively describes the dilemmas, as well as the advantages, of this rising class

---

[9] The tribute appeared in the *Ghanaian Times*, September 28, 1959, and can be found in the Lewis Papers, Mudd Library, Princeton University, Box 4. On Padmore, see James Hooker, *Black Revolutionary: George Padmore's Path from Communism to Pan-Africanism* (New York, 1967).

[10] Gordon K. Lewis, *The Growth of the Modern West Indies* (London, 1968), p. 150.

of educated black men and women. Gone were the days of slavery where "the social divisions were extremely simple: at the top of the pyramid was the small handful of whites—owners and overseers; the base was Negro slaves." In place of this rigid two-tiered racial system, following emancipation in the 1830s, there had appeared a "colored middle class ... usually light skinned, well educated, professional, and urban, ... colored Europeans, in dress, ... in tastes, in opinions, and in aspirations."[11] These pioneers had, however, prepared the way for second and third generations, now farther removed from the era of slavery, less subjugated to the European world, and less ready to belittle their African roots. To this new generation Lewis and Williams belonged.

Finishing school at the age of fourteen, Lewis had to wait two years before he could sit for a competitive government examination that provided entry to a British university. He spent his time well, working as a clerk and learning "to write, to type, to file, and to be orderly. But this was at the expense of not reading enough history and literature, for which these years of one's life are the most appropriate."[12]

One West Indian historian described West Indian education and the Island Scholarship system that was at its apex and that bright lads like Lewis aspired to as "a murderously competitive regime, with pupils exercised like race horses in a steeplechase, only a chosen few could hope to win and producing in those few the well known phenomenon of the colonial Oxonian only too often made unfit, by experience, for creative service for his own community." Of the few who wiggled "through the escape-hatch from the colonial prison ... it would be difficult to estimate who was damaged the most, the winners who themselves frequently collapsed from tension and exhaustion of new studies, or the losers who gave up hope as marked 'failures' and settled down desperately into the familiar routines of early marriage, a large family, debt, and heavy drinking on the West Indian cocktail circuit."[13]

Not only was education in the British West Indies highly competitive. It was severely classical and potentially highly alienating. Lewis seems not to have been as troubled by the rigid English orientation as his fellow West Indian, Eric Williams, also an island scholar of the same generation. Writing about his schooling in Trinidad, Williams commented that "the education provided is ... woefully unsuited to local conditions. ... It is really education for the sons of the middle classes, not for the sons of agricultural laborers." The examinations that Lewis and Williams sat for tested the young scholars' knowledge of English

---

[11] Eric Williams, *The Negro in the Caribbean* (Washington, D.C., 1942), pp. 57–58.
[12] Lewis, "Autobiographical Note," p. 2.
[13] Lewis, *Growth of West Indies*, pp. 87–88 and 230.

history, English colonial history, European history, Greek history, Roman history, Latin, French, and English literature, focusing on the plays of Shakespeare and the writings of Chaucer. Williams opined: "English examinations, set by English examiners in England, are the rule."[14] Although the educational system was intensely and purposefully Anglicizing, the career restrictions that faced educated black West Indians were palpable. Williams observed that blacks "could not aspire to positions in the civil service, which were held by whites . . . whom the British up to a point associated with them in the local administration of the island." Yet Williams noted that "good students held their own with their colleagues in England and the empire."[15] Perhaps it is a reflection on the temperaments of these two men—one mercurial and profoundly political and the other contemplative and inward-looking—that Williams railed against his West Indian schooling while Lewis embraced it.

However critical young West Indian students might be of their schooling, they were aware that their education met the highest British standards. This was as true of St. Mary's College on the tiny island of St. Lucia, located in the capital city of Castries, as it was of the elite school that Eric Williams attended on the larger and richer island of Trinidad, Queen's Royal College. Lewis studied the standard subjects of British secondary education, excelling in Latin, English history, and composition. Although St. Mary's College was a Catholic school, situated on an island where French influence had once predominated and founded at the end of the nineteenth century by Father Tapon, its headmasters and teachers ardently prepared their students for life in the English-speaking West Indies and beyond. Despite the fact that the school was small, graduating only a handful of students even as late as the post–World War II era, it offered excellent training in French, Latin, English history, geography, religion, arithmetic, geometry, and algebra.[16]

Lewis's success in winning the scholarship for study at a British university did not disturb his personal equilibrium as it did so many oth-

---

[14] Williams, *Negro in the Caribbean*, pp. 75–76.

[15] Eric Williams, *Inward Hunger: The Education of a Prime Minister* (London, 1969), p. 23.

[16] Extract from the newspaper, the *St. Lucian*, 1915, vol. 1, no. 1, and 1916, vol. 1, nos. 2 and 3, supplied from the national archives of St. Lucia and interview with Vaughan Lewis, St. Lucia, February 2, 2002. Charles Gachet's *A History of the Roman Catholic Church in St. Lucia* (Port of Spain, Trinidad, 1975) provides much detail on Catholicism in St. Lucia and includes some material on St. Mary's College. Bruce King's biography, *Derek Walcott: A Caribbean Life* (Oxford, 2000), contains excellent descriptions of St. Mary's College, which Derek Walcott attended about fifteen years after Lewis had left. The school was still small, provided a highly Anglicized but excellent education, and was regarded as the best secondary school on the island.

ers. Nor did it alienate him from his studies. It did, however, create a dilemma. What should his course of study be? His fondest wish, to become an engineer and to return home to serve his community, surely reflected a pragmatic bent and a social conscience. But he crossed this off, realizing that the West Indian governments and white firms did not hire black engineers. Faute de mieux, he decided to study for a B.A. degree in commerce with a view to returning to the West Indies in municipal government or private trade.[17]

Lewis and Williams formed part of a rising black intelligentsia catapulted to island and even imperial prominence on the wave of the depression and ferocious labor protests that swept through the West Indies in the 1930s. The Caribbean's "precocious modernity" had created a highly marginalized island population that, in the words of Sidney Mintz, was "illiterate rather than non-literate; countrified rather than rural; urbanized but nearly without cities; industrialized without factories—and often agricultural without land."[18] In the 1930s the British West Indies, having experienced widespread poverty, exploded in labor violence as the decline in world prices for primary products, gradual in the 1920s, but catastrophic in the 1930s, took a heavy toll on agricultural and industrial workers. Initiated by striking sugar workers in St. Kitts and British Guiana in 1933 and followed by coal employee strikes in St. Lucia and oil workers strikes in Trinidad, labor discontent boiled over on the island of Jamaica in 1938. There the colonial government reacted to a dockworkers strike by calling in the troops. The resulting clashes left 115 workers injured and 19 dead and a British colonial government deeply distressed and confused.[19]

These outbursts of violence swept the old, mainly government-appointed West Indian conservative politicians out of power, though not all at once, and brought to the fore new leaders who drew their support from powerful trade unions and the working classes. If not before World War II, then certainly in the decade after, new politicians espousing less accommodationist political agendas became leaders in all of the islands' political movements. Men like Norman Manley in Jamaica, Grantley Adams in Barbados, Eric Williams in Trinidad, and Cheddi Jagan in British Guiana came to office in this era. They remained prominent politicians for decades. Lewis did not consider himself part of these political elite, asserting that he lacked the tempera-

---

[17] University of the West Indies, *Special Awards Ceremony*, pp. 14 and 15; and *Nobel Laureates in Economic Sciences* (New York, 1989), p. 217.

[18] Sidney Mintz, *Caribbean Transformations* (Chicago, 1974), pp. 37–38.

[19] Franklin W. Knight, *The Caribbean: The Genesis of a Fragmented Nationalism* (New York, 1990), pp. 287ff.

ment for the life of politics and preferred the introspective world of scholarship. Still, he arose in the same milieu as these political figures, and as Mark Figueroa has argued, he was a part of the West Indian "social compromise" of the 1930s and 1940s. The nationalist movement, previously fragmented into two branches—unskilled workers and peasants on one side and skilled workers and aspiring professionals on the other—fused under a banner of anticolonial nationalism, with the less educated deferring to their better-educated brethren.[20]

The Caribbean just before and after World War II drew many of its contemporaries into radical politics and culture. Given the devastating poverty and powerlessness of the area and the experience that many young West Indian intellectuals of this generation had of savage racial discrimination when they went abroad for study and careers and experienced for the first time the status of a racial minority, it is little surprising that many of them, including Lewis, were angry. The European and North American worlds at the time made sharp and damaging distinctions between their white and black populations, allowing none of the modulating gradations of color that tempered racial prejudice in the Caribbean. One should hardly be surprised, then, at the demagogic tones of Marcus Garvey's pan-Africanism or George Padmore's flirtation with communism before he committed himself to a radical form of pan-Africanism that favored a union of black people against their imperialist oppressors. Nor should C.L.R. James's celebration of the Haitian revolutionary Toussaint-Louverture in *The Black Jacobins* and Eric Williams's linking of Britain's industrial revolution with the Atlantic slave trade in *Capitalism and Slavery* be hard to understand. The French Caribbean produced equally severe assaults on Western values, including Frantz Fanon's indictment of European imperialism and his call for peasant violence in *The Wretched of the Earth*.[21] The words of the Caribbean poet Claude McKay of his first haunting impressions of white America were surely as true for those men and women from the West Indies who traveled to Britain: "It was the first time I had ever come face to face with such implacable hate of my race.

---

[20] Mark Figueroa, "Class Issues in Industrialization Policy: Lewis's Ideas and the Case of Jamaica, 1945–1956," University of Salford, *Salford Papers in Economics*, 1991, no. 1, p. 5. One should also consult Mark Figueroa, "Socio-economic Analysis and the Development of Industrialization Policy in Jamaica, 1945–1960," Ph.D. diss., University of Manchester, 1993, and the articles on Lewis by B. Ingham, published in the *Salford Papers in Economics*.

[21] There is a rich literature on Caribbean political and cultural movements in the first half of the twentieth century. This paragraph, however, owes a great deal to Winston James, *Holding Aloft the Banner of Ethiopia: Caribbean Radicalism in Early Twentieth-Century America* (London, 1998); and David Macey, *Frantz Fanon: A Life* (London, 2000).

... I had heard of prejudice in America, but never dreamed of it being so intensely bitter."[22] In light of the slights and prejudices that Lewis encountered first in the West Indies and then in more overt ways in Great Britain, it took great courage, an unshakeable sense of self-worth, and deep-seated faith in the common humanity of all men and women for him to accept and to work within well-established imperial institutions, including that most visible agency of the British Empire, the Colonial Office.

Two factors stand out in Lewis's willingness to maintain his equipoise in such a stressful environment and even to work within its established institutions. In the first place, Lewis grew up in a household that inculcated respect for all human beings and that advocated bringing about change from within. His parents also instilled in him a belief in the higher values of Western culture—its democratic ethos, those parts of its ideology that stressed the virtues of equality and fraternity, and its rationality. They believed that implicit in the tenets of English liberalism was an underlying humanism and nonracialism. On many occasions, Lewis asserted that he was a child of the Enlightenment. He believed in the power of reason and the existence of natural laws that were knowable and capable of fashioning a universe that would be just and fair for peoples of all races and religions. The second factor was growing up on a small island, St. Lucia, and not in the turbulence of Jamaica or Trinidad, from which almost all of the political and cultural radicals came. Here racial divides and economic inequalities were pronounced and glaring; in St. Lucia they were further below the surface.

THE LONDON SCHOOL OF ECONOMICS

Great Britain in the early 1930s was a shock to Lewis, although he chose to write or say little about this part of his life. Consequently, the narrative must be assembled from bits and pieces and from inference. Class antagonisms were palpable. Britain was in the throes of the Great Depression, and unemployment rates were soaring. Britons lived in a predominantly all-white world, with a tiny and politically insignificant nonwhite population, of which the Caribbean element was barely visible. As a consequence, issues of race rarely made their way into formal political and social discourse. Nonetheless, without knowing it, most Britons were deeply racialist. For them, like whites in the United States, only two fundamental racial categories existed—whites and

---

[22] Claude McKay, "A Negro Poet and His Poems," *Pearson's Magazine*, September 1918, p. 275, as quoted in James, *Banner of Ethiopia*, p. 93.

nonwhites. The latter were thought to be social and intellectual inferiors, and they were treated as such in many humiliating ways, especially in access to public accommodations. For Lewis, raised on an island that had a large black population, a tiny white elite, and many gradations of color, this sharp division of people into two racial groups was a disturbing. Like Frantz Fanon, who was unsettled when a French youngster exclaimed, "Look a Negro! . . . Mama, see the Negro! I'm frightened," so the stares that followed his movements in London made him self-conscious about his skin color.[23] An early trip to the continent, where he had an opportunity to observe the different attitudes of the French and the Danish to people of color made him even more conscious of how racially stultifying British culture was.[24]

Academically, however, Lewis's arrival at the London School of Economics in 1933 to study for a B.A. degree in commerce could hardly have occurred at a more propitious moment. The school was in the midst of a dramatic expansion under the leadership of its new director, William Beveridge, who ran the school from 1919 until 1937. Beveridge expanded the faculty and brought in a new generation of professors, many of whom had been trained at the LSE itself. He also increased the size of the student body, which, including occasional students, numbered more than three thousand in the early 1930s, of whom seven hundred came from overseas.[25] Beveridge was also a frenetic bricks-and-mortar man, of whom it was said that "he ruled over an empire on which the concrete never set."[26] Had it not been for Beveridge, Lewis could not have entered the LSE, for it was the new director who decided to establish a commerce degree in spite of considerable criticism.

---

[23] Frantz Fanon, *Black Skin, White Masks*, trans. Charles Lam Markmann (New York, 1967), p. 112; and chapter 5, "Black Skin, White Masks," in Macey, *Frantz Fanon*.

[24] See the discussion of this trip later in the chapter. A useful overview of the formation of Afro-Caribbean identity in Britain may be found in Winston James, "Migration, Racism, and Identity Formation: The Caribbean Experience in Britain," in *Inside Babylon: The Caribbean Diaspora in Britain*, ed. Winston James and Clive Harris (London, 1993). Two studies on race relations in Britain during this period are especially illuminating: J. G. St. Clair Drake's University of Chicago 1954 Ph.D. dissertation, "Value Systems, Social Structure, and Race Relations in the British Isles"; and Kenneth Little, *Negroes in Britain: A Study of Racial Relations in English Society* (London, 1947). Both works dealt at length with the black, mainly West Indian seamen community living in the port city of Cardiff, Wales, where in 1935 racial tensions and rioting called attention to the profound racial discrimination existing everywhere in Britain at the time.

[25] F. A. Hayek, "The London School of Economics, 1895–1945," *Economica*, n.s. vol. 13, no. 49, February 1946, p. 16.

[26] Ralf Dahrendorf, *LSE: A History of the London School of Economics and Political Science, 1895–1995* (Oxford, 1995), p. 142.

Beveridge's energy carried over to the economics faculty, where its new, dynamic, young professor of economics Lionel Robbins was making a mark for himself at the moment Lewis arrived. Robbins was deep into a project to rebuild an economics faculty that, in his view, was in need of "substantial overhaul."[27] Among the many significant appointments that he engineered, none was more meaningful than that of the Austrian Friedrich Hayek, who in part appealed to Robbins because his free market orientation and his anti-Marshall stance on economic analysis challenged the Keynesian approaches that were coming to the fore in the LSE's archrival for economic influence, the University of Cambridge.

Lewis was an immediate success in his studies at the London School of Economics. In 1935, his first year at the school, he won the Director's Prize for the best undergraduate essay. He gained the runner-up award for the best research paper in the next year for his essay "The Evolution of the Peasantry in the British West Indies."[28] That his professors admired his work was clear. His first-year adviser, Brian Magee, wrote of him in 1933–34: "My best student, serious and hard working and remarkably intelligent. His essays show a maturity quite unusual in a first year student."[29] Following his graduation in 1937 with first-class honors, his primary professor, Arnold Plant, head of the commerce division, recommended that Lewis be admitted to the Ph.D. program. He provided a glowing testimony. "May I say deliberately and with emphasis that Lewis is the most brilliant of all graduates whose work I have seen since I returned to the school. He is already a mature, independent, and original thinker with a quite exceptional literary capacity."[30]

The London School of Economics in the 1930s was bustling with intellectual vitality and at the center of raging economic controversies. Europe and North America were in the throes of a depression, the likes of which had not been seen for decades, perhaps never before. Politicians and the public looked to the universities to explain the present condition and to offer remedies. Alas, there was an alarming lack of consensus, and, within the economics profession, a pole of opposition arose between the Cambridge economists, led by John Maynard Keynes, who favored state spending programs and cheap money, and the LSE senior faculty, led by Lionel Robbins, and Friedrich Hayek of the Austrian school of economics, who viewed government interven-

---

[27] Alan Ebenstein, *Friedrich Hayek: A Biography* (New York, 2001), p. 59.
[28] *The Keys: The Official Organ of the League of Coloured Peoples*, vol. 4, no. 3, January–March 1937, p. 6.
[29] Ibid.
[30] Ibid.

tion in the economy with great suspicion. The London-based economists expected price and interest rate mechanisms to cure the downturn.[31] Lewis observed the debates, providing his own perspective on the issues years later when he observed that "the school had not quite caught up with Keynesianism, which was taught by the young lecturers but denied by the big names. On the other hand the school was in the forefront of the development and worldwide expansion of neoclassical economics, especially with John Hicks, Ray Allen, Nicholas Kaldor, Friedrich Hayek, and Lionel Robbins."[32] Of his own mentor, Arnold Plant, Lewis wrote that "though he was a laissez faire liberal, and I a social democrat, I am indebted to him for his incisive, no-nonsense criticism and also his supporting me at crucial moments in the appointments committee."[33]

Although many historians of this period have not been kind to the analyses that the senior economics faculty at the LSE offered of the depression, no one would deny their distinction. Lewis's adviser after the first year, Arnold Plant, was an expert on business organizations. He headed up the commerce division of the economics department and was mentor to two individuals in the 1930s who went on to be awarded the Nobel Prize in economics: Lewis and his predecessor at the LSE, Ronald H. Coase, who is often credited with pioneering the new institutional economics and who called Plant "a wonderful teacher."[34] Although Lionel Robbins had just turned thirty when he arrived at the LSE, his reputation as a dynamic lecturer and a builder of first-rate economic faculties preceded him. Friedrich Hayek, whom the LSE had brought in to introduce the free-market Austrian approach to economic theory, ably assisted Robbins.[35] There were equally lustrous names outside the mainline field of economics, and given Lewis's catholic interest, it was not surprising that he took advantage of their presence on the faculty. Lucy Mair and Bronislaw Malinowski handled sociology

---

[31] Lionel Robbins, *Autobiography of an Economist* (London, 1971), provides an excellent account of the tensions between Cambridge University and the London School of Economics. Indeed, Robbins and John Maynard Keynes were often the chief protagonists in these disputes. See the biography of John Maynard Keynes by Robert Skidelsky, *John Maynard Keynes: A Biography, vol. 2, The Economist as Saviour, 1920–1937* (London, 1992), for the specifics of the differences between these two men. Robbins expounded his views on the causes, consequences, and cures of the depression in a book entitled *The Great Depression* (London, 1935).

[32] Lewis, *Lives of the Laureates*, p. 4.

[33] W. Arthur Lewis to Arthur Seldon, November 11, 1970, Lewis Papers, Box 11.

[34] Ronald H. Coase, "The Institutional Structure of Production," *American Economic Review*, vol. 82, no. 4, September 1992, p. 715.

[35] See the chapters on the London School of Economics in Robbins, *Autobiography of an Economist*.

and anthropology. Harold Laski was already a fixture in political science, and R. H. Tawney, Vera Anstey, T. S. Ashton, and Arnold Toynbee taught courses in economic, colonial, and world history.[36] Lewis, however, focused on the economic disciplines, offering the following fields for his final B.A. exam in commerce: the principles of economics, set by Phelps Brown, Hayek, and Robbins; applied economics by Jewkes and Plant; and the economic history of the Great Powers and the British Empire by Anstey, Ashton, and Beales.[37] Although the senior faculty examined Lewis and made decisions about his future, he was much influenced by his younger colleagues, notably Nicholas Kaldor, one of his teachers, and Paul Rosenstein-Rodan. Kaldor was beginning to question the LSE critique of Keynes, while Rosenstein-Rodan was an early advocate of state-planned industrialization for less developed countries.[38]

Lewis had entered the LSE with the intention of returning to St. Lucia in some useful capacity. His credentials were impeccable. He was one of only two individuals who had achieved first-class honors among the commerce B.A. degree candidates in 1937. Although he understood that certain occupations would be closed to him, he was unprepared for the rejections that he received. The Colonial Office passed over his application to work as a civil servant on the Port of Spain city council in Trinidad, and the *Economist* would not take him into their firm as a journalist. The Colonial Office did not offer an offer an explanation and did not think it was obligated to do so. Its hiring regulations stipulated that, except in unusual circumstances, positions in the colonial service were reserved for persons of European parentage. The *Economist* was more honest. They said that they could not hire a black journalist since he would have to interview people who might refuse to see him because of his color.

Lewis never wrote about these rejections, referring to them only in the presence of individuals with whom he had a personal friendship and whom he knew to be sympathetic. Yet they left their mark. His

[36] The calendars of the London School of Economics for the 1930s provide a complete listing of the faculty and may be found in the archives of the school.

[37] Archives, 27/16.

[38] See the highly influential article by P. N. Rosenstein-Rodan, "Problems of Industrialisation of Eastern and South-Eastern Europe," *Economic Journal*, vol. 53, nos. 210–11, June–September 1943, pp. 202–11. Kaldor was also one of the young economists who was fascinated by the classical economists, as was Lewis. Nicholas Kaldor, "Alternative Theories of Distribution," *Review of Economic Studies*, vol. 23, no. 2, 1955–56, pp. 83–100. Kaldor was a dynamic teacher and had a strong influence on all those who came into contact with him, including Lewis, who was deeply moved when he learned of Kaldor's death. Information supplied by Professor Angus Deaton, Lewis's colleague at Princeton University at the time.

comments revealed a man who bristled with anger at this treatment to the point of being "obsessed with racial problems" but through it all able to maintain "his objectivity." The journalist of the magazine *West Africa* who made this observation was surely right when he noted in his 1957 essay that there were, in fact, "two Lewises," one the brilliant and highly analytical economist and the other who "feels passionately on problems of colour, so passionately that at times rationality almost goes by the board; the careful statesmanlike utterances of the economist give way to excited denunciations."[39]

When, however, the Colonial Office rejected his application to join the colonial service for posting to the West Indies, he took the advice of his LSE mentors and enrolled in the Ph.D. program there. For all of its opposition to Keynesian economics and its devotion to the free market, the LSE senior faculty setting proved remarkably supportive of Lewis on this crucial and most agonizing occasion. Considering that the Colonial Office had brushed him aside, in spite of his stellar academic credentials and his passion to serve the people of the West Indies, it would have been devastating if the faculty of the LSE had also rejected him. Whatever their political opinions, they were committed to the integrity of their profession, and they had recognized Lewis's extraordinary gifts for economic analysis. For them, race was important, not to be overlooked, but talent was far more important.

In weighing his choices for a thesis topic, rather than pursue his original choice, a study of the economics of farming, Lewis opted to investigate customer loyalties and pricing policies in firms with high overhead costs.[40] Plant served as his thesis adviser, and his study, published first in a series of articles between 1941 and 1949, appeared in 1949 as a small book under the title *Overhead Costs*.

In 1938, while Lewis was still working on his thesis, the LSE staff took what at the time was a momentous decision. It invited him to join the faculty, apparently as its first black staff member. That the step was taken only after extended discussions indicates how sensitive the issue of race was and how radical the authorities thought their action was. So that they might extricate themselves should the appointment prove embarrassing, the school offered Lewis a post as a temporary one-year assistant in the economics department. The decision to hire a black fac-

---

[39] This material comes from a portrait entitled "Realistic Radical," in *West Africa*, October 12, 1957, p. 965, written by an obviously well-informed journalist. A roughly similar description of these events comes from the journal *Spotlight: Monthly Caribbean News Magazine*, March 1959, vol. 20, no. 3, pp. 9–12. It is of some interest that both correspondents who gained this inside information were likely to have been persons of African descent.

[40] Student dossier, W. Arthur Lewis, LSE Archives.

ulty member was referred to the highest authorities, making its way to the director, A. H. Carr-Saunders, who would ordinarily not have taken an interest in such a junior hire. In a letter to the head of the Board of Governors committee, Lord Stamp, the director indicated that Lewis would lecture and take classes as proposed by the professors of economics (Plant, Robbins, and Hayek), but he would not do any advising. "He [Lewis] would therefore not see students individually but only in groups. The appointments committee," Carr-Saunders added, "is, as I said, quite unanimous but recognize that the appointment of a coloured man may possibly be open to some criticism. Normally, such appointments do not require the confirmation of the Governors but on this occasion I said that I should before taking action submit the matter to you." Stamp agreed, adding that "it is just the kind of experimental and terminable appointment that is so valuable in a case like this."

In his letter offering the appointment to Lewis, Carr-Saunders removed the statement "but you will not be required to give any personal supervision to students under the first year advisory system," fearing that it would give offense. Lewis accepted with alacrity, promising to uphold the high standards of instruction for which the LSE was justly famous. Although he made no comment about the discriminatory terms of his hiring, his typically understated later account of this moment in his career revealed that he knew he was being discriminated against. He simply stated that at the time of his first appointment there was some fuss over his race.[41]

As a teacher Lewis was an immediate success. The school did not terminate him after his first year, but advanced him to the rank of assistant lecturer and extended to him a four-year contract. Moreover, the fears, expressed by senior staff, that British students would hesitate to work with a black man proved utterly unfounded. Moreover, as Lewis's obligations to the British government increased during the war, the LSE staff had to insist that he turn away advisees so that he could devote all of his LSE time to teaching the department's basic economics courses.[42]

The outbreak of World War II deprived the LSE of many faculty members.[43] Health reasons prevented Lewis from joining the British

---

[41] The entirety of this story and the later one on Lewis's relations with the University of Liverpool come from the Staff File of W. Arthur Lewis at the London School of Economics Archives. I am grateful to the school for allowing me to see these important and confidential records.

[42] W. Arthur Lewis to Carr-Saunders, April 1, 1943, Lewis Staff File, LSE Archives.

[43] The director, Carr-Saunders, turned down a request for Lewis's services from the Board of Trade in 1940 on the grounds that his teaching was vital to the LSE. Without

armed forces; they did not deter him from assuming a heavy teaching load at the school. Originally, Lewis's primary teaching responsibilities were concentrated in the field of transportation. But because he demonstrated great skill in exposition and an easy familiarity with a vast body of economic literature, he took on additional lecturing responsibilities. His teaching assignments soon included the introductory courses in economics and business economics. He also began to offer lectures on the evolution of the interwar economy in Europe and North America, which included a discussion of the Great Depression.

Lewis's critical role in the school's teaching did not go unnoticed by senior members of the staff. Hayek wrote the director about Lewis's "anomalous" position on the faculty. He argued that Lewis deserved an "exceptional promotion" since he was doing the work of senior members of the department "and doing it with conspicuous success." In Hayek's view, Lewis was "one of our best teachers," who, at the least, deserved formal recognition in the form of a teaching citation, for "uncommon versatility and by his teaching, ranging over practically the whole field of economics."[44]

Lewis's lectures on international economics were particularly well attended by students from Asia, Africa, and Latin America, who often asked their lecturer to deal with the issues of development that were of special interest to them.[45] Lewis responded by offering a course in colonial economics in 1943–44, the first such course to appear in the calendar of the LSE.[46] By 1947–48, his teaching of the economics of colonial territories had found a formal place in the curriculum of the school, so that when Lewis was promoted to the rank of reader in that year, he was given the title of reader in colonial economics.[47] Lewis's presence at the London School of Economics did not place the LSE ahead of other British universities in the teaching of this field. In 1946, Oxford University announced the appointment of S. Herbert Frankel as professor of colonial economic affairs. Many other institutions in Britain and the United States followed this lead in quick succession.[48]

---

him the school would be "unable to offer the teaching facilities which appear in our program." Carr-Saunders to G. S. Barley, November 14, 1940, Lewis Staff File, LSE Archives.

[44] F. A. Hayek to Director, June 3, 1941, Lewis Staff File, LSE Archives.

[45] Lewis, "Autobiographical Note," p. 3.

[46] London School of Economics, *Calendar*, 1943–44, p. 171, LSE Archives.

[47] London School of Economics, *Calendar*, 1947–48, p. 15, LSE Archives.

[48] Gerald M. Meier, "The Formative Period," in *Pioneers in Development: A World Bank Publication*, ed. Gerald M. Meier and Dudley Seers (New York, 1984), p. 8, n. 14.

Lewis's course on the economies of colonial territories represented a curricular breakthrough at the LSE, although the course materials that Lewis assembled at this stage were quite rudimentary and lacked theoretical readings. Previously the economics faculty had confined their teaching to standard economics courses (money and banking, the business firm, and the principles and theory of economics), supplementing these courses with topics in economic history that focused exclusively on British and European economies. Courses dealing with the rest of the world, particularly the colonial world, were taught in the history and anthropology departments.[49]

Lewis owed a great deal to the London School of Economics, perhaps more than even he was aware, though he had only praise for his instructors and their courses. The technical training that he received at the LSE was outstanding. By the 1930s, the school's standing in the field of economics had come to equal that of the University of Cambridge, which until then had been recognized as the preeminent institution in the world for the study of theoretical and applied economics. At the LSE Lewis benefited from exposure to some of the most outstanding advocates of liberal capitalism. His three main mentors and major undergraduate examiners, Lionel Robbins, Friedrich Hayek, and Arnold Plant, were dynamic teachers. Their flair as classroom lecturers was exceeded only by the time they devoted to their Ph.D. candidates. Although Lewis balked at what he regarded as an uncritical acceptance of free markets and price mechanisms and found encouragement to explore less market-oriented emphases from younger faculty, like Nicholas Kaldor, and fellow students, who were influenced by the Keynesianism of the University of Cambridge, he never discounted the power of profit motives, price signals, and free markets in any of his economic treatises.

Lewis would have read in his undergraduate studies Robbins's classic text on economics, *An Essay on the Nature and Significance of Economic Science*, originally published in 1932 and revised in 1935. Robbins's oft-cited definition of economics as "a study of the disposal of scarce commodities" found numerous reverberations in Lewis's own writings, as did Robbins's and Plant's insistence that the most effective way for a society to decide on how scarce commodities and resources were to be allocated was through the operations of price mechanisms in free market economies.[50]

---

[49] This paragraph is based on reading the *Calendars* of the London School of Economics for the 1940s.

[50] Lionel Robbins, *An Essay on the Nature and Significance of Economic Science* (London, 1935), p. 38.

Lewis's indebtedness to the nineteenth-century British economists and his knowledge of their works, apparent in nearly everything he wrote, but especially in *The Theory of Economic Growth*, also owed much to the teachings of Lionel Robbins, who regularly delivered powerful lectures on the classical economists in the 1930s, finally published in 1952 and revised in 1977.[51] While conceding that the examination of the history of economic thought had become "a very unimportant embellishment as inessential to the economist as the history of chemistry is said to be inessential to the chemist,"[52] Robbins insisted that Adam Smith, David Ricardo, Thomas Malthus, and James and John Stuart Mill had grappled with many of the same problems and policy issues that troubled contemporary societies and provided answers that continued to be relevant—an observation that Lewis had no difficulty accepting.

The ambience of the school held even deeper significance for Lewis. It confirmed his deep-seated belief, originally instilled in him in his childhood, that reason, liberal and rational discourse, tolerance of other people's of points of view, and moderation in all matters of the mind and emotion, however difficult these qualities might prove to adhere to in the face of unreasoning prejudice, were cherished ideals. Lewis admired the openness of his mentors and gratefully acknowledged the key roles that they played in his early career. Thus, already at this early moment in his career, exposure to the faculty and student body at the London School of Economics strengthened Lewis's beliefs in a middle way, to be maintained in spite of personal provocations and anguish.

Lewis's Early Publications in International Economics, Business Economics, and Planning

Publishing was hardly a decisive requirement of the academic establishment of the LSE at this time. Yet the school's faculty had a plethora of distinguished scholars, with enviable publications records and international reputations. Although Arnold Plant was not a prolific writer, Robbins and Hayek were. Laski, Malinowski, Tawney, Toynbee, and many others were luminous figures, whose publications gave them in-

---

[51] Lionel (Lord) Robbins, *Theory of Economic Policy in English Classical Political Economy* (London, 1978, but first published in 1952); and Lionel Robbins, *A History of Economic Thought: The LSE Lectures*, ed. Steven G. Medema and Warren J. Samuels (Princeton, 1998).

[52] Robbins, *Theory of Economic Policy*, p. 2. Lewis's magisterial *The Theory of Economic Growth* has numerous references to the work of economic historians. He regularly cited R. H. Tawney, who taught at the LSE, and Arnold Toynbee, a faculty member at the University of London.

ternational reputations. Lewis followed in their footsteps and sought from the outset of his career to acquire an international reputation through his writings. Although he was only in his late twenties and early thirties, his robust teaching obligations entailed lecturing in three distinct fields of economic specialization. These were the business firm, international economies, and development economics, or as he and others at the time named it, colonial economics—in all of which he managed to make immediate scholarly contributions.

Lewis's first publication as a faculty member was a set of essays for advanced high school students, *Economic Problems of To-Day*, published in 1940. Although the book was intended for the nonspecialist who "would like to have some knowledge of the economic problems which loom so large in contemporary discussions," it nonetheless contained in simplified form and language the core arguments that he later developed into his important and more scholarly work, *Economic Survey, 1919–1939*.[53] In this essay Lewis compared the economic systems of Britain, France, Germany, the United States, and Russia, arguing that the basic test of any economic system, capitalist or communist, unregulated or regulated, was entirely a pragmatic one: whether economies used resources "as fully as possible and to the best advantage," as Lionel Robbins always insisted. The key to economic success depended on the use of property. Economies that placed property "in the hands of those persons whose incomes vary directly with the efficiency they apply to their job" would be the most successful.[54] In this regard, Russia's managed economy was no different from the capitalist economies of the West. Managed economics, too, as the Communist leaders learned often through bitter experience, had to operate according to the iron laws of supply and demand.

Lewis's mentors, Arnold Plant and Lionel Robbins, had encouraged their protégé to write *Economic Problems of To-Day*. The book also grew out of a set of lectures on the international economy that Hayek had pressed Lewis to undertake. Lewis maintained an interest in the subject throughout his life, publishing the more scholarly work, *Economic Survey, 1919–1939*, in 1949 and then its sequel, *Growth and Fluctuations, 1870–1913*, in 1978. According to Lewis, the 1949 treatise was based on a course of lectures that he had been giving at the LSE between 1944 and 1947 "out of [which] has grown as the reader will see for himself an over ambitious attempt to interpret the interwar years in the setting of world economic history." Here, too, Lewis claimed that the study was not meant for professional economists but rather "for students of

---

[53] W. Arthur Lewis, *Economic Problems of To-Day* (London, 1940).
[54] Ibid., p. 40.

about a second-year level and the interested lay public." To make the work accessible to this larger audience, Lewis "banned" all footnotes.[55] In spite of his disclaimers, the study remains today the single best overview of these tumultuous years.[56]

Compared to his earlier *Economic Problems of To-Day,* Lewis dealt in greater detail and more economic sophistication with the interwar years, focusing much of his analysis on the Great Depression. He set for himself the task of understanding why this depression had proved to be so much deeper, longer lasting, and widespread than earlier depressions and why it had produced such severe declines in investment, banking crises, high levels of indebtedness, and massive unemployment. Drawing on his Caribbean perspective, Lewis gave his interpretation of the depression a non-Western focus. He stressed the importance of a decline in agricultural and raw material prices in 1930 that had prepared the way for the disintegration of the international monetary mechanisms in 1931. For Lewis the depression was deep and long lasting because Europe and North America had created a world capitalist system that lacked appropriate international instruments of control and regulation. Hence, a stock market collapse in the United States set off a chain of worldwide repercussions that the banking institutions and the main business organizations in the world could not cope with.[57]

Critical for Lewis, even though his individual chapters focused on the major industrialized countries in the world economy (Britain, France, Germany, Japan, the United States, and the Soviet Union), was the place of less developed economies in the world economic order. His text contained numerous references to non-European countries (Egypt, Colombia, China, Venezuela, Brazil, Manchuria, South Africa, and Turkey), not merely because Lewis identified with their plight, but because in his view they played a major role in the economic downturn of the industrialized parts of the world. Lewis observed that the twelve most industrialized countries of the world purchased 74 percent of the primary products put into world trade and also exported many of their manufactures to the less developed economies of the world. Hence a decline in the prices paid for primary products would result in a slowdown in the growth of the export trade of the developed parts of the world and increase unemployment all over the globe.[58]

---

[55] W. Arthur Lewis, *Economic Survey, 1919–1939* (London, 1949), pp. 9–10.

[56] That, at least, is the opinion of Professor Harold James of the Princeton University history department. See also Harold James, *The End of Globalization: Lessons from the Great Depression* (Cambridge, Mass., 2001), esp. pp. 104 and 105.

[57] Lewis, *Economic Survey 1919–1939*, p. 56.

[58] Ibid., pp. 149–55.

Lewis's second field of teaching and research was the business firm, the area of his undergraduate specialization. He published a steady stream of articles between 1941 and 1949, drawn from his dissertation chapters, which he published in revised form under the title *Overhead Costs*. In the latter publication, Lewis acknowledged the help that he had received from his dissertation director, Arnold Plant, praising him for his "inspiration, fresh insights, and much happy disputation."[59] The book examined firms that supplied basic services, like water and electricity, and that had large fixed costs and differential rating systems for recovering these costs. Some firms, notably electricity and gas companies, charged two sets of fees. Peak hour users paid higher fees, while those who consumed the services at off-hours were offered lower rates.[60] Other firms gave discounts to loyal customers, while still others refused to supply their services unless consumers agreed not to buy elsewhere.[61]

In a concluding chapter, the only one that had not been previously published, Lewis tackled a question that was central to his expanding research interests in development economics and international economic history, the conclusions of which would shape his later activities as a writer and consultant on colonial questions. He weighed the merits of public versus private ownership of quasi-monopolistic enterprises. He did not rush to the defense of the public ownership of public utilities, as one might have expected from a person with strong Fabian socialist beliefs, but took an equivocal position. The arguments for public ownership were that it was more democratic and efficient and promoted the public interest more effectively than private ownership. Yet "half a century of municipal enterprise and twenty-five years of public corporations have proved little more than that public operation has both advantages and disadvantages." A skeptic at all times, Lewis concluded that public corporations needed to be made "accountable to the public for their actions." Otherwise they would be run by a few individuals and would be delivered "into the hands of a tyranny more deadly than has ever been conceived."[62]

Although most of *Overhead Costs* had more to do with the field of industrial organization than with Lewis's other two research interests (international economics and colonial economies), these articles and

---

[59] W. Arthur Lewis, *Overhead Costs: Some Essays in Economic Analysis* (New York, 1949), p. 5.
[60] Ibid., p. 9.
[61] Ibid., pp. 44 and 70.
[62] Ibid., pp. 181–82.

the book revealed Lewis's technical and analytical skills.[63] They represented breakthroughs at the time and proved remarkably prescient. His essays on two-part tariffs and imperfect competition questioned much of the conventional wisdom and offered more efficient ways for companies, like utility firms, to employ differential rating structures to cover large fixed overheads and to realize fair profits. The essays were highly regarded at the time, stimulating other studies that soon superseded his contributions. In the late 1940s, however, they were state of the art and formed the basis of his reputation as one of the brightest young economists of his generation.[64] Reviewers praised the book, and one later commentator, when asked what qualified Lewis for the Nobel Prize in economics, other than his famous 1954 article, singled out *Overhead Costs*, calling it a jewel of economic reasoning.[65]

The third of Lewis's teaching and publishing preoccupations was economic planning, in which Lewis published a third work in 1949, a banner year in his publishing career. The study resulted from an unfavorable reaction to a paper that Lewis presented on inflation and the measures to overcome it at a Fabian Society conference in 1947, for which, he states, he was "roundly abused." He said to the secretary on the conference: "'You really ought to commission a study on the problems and pitfalls of administering a mixed economy.' 'Why don't you do it,' he [the secretary] said, and after thinking about the subject for a little time I agreed to do so."[66] Although *The Principles of Economic Planning: A Study Prepared for the Fabian Society* was meant to be a guide for the British Labour Party as its members undertook the nationalization of British industries, almost overnight and unexpectedly, from

---

[63] Joseph Stiglitz mentions that Lewis was still drawing on this work in his Princeton courses in economic development in the 1970s and 1980s. See Joseph Stiglitz, "Comment on 'Toward a Counter-counterrevolution in Development Theory,' by Krugman," in *Proceedings of the World Bank Conference on Development Economics* (Washington, D.C., 1992). Stiglitz in note 4 on page 42 writes: "Krugman seems to be unaware of the work that originally established Lewis's reputation as an economist (see, for example, Lewis 1949 [*Overhead Costs*]) the importance of overheads (non convexities and increasing returns) which he stressed throughout the 1970s and 1980s in courses on development economics at Princeton."

[64] I am indebted to Professor Mark Gersovitz for these insights. Professor Gersovitz, who now teaches in the Economics Department at the Johns Hopkins University, was a close friend and colleague of Lewis when the two were on the Princeton University faculty. Professor Gersovitz shared with me many valuable impressions of Lewis as a person and a scholar during a day-long interview on May 23, 2003.

[65] William Baumol, interview, September 15, 1998.

[66] "W. Arthur Lewis," *Lives of the Laureates: Thirteen Nobel Economists*, edited by William Breit and Roger W. Spencer (Cambridge, Mass., 1995), p. 6.

Lewis's perspective, the work caught on as a primer for any kind of state-planned economic development. Colonial officials and anticolonial nationalists alike read it with interest because they believed that, despite its brevity, it offered a program for planning the economies of Asian and African countries.

Although Lewis described the pamphlet as addressed "exclusively to the problems of Great Britain in the year 1948," it clearly had a much larger purview. It drew on the storehouse of experience that Lewis had accumulated over nearly a decade providing advice on the economies of the developing world.[67] The first of the factors that influenced the publication were the lectures on colonial economies that he delivered originally during the war at the LSE and that he continued to offer even more frequently when he moved to the University of Manchester in 1948. Equally important were his activities as a consultant to the British Colonial Office, where in the latter stages of the war he evaluated many of the draft plans for postwar colonial economic development.

A third influence was even more decisive, for it reflected all of the thinking, lecturing, and writing that he devoted up to that time on the future of his native lands, the West Indies. In 1944, Lewis had published *An Economic Plan for Jamaica*, and five years later, in 1949, he served as a consultant to the four-nation Caribbean Commission that made recommendations for Caribbean-wide development projects. As he had insisted in *Economic Problems of To-Day*, wasting resources was the greatest of economic sins. Lewis believed that the projects being recommended by the Caribbean Commission, though well meaning, lacked an overall plan. He feared that the funds earmarked for Caribbean development would be "frittered away on a number of schemes, mostly unrelated," which when terminated would leave the colonies "with a structure of social services beyond their capacities to meet from their own resources."[68] He favored closely coordinated projects that would, in the first instance, generate economic progress and lead to the rising income levels and larger tax revenues that would enable governments to find the resources for the much-desired social services.

Not surprisingly, *The Principles of Economic Planning* placed Lewis in the forefront of an evolving group of scholars dedicated to investigating the problems of economic development in colonial and previously colonized territories. To this point the field hardly existed. If it had a name, it carried the more prosaic term "colonial economics," which

[67] Ibid.
[68] W. Arthur Lewis, "An Economic Plan for Jamaica," *Agenda: A Quarterly Journal of Reconstruction*, vol. 3, no. 4, November 1944, p. 154.

Lewis had employed when offering the first such course at the LSE. As Lewis himself indicated, this field owed its inception to the demands of colonial students and prospective colonial officials, who having come to the major universities of Britain to acquire skills that they could carry to these territories, expressed dissatisfaction with the thoroughly European and North American orientation of their training. In the context of the 1950s and 1960s, by which time the field of development economics had acquired a solid place for itself in the curriculum of economics departments, *The Principles of Economic Planning* would not have attracted much attention. The only part of the text that dealt with colonial areas was an eight-page appendix, entitled "On Planning in Backward Countries." Yet a work written by an intellectual from the Caribbean, laying out the techniques of planning and highlighting the advantages and pitfalls of state intervention in economic affairs, aroused great interest and brought attention to its author among colonial government officers and nationalist leaders, both eager to promote the economic development of their territories.

Lewis commenced *Principles* by conceding that the free market was a powerful engine of economic progress. Still, he wondered "whether state control could do better either as alternative or as a supplement."[69] As usual, Lewis worried about waste and misuse of resources, problems that seemed even more compelling for countries that could not afford to misuse resources in their efforts to catch up to the developed nations. Lewis did not believe that markets and prices were infallible mechanisms for distributing goods and services, guaranteeing living wages, handling foreign exchanges, and coping with major structural economic changes. He concluded his introductory chapter with a ringing affirmation: "We are all planners now."[70]

Lewis was under no illusion that planning was a panacea. It could be "inflexible" and was certainly "imperfect"; it could also have a "stifling effect on the direction of enterprises."[71] The growth of large civil bureaucracies worked inherently against democracy. Since neither the people nor parliament could plan, only a small cadre of technicians would. Hence, a few individuals could exercise great unchecked economic power. For Lewis the proper balance between the private and the public was "to preserve free markets wherever possible," confining the operations of the state to regulating markets and prices, especially through the use of tax codes, subsidies, and exchange rates.[72] Price con-

---

[69] W. Arthur Lewis, *The Principles of Economic Planning: A Study Prepared for the Fabian Society* (London, 1949), p. 8.
[70] Ibid., p. 14.
[71] Ibid., pp. 17–18.
[72] Ibid., p. 20.

trols and rationing were desirable only as temporary measures, to deal with short-term problems and to be removed as quickly as possible. Indeed, the principal vehicle for state planning was the state budget, which used taxation rates and the state as consumer to influence the actions and decisions of the private sector.

Although Lewis thought of himself as a socialist who favored equality as a social good, claiming that no man was worth £10,000 a year, he also believed that some income inequality was needed to reward hard work and skill. Taxation and monetary policy were the best instruments for redistributing income, achieving full employment, and checking inflation and deflation.

The primary reason for planning, according to Lewis, and especially in less developed economies, was "to achieve a much higher level of income" than is possible in an unplanned society.[73] Planning could create levels of investible funds that would not occur if investment depended on the voluntary savings of private individuals. On the basis of his work in economic history, Lewis asserted that "domestic savings are always insufficient in a country which seeks to achieve rapid progress."[74] Only the state can insure the requisite savings rates of 15 to 20 percent of national income that are vital to rapid economic progress.

In Lewis's appendix, where he dealt with "backward countries," the author argued that planning was "much more necessary and much more difficult to execute" than it was in developed economies.[75] The dilemma was that planning required "a strong, competent, and incorrupt administration." This is "just what no backward country possesses, and in the absence of such an administration it is often better that governments should be laissez faire than that they should pretend to plan." Often governments can hardly carry out "the normally accepted functions of government," such as roads and schools, filtered water, electricity, and public health.[76] What the state can do is "to arouse the enthusiasm of their people for new knowledge and new ways of life,"[77] and what they must do is to effect an agricultural revolution even if this requires breaking up the estates of large and powerful landlords.

Lewis was unprepared for the groundswell of praise and criticism that greeted the publication of the book. He should not have been because planning had become such a catchword among politicians and

---

[73] Ibid., p. 52.
[74] Ibid., p. 53.
[75] Ibid., p. 121.
[76] Ibid., p. 122.
[77] Ibid., p. 123.

social scientists. Britain's Labour Party was nationalizing the country's major industries, and British and French colonial governments were being pressed to produce five- and ten-year documents. In Latin America Raúl Prebisch and other highly regarded economists were extolling the virtues of closed and planned economies, and even political scientists and economists in the United States, the bastion of free market economics, held up the Tennessee Valley Authority as an example of planned economic growth. Condemned on the left as not sufficiently enthusiastic about planning and even as antiplanning, on the right as excessively government-centered, and embraced by economic planners in colonial territories as a sure guide to planning, Lewis drafted a new preface in July 1951 when the book was reissued in 1952. In it, he argued that the study was never intended to be a full-scale book since the Fabian Society had "asked for a pamphlet on the economic perplexities and this is what I set out to write."[78] Lewis also used the new preface to disavow the impact that the book had generated among scholars and persons concerned with planning. The book, he insisted, was "not as its title suggests, an academic study of theoretical principles, but is rather a political statement." Lewis reminded his readers that he had written the treatise in the summer of 1948 to cover "some topics which happened to be of special interest [at the time]."[79]

Taken in their entirety, Lewis's publications during and after the war up to 1949 revealed a person struggling to find a middle ground. His socialist predilections made him an advocate of regulated economies. So did his ties with the Fabian intellectual elite of Britain. Yet his liberalism and belief in the value of individual initiatives, some of which must have been pounded into him at the LSE, caused him to see the problems that powerful, centralized state institutions could cause for personal freedom and economic progress. Extreme inequalities repelled him, but he was no egalitarian. He believed that men and women needed profit incentives to produce their best work.

In 1947 Lewis married Gladys Jacobs. The daughter of a headmaster from the island of Grenada, Jacobs had gone to London to pursue university training, where she completed a teaching degree and became a teacher in government schools during the war. She had introduced herself to Lewis at one of his public lectures on colonial development after the war, mentioning that the two families knew each other. Their parents had similar backgrounds in education, and both had migrated to their present locations from the island of Antigua. Later, they married

---

[78] Preface for the third impression of *The Principles of Economic Planning* (London, 1952), p. 1 of an unnumbered preface.
[79] Ibid.

on Grenada. On many later occasions, Lewis remarked that he owed much of the equanimity that he possessed as a public figure to the loving support that his wife and their two daughters gave him. Elizabeth was born in 1949, and Barbara in 1951.

RACE IN LEWIS'S EARLY CAREER

Race had been a factor in Lewis's first appointment to the faculty of the London School of Economics. Race continued to impinge on his career at this stage. He wrote frequently about race during his London days and did so with obvious passion. He also protested against racial discrimination with intensity and extraordinary personal courage. Having been brought up to believe that individuals should be judged by their works and their attainments, he felt deeply the slights that were part of his day-to-day existence in London. Yet, as was his custom, he kept much of the hurt within himself. Only when he was with close friends and able to relax was he willing to "recount the incidents when he has experienced colour discrimination. . . . Every such incident, a sensitive listener will feel, has wounded him, even if he can be so understanding about colour prejudice."[80]

Just as the London School of Economics was brimming with intellectual excitement when Lewis entered its doors as a student, so the West Indian immigrant community in the British Isles was alive with intellectual disputations and political vitality. West Indians living in London at the time, many of whom associated with Lewis at one time or another, were nothing less than an aristocracy of talent. Among those whom Lewis knew was C.L.R. James, who was just discovering his latent West Indian nationalism and Marxism and was in the midst of studying and writing about that hero of West Indian nationalism, Toussaint-Louverture. Another of Lewis's London companions was George Padmore, like James an avowed Marxist and a pan-African activist, who had been involved in the Communist International. Amy Jacques Garvey, the second wife of Marcus Garvey, was promoting her husband's pan-African vision, and fellow student Eric Williams was making his mark at Oxford University in the same fashion that Lewis was advancing at the London School of Economics. Although Paul Robeson was not a West Indian, he was a powerful presence within this group, a man whom C.L.R. James succeeded in persuading to play the role of

---

[80] This observation comes from a remarkably personal and informative interview conducted by the staff of the journal *West Africa*, October 12, 1957, p. 965.

Toussaint-Louverture in the play that preceded the publication of James's classic work, *The Black Jacobins*.

All the same, ideological preferences divided this overseas West Indian community of students and intellectuals. Lewis, with his humanism and belief in the inherent goodness of humanity, found no appeal in the strident Marxism of some of his friends. Nor did he admire the Soviet Union the way that Padmore, James, and Robeson did at this stage in their lives. Even their shared belief in pan-Africanism revealed differences, for Lewis was less drawn to the trade unionist and Marxist orientation of Padmore and his colleague I.T.A. Wallace-Johnson.[81] Yet he eagerly joined them in the formation of the International Friends of Ethiopia, which was founded in 1935 to protest the Italian invasion of Ethiopia. He, too, worked to bring educated Africans into the pan-African movement and saw the invasion of Ethiopia as providing an ideal rallying point.[82]

Lewis's closest associates, however, came from a group of West Indians resident in Britain who looked to Dr. Harold Moody and his League of Coloured Peoples for their sociability and their political inspiration.[83] As was common among new immigrants to Britain, Lewis sought out the companionship and advice of other West Indians as soon as he arrived in London. He found a warm welcome in Dr. Harold A. Moody's home. Moody was the head of the League of Coloured Peoples, a predominantly West Indian organization, and was a dynamic figure in the still small West Indian community living in the British Isles. A Jamaican, born in 1883, he had received a medical degree from the University of London. The League that he was so instrumental in organizing provided social outlets for the West Indian com-

---

[81] See the discussion of the calling of the Pan-African Congress that met in Manchester in 1945 and that involved the two wings of the Pan-African movement—the conservative wing as represented by Dr. Harold Moody of the League of Coloured Peoples, including at that time W.E.B. DuBois, and the radical Marxist element, led by George Padmore—in Penny Von Eschen, *Race against Empire: Black Americans and Anti-colonialism, 1937–1957* (Ithaca, N.Y., 1997), pp. 45–53.

[82] For descriptions of the West Indian community residing in London during the 1930s, see in particular Peter A. Hill, "In England, 1932–1938," in *C.L.R. James: His Life and Work*, ed. Paul Buhle (London, 1986); James R. Hooker, *Black Revolutionary: George Padmore's Path from Communism to Pan-Africanism* (London, 1967); C.L.R. James, *Beyond a Boundary* (London, 1963); and Williams, *Inward Hunger*.

[83] See Immanuel Geiss in *The Pan-African Movement*, trans. Ann Keep (London, 1974), especially chapter 17, entitled "Conservative and Radical Pan-Africanism in England (1934–9): Harold Moody and George Padmore." In analyzing what Geiss considered to be the two most important political and intellectual pan-African strains in Britain at the time, he points out that both tendencies were energized by the Italian invasion of Ethiopia, but Moody's League of Coloured Peoples remained committed to a Christian, nonracial approach.

munities throughout Britain, sponsoring dinners, dances, and celebrations of various kinds. It also engaged in political action, particularly following the Italian invasion of Ethiopia, when it began to work energetically to call attention to problems of racial discrimination while always espousing racial harmony.[84]

During the 1930s, the League published a journal, entitled *The Keys*, named for the Reverend J. Aggrey's famous analogy of the piano and its black and whites keys. According to Aggrey, one could play simple tunes on the piano using only the black or the white keys, but a concerto was possible only by making use of both sets of keys. *The Keys* was the most visible organ of West Indian immigrant opinion in Britain at this time, and it is not surprising that the young Lewis became its most effective writer and editor. He assumed responsibilities for editing the journal in the mid-1930s and used it not only to publicize West Indian issues but also to awaken the West Indian community to alliances that it could form with Africans living in Britain.

In one of the issues in 1937 Lewis called attention to African problems. Lewis's article entitled "African Economic Problems" described the evils of uncontrolled and unregulated industrialization, which had brought misery to England during the industrial revolution and was also threatening to impoverish the African continent. Industrialization itself was not the villain. Rather it was "a reckless quest for wealth, leaving others to reap a rich harvest of vice and woe." In Africa the countries that were moving in the most distressing directions were dominated by European settlers. Lewis feared that the Rhodesias and Kenya were likely to follow the same pathway that had led South Africa to solidify white power and privilege at the expense of the black population.[85]

Lewis's articles on race in *The Keys* are the most passionate and articulate of all the essays that appeared in the journal in this decade. In addition, they offer a rare and intimate glimpse into the racial experiences of a man who throughout his life was intensely private, rarely permitting outsiders to penetrate his innermost feelings. Reviewing Margery Perham's book *Africans and British Rule*, Lewis spotted pas-

---

[84] A useful treatment of racial prejudice against West Indians living in Britain and the place of the League of Coloured Peoples in combating it may be found in Laura Tabili, *"We Ask for British Justice": Workers and Racial Difference in Late Imperial Britain* (Ithaca, N.Y., 1994). Lewis took an active part in the League's political activities in the British seaports of Cardiff and Bristol, where a large number of West Indian sailors resided. The narrative of these events can be followed in the journal of the League of Coloured Peoples, entitled *The Keys*. See particularly *The Keys*, vol. 3, no. 2, October–December 1935.

[85] W. Arthur Lewis, "African Economic Problems," *The Keys*, vol. 5, no. 1, July–September 1937, p. 16.

sages and attitudes that revealed what he surmised were Perham's underlying paternalistic and racialist biases toward African peoples. The Perham review has a hard edge to it that is markedly different from most of Lewis's other writings, even those on race. Although Lewis had solicited financial support from Perham for the League and its journal, he spared nothing in his criticism of the book. "However inferior we [black people] may be," Lewis wrote, "however barbarous, inferiority and barbarity cannot justify the admitted exploitation of our people in all the areas where Europeans are firmly established." He went on in the same vein: "To Miss Perham it is from his own savagery that the African needs protection; white exploitation is to be seen merely as the inevitable if unfortunate accompaniment of the effort to civilize him."

Lewis concluded the review on a remarkably sour note. *Africans and British Rule* is not even "good propaganda," he wrote. "Good propaganda identifies itself with those whom it addresses. But Miss Perham writes from the heights of her civilized eminence to the depths of our savagery. The book is not merely smug and self satisfied; it reeks of that self-conceit which typifies the colonial Englishman and which is doing more than anything else to poison the relations between the races. From the prosperous seclusion of Oxford it is easy to ride the high horse of cultural superiority, to belittle the wrongs of a people and magnify their faults. The book will go down well in the Colonial Office; it will please the settlers and doubtless be subsidized by one or two colonial governments. Africans fortunately are accustomed to being insulted. They will merely hope that Miss Perham will have learned a little manners before she settles down to write her next apology for imperialism."[86] These statements from a twenty-six-year-old, decidedly junior faculty member at the LSE are remarkable indeed.

Equally revealing was his article describing a visit that he had made to the European continent in 1936. As a shy, young overseas student in London, Lewis admitted to being unnerved by the stares that accompanied his every movement. These had made him "extremely self-conscious." Paris was a relief. There no one paid him any heed. "It took some time to grow accustomed to an atmosphere in which I was no longer the great center of attention." But if Paris was liberating, Denmark was a revelation. There, instead "of the supercilious stare which

---

[86] League of Coloured Peoples, *Newsletter*, September 1941, pp. 128–29. In the next issue of the *Newsletter*, October 1941, M. M. Green, a distinguished British anthropologist with numerous professional interests in Africa and a friend of Margery Perham, wrote to the journal in criticism of the Lewis review. Lewis held his ground, however, asserting that he "did not expect my review to please Miss Perham's friends any more than the book itself pleased me" (p. 8).

you got in London, Cardiff, or any of the seaport towns of Britain, you get a smile of welcome." This was at first surprising because, unlike the English and the French, the Danes did not live alongside persons of African descent as the British and French did. By most conventional reckoning, they should have done the gawking at a person with black skin. He concluded that the Danes were free of racial prejudice because they had neither a powerful navy nor colonies and consequently were able to live in a "true democracy."[87]

In an earlier issue of *The Keys*, Lewis had directly tackled the question of European racism and had concluded that it stemmed from nothing more exalted than an unbridled and amoral pursuit of economic gain. Denying that race prejudice sprang from ignorance as some apologists claimed, Lewis pointed out that blacks had lived in Europe for hundreds of years. They had proven themselves "to be both harmless and cultured." On the contrary, prejudice was "the result of a deliberate policy, executed for sound economic reasons. Colour prejudice is the active expression of the theory of racial superiority and the foundation and modern excuse for imperialism." Empires existed, Lewis claimed, to provide cheap raw materials and cheap labor and to ensure Europeans with high living standards. "But the methods by which this is achieved—forced labor, taxed labor, 'alienation' of native land, compulsory cultivation—are so barbarous that empires would not be allowed to exist unless both the exploited race and the Europeans at home were taught to be docile—were duped with the theory of civilizing backward peoples." For Lewis, at least at this stage of his career, empires and racial discrimination went hand in hand. The closer one got to "the scene of exploitation—the colonies," the more virulent became the racist ideologies.[88]

A final story of overt race discrimination rounded out Lewis's early career in London. Recognizing that his prospects for promotion to the rank of professor could not be realized because the senior positions in the economics faculty at the London School of Economics were held by relatively young faculty, not soon to retire, Lewis applied for and was recommended by the selection committee for the prestigious Chaddock Chair of Economics at the University of Liverpool. Although he was the unanimous choice of the selection committee, his appointment was challenged over the issue of race. Even Carr-Saunders's glowing recommendation that "few appointments which have been made in my time at the School have been better justified" failed

---

[87] *The Keys*, vol. 4, no. 1, July–September 1936, p. 21. He did, of course, overlook the important role that the Danes had played in promoting the Atlantic slave trade.
[88] *The Keys*, vol. 3, no. 3, January–March 1936, p. 30.

to persuade J. F. Mountford, Liverpool's vice-chancellor, who took an active interest in the search.[89] While conceding that Lewis had established a first-rate reputation as an economist, Mountford, in writing to Carr-Saunders, a fellow Liverpudlian, worried about "other considerations than high academic standing." The vice-chancellor pointed out that the situation in Liverpool was quite different from that at the London School of Economics. Not only would Lewis have to deal with a less sophisticated and worldly-wise business community, but he would have to teach all the economics students enrolled in the university. In London, students had the option of attending other universities. In Liverpool they did not.[90]

Carr-Saunders maintained his support of Lewis, observing that while he could not make any final prediction about how the appointment would turn out, "short of the existence of any colour prejudice such as nothing could get over, I should have thought that he [Lewis] would have done well in this sort of outside work at Liverpool."[91] Mountford remained unconvinced, and despite the continuing support of the selection committee he rejected their nominee. In a most demeaning fashion, he suggested to Lewis that he visit Liverpool several times during the next academic year so that the faculty, students, and community could get to know him. Admitting that he was tempted to show the vice-chancellor just how wrong he was, Lewis recoiled from the proposal that he visit "so that the public may be able to look at me and decide whether they can stand my appearance."[92] Carr-Saunders concluded that the opposition to the appointment did not arise from the local business community, which the director knew to be liberal, but from within the university community itself.[93]

Manchester did not make the same mistake that Liverpool had. In 1946, following the departure of J. R. Hicks, the noted economist, for Oxford University, the vice-chancellor, John S. B. Stopford, oversaw the search for Hicks's replacement. In light of the fact that the faculty had already appointed a senior lecturer in Hicks's field of economic theory, the members of the selection committee decided to conduct their search "without restriction" on field. Their interview with Lewis convinced the committee members that he was the outstanding candidate. They offered the position to him, and he immediately accepted.

[89] Carr-Saunders to Stanley Dumbell, Registrar, University of Liverpool, May 14, 1947, Lewis Staff File, LSE Archives.
[90] J. F. Mountford to Carr-Saunders, May 19, 1947, Lewis Staff File, LSE Archives.
[91] Carr-Saunders to Mountford, May 21, 1947, Lewis Staff File, LSE Archives.
[92] W. Arthur Lewis to Carr-Saunders, July 4, 1947, Lewis Staff File, LSE Archives.
[93] Carr-Saunders to W. Arthur Lewis, July 14, 1947, Lewis Staff File, LSE Archives.

The choice of Lewis had powerful implications for the teaching of economics at Manchester. Although the selection committee recognized his all-round competence in economics, noting that he had taught courses at the London School of Economics in general economic theory and in "industrial problems," they also observed that he had won a Leverhulme Fellowship to do research in the West Indies, where he had been collecting materials "for a projected volume in the economic history of the region since the abolition of slavery."[94]

Lewis found the Faculty of Economic and Social Studies a congenial setting. The economics faculty's long-serving and prestigious professor John Jewkes preferred to operate by consensus. He encouraged the other three professors (Michael Polanyi, Ely Devons, and Lewis) to take part in all the decisions, meeting with these men every Wednesday morning to discuss departmental matters. They were a busy group, implementing a program to expand the faculty of economic and social studies by sixteen new faculty positions in less than a decade.[95]

When Jewkes moved to Oxford as the chair of Economic Organization, Lewis took his place as the Stanley Jevons Professor of Political Economy and the Cobden Lecturer.[96] Under Lewis's leadership, Manchester rapidly emerged as the leading place to study development economics in Britain. He and his colleagues, Ely Devons, a specialist in economic statistics and applied economics, and Kurt Martin (né Mandelbaum), whose book *The Industrialization of Backward Areas* put forth the idea of unlimited supplies of labor, created "what was probably one of the first specialist postgraduate programs in development, establishing what has since become the standard curriculum in courses of this kind."[97] Lewis's course, entitled "The Theory of Economic Development," was the core offering in this curriculum. It featured the most important books on economic development, including P. T. Bauer's *West African Trade*, Lewis's *Theory of Economic Growth*, W. W. Rostow's article on the takeoff into sustained economic growth, selections from the writings of Joseph Schumpeter on economic change, and

---

[94] Minute of November 13, 1947, Senate Minute Book, vol. 60, University of Manchester Archives.

[95] Minute of December 11, 1947, Minutes of the Senate, vol. 29, and W. A. Lewis to the Vice-Chancellor, June 8, 1948, VCA 17/357, 2/3, Economic and Social Studies in the University of Manchester Archives.

[96] Minute of October 14, 1948, Senate Minutes, vol. 30, pp. 123–124, and Report of the Council of the University of Manchester to the Court of Governors, 1949, p. v, University of Manchester Archives.

[97] E.V.K. Fitzgerald, "Kurt Mandelbaum and the Classical Tradition in Development Theory," in *Strategies of Economic Development: Readings in the Political Economy of Industrialization*, ed. Kurt Martin (London, 1991), p. 11.

Colin Clark's book *Conditions of Economic Progress*. Lewis described the course as an examination of "the causes of economic progress, stagnation, decadence, and decay."[98]

. . .

The early years growing up in the West Indies and studying and teaching in Great Britain left a deep imprint on Lewis and shaped personality traits and intellectual activities that stayed with him throughout his life. The son of upwardly mobile school-teachers, he took advantage of the escape hatches that the West Indies system of education afforded to persons of exceptional intellectual merit. Unlike some of his peers, he did not allow the ferocious academic competition to gain a West Indian government scholarship or the many overt acts of racial discrimination and the daily routine of bias that his generation of young intellectuals experienced to rob him of his humanity. He continued to believe in and work for liberal, evolutionary change. Radical approaches held no appeal. Although he was profoundly aware of the injustices of colonial rule and could be as caustic about them as any of the critics of colonial rule, he was nonetheless prepared to work within the imperial system in hopes of making it more responsive to the needs of the colonized. In turn, at a time of rapid and wrenching imperial transformation, the colonizers were prepared to seek the advice of this educated man from the colonies. His mastery of a field of economic knowledge vital to the colonizers made him immensely attractive to the colonial elite. Yet he desperately wanted to use his skills to advance the cause of racial and political equality; he assuredly did not want to yoke his talents so that Europeans could solidify their power over non-European peoples.

Even at this early stage, Lewis's life abounded in contradictions and tensions, clearly manifested in his writings. He struggled to articulate a middle position between the free market economics that he learned at the LSE and the planned and regulated economies that John Maynard Keynes had made appealing and were attracting political leaders and economists in many parts of the world. He could hardly have known in the 1940s that Europe's imperial mandate would run out in the decade of the 1950s, so his willingness to advise officials who administered an empire that he regarded as grossly exploitative of colonized peoples and extremely racist was fraught with personal anxieties. He blanched at racial discrimination but believed that liberal and rational measures could persuade men and women of goodwill that

[98] Prospectus of General Information, 1956–57, University of Manchester Archives.

their racial views were misguided. Nevertheless, he could not avoid the worry that his belief in liberal reform was naively unrealistic and that racial biases were too deep-seated to yield to rational argument or that his own merits as a young economist would be ignored. These tensions came to the fore and his beliefs were put to the test when he agreed to become a consultant with the Colonial Office in the 1940s.

CHAPTER 2

The Colonial Office

DATING THE BEGINNINGS OF DECOLONIZATION in British Africa cannot be done with exactitude. Some would argue that decolonization was always on the agenda of the colonial rulers, especially the British, since their officials expected colonial territories to go the way that the American colonies had in the 1770s. Robert Pearce has identified the late 1940s as the "turning point" in African colonial thinking, timed to the rise of the Gold Coast nationalist movement and to the labor riots that swept through the major Gold Coast cities in 1948.[1] There is little doubt, however, that World War II sharply accelerated the planning of British officialdom for an Africa that would have an altered political and economic future and for placing Africa's nonsettler territories on a fast track to independence. During this decade of feverish activity, W. Arthur Lewis was intimately involved in commenting on and drafting many of these plans.

Viewing decolonization through Lewis's career makes it clear that the outbreak of World War II was a decisive turning point for imperial relations. The British were required to call on imperial resources, including colonial troops, as they had during the First World War, to defeat a powerful foe. To rally support at home and around the world, they compared Britain's commitment to freedom and democracy to the fascists' autocracy and repression. In their colonial territories, they spared no effort to publicize the vile racist visions of the Nazis, and they promised an improved, less autocratic form of colonial authority after the war had been won. Many critics of colonialism took this as pure propaganda, certain to be discarded once the military victory had been secured. Others did not. African nationalist leaders, mainly supportive of the allied war effort during the war, were emboldened at its close to intensify their demands for greater economic and political autonomy. They found an ally in Britain in Lewis, who believed that under the right circumstances and with prodding from liberals and socialists in Britain and nationalist critics in the colonies, British officials could be persuaded to live up to the higher ideals of colonial authority.

---

[1] Robert Pearce, *The Turning Point in Africa: British Colonial Policy, 1938–1948* (London, 1982).

The British perspective accorded with his sense of what rightly guided liberal democracies were capable of achieving. Thus, he was more than willing to make his talents available to a war effort that pitted, in his view, the forces of civilization battling barbarism, even, if called upon, to collaborate with that instrument of colonial domination, the British Colonial Office.

Indeed, from the late 1930s until 1953 Lewis had frequent contacts with the British Colonial Office, first as a member of West Indian delegations seeking to alter the hiring policies of the British government and after that as an adviser and consultant on projects designed to promote colonial economic development. Later in his life he shuddered as he recalled the arrogant and snobbish ways of the officials at the Colonial Office. He would not deny, however, that his work at the Colonial Office had been pivotal for his career as a development economist. During this decade and a half, he often found himself battling with the Colonial Office over development priorities. Still, he remained a much sought after expert whose memorandums on development and planning produced both admiration and criticism and invariably stirred debate.

Despite the strained personal and intellectual relations with officials at the Colonial Office, Lewis's experiences with the Colonial Office provided privileged access to information on colonial economies and spurred his thinking and writing about development economics. Lewis first elaborated many of his most influential concepts in the field of economic development and staked out his reputation as the founder of development economics through the countless reports and memorandums that he wrote for the Colonial Office. Many of these documents, some of them not published, are still not well known to economists. Access to published and unpublished materials at the Colonial Office enabled Lewis to review nearly every five- and ten-year development program that the colonial governments produced during the war and immediately after it. The titles of his Colonial Office memorandums, such as "Principles of Economic Planning," were often the same as those he chose for the formal essays that he later published.

Lewis and the Colonial Office drew together during World War II, a time when the European imperial powers were reevaluating their relations with colonial territories and had begun to realize that the end of the war would bring changes in the international balance of power, a growth in nationalist sentiments, and demands for political freedom. At the least, metropolitan attitudes toward empire would require adjustment. While Lewis and Colonial Office officials were hardly aware that formal colonialism was in its last stages, they knew that the authoritarian and highly paternalist policies that had once prevailed would have to be altered. As a person of color, trained in "colonial economics," and holding a position at the London School of Economics and later a prestigious professorship at the University of Manchester, Lewis had impeccable credentials for advising on these issues. Throughout the decade in which his contacts with the Colonial Office were intense and colonial nationalist movements were gaining in intensity (1943–53), Lewis agonized over what he regarded as the slow pace of political and economic reform. He chafed at the frequent sacrifice of effective programs for colonial development on the altar of metropolitan well-being. He was especially distraught about white settler areas, like Southern Rhodesia and Kenya, where colonial administrators seemed destined to replicate the experience of South Africa, safeguarding white privilege at the expense of the black majority.

Lewis and the Moyne Commission

Lewis's contacts with the Colonial Office did not begin auspiciously, however. It is some measure of the man's talent and his desire to find a middle ground as well as the shrewdness of the Colonial Office that these early relations did not poison the atmosphere between them. Lewis's first dealings with the Colonial Office occurred, fittingly, during the investigations of the West Indies Royal Commission, known as the Moyne Commission, after Lord Moyne, who headed it. The commission, created in 1938 by the British Parliament, was charged with the task of investigating the labor agitation, strikes, and clashes with the police that had swept through the West Indies during the 1930s and that had culminated in a series of bloody confrontations between police and labor organizers in Jamaica in 1938. Lewis had first come to the attention of leading Fabians in Britain when he wrote an essay elucidating the underlying causes of what to an alarmed British public seemed a stain on the country's imperial mission. Thus, having already written about West Indian conditions before the Moyne Commission came into being, Lewis, not surprisingly, submitted his own memorandum to the commissioners and requested an interview. The Colonial Office responded that since the commissioners had already left for the Caribbean, it would not be possible to grant him an interview. It forwarded his written report.[2]

Lewis's seventeen-page, single-spaced document went over familiar ground. He expounded on the extreme poverty of the West Indies, which he believed was the root cause of the labor discontent, re-

---

[2] T.I.K. Lloyd to W. Arthur Lewis, September 28, 1938, Records of the British Colonial Office, Public Records Office, London (hereafter PRO CO) 950/56.

marking that "there can be few places in the world which touch the depths of West Indian poverty or show so little progress." Much of this poverty Lewis attributed to the low prices for the West Indies' major exports of sugar and bananas. He chided the British government for refusing to pay a premium for these products, especially in light of the contribution that the Caribbean had made to British prosperity in the eighteenth century when slavery flourished. He compared Britain's hands-off economic relationship with its Caribbean possession unfavorably with that adopted by the French and Americans, both of whom provided protected markets for the major exports of their West Indian possessions. No matter, he concluded, developing an argument that he was to return to over and over again in his writings, raising the prices for West Indian exports would be a weak palliative. The only long-term solution for an area that had already a large population and a relatively efficient agricultural sector was industrialization, which was possible, in his view, only if accompanied by a radical program for redistributing income from the inordinately rich to the large number of impoverished—a situation that he also regarded as a "legacy of West Indian slavery."

Lewis did not limit his discussion to economics. Political and social concerns also underlay the violence. Only suffrage reform would break the power of the small, white, ruling elite that inhibited the redistribution of wealth and blocked true economic development. Lewis also put forward a concept that he was to champion throughout his life: a West Indian political and economic federation. At this stage he favored a union of Trinidad and Tobago, Barbados, the Windward and Leeward Islands, and possibly British Guiana. Jamaica and the Bahamas would have to remain outside the federation until a better-developed system of ocean and air transportation shrank the distances that separated them from the rest of the British West Indies. An additional and indispensable benefit that would flow from political and economic amalgamation would be the weakening of the position of "small local potentates fearful that their voices, all powerful in a small island, will be unheard in a large federation."

Predictably, Lewis was savage in his criticisms of the Moyne Report when it was published in an abridged form in 1939. The Colonial Office had decided to hold back the full report until 1945 lest its many criticisms of the colonial system arouse antagonism to Britain in the United States and further inflame West Indian sentiment at a time when Britain's control of this strategic area was of military importance. The main recommendation of the Moyne Commission was that the British government establish a West Indian Welfare Fund that would be financed through the British Treasury by annual grants of £1 million for a period of twenty years. This fund would be used to improve education, public health, and housing and to promote moderate leaders in the trade union movement. In the economic sector, the report favored, on the one hand, "an intensification of the agricultural system through a reorientation in the direction of mixed farming, with the greater home production of essential foodstuffs and on the other to take whatever steps are practicable to improve the position of agricultural exporting industries."[3] The commission claimed that the West Indies were primarily agricultural territories and that improvements in standards of life depended on "the intensive use of the soil." Finally, the commission spoke against both of "the extreme proposals put before us for the grant of immediate and complete self-government based on universal suffrage, or for the wide increase of the authority of Governors which would convert the existing system into a virtual autocracy."[4] The commission did recommend closer economic and political ties among the islands, although it did not believe that the West Indies were yet ready for political federation.

Lewis's chief objection was that the report was weak on economics and that its one, paltry reference to the West Indies' prospects for industrialization was negative. He objected to Moyne's claim that the industrial prospects for the West Indies were not bright. Not only did the islands have cheap energy sources but, in Lewis's opinion, they also had vital raw materials and easy access to the rich consumer markets of North and South America. What the area lacked, namely skilled manpower and investable capital, could be overcome by encouraging skilled personnel and capital to come from the outside.

In Lewis's opinion, the Moyne Commission Report had many other defects. It was not attentive to the educational dimension of economic development. In educational resources, the British West Indies lagged far behind Cuba, Haiti, Santo Domingo, and Puerto Rico, all of which had universities. He faulted the Moyne commissioners for failing to recommend the establishment of a university for the West Indies, the foundations for which were already in place. The Imperial College of Tropical Agriculture at Trinidad could be expanded into a faculty for the study of the natural sciences. Likewise, Codrington College in Barbados could become a college of arts and sciences, while Jamaica could become the center for the study of engineering and medicine. Al-

---

[3] West India Royal Commission, 1938–39, *Recommendations, House of Commons Sessional Papers*, 1939–40, cmd. 6174, vol. 5, p. 18. The full report was not published until 1945. West India Royal Commission, 1938–39, *Statement of Actions Taken on the Recommendations, House of Commons Sessional Papers*, 1944–45, cmd. 6656, vol. 10.

[4] West India Royal Commission, 1938–39, *Recommendations, House of Commons Sessional Papers*, 1939–40, cmd. 6174, vol. 5, p. 25.

though the later development of the University of the West Indies diverged slightly from these recommendations, Lewis's suggestions for building on already existing schools were prescient.

Lewis concluded his critique with comments on social tensions, which he thought had been ignored. Above all, Moyne had omitted any discussion of the long history of West Indian slavery, which had stamped its imprint on the islands' social makeup. "That pattern was a society in which a handful of peoples owned most of the wealth while the vast masses laboured in poverty on the property of the minority." Only if the British governors made education and public health widely available, empowered trade unions, and redistributed wealth would the power of the monopolists be broken and the West Indies find its way out of poverty.[5]

Lewis's criticisms jolted the Colonial Office, all the more so because its officials resented the fact that Lewis had published his objections rather than shared them privately with the Office. Even though Sydney Caine, the top economic expert at the Colonial Office, agreed with many of Lewis's observations, he challenged Lewis's claim that the West Indies possessed natural advantages for industrial development.[6] Thus, Lewis's first interventions in the debate about the political and economic future of colonial territories, in this case the British colonies in the West Indies, stressed the economic dimensions of West Indian development, in line with the Moyne Report, but were hardly silent about the political context. Lewis favored a political federation that would be based on democratic elections and would proceed quickly to a considerable degree of political autonomy.

LEWIS, THE LEAGUE OF COLOURED PEOPLES, AND THE COLONIAL OFFICE

A second area of contact between Lewis and the Colonial Office boded even less well for their future relationship. Having been spurned by the Colonial Office for employment, Lewis joined with the League of Coloured Peoples to protest the British government's barriers to hiring persons of color. This was an especially contentious and emotional issue for the League since the son of its president, Dr. Harold Moody, was himself seeking employment in the British armed forces and experiencing many problems.

---

[5] Lewis's critique of the Moyne Commission Report may be found in a document submitted by the League of Coloured Peoples in PRO CO 318/445/47.

[6] Minute by Sydney Caine, May 29, 1940, PRO CO 318/445/47. The document that criticized the Moyne Commission Report and was written by Lewis was formally sub-

The League's approach to the Colonial Office could not have come at a more propitious moment for the West Indians. The British Government had declared war on Germany and had launched a propaganda campaign against the Nazi regime, with particular emphasis on Germany's racialist policies. It now found itself in the awkward, if not to say hypocritical, position of denying military commissions and Colonial Office appointments to colonial subjects. Moreover, at a time when the British needed to draw on all of the resources of the empire to battle the German military machine, restrictions against commissioning colonials were not just offensive; they were self-defeating.[7]

The war was not more than a month old before the League sent a delegation, headed up by President Moody and including Lewis, to meet with the colonial secretary on behalf of four colonial subjects who had applied for commissions in the British army.[8] One of the applicants was a Southern Rhodesian who wished to join the army. Two others were West Indian doctors who sought officer status in the medical corps. The fourth was Moody's son, who, according to an internal Colonial Office note, was "so outstandingly suitable for a commission on every possible ground (except his colour) and moreover has all the standard qualifications (including certificate "A") that he [Dr. Moody] has been pressing this case as hard as he can as a 'test case.'" The War Office, however, admitted to being "up against the practical difficulty of where they can possibly place him without giving rise to all the reactions which have of course always been lurking in the background."[9]

The League delegation must have had some impact because within weeks the four applicants were given commissions. But the War Office and the Colonial Office refused to treat these appointments as test cases or to issue a formal declaration against discrimination in the armed services. Moody and the others from the League had demanded in December 1939 that the British government endorse their statement "that there should be no discrimination in government appointments (whether civil or military) on the grounds of colour, caste, or creed."[10] They did, however, pry from British officials a statement that British

---

mitted on behalf of the League of Coloured Peoples and published as a *Parliamentary Paper*, cmd. 6174, May 1939.

[7] David Killingray provides a useful overview of this issue in "Race and Rank in the British Army in the Twentieth Century," *Ethnic and Racial Studies*, vol. 10, no. 3, July 1987, pp. 276–90.

[8] No. 1, Moody to Malcolm MacDonald, November 8, 1939, PRO CO 323/1692/4.

[9] Minute by J. J. Paskin, November 9, 1939, PRO CO 323/1692/4.

[10] No. 30, Note of Discussion between the Secretary of State and a Deputation from the League of Coloured Peoples Held at the Colonial Office on December 14, 1939, PRO CO 323/1692/4.

subjects and protected persons living in the United Kingdom would be eligible for voluntary enlistment in the armed forces and for consideration for the grant of *emergency* commissions on the same footing as British subjects in the United Kingdom. But these commissions were not permanent. They would lapse when the emergency was over, that is to say at the end of the war. At this time, these men would be decommissioned and the old practice of limiting commissions to persons of European parentage would be reinstated.[11]

Even before the issue of the commissioning nonwhite officers in the British armed forces had come to the fore, the League had raised with the Colonial Office the question of the eligibility for colonial service of persons whose parents were not Europeans. Employing colonials was already a complicated and disputatious issue, made even more so in 1930 when the Colonial Office created a unified colonial service. By establishing a single bureaucracy for all of Britain's colonial possessions in Asia, Africa, and the West Indies, the Colonial Office made it possible for colonial officials to transfer freely from one colonial territory to another. Intentionally or unwittingly, the reform had a racial dimension. It made the hiring of nonwhite officers into these higher administrative positions more difficult. Indeed, the 1930 regulations openly stated that applicants had to be of European parentage.[12]

The League of Coloured Peoples took dead aim at these hiring restrictions. Perhaps because Lewis had himself suffered discrimination at the hands of the Colonial Office and was influential in setting the agenda of the League, the League redirected much of its energies from overt cases of discrimination against persons of African and Asian descent in the hotels and other establishments of the British Isles and mounted a campaign against racism in the colonial service. A ready-made issue was at hand. In May 28, 1938, the *British Medical Journal* ran a Colonial Office advertisement for a Jamaican medical officer, stating that applicants had to be of European parentage.

Thus, the Colonial Office was embarrassed and largely defenseless when the League approached it. In previous correspondence and meetings with West Indian delegations, Colonial Office officials had routinely expressed their dismay at the humiliating acts of racial discrimination that individuals of color encountered in Great Britain. They had dispatched numerous letters of apologies to distinguished visitors,

---

[11] Colonial Office Note on Moody's Memorandum of Complaints, November 1939, PRO CO 323/1692/4.

[12] There is a Colonial Office minute by C. J. Jeffreys on April 2, 1941, that provides a historical overview of the creation of the unified colonial services and lays out the reasons behind this reform. PRO CO 850/193/2.

pointing out that there were no legal steps that could be taken against offending proprietors and counseling patience as better education changed long-established racial stereotypes. Now, however, the Colonial Office was the discriminator. In an internal note, N. L. Mayle observed that there was no need to have inserted an obviously inflammatory condition in the advertisement since "it [the restriction against hiring applicants of color] could have been applied later, if necessary, when the selection was made."[13]

The League pressed its case and others in a series of meetings and letters between 1938 and 1941. Lewis was involved in all of the meetings that took place at the Colonial Office, and he was the general editor of the League of Coloured Peoples' issue of *News Notes*, in which the League, to the dismay of the Colonial Office, published the whole of the correspondence. What the League wanted was an unequivocal statement against discrimination in hiring and promoting persons of color in the unified colonial services. The Colonial Office was unwilling, believing that while local colonial peoples could serve effectively in their own countries, they would be ineffective and unwanted in other colonial areas. It would not do, the Colonial Office officials reasoned, to have a Nigerian administering Gold Coast peasants, not to mention Indian or West Indian officials moving from one African colonial posting to another as freely as administrators of European parentage. Indeed, the Colonial Office never wavered in its belief that the indigenization of the individual colonial services was the correct route for transforming colonial bureaucracies and that so long as local talent was not available to staff the colonial bureaucracies, white Britons were preferred.

During the discussions with the representatives of the League of Coloured Peoples, the Colonial Office relied on its most prominent officials and employed the full panoply of imperialist rhetoric in defense of its policies. Lord Lugard stepped forward to argue that opening up the colonial services to every British subject, white and nonwhite, would violate the principle of Africa for the Africans.[14] Alternatively, the Colonial Office tried to mollify its critics by apologizing for the overt racial statements in the advertisement and by promising to find "a term less likely to cause offense."[15] Some officials even went so far as to deny the existence of racial barriers since the secretary of state for the colonies had the right to make exceptions and, according to the apologists, often did.[16]

[13] Minute by N. L. Mayle, August 20, 1938, PRO CO 137/828/68924/38.
[14] Lugard to Moody, September 1, 1941, PRO CO 850/193/2.
[15] Minute by E. Lloyd, PRO CO 323/1692/4.
[16] See the note by A. J. Dawes, December 22, 1939, who, however, conceded that the Colonial Office could not afford "to go beyond the designedly anodyne phraseology of my version," adding that "this question is absolutely seething with politics."

The League did not agree. In its frustration it demanded the right to publish what was by then a lengthy correspondence. Unable to find good grounds to object, the colonial secretary insisted that the League publish the whole of the correspondence, including the Colonial Office's defenses of its hiring policies. The League designated Lewis to prepare the issue of *News Notes*, in which the correspondence was published, and Lewis wrote a blistering attack on the stance of the Colonial Office. In introducing the subject, Lewis held nothing back. He quoted George Bernard Shaw's statement that the colonial service was "a system of outdoor relief" by virtue of providing "good jobs retained exclusively for the English middle classes. Now the finest medical specialist from Vienna, the greatest soil chemist from Germany, or the best engineer from the United States need not hope to enter the service despite the fact that some of the best medical work in the tropics has been done by foreign scientists. The colonial service is a British preserve."

In this same vein, Lewis observed: "Ever since its inception it [colonial employment] has to all practical purposes been reserved to white men to the exclusion of those born within the colonial empire itself." To the Colonial Office's claim that it had no need to issue a statement against racial discrimination since there was none, Lewis quoted the many references that the League had uncovered to demonstrate that being of European parentage was essential. He referred to a long list of statements by eminently well-qualified applicants who had been rejected on racial grounds. He cited the aforementioned advertisement in the *British Medical Journal*, a Colonial Office memorandum entitled "General Information regarding Colonial Appointments," and an extract from a *Colonial Service Recruitment Manual*, No. 1, ninth edition, page 64, all of which made specific reference to the need for applicants to be of European parentage. Although the secretary of state, Moyne, had claimed that he could set aside this restriction, Lewis observed that even this claim showed that race was a significant factor in the decision about hiring. Lewis, citing Moody's letter to Moyne of June 12, 1941, asserted that "the words [about race] are an unnecessary offense which would be more in place in a German document than in a British one." In conclusion, Lewis stated that the correspondence left no doubt that race matters. "Until that determination is done away with and people are chosen on merit alone and posted on merit alone in a colony ... the basic problem persists."[17]

It is hard to imagine that the publications of the League of Coloured Peoples ordinarily attracted a great deal of notice. This one did. In the

---

[17] See pages 97 to 118 of the August 1941 issue of the *Newsletter*, published by the League of Coloured Peoples for Lewis's introduction and the correspondence between the League and the Colonial Office.

next edition of the *Newsletter,* the League observed that the exchange of correspondence with the Colonial Office had brought press comments in the *Manchester Guardian,* the *Yorkshire Post,* the *Liverpool Daily Mail,* the *Western Mail,* the *Bulletin and Scots Pictorial, West Africa,* the *New Statesman and Nation,* and many others. It also published letters of appreciation from numerous religious and intellectual British dignitaries, including the archbishop of York, Frank Owen, the Reverend L. J. Kerr, J. H. Oldham, and Margaret Read. Calling the correspondence "a classic," Kerr noted that "he [the colonial secretary] tried all he could to evade you [the League of Coloured Peoples], but you brought him to the point where at least he exposed a few of his conditions." The archbishop of York volunteered to help the League in its struggle to expose and combat racial prejudice, but "was afraid that the 'volume of prejudice to be broken down is very great.'"[18]

Lewis's Early Contacts with the Colonial Office

Under ordinary circumstances Lewis's frequent confrontations with the Colonial Office between 1939 and 1941 would have precluded any long-term relationship. But circumstances were far from ordinary. Lewis retained the confidence of his mentors at the London School of Economics, to whom the government frequently turned for advice. The senior faculty of the LSE saw Lewis as a rising star, and when government officials approached them, asking who on their staff could help in the war effort, they had no hesitation in recommending Lewis. The young economist did, indeed, have unique qualifications in the increasingly important and technically demanding field of colonial economies, as it was then called. Not only was he making himself a leading expert on the problems of these economies, which thus far had attracted few theoretical economists, but he was a person from the colonies themselves—a West Indian in a field of study hitherto the exclusive domain of persons of European descent. The Colonial Office had heard the protests of racial discrimination, and not just from the League of Coloured Peoples. It had been stung when West Indian intellectuals castigated the Moyne Commission for failing to include a West Indian among its ranks. If, therefore, Lewis was willing to work with the Colonial Office, hardly a foregone conclusion, the Colonial Office was prepared to swallow its pride (though its members never forgot the earlier run-ins) and take him on as an adviser.

[18] Ibid., p. 122.

The Colonial Office's most trusted official at the time, Lord Hailey, made the opening overture to Lewis. Ironically, it came at the very moment when Lewis was composing the issue of the *Newsletter* that called attention to the racist stances at the Colonial Office. Hailey had written to P. B. Whale, an economist on the faculty of the London School of Economics, to ask if Whale was available to carry out vital researches on investment capital, mining, and industrial development in colonial territories. Although it was only 1941 and the German army was driving the British forces further and further eastward across North Africa toward Egypt, the Colonial Office was nonetheless preparing for the end of the war and a restored and strengthened British Empire. Whale excused himself on the grounds that he had too many other obligations. He recommended Lewis.[19] Hailey was not deterred by Lewis's reputation as a critic of the Colonial Office. After ascertaining that Lewis was willing to be a consultant, Hailey asked the young man, who had just turned twenty-six, if he would prepare "a factual statement for the Committee [for the Post-War Reconstruction of the Colonies attached to the Colonial Office] on the subject of the financing of mining and industrial undertakings in the colonies."[20] Hailey insisted on total confidentiality since he wanted to keep unofficial and interested parties "from influencing the recommendations at this stage."

That the research was to be done in secret at first proved a stumbling block to Lewis and his superiors at the LSE. But by creating an oversight committee composed of top school faculty (Anstey, Beales, Benham, Firth, Paish, and Whale) "to assist Dr. Lewis and to read through and approve the reports submitted to Lord Hailey," the administration of the London School of Economics gave Lewis its approval to undertake the assignment.

Lewis's decision to make himself available to the Colonial Office was entirely consistent with the nonconfrontational approach to the political world that he had taken to this point in his career. He had always pictured himself as working from within. As a deeply committed Fabian socialist, who had established a relationship with the Fabians when he arrived as a student and enjoyed their confidence, he regarded the outbreak of World War II as a compelling moment to rally behind the British nation and empire. Britain was standing alone against racist and expansionist fascist enemies, for whom Lewis had only contempt. Moreover, the young and idealistic Lewis believed that the world was in a period of radical transformation. The European imperial systems were certain to be reformed. Even if empires did not

---

[19] Hailey to P. B. Whale, LSE Archives, Central Filing Registry 288/6.
[20] Hailey to Lewis, September 4, 1941, LSE Archives, Central Filing Registry 288/6.

give way to independent nation-states once the war was over, they would become more open and less racially structured than they had been in the past. Lewis could work with the Colonial Office with a clear conscience because he expected the defeat of the Axis powers to promote political freedoms, egalitarianism, and racial harmony.

Although he was ready to work from within the system, Lewis insisted that he be taken on not to address relatively modest day-to-day economic problems, but to formulate new, long-range policies that he believed would promote the economic development of the British colonial world and transform the relations between developed and developing regions of the world.[21]

Any doubts that the officials at the Colonial Office might have had in asking Lewis to take on this first assignment were quickly put to rest. Lewis's thirty-one-page, single-spaced typescript, entitled "Some Aspects of the Flow of Capital in the British Colonies," was a work of extraordinary quality. Gerard Clauson, one of the leading experts at the Colonial Office, called the essay "much the best paper which the Committee has yet received. By his intellectual capacity and his power of analysis, compression, and clear expression the author has succeeded not only in giving a clear picture of a complicated situation but also in stating the problems which have to be solved. . . . Considering its expanse of ground offered, he has made amazingly few mistakes."[22] Hailey added his own note of praise, observing: "This is first class, and I have read it with great interest. I wish we could get a few more outside contributors of this intellectual standard."[23]

The paper on capital flows was a tour de force. It featured Lewis's skill in the collection of data and the formulation of recommendations on the basis of finely-grained analysis. Obtaining permission to consult confidential files in the Colonial Office, to broaden his inquiry to include investments in plantations as well as mines and industries, and to extend the scope of the project beyond fact-finding so that he could make proposals about future policy, Lewis identified five major streams of capital flow into colonial territories: British capital markets, the British Exchequer, foreign investors, immigrants, and local earnings. These findings were hardly novel. What was new, however, was Lewis's breakdown of how different parts of the empire attracted different capital flows. Mines appealed to one group of investors; planta-

---

[21] See No. 47 (CPP [Convention People's Party] 47), Lewis to Hailey, September 23, 1941, PRO CO 852/503/7; and Hailey to Lewis, October 1941, LSE Archives, Central Filing Registry 288/6.

[22] Clauson's note is attached to the report, which can be found in CPP 152, PRO CO 852/503/3.

[23] Note by Hailey, September 14, 1942 in CPP 152, PRO CO 852/503/3.

tions to others. On the basis of these findings, the Colonial Office and colonial governments would be in a better position to create tax and tariff codes likely to promote the kinds of capital flows that they favored for specific territories.[24]

Because of his excellent study of capital flows, the officials at the Colonial Office next entrusted Lewis with the more delicate task of making recommendations about long-range mining policy in the colonies. By 1942 Britain's wartime coalition had a strong contingent of Labour and Fabian representatives, for whom the private ownership of vital assets, like mines, was troubling. These officials were even more greatly disturbed by some of the concessions that earlier colonial governments had made to private firms to gain control over mineral resources. It was a measure of the confidence that the Colonial Office placed in Lewis that they asked him to investigate an issue likely to roil relations between colonial governments, big business firms, and nationalist critics.

The final Colonial Office report on mining, issued as Colonial Note No. 206 in 1946, "Mining Policy in Africa," had a large dose of Lewis's views but was at the same time a compromise document, designed not to antagonize any of the interested parties.[25] While asserting the principle that the state should own and operate mines, it recognized that nationalizing all of the colonial mining companies and compensating their shareholders would place a heavy financial burden on the British Treasury. Instead, the document proposed that the state own and operate all new mines and buy out the old mines in a gradual fashion using funds supplied by the metropolitan government. The colonial governments were not to be saddled with these financial obligations. As Lewis observed in an earlier memorandum, colonial states, with the sanction of the British government, had often given away what had never belonged to them (mineral and land rights); hence the metropolitan tax payers rather than colonial subjects should shoulder the expense.[26]

---

[24] The report is in CPP 152, PRO CO 852/505/3. Clauson and Caine had quibbles with parts of the report and asked Lewis to make minor revisions. He did that, and the revised report was originally located in CPP 163, PRO CO 852/505/5. It was, however, removed and sent to a Colonial Office official, P. A. Wilson, on November 18, 1947.

[25] The document may be found in Great Britain, *Colonial Office Paper*, No. 206, 1945.

[26] Two Lewis memorandums on mining policy may be found in "Mining in the British African Colonies," October 31, 1942, Fabian Colonial Bureau, mss, Brit. Emp. S. 365, Box 48/2 and in the same collection, Box 46/2. In the 1942 memorandum, Lewis warned about the widespread influence of a few conglomerates and the individuals who controlled them. "It is pretty clear, however, that the shadow of half a dozen of these millionaires engulfs the entire continent."

Lewis and the Colonial Economic Advisory Committee (CEAC)

In 1941 Lewis joined the Board of Trade to help in its wartime preparations. It was only a matter of time, however, before he found himself back at the Colonial Office. On this occasion his duties were far greater. By the middle of 1943, the prospects for winning the war had brightened, and the Colonial Office now had to look more seriously at how it would deal with the colonies after the war was over. Two Colonial Office officials who commanded the most respect in economic matters, Gerard Clauson and Sydney Caine, were asked to create a new economic advisory body, which was given the name Colonial Economic Advisory Committee (CEAC). This body was expected to bring together expert economists and important businesspersons with knowledge of colonial areas and put them in dialogue with the most competent young economic experts at the Colonial Office. Clauson insisted that the new committee have at least two professional economists and proposed Hubert Henderson and Lionel Robbins, with Arnold Plant as a backup.[27] Clauson also wanted to include on the committee an economist with a specialized knowledge of colonies and colonial economies and suggested either Professor Keith Hancock or E.A.G. Robinson.

Caine and Clauson also agreed that "the committee should have a really competent secretary. Either we should get a good young economist with some experience of administration from one of the other departments [of the government] or we should put on to the job a really good principal of our own."[28] As it turned out, they chose a person entirely from the outside. Once again they reached out to the London School of Economics and plucked Lewis from the faculty. Both Colonial Office individuals were aware that Lewis was as independent in his opinions as he was talented and that as secretary of the committee he would insist that the body explore questions of colonial economic development in the widest and most open way.

Secretaries of government advisory committees were not meant to be clerks. Their true analogs were the recording secretaries of British limited companies. Not only were the secretaries of business firms required to assist the chairs of the business firms in all of their duties, but typically they prepared the major reports and memorandums for submission to the boards of directors for discussion. If ever a personnel

---

[27] Memorandum by G. Clauson to George Gator, April 23, 1943, PRO CO 852/510/29.
[28] Note by A. M., May 13, 1943 in E. Gent to G. Gator, May 5, 1943, PRO CO 852/510/29.

choice was fraught with tension and likely to bring to the surface problems between the consultants and the Colonial Office, this was one.

The Colonial Economic Advisory Committee, when finally assembled, was indeed a formidable body. It had a first-rate team of economists, including left-leaning (Evan F. M. Durbin) and right-leaning (Lionel Robbins, the free trade and free market advocate) faculty members from the London School of Economics, "practical men" of business (though none representing the big West African firms, like the United Africa Company or the shipping conglomerates), and representatives of labor and the British consumer. Lewis would find among the appointees a corps of individuals who were sympathetic with his evolving statist views. Nonetheless, the Colonial Office remained in the dominant position within the committee. Not only was the chair of the committee to be the parliamentary under-secretary of state for the colonies, the duke of Devonshire, but the committee's vice-chair was Gerard Clauson, the assistant under-secretary of state for long-term colonial planning. Hailey was the third official Colonial Office representative to sit as a voting member. In addition, many other Colonial officials, including Sydney Caine, were expected to participate in the meetings.[29]

The preliminary statements that accompanied the creation of the committee and the selection of its members suggested that the committee would take on large responsibilities, including laying out a framework for colonial economic development that would be ready for implementation once the war was over. According to the memorandum circulated in May 1943, the committee was "to advise the Secretary of State in such questions of economic policy in relation to the colonial dependencies as he may refer to the committee, including particularly matters of general policy arising on programmes of economic development."[30]

Things did not go as expected, however. The colonial secretary, Oliver Stanley, whose ambition was to use success in this position to catapult himself to greater political prominence, was unable to attend the first meeting and asked the committee members to await his statement of principles before they got down to work. In anticipation of this important speech, which Stanley planned to deliver at the second meeting, Caine and Clauson prepared an advanced draft and circulated it for comment to Lewis. Lewis could not have been more critical or outspoken. The proposed speech contained the very approach that Lewis feared and that had caused him to hesitate about taking on the secre-

[29] No. 11, C. G. Jarrett to I. Beamish, June 23, 1943, PRO CO 852/210/29.
[30] No. 2, Recommendations for an Economic Advisory Committee, May 1943, PRO CO 852/510/29.

taryship in the first place. The draft speech proposed that the committee "concentrate as far as possible on specific practical issues as examples of theoretical policies." Caine continued in this vein, writing that "however attractive it might be to try and work out from first principles a complete new economic system for the colonies, I imagine that the committee would agree that that is not even remotely practicable in the world in which we live, particularly having regard to the diverse states of political and economic progress in different colonial dependencies and that in practice the committee's recommendations are likely to be concerned with specific issues." Caine's view was that the new committee would operate in an ad hoc way, "confining itself to answering the specific questions that the Office chooses to ask."[31]

Lewis disagreed "fundamentally." This was, he was certain, the wrong use of such a talented group. In his view the Advisory Committee should "set about making a systematic review" of colonial economies. To this end, he proposed the creation of hard-working subcommittees to investigate the most critical areas of economic development. In his mind these were mining, secondary industries, agricultural finance, trade relations, agricultural marketing, public finance, and the machinery for economic development. If the secretary of state would provide the CEAC with this kind of broad mission, within two years the secretary "will have before him a well thought-out body of principles which can be the basis of a series of reconstruction dispatches." Being the secretary of such a dynamic committee, Lewis added, "would be a job into which anyone would be glad to throw all of his energies; but if the Economic Advisory Committee is merely an appendage to the Office, it is a waste of resources to use an economist as its secretary. All it needs is a competent clerk."[32]

Needless to say, Caine and Clauson were shocked by this strong challenge to their ideas, coming, as it did, from a man not yet thirty years old, who was prepared to throw himself in opposition to the senior economic experts of the Colonial Office. Sydney Caine was himself a graduate of the LSE, one of Robbins's prized pupils. Like Lewis he had won first-class honors in the 1920s. He had risen to prominence in the Colonial Office as Clauson's protégé during the 1930s and World War II. In 1942, Caine became the chief financial adviser in the Colonial Office. His ascent after that was meteoric. In August 1943, he wrote what was regarded as the new manifesto of colonial economics, a three-thousand-word memorandum that called for economic planning in the colonies, stressed the large role that colonial states would need

---

[31] Note from M. M. to Secretary of State, December 2, 1943, PRO CO 852/510/30.
[32] Note by W. A. Lewis to Caine, November 22, 1943, PRO CO 852/510/30.

to play in promoting economic growth, and even cited the Russian five-year plans and the TVA project in the United States as models for the kind of centralized state intervention in the economy that Britain's colonies needed.[33] In 1944 he became assistant under-secretary of state for the colonies; then, three years later a deputy under-secretary of state. In 1957, he left the Colonial Office to become director of the London School of Economics.[34]

The irony of Caine's and Clauson's reaction to Lewis's critique was that Lewis was elaborating on the very themes that Caine had extolled in his August 1943 memorandum. The two officials felt duty bound to share Lewis's criticism with Stanley. Much to their chagrin, Stanley discarded virtually all of the cautionary language that Caine had written into the original speech and instructed the drafters to incorporate the main points that Lewis had insisted on, even going so far as to instruct the speech writers to use much of Lewis's phraseology.

The speech that Stanley delivered to the second meeting of the CEAC clearly bore Lewis's imprint. It stressed the need to identify the first principles of economic development for the not yet industrialized parts of the British Empire. While not denying an important role to private enterprise, Stanley stated that "in the future we have got to have developments by the government of colonies on a scale quite unknown in the past. From time to time, the Secretary might need to refer specific questions to the committee for immediate and urgent advice." But echoing Lewis's vision of the larger role that the committee should take on, Stanley instructed the committee members to focus "on questions of principles rather than questions of detail."[35] In short, Lewis had bested the colonial bureaucrats. The Colonial Economic Advisory Committee was to be a "think tank," invested with the duty of developing long-range plans and laying out the general terms for promoting colonial economic development.

This dispute with Colonial Office officials was altogether predictable and was followed by similar crises that inevitably frustrated Lewis and ultimately led him to resign. He was a pragmatic man only in the sense that he eschewed violent and radical solutions to problems. He was an idealist, however, believing that men and women of goodwill and generosity to one another could reason their way to a better world. As a pragmatist, he understood that he needed to present his ideas to people

[33] J. M. Lee and Martin Petter, *The Colonial Office, War, and Development Policy: Organisation and the Planning of a Metropolitan Initiative, 1939–1945* (London, 1982), p. 170.

[34] Martin Petter, "Sir Sydney Caine and the Colonial Office in the Second World War: A Career in the Making," *Canadian Journal of History*, vol. 16, no. 1, April 1981, pp. 67–85.

[35] The speech may be found in the minutes of the second meeting of the Colonial Economic Advisory Committee that occurred on December 9, 1943. PRO CO 990/2.

in power if they were to be implemented. As an idealist and a believer in the power of reason, however, he was not willing to compromise on the big principles when he believed that his conclusions were right. This approach to power first put him at odds with the Colonial Office, cropped up again when he was chief economic adviser to Kwame Nkrumah in Ghana, and brought his public career to an end when he tried to save the federation of the British West Indies in the 1960s.

The secretary's speech did not, however, put to rest the simmering conflict between the officials of the Colonial Office and the Advisory Committee. Even while Lewis was disputing Caine's and Clauson's understanding of the role of the committee, these two bureaucrats were drafting a memorandum on the most critical question of colonial development—the nature of economic planning that the Colonial Office wished to implement in its possessions. Entitled "Social and Economic Planning in the Empire," the document described two kinds of planning. The first kind, labeled "'all-in' planning, would aim at a single comprehensive plan for the whole community and would exclude the possibility of 'planning' by private individuals." It should be avoided. Instead, Caine and Clauson favored what they described as "'outline planning,' leaving ample scope . . . for the private planning or initiative of individuals." The economic role of the state, in "outline planning," was to be a limited one. The state would confine itself to creating a "framework within which the individual plans can operate in proper harmony." Indeed, the primary economic responsibilities of the state were the traditional ones, "law and order, communications, and the general services," leaving "to private individuals or groups of individuals the machinery of the great bulk of decisions on production, in the light of estimates of market prospects."[36]

To say that this memorandum alarmed the leftist members of the Advisory Committee would be an understatement. Lewis hardly needed to register his disappointment. Two of the economists on the committee, Henderson and Durbin, with varying support from three noneconomists (Bourdillon, McFadyen, and Dalgleish), were appalled by the prospects of presenting this document as the committee's statement of purpose. Henderson could hardly contain his anger, claiming that the Caine-Clauson vision "was based on a certain economic philosophy quite unsuited to the conditions of the modern day and more appropriate to fifty-years ago; it was particularly ill-suited to the interest of the colonies." In light of the fact that Colonial Secretary Stan-

---

[36] Memorandum, "Social and Economic Planning in the Colonial Empire," November 1943, PRO CO 990/2.

ley had underscored a much-expanded role for the state, Henderson was surprised that the document lacked "the spirit of planning." It seemed to him "to recommend a combined policy of financial profligacy and economic laissez-faire." Social services were to be expanded without reference to economic resources. The proposals ignored economic diversification.

Durbin endorsed Henderson's critique, observing that "the general spirit of the document suggested that the business of government in colonial territories was to create a system in which 'private enterprise' (which must mean private foreign enterprise from the point of view of native peoples) could develop." Lewis's views are not recorded. But he clearly shared the perspectives of Durbin and Henderson. While he was at no time against private enterprise, he entirely supported Stanley's earlier view that colonial states must play a much larger role in economic affairs. In addition, he would have been uncomfortable with the slippery terminology that Caine and Clauson used when they differentiated between all-in planning and outline planning, particularly their suggestion that the private sector often engaged in a form of centralized planning. No doubt Lewis was pleased when the Advisory Committee created a special subcommittee consisting of Henderson, Durbin, and Robbins to work with Caine and Clauson to redraft the document.[37]

The revised document, like Stanley's revised speech, was a victory for those who favored more radical and state-centered approaches to colonial economic development. The new statement was a far cry from the tepid report that Caine and Clauson had put forth. Planning could be "all-in" or "outline," depending on the circumstances in individual colonial territories. The report favored a wide variety of methods, though it did aver that the state should never "attempt to lay down over the whole field of production how much every individual product should be made over the whole period but only to lay down whatever framework is thought to be necessary to ensure that individual decisions in such matters are made in proper harmony." But the document demanded that the state go beyond its traditional responsibilities for law and order, communications, and general services. Where the private sector was unlikely to take the lead, particularly in industrialization, the state must step in.[38]

[37] The discussion of the Caine-Clauson memorandum is contained in the minutes of the second meeting of the Colonial Economic Advisory Committee of December 9, 1943. PRO CO 990/2.

[38] No. 11, "The Planning of Social and Economic Development in the Colonial Empire," January 1944. PRO CO 990/2.

Emboldened by these two victories over entrenched elements, Lewis eagerly began "to review the whole field of colonial economic problems and to formulate general principles, within which the framework of colonial economic policy should fit."[39] He was now more than ever convinced that this high-powered team of experts could produce reports that would transform the relationship of Britain to its colonies and generate rapid economic growth after the war. In Lewis's formulation, economics would lead political progress, laying the foundations for independent African governments. To this end, the Advisory Committee established five subcommittees: on agenda, with the responsibility for elaborating the general principles that would guide colonial economic development; on research; on production and development; on marketing; and on public finance. Four additional subcommittees were attached to the production and development subcommittee: minerals, primary production, secondary industries, and communications.

The chair of the Colonial Economic Advisory Committee, the duke of Devonshire, defended the existence of so many subcommittees, observing: "After all, the task of the committee was considerable—nothing less than to frame an economic policy for one-fifth of the earth's surface, comprising countries as various as Malta and Somaliland."[40] No doubt there were echoes of Rhodes's imperializing vision and Britain's image as the world's great policeman and ruler in Devonshire's inflated rhetoric. Yet Lewis thrilled to the prospect of participating in efforts to lead Britain's colonial territories out of poverty and economic backwardness.

Even as Lewis was teaching his classes at the LSE and publishing a series of research articles in important journals, he was drafting the memorandums and reports for all of the subcommittees that he was sure would lead to dramatic economic transformations. One of the first documents that Lewis laid before the full Advisory Committee bore the title "Machinery for Economic Planning." At this stage of Lewis's thinking, the document was no more than a rudimentary effort to pull together his thoughts and those of others about the place of state planning in colonial economies. For the secondary industries subcommittee, Lewis produced a report called "The Development of Manufacturing Industries" that laid out the bases for judging which kinds of industries would be suitable in different colonial settings and what role the state should play in stimulating industrial progress. His third report was entitled "Colonial Economic Development." It was the most

---

[39] No. 12, Colonial Economic Advisory Committee, Agenda Sub-Committee, First Report, Work on the Economic Advisory Committee, February 1, 1944, PRO CO 990/2.
[40] Ibid.

mature and finished essay of all the documents that he submitted to the Advisory Committee.

In the latter report Lewis elaborated themes that were becoming the core of his development philosophy.[41] In earlier essays on the West Indies, he had argued that only industrial development could lift heavily populated territories out of poverty. Confronted with a much larger, less populous colonial world, Lewis modified his stress on industrialization. Claiming that good economic plans had to promote balanced growth, he now asserted the primacy of agriculture for those parts of the world that had not yet experienced an agricultural revolution. Agricultural expansion must in most cases precede industrial growth since it was the key to overcoming malnutrition and creating a healthy and productive workforce. Lewis's approach to the industrial sphere stressed what economists later would label import-substitution industrialization. Lewis expected local entrepreneurs, with the state providing tariff protection, purchasing agreements, and favorable taxation rates, to establish factories for the production of consumption goods—clothes, shoes, household utensils, and the other products that were already in high demand in these countries. Yet, here, too, Lewis expressed reservations about a free market, laissez-faire approach. He wrote: "There are no 'natural' economic forces that we can rely on to produce industrial development in Africa at the necessary rate. Both capital and entrepreneurship are absent; either the government must take an active part in planning development or there will be little or none."

Lewis's generalizations about the limitations of the free market and the significance of the state in economic development ran counter to the prevailing sentiments at the Colonial Office. So did his emphasis on speed, for Lewis believed that Africa must be set on the high road to development as swiftly as possible lest it experience the economic stagnation and poverty that characterized the West Indies. Development could not be done on the cheap. It would require a huge outlay of capital, and Lewis saw no alternative but to encourage foreign capital, notably American capital, to join in the effort. Nor could development be carried out equally over the whole of British Africa, which was an immense area with enormous needs. Rather, Lewis wanted to designate specific colonies and even regions within colonies as model areas

---

[41] The report "Machinery for Economic Planning" may be found in CEAC (44) 31, CEAC, Agenda Sub-Committee, Second Report, PRO CO 990/2. "The Development of Manufacturing Industries" was written for the Industry Sub-Committee for the CEAC, July 28, 1944, PRO CO 990/2, and the report "Colonial Economic Development" was the Third Report for the Agenda Sub-Committee of the Colonial Economic Advisory Committee, CEAC (44) 38, September 14, 1944, PRO CO 990/2.

for development and as magnets of economic progress from which the new techniques would spread outward.[42]

The selective approach to development—favoring southern Nigeria over the north or Uganda over Kenya and Tanganyika—was anathema to British officialdom. In their minds, nothing would be more politically destabilizing and more likely to produce tension in the postwar years than privileging certain regions over others in British development spending. Colonial Office officials regarded Lewis's proposal in favor of foreign assistance, by which was understood American assistance, as nearly treasonous. The Colonial Office viewed the development project as something that would reflect on Britain's imperial glory, not reveal the limitations of empire. Development plans were intended to prolong the life of the empire and support the balance sheets of British firms, not ease the Americans into territories once controlled by the British.

In particular, Lewis's document raised the ire of Sydney Caine, whom Lewis had already challenged in two earlier disputes and who had by now become Lewis's sternest critic at the Colonial Office. It is hard to say whether Caine deliberately set about to undermine the effectiveness of the committee, as Lewis suspected, or the committee simply ran out of energy and lost its vision. But not soon after submitting his report on development, Lewis felt compelled to resign his appointment. In his first official explanation of his resignation and in his note to Carr-Saunders, director of the London School of Economics, to which Lewis was about to return, he simply stated that he felt underused as the secretary of the committee and believed that he could make a greater contribution professionally by returning to the classroom.[43]

This anodyne explanation did not suffice. Rumors circulated that Lewis had resigned because of unbridgeable ideological differences with the staff of the Colonial Office. Once questions were asked in Parliament, Lewis felt obliged to state his side of the case, which he did in a note to the colonial secretary. In his opinion the Colonial Office had so hemmed in the Colonial Economic Advisory Committee that "the secretaryship was largely a waste of time." As for specific differences, Lewis reiterated his belief that regional industrialization centers and foreign financing were the only sure ways to generate rapid economic progress. Unfortunately, these proposals "frightened Mr. Caine

---

[42] "Colonial Economic Development," Third Report of the Agenda Sub-Committee of the Colonial Economic Advisory Committee, September 14, 1944, CEAC (44) 38, PRO CO 990/2.

[43] The stresses also caused Lewis to come down with an ulcer. Lewis to Carr-Saunders, October 31, 1944, Lewis Staff File, LSE Archives.

because of [their] 'political' implications." According to Lewis, Caine used "passive resistance" to subvert his ideas and to undermine the work of the committee. Subcommittees passed into disuse. Moreover, committee members, unsympathetic to Lewis's ideas, rarely attended meetings. Those who were faithful in attending expressed their disappointment with the actions of the committee.[44]

On this occasion Caine was ready with a defense when the group, whom Caine identified as "rebels," asked the secretary of state to adjudicate on five issues that were roiling the committee: the pace of social change in the colonies, the need for larger agricultural units in place of peasant agriculture, the channeling of the bulk of industrial funds to a few areas, the power of planning agencies, and the place of foreign capital in the development projects. In Caine's view, the approach favored by Lewis and his supporters in the committee was "revolutionary." "It would raise political and social problems of the first importance and ... the committee could not therefore usefully consider them without making assumptions on political and social policy which were really outside their competence." No doubt Caine was politically correct. What some of the committee members were recommending would have generated howls of disapproval from colonial governors and other officials in the colonies, especially in territories not favored with large allocations of development funds. In this case, the colonial secretary could hardly afford to stand against the top officials at the Colonial Office, especially since embracing Lewis's directions would have produced strong opposition in the colonies. Lewis's proposals were altogether too radical for the Colonial Office. Stanley could no longer afford to back recommendations that hardly any officials favored. Lewis had to go. His resignation was accepted.[45]

Looking back at these events several years later, Lewis held that a significant opportunity had been missed. In a note that he composed for colleagues at the Fabian Colonial Bureau, Lewis complained that the Colonial Office lacked individuals who had the necessary economic expertise to understand colonial economies. The leading figures at the Office—individuals like Caine and Clauson in particular—were well trained in neoclassical economics, having studied at the best British universities. But they were at a loss when it came to using the tools

---

[44] Note by W. Arthur Lewis, November 30, 1944, PRO CO 852/586/9.

[45] These are from a Colonial Office Minute by Caine, November 2, 1944, PRO CO 852/588/19260. They are cited in Martin Petter, "Sir Sydney Caine and the Colonial Office in the Second World War: A Career in the Making," *Canadian Journal of History*, vol. 16, no. 1, April 1981, p. 83.

fashioned for analyzing developed industrialized societies for more subsistence, agriculturally oriented economies.[46]

For Lewis the second reason for the failure of the Colonial Economic Advisory Committee was the overbearing influence of Sydney Caine. According to Lewis, Caine, as head of the Office's Economic Department, was out of his economic depth. He "is a charming person, very liberal in outlook, progressive in many things, and just the sort of person to put in charge of East African affairs to achieve the much needed New Deal there (what higher praise can I give him?). A contemporary of Robbins and Plant as students of Cannan at the LSE, he is a religious devotee of laissez-faire, and his headship of the Economics Department at this juncture is fatal. . . . His laissez-faire approach is fatal not only in the decisions he makes, especially on secondary industry, on marketing, on cooperative organization, but also on the appointments he recommends to important jobs in the colonies, for which he chooses almost invariably people as laissez-faire as himself."

Lewis continued in this vein, pointing out that the Colonial Economic Advisory Committee had been Stanley's favored project. Only through the colonial secretary's interventions had the subcommittees actually come into existence. But only three ever functioned effectively. One was the research committee, which, because it undertook long-term, rather theoretical, research projects, was not seen as a threat to Colonial Office policy. The second was the mineral policies subcommittee, which led ultimately to the important Colonial Office statement on mining policy in 1945. The third dealt with industrial development. Yet as soon as the subcommittee on secondary industries got underway, Caine and others at the Colonial Office "sabotaged" it.

Lewis concluded his critique by reminding his readers that the Colonial Office had stacked the committee so that it would not challenge the colonial status quo. "Some represented vested interests; others were laissez-faire economists; others, too busy. A minority were aware of what was happening and resented it."[47]

Service with the committee took its toll on Lewis's health. By the time of his resignation he was suffering from a duodenal ulcer. Yet this was a critical phase in the evolution of Lewis's thinking about colonial economies. Constantly at odds with the men and women at the Colonial Office who were well schooled in neoclassical economics, some of whom, like Robbins, had been his mentors at the London School of

---

[46] Lewis's blistering critique, which is summarized here, can be found in a paper he wrote for the Fabian Colonial Bureau, entitled "Colonial Economic Development." Fabian Colonial Bureau Papers, n.d., but probably 1945, mss. Brit. Emp. S 365.

[47] Ibid.

Economics or his predecessors as students, like Sydney Caine, he concluded that the standard approaches to economic analysis offered little hope for the economic development of colonial areas. The poverty was deep-seated; the resources limited; the populations growing rapidly; and the time frame too cramped for the free market to function as the primary motor of economic growth. The state would have to take the lead, accelerating income growth, centralizing economic decision-making, and allocating scarce resources more efficiently than private businesspersons could. The general field of economics would need to be refashioned as its practitioners moved their research agendas away from the developed parts of the world and focused on Asia, Africa, and Latin America. In all likelihood the study of the economies of colonial territories would require a special field of economic analysis capable of offering new programs and inspiring new hope throughout the colonial world.

LEWIS AND THE COLONIAL ECONOMIC DEVELOPMENT COUNCIL

The winding down of the Colonial Economic Advisory Committee and the bitter recriminations that hung around Lewis's resignation did not terminate Lewis's dealing with the Colonial Office. An additional feature of Stanley's ambitious proposals for transforming the colonies was an enhanced fund to promote large-scale colonial development projects. In 1929 the British government had created the Colonial Development Fund, to which the British Treasury was supposed to allocate monies for long-range programs of social and economic development in the colonies. Although the fund came into existence, the Great Depression starved it of resources. In 1940, the British Parliament created a new body, called the Colonial Welfare and Development Fund, and set aside £5 million per year for projects after the war. Stanley doubled the amount to be spent, raising it to £10 million per year over a twelve-year period.[48] As the Colonial Welfare and Development Fund moved into action after World War II, under the tutelage of a new Labour government and a new secretary of state for the colonies, Arthur Creech Jones, a dedicated Fabian socialist and a person with strong credentials in colonial affairs, the expectations were high. Not surprisingly, the colonial secretary turned to Lewis for advice, and once again Lewis agreed to help.[49]

[48] C.H.M. Wilcox, Note on Colonial Development and Welfare Fund, August 28, 1944, and record of meeting at the Treasury, September 1, 1944, between Colonial Office and Treasury officials. PRO T 161/1199.
[49] Lee and Petter, *The Colonial Office, War, and Development Policy*, passim.

The successor body at the Colonial Office to the Colonial Economic Advisory Committee was an organization called the Colonial Economic Development Council. It was charged with two primary and interrelated duties. First, it was to review the specific ten-year development plans that each of the colonies was required to draw up for the use of funds from the Colonial Development and Welfare Fund. Second, it was to evaluate the specific and large-scale development projects that were part of the ten-year plans.

Although this was a period of rapid political change in Britain's colonial territories, especially those in Africa, where new African nationalist parties were coming into being and new dynamic political leaders coming to prominence, the Colonial Economic Development Council got off to a slow start. Its level of activity did not impress Lewis at first. He attended a few meetings right after his appointment, but he was absent throughout most of 1947.[50] The council did not begin to work at full speed until it entered its second full year (1948) when once again Lewis thrust himself into the center of its activities and produced yet another crisis.

The cause of the crisis was a memorandum that Lewis submitted to the Colonial Office in April 1948. It bore the bold title "The Principles of Development Planning," and it started off ominously. Lewis pleaded with the members of the council "to consider urgently the principles of development planning because in my view the ten-year colonial development plans, most of which have already been approved, constitute a grave waste of money." In his estimation, the plans had made a fatal mistake of separating economic and social matters when, in fact, they were inextricably linked. Education and public health were dealt with exclusively as social programs when in truth they were as vital to economic development as economic development was vital to them. In addition, the plans were too "authoritarian." Lewis returned to a theme that he had first articulated as a member of the League of Coloured Peoples when he complained that the British colonial service was a vehicle for employment for the educated British middle class. The colonial development plans would generate many jobs for British officials. The lion's share of the British grants would go to pay the salaries of British consultants and experts, or they would be eaten up in big road and building projects that would be contracted out to British firms.[51]

---

[50] Lewis attended meetings number 9, 10, 11, and 13, but was absent for 12 and 14 through 21. PRO CO 852/866/6.

[51] No. 1, Lewis to Newsam, April 2, 1948, PRO CO 852/941/3.

Lewis then elaborated what for him was a new anthem in his approach to development—mass education. The concept, mass education, was already a shibboleth in colonial discourse. As the day of independence seemed to be drawing ever and ever closer, colonial officials had begun to stress the importance of educating colonial populations for the duties of self-government. In 1946, the colonial secretary had sent out a circular calling on all of the colonies to compile figures on literacy and the proportions of the population who had access to elementary education.

Lewis took pains in his memorandum to point out that his concept of mass education was radically different from that current in the Colonial Office. For him mass education meant the training of all the peoples of colonial territories for the monumental task of rapid economic and social change. It meant educating farmers to be more productive cultivators and training young men and women to be medical auxiliaries, sanitary inspectors, midwives, and pharmacy dispensers. Colonies were poor because "peoples have not learnt how to master their environments. Their techniques and their tools are primitive; their hygiene deplorable; and their attitudes are frequently a fatalistic acceptance of their conditions as inevitable." Knowledge was the critical shortcoming standing in the way of prosperity. "If a mass attack is to be made on colonial conditions, it must be by mass employment of the partially qualified." Mass education entailed reaching into every village and demonstrating new ways of doing things; hence it must be directed at adults as well as children so that private citizens could energize their rural communities and get behind the development push that was coming from above.

Lewis highlighted his complaint with the conventional Colonial Office view of development by examining in detail the Nigerian development plan. In his view the plan was weighted too heavily in favor of expensive outside experts and provided little training for an African staff. If the Nigerian government would take £1 million from the development budget that had been earmarked for harbors and spend this sum in the countryside disseminating new agricultural techniques, the economic and social payoffs would be dramatic. The expenditure of 17 percent of Nigeria's development budget on buildings alone was a gross misallocation of funds.

Lewis's approaches to development were ordinarily cold, analytical, and spare. This document, in contrast, while spare, had a lyrical and emotional quality and a populist emphasis that was rarely evident in Lewis's writings. To be sure, his statement about the hygienic and the fatalist habits of uneducated Africans was harsh, though it undoubtedly reflected views that were common in the colonial metropole about

Africans at the time and that Lewis thus far had had little opportunity to test against realities on the ground. Yet his eloquence about the way that Africans could transform their environment if given only a fraction of the development funds and a partial exposure to new practices bespoke an optimism that bordered on utopianism. The document had parallels with the kind of peasant glorification that was appearing in the programs and writings of East Asian and Southeast Asian socialists, though there is no evidence that Lewis had the ideas of Mao Zedong or Ho Chi Minh in mind when he composed his memorandum. He was far more familiar at the time with the new school of modernization theory that was taking shape on both sides of the Atlantic in social science departments.

The Lewis memorandum engendered a cool, if not hostile, reaction at the Colonial Office. How could it have been otherwise? No fewer than seventeen development plans had already been drawn up and vetted. No one was prepared to start over again, let alone concede that the original plans represented "a waste of money." Moreover, the British economy at home was under great pressure. The value of the pound sterling was not holding up well, and so the prospect of reworking these plans attracted no interest. Nonetheless, rather than opposing Lewis's suggestions outright, officials at the Colonial Office endeavored to co-opt the proposals without altering their own underlying approaches to education and economic change in the colonies. The Office sent the Lewis document for comment to the Mass Education Sub-Committee of the African Colonial Education Committee before laying it before the Colonial Economic Development Council.[52] The most powerful figures in the Colonial Office, Sydney Caine on the economic side and Andrew Cohen, the leading political adviser, marshaled their arguments against Lewis's ideas. They claimed that without large expenditures on roads, buildings, and industries, mass education would itself suffer.[53] The African Colonial Education Committee also joined in, expressing deep reservations about Lewis's vision, claiming that Lewis had overlooked the pitfalls and the costs of trying to reach peasants.[54] Lewis hardly helped his case in Colonial Office circles when he published an article in the *Manchester Guardian* on July 21, 1948, under the provocative title "Colonial Development: The Defect of the Plans," in which he concluded, "The ten-year plans have been a failure."[55]

[52] Memorandum by W.E.F. Ward, April 21, 1948, PRO CO 852/941/3
[53] No. 6, A. Cohen Memorandum, April 26, 1948, PRO CO 852/941/3.
[54] Colonial Office Note, May 7, 1948, PRO CO 852/941/3.
[55] *Manchester Guardian*, July 21, 1948.

The final resolution to the issues that Lewis raised was entirely predictable, however distasteful to him. After making its way through various subcommittees, the Lewis memorandum resurfaced as a compromise document. Reaffirming its long-standing commitment to the education of colonial masses but now embracing Lewis's notion that mass education must have a broader purpose than the provision of elementary education to youngsters, the Colonial Office announced that education and the development of social services, like public health, must go hand in hand. In a circular dispatch sent to all of the colonial governors, the secretary of state for the colonies proclaimed that without big development projects, many of which had already been identified in the ten-year development plans, mass education could not advance. Equally important, however, the training of partially educated adults for new roles in a rapidly expanding economy was indispensable.[56]

Lewis had spurred the Colonial Economic Development Council into activity in 1948. His championing of mass education was as galvanizing as the reports that he had submitted to the Colonial Economic Advisory Committee in 1943. But once his document had made its way through the committee structures and had come out in a Colonial Office circular dispatched to all of the colonies, the council lost its focus. Lewis left in 1950. By 1951, the council had wound up its work. Outside members rarely attended meetings. The ten-year plans had already been elaborated and vetted, and most of the Colonial Development and Welfare Fund monies had been allocated.[57]

Lewis and the Colonial Development Corporation (CDC)

Lewis had one last opportunity with the Colonial Office. It, too, ended unhappily. At the end of 1947, the colonial secretary, Arthur Creech Jones, created the Colonial Development Corporation, endowing it with borrowing powers of up to £100 million and charging it with the task of investing funds and providing technicians for commercially viable projects in the colonies. The Colonial Development Corporation

[56] Despatch No. 86, Secretary of State for Colonies to all Colonies, November 10, 1948, PRO CO 852/941/3.

[57] The Colonial Office official A. Emmanuel wrote to his colleague, E. Newsam, in 1949 that "if we do not have a meeting fairly soon, some of the existing members may begin to ask whether the council has gone out of business." No. 8, A. Emmanuel to E. Newsam, April 6, 1949, PRO CO 851/1040/4. See also Note by Emmanuel from Roberts on the winding up of the Colonial Economic Development Council, November 8, 1951, PRO CO 852/1341/2.

was modeled on other parastatal organizations in postwar Britain that appeared when the Labour Government nationalized large-scale enterprises. Like the British railways and the coal and steel industries, the CDC was to be run by its own independent board of advisers, in this case a group selected by the Colonial Office but largely autonomous from it. The CDC was to invest in projects that would make profits, which were to be plowed back into the capital of the corporation or expended on other projects. The corporation was not expected to make a loss overall, even though it was understood that some of the undertakings might incur losses in the early stages.[58]

In justifying the CDC, the colonial secretary argued for its benefits to Britain as well as the colonies. Not only would it exploit underutilized colonial resources, but it would also "help to strengthen the resources of the sterling group as a whole and thus prove of considerable benefit to all of the members of that group and not only to the colonies themselves."[59] Although Creech Jones saw no contradiction between promoting the economic development of the colonies and strengthening the pound sterling, contradictions were bound to arise. If the projects supported by the CDC drew down the sterling balances of the British government rather than adding to them, they became easy targets for political criticism.

In 1948 Lewis turned down an invitation to serve on the CDC board on the grounds that he had many other obligations.[60] He had just taken up his professorship at the University of Manchester. But he lent his support to the committee. In articles composed for the West Indian journal *Jamaica Arise* in late 1947, he lauded the CDC for filling an important gap in the British development programs designed for colonial areas. In Lewis's opinion, the largest share of Colonial Development and Welfare monies was going into social projects. Thus, the Colonial Development Corporation could make a difference by identifying projects that held out great potential for sharply increasing the productivity of colonial territories but had failed to attract private capital. Placing education and public health ahead of agricultural and industrial schemes was often counterproductive. Commenting on what was then and continues to be the great dilemma of development, whether to favor welfare activities over programs that spur immediate economic growth or the other

---

[58] There are two general histories of the CDC: William Rendell, *The History of the Commonwealth Development Corporation, 1948–72* (London, 1976) and Michael McWilliam, *The Development Business: A History of the Commonwealth Development Corporation* (New York, 2001).

[59] Circular, Colonial Office to Governors of Colonies, December 17, 1947, PRO CO 852/1347/9.

[60] Note by G. C. Eastwood, October 28, 1948, PRO CO 537/4498.

way around, Lewis concluded: "The horse of development should go in front carrying the cart of welfare behind it." In dire need of rapid economic growth, colonies needed foreign investment for a critical boost, without which "we are condemning ourselves to backwardness." Moreover, the Colonial Development Corporation had a major advantage over other forms of foreign investment. Because the corporation enjoyed the backing of the British government, it could afford to underwrite long-range and ambitious projects that private investors were reluctant to back. Nor did it have to worry about the profitability of its investments, only their capacity to break even.[61]

Alas, the CDC's first director, Lord Trefgarne, handpicked by Fabian sympathizers in the Colonial Office, not only insisted on complete autonomy from the Colonial Office but was so eager to move ahead as rapidly and with as little regard for risk as possible that the CDC got into financial difficulties. Within the first three years of its operations, the CDC had created fifty projects, scattered all over the globe, many of which were not expected to show a profit for a very long time, if at all. Lewis commented that the corporation had tried to do too much too quickly. It had invested £35 million in programs for which it lacked detailed information. In addition, according to Lewis, Trefgarne had assembled a weak board whose members were unwilling to stand in the way of the ambitious but highly unrealistic schemes of their leader.[62]

By the third year of its existence the relations of the CDC with the Colonial Office and the British Parliament had deteriorated. The Conservative Party, ever anxious to demonstrate that the Labour Party's nationalizing experiment was flawed, employed the CDC's financial record and that of its even more colossally failed Overseas Food Corporation, which had incurred massive financial losses in its groundnuts scheme in Tanganyika, as evidence that the Labour Party misunderstood economic principles.

When Trefgarne stepped down in 1950, just before the parliamentary elections that would bring the Tory party back into power, relations with the Colonial Office had reached a nadir. The number of nonperforming projects was on the rise. Programs like the Gambia Poultry Scheme and the Tanganyika Railways had entered the vocabulary of newspaper editors and parliamentary critics as examples of government waste and mismanagement. The losses mounted each year, destined to rise to £8 million by 1951.[63] Perhaps sensing loss in

[61] W. Arthur Lewis, "The Colonial Development Corporation," *Jamaica Arise*, vol. 1, no. 6, August 1947, and vol. 1, no. 7, September 1947.

[62] Lewis gave an overview of the Trefgarne years in a letter to Marjorie Nicholson that he wrote on May 28, 1953. Fabian Colonial Bureau, Mss. Brit. Emp. S. 365, Box 54, file 1.

[63] Note by A. Emmanuel, October 3, 1950, PRO CO 537/7595.

the next election, the Fabians installed one of their own supporters, Lord Reith, as Trefgarne's replacement to head the CDC. If they expected Reith to be more cooperative with the officials at the Colonial Office, however, they were quickly disillusioned. Not only did Reith insist on all of the prerogatives of power that Trefgarne had fought for, but he also used his formal publications, notably the CDC's annual report, to criticize the decisions of his predecessor and to defend the corporation from its critics.[64] The CDC's relations with the Colonial Office became more combative once the Tory party had returned to office in 1951. Indeed, the CDC became a special object of Tory complaint, as one of the most vulnerable of the Labour Party's creations.[65]

It was under these profoundly troubling circumstances that Reith asked Lewis to join the board. Lewis agreed to serve and did so with enthusiasm since he had always believed in the mission of the CDC and shared Reith's vision that the corporation should function autonomously from the Colonial Office. But he was not blind to the tensions that surrounded the CDC and the bad start that it had gotten off to. In addition, he was aware that the assignment placed heavy demands on his time. Prior to each of the formal board meetings, which occurred usually on weekends, once or sometimes twice a month, he would receive a large packet of reading materials. His compensation was £500 a year, not to be taken lightly in view of the pay of university professors, even those who held chairs in prestigious universities.

Lewis was diligent and hard-working as a board member, always faithful in attendance, though deeply frustrated because, as he mentioned on many occasions, the task of the Reith board was not to undertake new initiatives but to bring order and financial stability after a period of too rapid expansion and profligacy. Lewis was, therefore, understandably upset and even bewildered when in 1953 his term as a board member was not extended. As he saw it, for the first time in his life he had been fired. He demanded an interview with Reith and sought an explanation. Reith pointed out that Lewis was not being fired since his term had expired. He was simply not being renewed.

Under pressure from Lewis to provide more information on his non-renewal at the board, Reith speculated that the colonial secretary had objected to a talk that Lewis gave on the BBC in July 1952 that dealt with the Central African Federation. The talk, entitled "When the Trustee Becomes a Partner," was intensely critical of the Colonial Office proposals to create a federation in central Africa, which, in Lewis's

[64] Note by M. Willard, March 14, 1959, PRO CO 852/1348/7.
[65] Note by M. Willis, January 2, 1954, PRO CO 852/1512.

opinion, would spread the influence of white settlers at the expense of the African majority and impede the transfer of power to the black majority. Naturally, Lewis countered Reith by stating that when he had come onto the board he had been assured that as a part-time member he was free to express his opinions as he saw fit.[66]

That Lewis should have been as surprised and distressed as he was seems surprising in hindsight. The new Conservative government was unsympathetic to the directions that the CDC had taken under Trefgarne. They were even more displeased with Reith's insistence on the autonomy of his board. The Tories were eager to purge the board of its earlier Fabian leanings, and they saw Lewis as a powerful Fabian voice within the board. Moreover, Lewis had given many grounds for complaint. His steady criticism of government policy toward Kenya and the Central African Federation and his note suggesting that there were grounds for viewing the CDC as a vehicle of colonial exploitation were only the most visible instances of his anti-imperialism. No doubt Lewis was right in his parting words to Reith: "He was sure that it would be harmful to the CDC not to have someone like himself on the board."

Lewis's decade-and-a-half-long relations with the Colonial Office produced a string of personal disappointments. The efforts of the League of Coloured Peoples to end racial discrimination in the commissioning of military officers and the employment of colonial officials of color set in motion reforms that led eventually to precisely the statements banning racial discrimination in hiring in the British government that the League demanded. But the early steps taken during World War II were halting and deeply distressing to Lewis and his colleagues at the League. Lewis's masterful reports to Hailey's Committee for the Post-War Reconstruction of the Colonies resulted in his selection as the secretary of the Colonial Economic Advisory Committee. But his early triumphs over the conservative economists in the Colonial Office proved illusory. Marshalling opposition to the Lewis approaches inside the colonial bureaucracy, Sydney Caine and his clique led Lewis to resign as secretary. Later Lewis revived the spirits of the Colonial Economic Development Council with his imaginative views of economic development springing from the energy of the peasant farmer and the rudimentarily educated city dweller. But once this report had wended its way through the multitude of Colonial Office subcommittees and had been adapted to the wishes of officials in London

---

[66] The text of the interview can be found in Aide-Mémoire of a conversation with Professor Lewis, May 8, 1953, PRO CO 967/194. Lewis's talk on the BBC may be found in the Lewis Papers, Prudence Smith, BBC, to W. Arthur Lewis, February 21, 1952, and R. O. Davies to Lewis, July 19, 1952, Box 3.

and the colonies, it had lost most of its originality. Lewis's coup de grâce occurred when he was unceremoniously dismissed from the CDC just as he was beginning to understand the job.

Yet it would be a mistake to form a negative view of these years in Lewis's life. Although he failed to win approval for his programs from the powerful men and women in the Colonial Office, these were years of robust intellectual growth as an economist. It is inconceivable that he could have produced the major works of economic analysis that he did in the early 1950s, particularly his book *The Theory of Economic Growth* and the article "Economic Development with Unlimited Supplies of Labour," had he not had access to the reports and memorandums at the Colonial Office and had he not had to think deeply about colonial economies and to defend his arguments in front of his critics.

Lewis's writings for the Colonial Office were brief and not highly theoretical, precisely because Lewis intended them to be read by busy officials who were not interested in the theoretical underpinnings or the vast database on which these propositions rested. But during these years as a consultant Lewis consolidated many of the basic arguments concerning economic growth in less developed areas that he was to expound in his scholarly writings at great length throughout the rest of his life. Drawing on his experience advising the Colonial Office and his wide reading about Britain's colonial territories, Lewis was certain that the economic discipline itself, at least as it was taught in the universities at the time, was an inadequate tool for understanding and promoting economic growth. His memorandum on mass education, a forerunner in many respects to the modernization theory of the 1950s, asserted that economic systems could not be studied in isolation from the larger cultural, social, and political institutional frameworks within which they operated. The arguments of this powerful and pithy document were to form the core of one of his most widely acclaimed books, *The Theory of Economic Growth*, which he published in 1955.

He also used these years to consolidate five of his primary arguments concerning the economic aspects of growth in less developed economies. The first and most overarching of his insights was that development in colonial and ex-colonial territories required a specialized economic analysis and a different approach from that which worked in the developed parts of the world. It is here that he and Caine so often clashed, and here where he insisted that Caine's perspectives would fail.

The four other principles derived logically from the first general observation. The first of the four additional principles was that because rapid economic development was critical and poverty so widespread and now so intolerable, laissez-faire, free market policies would not suffice. Second, development needed to be given the highest priority, and all of a society's resources needed to be exploited in the most efficient fashion to achieve high growth rates. The market had proved to be a cumbersome and often wasteful vehicle for allocating resources. Third, planning was called for, and the state was not only the primary organization to lay out the plan, but it could also step forward and carry out projects that the private sector was unable to do because of a lack of capital or entrepreneurship. The fourth and final ingredient was a belief in education and knowledge as the key component for instilling new methods, new wants, and new hopes. By education Lewis, of course, meant Western education at all levels, including university training. But he also meant the inculcation of the development ethos and the techniques of advanced productivity among the rank and file of the population. These principles were to appear over and over again in all of Lewis's subsequent writings. It is hardly surprising, then, that Lewis's most productive years of writing and, indeed, the establishment of his reputation as the founding figure in development economics coincided with his long, close, and tempestuous relationship with the British Colonial Office.

During the early stages of World War II, Lewis had to decide whether he would work within Britain's imperial system, consulting for its primary organization, the Colonial Office, rather than outside it and against it. The choice proved easy. Britain was struggling against fascism, which left him in no doubt where he stood. From the inside, he used his influence, first, to promote the economic well-being and political opportunities of colonial peoples, and then after the pace of decolonization accelerated following the war, he rallied to the side of those who favored a fast pace toward African and Asian political independence. He was outspoken against British policies that promoted the interests of European settlers in Africa, and he often made economic recommendations that officials at the Colonial Office rejected as being too radical. But the reports that flowed from his pen during these years provided British officialdom at home and in the colonies with blueprints for how to make the impending political independence economically feasible. In this way, he was an effective advocate of decolonization, working within the British establishment, proof, indeed, that a person of color on the inside could make a difference.

Yet the personal frustrations that he experienced in his dealing with the officials of the Colonial Office were as obvious as the intellectual gains that he made. When he resigned from the Colonial Economic Advisory Council, he was suffering from an ulcer. He believed that he had been unceremoniously dismissed from his position with the Colonial Development Corporation. The experiences at the Colonial Office should have made him more skeptical about people in power and more aware that sound economic programs often had to be subordinated to political concerns. Even so, when Kwame Nkrumah approached Lewis to be Ghana's chief economic adviser, Lewis accepted.

CHAPTER 3

Unlimited Supplies of Labor

THE NOBEL AWARD THAT WAS PRESENTED to W. Arthur Lewis in 1979 cited the Princeton economist for his luminous article "Economic Development with Unlimited Supplies of Labour," which the journal *Manchester School* had published in its 1954 issue. It was unquestionably his outstanding scholarly achievement. A few individuals, perhaps resentful critics, would go even further, contending that only this publication was worthy of the Nobel award. This would be unjust since such a comment ignores Lewis's many important contributions in economic analysis and economic history. But it is true that the article galvanized the new field of development economics, providing it with a legitimacy that it had not previously enjoyed. Moreover, nearly all of his later studies in economic history bore the imprint of the article.

The field of development economics came of age in the decade and a half that followed World War II. Lewis was the acknowledged pioneer of this field, although many other scholars and groups made contributions. Among the groups in the forefront was the Economic Commission for Latin America (ECLA), founded in 1948 under the auspices of the United Nations and charged with the task of promoting growth in the Latin American economies. As its executive secretary and driving force from 1950 onwards, Raúl Prebisch was responsible for assembling an impressive team of social scientists and articulating a distinctive strategy for spurring economic development, based on the premise that primary product exporters like the Latin American states were disadvantaged in their trade with the industrialized parts of the world. The ECLA formula was local industrialization behind protective tariff barriers, coupled with less reliance on the cultivation and export of cash crops. These initiatives, they contended, would lead to rapid economic growth and ultimately to prosperity.

Equally influential was Paul Rosenstein-Rodan, Lewis's colleague at the University of London, whose early work on development economics and article on industrialization in Eastern and central Europe were frequently cited in the very early evolution of the field of development economics. Rosenstein-Rodan sketched out an industrialization program for Eastern and Central Europe that he believed would catapult these war-ravaged territories into the front rank of developed countries.¹ Inspired by this article, economists, dealing with colonial and postcolonial societies, sought to adapt Rosenstein-Rodan's formulations for industrial change, based on the notion of a "big push" into industrialization to their regions of the world. If not towering above the others, then certainly primus inter pares was Lewis himself.² He was not merely the most rigorously trained economist from the less developed world. His publications focused sharply on the critical issues of poverty and development. His ideas were persuasive and compelling, his arguments powerful, and the corpus of his writings suffused with the optimism that marked this era of political decolonization.³ Of the pioneers of development economics, he was the best synthesizer, the best able to handle multicausal relationships. His book *The Theory of Economic Growth* masterfully merged economic theory with social and political analysis.

Although development economics endeavored to make itself into a distinct subfield of the larger discipline of economics, in fact, it was closely tied with a worldwide concern with economic growth. In the words of Amartya Sen, "growth was everybody's concern [after World

---

¹ P. N. Rosenstein-Rodan, "Problems of Industrialization of Eastern and South-Eastern Europe," *Economic Journal*, vol. 53, nos. 210–11, June–September 1943, pp. 202–11.

² This is at least the view of Jagdish N. Bhagwati, who identified Raúl Prebisch, Paul Rosenstein-Rodan, Ragnar Nurske, and Lewis as belonging "to a most distinguished *small* group of pioneers." He singled out Lewis and Prebisch for shattering the myth that "fundamental thinking [on economic issues] required that one belonged to the center, not the periphery." Jagdish Bhagwati, "Comment," in Meier and Seers, *Pioneers in Development*, p. 197.

³ The literature on the rise of development economics in the aftermath of World War II is voluminous. H. W. Arndt has written two overviews, though of a decidedly negative cast: *Economic Development: The History of an Idea* (Chicago, 1987) and *The Rise and Fall of Economic Growth: A Study in Contemporary Thought* (Melbourne, 1978). Frederick Cooper focuses on the uses of the ideas of development theory in Africa in "Modernizing Bureaucrats, Backward Africans, and the Development Concept," in *International Development and the Social Sciences: Essays on the History and Politics of Knowledge*, ed. Frederick Cooper and Randall Packard (Los Angeles, 1997). A. T. Killick's *Development Economics in Action: A Study of Economic Policies in Ghana* (New York, 1978) is a brilliant case study of the panoply of ideas that formed the consensus behind economic development from the 1950s through the 1970s as these ideas were applied to the state and economy of Ghana. I will draw on it freely but also critique it in chapters 5 and 6 of this book. First-rate sketches from the leading development economists of this period, including one by Lewis himself, can be found in Meier and Seers, ed. *Pioneers in Development*. Here the reader can note the different emphases that each one of the pioneers in this field brought to his or her work. The volume contains essays written by P. T. Bauer, Colin Clark, Albert O. Hirschman, Arthur Lewis, Gunnar Myrdal, Raúl Prebisch, Paul N. Rosenstein-Rodan, Walt Whitman Rostow, H. W. Singer, and Jan Tinbergen; in short, the true movers and shakers of the development revolution in economics.

War II], and it is no wonder that in such a milieu growth theory was pampered by the attention of economists."[4] Not only were colonial officials and nationalist leaders concerned about the development of colonies, but Europeans wanted to rebuild their war-torn economies as rapidly as possible. Economic growth also became one of the defining issues of the Cold War. The leaders of socialist and Communist countries were determined to show the rest of the world that their formulas for rapid economic development were better suited to the third world than those being propounded by the capitalist West. Economists trained in Soviet institutions insisted that planned and centrally regulated economies used resources more efficiently than free market capitalist economies and would, thus, close the economic gap that separated the less developed countries from those that had gone through their industrial revolutions.

By the late 1940s and early 1950s Lewis was preoccupied with the very questions that were stirring the political and business elites in Europe, North America, the Soviet bloc countries, and the decolonizing world: economic growth. Personal interest, repeated student pleas for courses on colonial economic growth, and Colonial Office consultancies had already focused his scholarship precisely on those questions that had vexed him since his days growing up in the West Indies. Why was one part of the world, the West, so rich while the rest was so poor? Was the wealth of the industrialized countries the result of the poverty of other parts of the world? Were there formulas to be found for breaking the "vicious cycles of poverty" that seemed to trap so many Asian, African, and Latin American countries? Could new economic programs set a process of sustained development in motion? Lewis was now able to devote himself exclusively to these personal and intellectual passions. With the war at an end and his secondment to government agencies finished, he could concentrate his teaching, research, and government consultancies on this research agenda. His appointment in 1947 to one of England's most prestigious economic chairs provided him with a secure academic position at an extraordinarily young age. He consulted with the Colonial Office, the United Nations, and foreign governments on his own terms and at his own choosing, benefiting from a growing reputation as an expert on economic development. His years as professor of political economy at the University of Manchester, 1947–1957, were to be his most productive in research and teaching.

[4] Amartya Sen, introduction to *Growth Economics: Selected Readings*, ed. Amartya Sen (Harmondsworth, Eng., 1970), p. 9.

Lewis's Preparation for "Unlimited Supplies of Labour"

What made Lewis's most influential article, "Economic Development with Unlimited Supplies of Labour," published in the journal *Manchester School* in 1954, such an overnight sensation with a wide readership is that it was short, well written, easy to understand, original, and self-evident, at least to nonspecialists. A lay reader could grasp its basic argument. But so too could professional economists who were impressed with Lewis's rigorous use of data and the clarity of his economic analysis. Of all the approaches being put forward at the time (big push, unbalanced growth, forward and backward linkages, and takeoff into sustained economic growth), many preferred Lewis's on the grounds that it was the most rigorous and the most easily modeled. Thus, it appealed even to those economists who were suspicious of the new field of development economics on the grounds that the field lacked mathematical rigor and could not be formally modeled.[5] Moreover, its major tenets fit comfortably within the economic consensus of the period.

Lewis started from a premise that most noneconomists accepted without question. The poor countries of Asia and the Caribbean were characterized by two separate and distinct economic sectors—a traditional agrarian sector and a capitalist industrial sector. The agrarian or traditional sectors were burdened by a large pool of surplus or redundant workers who contributed little or nothing to output. Indeed, in some cases, their output was thought to be negative. This situation of stagnation, however, had a silver lining since workers could move out of this sector with no loss of agricultural output and at near subsistence rates into the modern sector, turning the latter into an engine of economic change. Critical to this process of labor transfer were the activities of a nascent entrepreneurial class or an emergent interventionist state, so long as both groups were capable of recognizing the opportunities that an "unlimited supply of cheap rural labor" created for rapid industrialization.

The attraction of the Lewis article was that it stressed a factor—labor—that other economists had considered important and that Lewis

---

[5] Paul Krugman, "Toward a Counter-counterrevolution in Development Theory," *Proceedings of the World Bank Annual Conference on Development Economics*, p. 22. Krugman is particularly critical of Lewis's work in development economics. Of Lewis's best-known book, *The Theory of Economic Growth*, he comments that the "1955 text on economic growth seems fairly innocent of the whole idea of external economies; indeed, the term does not even appear in the index." While conceding that Lewis's article on unlimited supplies of labor was "probably the most famous paper in the literature of development economics," he added, "in retrospect, it is hard to see exactly why."

now elevated to the highest prominence. In his critically important 1943 article, Paul Rosenstein-Rodan had posited "a country in which 20,000 'unemployed workers ... are taken from the land and put into a large new shoe factory. They receive wages substantially higher than their previous income *in natura.*"' Indeed, Lewis's earlier writings from the late 1940s and early 1950s regularly described societies characterized by unlimited supplies of labor. Even his undergraduate essays on labor in the West Indies had promoted industrialization as the solution to employment for the large peasant workforces trapped in the countryside. So had his important writings on the economic problems of the West Indies that he had contributed to the Caribbean Commission in the late 1940s.

Between 1949 and 1954 Lewis began to identify the linkages between surplus workers in the traditional sector and industrialization, thereby laying the analytical foundations for his 1954 article. In doing so, he shifted his gaze from the West Indies and turned instead to the writings of the classical British and European economic historians of the nineteenth century, whose essays, he asserted, demonstrated that the British industrial revolution and the subsequent European industrial revolutions had used the very same elements of surplus labor that now existed in many less developed countries. Lewis's advice to his economist colleagues was brief and to the point. Surely drawing on Robbins's famous LSE lectures on the nineteenth-century classical economists, Lewis urged his colleagues in development economics to return to the classics. Lewis counseled his colleagues to revisit the works of the great nineteenth-century economists, in particular Adam Smith, David Ricardo, Thomas Malthus, and Karl Marx, where they would encounter an English economy that had many of the same characteristics that now pertained in Asia and the Caribbean. Equally large and unproductive reservoirs of cheap, unskilled labor that Lewis observed in contemporary Asian and Caribbean societies had been trapped nearly a century and a half ago in the English countryside. British labor surpluses had made possible the industrial revolution and burnished the reputations of Britain's entrepreneurs. Adam Smith in his *Wealth of Nations* and Karl Marx in *Capital,* properly read, offered nothing less than a blueprint for contemporary industrialization.

The first of four essays that reveal the direction of Lewis's thinking on labor supplies and industrialization between 1949 and 1954 was a brief note, entitled "Colonial Development," which he published in 1949. In the introduction he noted that his article was intended to do no more than "clear my own mind." It would lay out "a road map of the whole area [of colonial development] as a guide to further exploration."⁶ Not infrequently, Lewis wrote summary, state-of-the-art essays to force himself to see where the field of study was and what large questions still needed to be solved. Lewis's essays of this genre tended to be short and deceptively simple. Yet not only did they give Lewis and other scholars a chance to take stock, but in retrospect they offer markers to the evolution of Lewis's thinking for outsiders looking back on these years.

The 1949 essay displayed his penchant for viewing issues of development as a whole. Lewis was at heart a general equilibrium theorist, believing that no part of the development picture could be separated from the rest and that economic imbalances, say a rapid increase in investable capital or large, unproductive labor forces in the countryside, would reverberate through the economy until a state of balance was achieved. Lewis also held to a view of an economy that incorporated many noneconomic factors and that drew upon his broad training and teaching in economics and economic history at the London School of Economics and Manchester.

As a summing-up essay, the 1949 work was full of the immediate postwar feelings of optimism toward colonial economic development. Lewis continued to stress the need for mass education that would mobilize all segments of colonial societies in the development effort, adults as well as children. Caught up in the enthusiasm about the new generation of Asian and African nationalist leaders, he looked to this dynamic political elite, whom he labeled "real democrats," to energize the rank and file of the population and enlist them behind the goals of economic development. Lewis believed that the highly charged political atmosphere of late colonialism and the five-year development plans that colonial governments were devising would lead to visible and immediate improvements for the people. "The colonies," he exclaimed, "will have planning, plenty of planning, and planning of the highest order."⁷

The second publication in this period resulted from a United Nations committee formed to examine employment and economic growth in the less developed parts of the world. In 1951 the United Nations asked five leading economists to provide advice on the prerequisites for full employment in the less developed countries of the world. The study was a follow-up to an earlier report that had examined the national and international measures required to achieve full employment in in-

---

⁶ W. Arthur Lewis, "Colonial Development," *Transactions of the Manchester Statistical Society,* Section 1948–49, January 12, 1949, p. 3.
⁷ Ibid., p. 22.

dustrialized countries. Lewis exercised the dominant influence within the committee. The major findings of the report represented his views.

Not only did the report elaborate a framework that was becoming the hallmark of Lewis's thinking, namely that economic development could occur when supplies of labor were "unlimited," but the tension within the committee over this issue, particularly between Lewis and another committee member, Theodore Schultz, became well known. Schultz was a specialist in agricultural economics and a passionate defender of the rationality and efficiency of peasant farmers. Later he regretted signing the report because of its emphasis on disguised rural unemployment. John P. Lewis, a fellow development economist and later a colleague of Lewis's at Princeton University, believed that the vehemence of some of Schultz's subsequent writings concerning Lewis and the concept of unlimited supplies of labor stemmed from his having agreed to a document that claimed that "the marginal product of farmers could be zero (that was heresy for a Chicago economist . . .)."[8] Ironically, both men shared the Nobel Prize for economics in 1979.

The task of the five-person committee was to make recommendations that would enhance third world employment. To this end, the report identified four categories of unemployment: cyclical, seasonal, technological, and disguised. The first three were standard terms in the economic literature at the time. It was, however, the fourth category of unemployment—disguised unemployment—that was to prove the most controversial and that reflected Lewis's own predilections. To be sure, the term *disguised unemployment* was hardly new, having appeared in the economic literature as early as the 1920s, but it had yet to acquire the formal status that it took on later in the decade. According to the report, "the disguised unemployed are those persons who work on their own account and who are so numerous relative to the resources with which they work that if a number of them were withdrawn for work in other sectors of the economy, the total output of the sector from which they were withdrawn would not be diminished even though no significant regionalization occurred in the sector."[9]

On the surface, the statement seemed both an accurate and an unobjectionable description of poor countries with large rural populations, like those that existed in Asia and many parts of Latin America. But the implications of this concept, barely spelled out in the UN report, were far-reaching. They implied that the marginal productivity or the

[8] J. Lewis, "William Arthur Lewis," p. 159.

[9] United Nations, *Measures for the Economic Development of Under-developed Countries: Report by a Group of Experts Appointed by the Secretary-General of the United Nations* (New York, 1951), p. 7.

additional product of many rural workers was zero, perhaps even negative—a stance that should have been anathema to free market, neoclassical economists, especially those who specialized in agriculture, like Schultz.

The committee went on to argue that only dramatic increases in economic growth could reduce the high levels of unemployment and underemployment and the alarming rates of population increase characteristic of underdeveloped economies. The Lewis formulas for spurring economic growth were as clear in this section of the document as was his concept of disguised unemployment. These entailed a broad range of economic and noneconomic factors that had been high on his agenda since the 1930s.

Among the crucial claims of the report was a finding that rapid growth occurred when capital formation doubled from roughly the 5 percent of GDP that characterized most traditional economies to 10 percent or even more.[10] In the West, population growth had proven a spur to economic progress, but this was because in the nineteenth century it had rarely exceeded 1 percent per year, at which level it was a powerful stimulant of consumer demand. Not so in the economies of the rest of the world. Here population growth rates of 2 and even 3 percent threatened to wipe out the gains of even the best-laid economic plans and to force late-developing societies to aim for nearly impossible growth rates of 5 percent per year.

The third of Lewis's four publications in this period stemmed from his visit to Egypt in the spring of 1953—a visit arranged at the invitation of the Egyptian Society of Political Economy, Statistics, and Legislation, where so many of the intellectual elite of the country gathered. Lewis had agreed to deliver three lectures on industrialization. Yet he began his lectures by offering advice on the agricultural side of the economy that he felt was as important as any recommendations he might have on industrial development. He reminded his audience that industrialization required a home market and that the surest way to create a home market was to improve agriculture, particularly foodstuff productivity. Cash crops, like cotton, which had undergirded the Egyptian economy for nearly a century, could provide only limited help, particularly if farmers failed to increase the overall productivity of food production and achieve greater farm output. Balanced industrial and agricultural growth was essential to sustained economic progress. To industrialize without promoting agricultural improvement "is to ruin the industrialists (who won't have enough workers or consum-

---

[10] Ibid., p. 35.

ers) and to improve agriculture without industrialization will ruin farmers (who will live in a society with vast hordes of unemployed)."[11]

Having treated agriculture, the importance of which he believed to be greatly underrated, Lewis devoted the remainder of his remarks to industrialization. In his view, Egypt and India were alike in having large labor surpluses, which depressed the wages of workers yet created opportunities for entrepreneurs to establish labor-intensive industries. In Lewis's calculations, roughly one-quarter of the agricultural populations of these two countries could be regarded as surplus, which meant that "the marginal productivity of labor in agriculture is zero. It may even be negative."[12] A country as populous and urbanized as Egypt had great potential for industrial expansion, however. Lewis identified the following industries as having a large enough domestic market to support local manufacturing: cement, brick-making, glass, pottery, wood, leather, processed food, textile, clothing, shoe, and tobacco industries. Although he did not employ the term *import-substitution industrialization*, he was promoting precisely that strategy. He also believed that Egypt's abundant supply of cheap labor would put the country in a position to become an exporter of a small, but potentially lucrative range of labor-intensive manufactures. Provided that industrial labor costs remained competitive with surrounding countries—and they should in the case of Egypt (or, say, India) because it was "overpopulated" in relation to agricultural resources—the prospects for exporting textiles, processed foods, shoes, and other items were "unlimited."[13]

In many ways, the Egyptian lectures previewed the main ideas in Lewis's 1954 article. But the fourth article of this period, based on Lewis's first extended trip to South and Southeast Asia in 1952, truly crystallized his ideas on labor surpluses. Commenting on his impressions of Malaya, Iran, Burma, India, and Ceylon in an article published in the *District Bank Review* in December 1952, he remarked that the "dominating problem . . . [in this area of the world] is the shortage of food."[14] At the time Burma, Thailand, and Indochina exported their food surpluses to India, Ceylon, and Malaya. But time was not on the side of the food-importing countries, and unless the countries of the region dramatically increased their agricultural productivity food shortages were inevitable. India's population problems impressed him

[11] W. Arthur Lewis, *Aspects of Industrialization: National Bank of Egypt, Fiftieth Anniversary Commemoration Lecture* (Cairo, 1953), p. 7.
[12] Ibid., p. 8.
[13] Ibid., p. 7.
[14] W. Arthur Lewis, "Reflections on South-East Asia," *District Bank Review*, no. 104, December 1952, p. 3.

profoundly. Already the subcontinent had exhausted its reservoirs of uncultivated land, and a population of 350 million now toiled on only 250 million acres. In Britain, with its high levels of agricultural productivity, it took an average of one acre of land to feed one person. Of all the countries that Lewis had seen, none struck him more forcefully as having a "surplus" agricultural population or being more desperately in need of industrialization than India.[15]

The "Unlimited Supplies of Labour" Article

In one of Lewis's brief autobiographical musings, he identified August 1952 as the moment when his two-sector model of economic development sprang into his mind. At the time, and, indeed, for some time, he had been wrestling with two questions. The first was why industrial products (in Lewis's thinking, steel was the exemplary product) sold for such high world prices compared to agricultural products, such as coffee. The second was why so many of the countries in the less developed world had large and impoverished populations. "Walking down the road in Bangkok, it came to me suddenly that both problems (the relative prices of coffee and steel and the wealth and poverty of nations) have the same solution. Throw away the neoclassical assumption that the quantity of labor is fixed. An 'unlimited supply of labor' will keep wages down, producing cheap coffee in the first case and high profits in the second. The result is a dual national or world economy where one part is a reservoir of cheap labor to the other."[16]

When Lewis's article on unlimited supplies of labor appeared in 1954, it created a sensation. It did precisely what Lewis hoped: it placed the emerging field of development economics squarely on the map of the economics profession, providing it with a set of bedrock working theorems, however controversial they might be. Moreover,

---

[15] Ibid., p. 11.
[16] Lewis, "Autobiographical Note," p. 3. The development economists Raúl Prebisch and H. W. Singer had investigated the terms of trade between primary exports and manufactures and concluded that the terms worked against primary product exporters. Their studies purported to show that the world demand for foodstuff exports, such as cocoa, coffee, and tea and other agricultural products, like cotton, would not expand as rapidly as the demand for manufactures. Hence, primary product exporters would never have the high growth rates that the industrialized parts of the world enjoyed. Lewis accepted this view up to a point; yet his researches also convinced him that the ratio of third-world trade in world trade was a fixed percentage. Primary product exporters would share in the benefits of an expanding world economy as much as the industrialized parts of the world. Asia, Africa, and Latin America needed industrialization because this was the only way to achieve rising standards of living.

just as he had intended, his hypotheses set the field of development economics apart as a distinctive branch of study, particularly because, according to Lewis, it was not governed by neoclassical assumptions concerning the marginal product of labor.[17]

Still, Lewis did not intend to unmoor development economics from the discipline, only to establish it as a distinct subfield, requiring its own specialized training. He was not prepared to follow the lead of certain economic anthropologists, who were arguing at this time that *homo economicus*, or the rational economic actor, was a unique historical creature, a personality type that had emerged only out of the capitalist ethos of the West. Lewis had little patience for scholars who contended that peoples in the less developed regions of the world behaved differently from peoples of European descent, that they valued communal solidarities over individual achievement, even at times scorning economic gain. Rather, he sought to connect the new field of development economics with classical economics, whose earliest practitioners he thought dealt with problems similar to those that faced contemporary Asian and African countries.

Over and over again, as Lewis worked through the principal ideas that informed his pathbreaking article, he felt certain that the existence of unlimited supplies of labor in certain parts of the world explained why products exported from the industrialized parts of the world and requiring no more backbreaking labor than cash crops from Asia and Africa required so much more of a third-world farmer's work time to purchase than the coffee, tea, and cotton that a factory worker bought. It also explained why the primary producing countries of the world, whose populations were not lazier than those of the industrialized communities, were so much poorer. Neoclassical economics, in his view, offered no answers. Reflecting back on his thinking in this period, Lewis wrote: "From my undergraduate days I had sought a solu-

---

[17] Lewis's claim that neoclassical economics did not work in understanding the British industrial revolution and was leading economic planners astray in developing plans for less developed economies did not arouse as much opposition as his argument about the zero marginal productivity of workers in the traditional sector. But it did not go unchallenged. The economic historian Jeffrey G. Williamson wrote a series of articles in the 1980s claiming that standard neoclassical analysis was superior to the Lewis labor surplus model for explaining Britain's industrial revolution. In his view any labor surpluses that existed in the British economy at the time were not crucial to the country's industrialization. Nor was there any rapid rise in the British savings rate, as Lewis assumed. See in particular, Jeffrey G. Williamson, "The Historical Content of the Classical Labor Surplus Model," *Population and Development Review*, vol. 11, no. 2, June 1985, pp. 171–191, and Jeffrey G. Williamson, "Why Was British Growth So Slow During the Industrial Revolution?" *Journal of Economic History*, vol. 44, no. 3, September 1984, pp. 687–712.

tion to the question what determines the relative prices of steel and coffee. The approach through marginal utility made no sense to me."[18]

Lewis's search for insight into the pressing question of why some countries were wealthy and others were poor and his dissatisfaction with neoclassical marginal utility methods drove him back to the classical economists, whose writings the economics profession were rediscovering at this time.[19] Equally eye-opening for fathoming the mainsprings of the English industrial revolution were the works of British economic historians. Heading the list of studies that influenced Lewis was Barbara and John Hammond's three-volume examination of British workers at the end of the eighteenth century.[20] Their study, coupled with the copious statistical data that Phyllis Deane and G.D.H. Cole were gathering at the time on all aspects of the British economy from the end of the seventeenth century to the middle of the twentieth century, provided powerful evidence that contrary to the assumption that informed much of neoclassical economics, workers' wages had stagnated even as the industrial sector expanded.

Another economic historian to influence Lewis was T. S. Ashton, whose work *The Industrial Revolution, 1760–1830*, published in 1948, was a brief but authoritative overview that most scholars at the time regarded as the best study of the period.[21] Ashton held the chair in economic history at the London School of Economics during part of the time that Lewis was on the faculty there. They would have had many conversations about British economic history. The final two sentences of Ashton's book, frequently cited in favor of industrialization, made clear the need to spread the benefits of industrial development throughout the world. "There are today on the plains of India and China men and women, plague-ridden and hungry, living lives little better to outward appearance, than those of the cattle that toil with them by day and share their place of sleep at night. Such Asiatic standards, and such unmecha-

---

[18] Lewis, "Autobiographical Note," p. 3.

[19] See the biography of Nicholas Kaldor by Ferdinando Targetti, *Nicholas Kaldor: The Economics and Politics of Capitalism as a Dynamic System* (Oxford, 1992), particularly chapter 5, where the author describes the efforts of leading Cambridge-based economists such as Piero Sraffa, Joan Robinson, and Kaldor to revive an interest in the writings of Smith, Malthus, Ricardo, and Marx. What fascinated these scholars, as well as Lewis, was the attention the classical economists paid to issues of economic growth and the distribution of wealth.

[20] Barbara and J. L. Hammond, *The Village Labourer, 1760–1832: A Study of the Government of England before the Reform Bill; The Town Labourer, 1760–1832*; and *The Skilled Labourer, 1760–1832* (London, 1911–19).

[21] T. S. Ashton, *The Industrial Revolution, 1760–1830* (London, 1948).

nized horrors, are the lot of those who increase their numbers without passing through an industrial revolution."[22]

On the basis of his reading of British economic history and the classical economists, Lewis believed that he had been able to identify two critical ingredients that had produced the industrial revolution and that could be transported successfully to the third world. The first stemmed from his readings of the Hammonds. British industrialists had benefited from vast supplies of cheap labor released from the agrarian sector. The second, drawn mainly from the statistics that Cole and Deane were assembling, was that the availability of cheap labor caused industrial profits to soar and enabled businesspersons to reinvest their profits in business expansion. Citing the work of the Hammonds, Deane and Cole, and Ashton, Lewis concluded that the British industrialists represented a new element in European society. Unlike landlords and peasants, who used increases in wealth to purchase more land, or merchants, who sought to expand their sales of merchandise, or government officials who used gains that came to them to purchase items of conspicuous consumption and markers of wealth and prestige, the industrialists, perhaps because of their Protestant ethic (though Lewis never developed this critical part of his argument at any great length), became infatuated with their industrial successes. They plowed business profits back into their firms, thus becoming the engine of rapid economic growth in the early stage of industrialization. Moreover, as their proportion of the national income rose, so the industrial revolution advanced until finally the whole of the surplus labor force, once trapped in the agrarian sector, was absorbed. At this point, the theories of the classical economists, resting on assumptions of unlimited supplies of labor, no longer pertained. Neoclassical economics, as enunciated by Alfred Marshall and his disciples, took over, based as it was on limited supplies of labor, marginal utility rates, and intersecting curves of supply and demand.

Lewis's belief that Britain's industrial revolution offered guidelines for the industrialization of the third world did not mean that this experience had to be replicated in third world industrialization. In a 1937 article that he wrote for *The Keys*, entitled "African Economic Problems," he stated: "This much is clear: uncontrolled industrialism destroys more happiness than it creates. Study England in the throes of the Industrial Revolution or any country from America to Japan, and we find always that legacy of slums and misery, which uncon-

[22] Ibid., p. 129.

trolled industrialism hands down to future generations."[23] Planning, which had also featured prominently in Lewis's writings in these years, was the instrument for avoiding the excesses of the early industrial revolutions. Knowledge of the gross injustices would enable planners to implement economic programs that were mindful of the welfare of all classes. Successful industrialization, in Lewis's formulations, did not necessarily require an industrialist class hiring workers at subsistence wages and benefiting from a rise in the proportion of profits in national income accounts. It could be advanced by forward-looking state bureaucrats.

A careful reading of Barbara and J. L. Hammond's three-volume study of the English working classes during the industrial revolution (*The Village Labourer*, *The Town Labourer*, and *The Skilled Labourer*, published between 1911 and 1919) demonstrates how steeped Lewis's 1954 article was in the English historical tradition. The Hammonds were Fabian socialists, members of an intellectual elite that emerged at the turn of the twentieth century. Their nonrevolutionary and economically driven predispositions appealed to Lewis. They dedicated their second volume, *The Town Labourer*, to two leading contemporary Fabians, J. A. Hobson and Leonard Hobhouse. This volume is particularly revealing. Remove the Hammonds' passionate embrace of the working classes and the authors' moral outrage at the ruling industrial elite and the landed aristocrats, add a pinch of dispassionate economic analysis and a modicum of empirical validation, and one has the framework of Lewis's 1954 article.

Certainly Lewis's belief that the English industrial revolution arose out of an abundant and cheap workforce paid at subsistence wages and a dynamic, emerging new class of business innovators is writ large on all of the Hammonds's pages. The subtitle of the second volume, *The New Civilisation*, also reverberates through Lewis's writings of the 1950s and 1960s. The Hammonds claimed that the new industrialists "had only to stamp on the ground to turn empty valleys into swarming hives of work people."[24] Surplus labor came from Ireland, the demobilization of troops following wars with France on the continent, the exodus of villagers from the countryside following the enclosure movement, and natural population increase. They came en masse, willing to work for the going wages "as they were accustomed to low wages."[25] The new industrialists were able to make themselves into a group apart. They were the forgers of this new civilization, "in which human life seemed

---

[23] W. Arthur Lewis, "African Economic Problems," *The Keys*, vol. 5, no. 1, July–September 1937, p. 15.

[24] Hammond and Hammond, *The Town Labourer*, p. 11.

[25] Ibid., p. 12.

a good deal less important than the profits of capital." These individuals had raised themselves "by their own efforts commencing in a very humble way, and pushing their advance by a series of increasing exertions.... Competing wildly for the new opportunities of wealth and enabled by law successfully to resist the claims of the workmen to a living wage, [the capitalists] forced the new society into this mould."[26] From the vantage point of the 1950s, Lewis found the ire that led the Hammonds to assert that "the general feature of the times was the rise of a class of rich employers and the creation of a large and miserable proletariat" less persuasive than the vivid descriptions of just how this new industrial world had come into being.[27]

An additional feature marked Lewis's intellectual breakthrough. By positing traditional and modern sectors, admittedly abstractions and ideal types rather than precise descriptions of any less developed economy or the economies of Europe at the beginning of the nineteenth century, Lewis aligned himself with a vast body of noneconomic, social scientific literature, loosely labeled at the time *modernization theory*. Lewis rarely cited the works of noneconomists in his articles or books, but he was a voracious reader of works in history, political science, and sociology and would have been entirely familiar with the main tenets of modernization theory that was establishing itself as the dominant paradigm in the 1950s. Social scientists like Daniel Lerner, whose book *The Passing of Traditional Society* reflected the mantra of this school, as well as others like David Apter, Talcott Parsons, Cyril Black, and Marion Levy, to mention only a few of the prominent figures who were publishing in this decade, believed that the world was divided between the modern countries, mainly to be found in Western Europe, Australasia, and North America, and the traditional ones. The great challenge of the postwar era was the transition of traditional countries to modernity—a process that these scholars labeled modernization. Thus, although Lewis saw himself as breaking molds, founding a new field, and challenging prevailing assumptions of an established field, his formulations were deeply rooted in European experience and dovetailed with the predominant social scientific vision of the period.

THE ARTICLE ITSELF AND ITS IMMEDIATE IMPACT

Lewis began his article on unlimited supplies of labor by defining his crucial, underlying concept. Unlimited supplies of labor existed where "the marginal productivity of labour is negligible, zero, or even nega-

[26] Ibid., p. 14.
[27] Ibid., p. 96.

tive."[28] This was to prove one of the most disputed parts of the article and to cause him no end of grief for the rest of his career. The United Kingdom, northwestern Europe, and parts of Africa did not have unlimited supplies of labor. But India, Egypt, and Jamaica did, and for these parts of the world Lewis proposed "to elaborate a different framework . . . which the neoclassical (and Keynesian) assumptions do not fit."[29] In these areas labor could be withdrawn from the sector where it was in surplus without any effect on the product. Such conditions were most apparent in the agricultural sectors of Asian and Latin American countries, but they were not confined to agriculture. They existed as well, though they were not so visible, in casual jobs, petty trading, and domestic service. In all of these activities labor was paid a subsistence wage, and yet even at this meager level the supply of workers exceeded the demand.

This otherwise depressing state of affairs—for Lewis the essence of a stagnant traditional economy—had potentially beneficial consequences. Once a modern, forward-looking sector had come into being, for example through the creation of new industries, a ready-made pool of cheap, albeit unskilled, workers was available, consisting, of course, of redundant peasant farmers, petty traders, retainers, wives and daughters of the household, and that part of the population which was expanding. As soon as a modern economic sector arose, a dual economy existed, which Lewis described as "heavily developed patches of the economy, surrounded by economic darkness."[30] Lewis believed that wages in the modern sector would need to be only about 30 percent above subsistence to attract workers from the traditional sector and to facilitate their migration to the cities and their settling in.

This, then, was the mechanism of economic modernization. As Lewis so aptly put it: "Now the play begins. For we can now begin to trace the process of economic expansion."[31] Two critical ingredients characterized the growth of the economy at this stage. First, labor moved from the traditional to the modern sector, and, second, the entrepreneurs accumulated capital from the profits of their businesses in the modern sector. If these profits were reinvested in the modern sector, they would cause the modern segments of the economy to grow over time until the modern wage sector had absorbed all the cheap and surplus labor that had once been trapped in the traditional sector.

---

[28] W. Arthur Lewis, "Economic Development with Unlimited Supplies of Labour," *Manchester School*, vol. 22, no. 2, May 1954, p. 141.
[29] Ibid., p. 141.
[30] Ibid., p. 148.
[31] Ibid., p. 151.

At that point labor was no longer in surplus. The dual nature of the economy would cease to exist. Workers would now labor for above-subsistence wages, labor shortages would exist, higher and higher levels of labor productivity would begin to take place, and, in short, all of the ingredients of the neoclassical and Keynesian economy would now exist.

During this transitional phase of economic change the levels of investment rose from 4 to 5 percent of national income to 12 to 15 percent. They did so because the ratio of profits in national income accounts ascended steeply, based, as it was, on the expansion of modern economic activities, in turn fueled by cheap labor. Here, the reader can see a strong element of the classical theory of labor value, even the Marxist notion that the capitalist class captured the largest share of the economic gain of development. Yet Lewis did not deplore the ascent of the profit rate in national income accounts, as many of the Fabians did. He saw this development as highly progressive. As a Fabian socialist, he believed that income levels would ultimately become more equal, especially as a consequence of democratic politics and trade union activity.

The Lewis model not only expected gross income disparities in the early stages of economic change. It demanded them. The real driving force behind economic growth was the modern sector entrepreneur. Backward countries saved little, according to Lewis, not because they were poor but "because their capitalist sector is too small. Inequality in and of itself was no guarantee of development. Inequality is omnipresent in the world. It is only useful when it creates a capitalist class, that is to say, ... a group of men who think in terms of investing capital productively."[32]

In the 1954 publication, Lewis was buoyantly optimistic. Economic growth had an aura of inevitability, as if the processes of economic change that he had outlined would follow automatically, even mechanistically, wherever labor surpluses existed. Lewis was soon forced to explain the disappointing record and the obvious difficulties that most less developed countries experienced in the 1960s and 1970s. There was no gainsaying that change was neither automatic nor easy. One of the problems that soon became apparent to him and others was the failure of a dynamic capitalist class to emerge. Experience revealed to Lewis that, in many of the poorer countries of the world, leaders in the modern sector were not so liberated from traditional values and ways of doing things as he had predicted. Often these individuals came from the old landed elites and had not shed their agrarian and traditionalist

[32] Ibid., p. 159.

ways in favor of a profit-maximizing mentality. They were not willing to reinvest profits in their modern enterprises, preferring instead to purchase land, engage in conspicuous consumption, and curry political favor. Lewis also admitted that the creation of this capitalist class in England, Western Europe, and North America was a profound historical riddle. He thought it likely that the early capitalists in the West were drawn from marginal, immigrant groups.

Lewis defined a capitalist class as having "a passion . . . for ruling over bigger and better factories." Priests, traders, landlords, soldiers, and princes did not work for this goal. They hoarded money or speculated or invested in real estate. While "the banker wants more deposits, only the industrialists' passion drives toward using profits to create a bigger empire of bricks and steel."[33] Having observed the industrial achievements of the Soviet Union under Stalin's five-year plans, Lewis believed that a class dedicated to economic growth could arise even within the public sector. There, too, bureaucrats had become as ardent for economic growth and for the reinvestment of public sector profits in economic enterprises as their private sector counterparts elsewhere in the world.

The article had an immediate impact. It was regularly cited in other studies and was featured in the first edition of the standard sourcebook on economic development, Gerald M. Meier's *Leading Issues in Economic Development*, which first appeared in 1964.[34] Yet unlike many other essays, it continued to be influential decades after its original date of publication. Reflecting on the immediate and long-term impact of the 1954 article, Lewis observed that the essay "was greeted with applause and with cries of outrage. In the succeeding twenty-five years other scholars have written five books and numerous articles regarding the merits of the thesis, assessing contradictory data, or applying it to resolving other problems. The debate continues."[35] Although it encountered some rough water and incisive criticism, the development economist and Lewis's colleague John P. Lewis was not far from the mark when he commented that "most development economists consider it the single most influential article in the history of the field."[36]

As Rosenstein-Rodan had pointed out long before Lewis published his article, "the concept of 'agrarian excess' or 'surplus population' or

---

[33] Ibid., pp. 160 and 169–70.
[34] Gerald M. Meier, *Leading Issues in Economic Development* (New York, 1964). Gerald M. Meier and Robert E. Baldwin also featured Lewis's ideas on unlimited supplies of labor prominently in their highly regarded book on economic development, *Economic Development: Theory, History, Policy* (London, 1957).
[35] Lewis, "Autobiographical Note," p. 4.
[36] Lewis, "William Arthur Lewis," p. 158.

'disguised unemployment in agriculture' was hardly new, having appeared in the economic literature as early as the late 1920s."[37] Lewis, however, made it central. From 1954, developmentalists could not avoid it when describing barriers to development and potentials for growth. According to Albert Hirschman, "there was . . . something arcane about the concept [of unlimited supplies of labor], often also referred to as 'disguised unemployment,' that served to enhance the scientific aura and status of the new field."[38]

The Lewis article also fit comfortably within a new orthodoxy in British economic thinking—growth economics that was associated with the writings of R. F. Harrod and Evsey Domar. Both economists had spurned much of the conventional economic analysis, even Keynesianism, on the grounds that earlier studies concentrated on conditions of equilibrium and ignored "steadily continuing" economic change. In his 1939 article, "An Essay in Dynamic Theory," published in the *Economic Journal*, Harrod stressed the need "to give the outline of a 'dynamic theory' in contrast to 'static theory.'" His goal was "to develop a similar classification and system of axioms to meet the situation in which certain forces are operating steadily to increase or decrease certain magnitudes in the system." He proposed "the study of change analogous to that provided by static theory for the study of rest."[39] By the early 1940s Harrod and Domar had concluded that the essential ingredient responsible for disequilibriating economic change and dramatic economic growth or decline stemmed from changes in the rate of savings. Although Harrod and Domar did not work on developing economies, their equation that economic growth (g) equaled savings (s) divided by capital output meant that a high savings rate and low capital intensity industrialization would result in extremely high economic growth rates. This was precisely the argument that Lewis was making in his article on unlimited supplies of labor and thus made the essay immensely attractive to economists and policymakers.[40]

Like all powerful and novel approaches, Lewis's article came in for searching criticism, which he addressed over the remainder of his life

---

[37] Paul N. Rosenstein-Rodan, "*Natura Facit Saltum*: Analysis of the Disequilibrium Growth Process," in Meier and Seers, *Pioneers in Development*, p. 212.

[38] Albert O. Hirschman, "The Rise and Decline of Development Economics," in *Essays in Trespassing: Economics to Politics and Beyond* (Cambridge, 1981), p. 10.

[39] R. F. Harrod, "An Essay in Dynamic Theory," *Economic Journal*, vol. 49, no. 193, March 1939, p. 14. One should also consult R. F. Harrod, *Towards a Dynamic Economics: Some Recent Developments of Economic Theory and Their Application to Policy* (London, 1948).

[40] Dudley Seers, "The Birth, Life, and Death of Development Economics," *Development and Change*, vol. 10, no. 4, October 1979, p. 711.

in a series of further statements and reformulations. Even though nearly everything that he published after 1954 bore some relation to the original article, Lewis dealt specifically with his critics in articles published in 1958, 1968, and 1979, the last occasion being the twenty-fifth anniversary issue of the publication of the original article.

No statement in Lewis's article provoked more opposition than his contention that the supplies of labor were unlimited in many traditional economies and that the marginal product of workers in the traditional sector was negligible, zero, or even negative. One of the first to criticize this argument was a fellow development economist, P. T. Bauer, who, in reviewing Lewis's book *The Theory of Economic Growth*, published only one year after the *Manchester School* article, claimed that while the author purported to eschew any general theory of development, in fact, "there is a particular model from which his main theme springs."[41] This was Lewis's belief in labor surpluses, which has "misled Lewis on some fundamental issues." To begin with, Bauer believed that Lewis drew too sharp a distinction between the traditional and modern sectors. He was blind to the innovativeness existing within peasant farming. He also attacked Lewis for ignoring "the opportunity cost of labour in the subsistence sector," which can involve "seasonal activity, various other activities, and also . . . preferred leisure."[42]

Theodore W. Schultz, who had worked with Lewis on the UN report on unemployment in underdeveloped countries and had reluctantly signed the final report that recognized disguised unemployment as a condition in these countries, now joined the chorus of protest. He wrote a series of articles, culminating in his celebrated 1964 book, *Transforming Traditional Agriculture*, which incorporated a reasoned critique of labor surpluses and argued in favor of the rationality, efficiency, and creativity of the small farmer. In Schultz's view, numerous case studies of the agricultural sector in less developed societies showed that when labor was withdrawn from the agrarian sector, "the output of the traditional sector falls."[43]

Finally, econometricians and economic logicians entered the debate. A Princeton-based economist made a telling critique of the Lewis argument in a statement that critics of the Lewis model have cited over and over again. Jacob Viner wrote: "As far as agriculture is concerned, I find it impossible to conceive a farm of any kind on which, other fac-

---

[41] Bauer's review first appeared in the *American Economic Review*, in June 1956, but I am quoting from his reissue of the review in his book, *Dissent on Development: Studies and Debates in Development Economics* (Cambridge, 1972), p. 435.

[42] Ibid., p. 437.

[43] Theodore W. Schultz, *Transforming Traditional Agriculture* (New Haven, 1964), p. 56.

tors of production being held constant in quantity, and even in form as well, it would not be possible, by known methods, to obtain some addition to the crop by using additional laborers in more careful selection and planting of the seed, more intensive weeding, cultivation, thinning, and mulching, more painstaking harvesting, gleaning, and cleaning of the crop."[44] Nor could he believe that employers of agricultural labor would be willing to "hire at any wage-rate additional units of labor beyond the point at which they know the labor will add less in value to the product than the wage-cost, to say nothing of the case where the labor will add nothing to and may even subtract from the product."

Lewis had obviously struck a raw nerve. But he did not give way. His 1968 pamphlet provided a set of comprehensive answers to his critics. He assured detractors that his dual model did not posit a traditional agrarian sector and a robust industrial one. Industrialization was not the only vehicle of economic growth since the agrarian sector could also provide the capitalist lead. A capitalist for Lewis was not necessarily an industrialist. He was quite simply an individual "who hires labor and resells its product for a profit."[45] Nor was the model antisocialist or antiplanning since the capitalist innovator could operate as energetically in a public sector economy as in a private sector. Lewis had, in fact, made all of these points in his original statement, though he had not stressed many of them. He felt that he had a right to be annoyed, believing that critics had not given his original essay a careful reading.

Lewis took pains to deal with the criticism of the marginal productivity of labor, particularly his claim that it could be negligible or even zero. He admitted the veritable groundswell of opposition to the claim that labor productivity might be negligible. His defense was that he was not dealing with the marginal productivity of man-hours. Viner was, of course, right that better weeding and more careful seed selection would increase output. But he was referring to workers, not man-hours. Individuals could be withdrawn from the traditional sector without any diminution of the product because those who remained behind would and could work longer and make up for the missing individuals. Nonetheless, he reformulated the notion of unlimited or surplus labor supplies by asserting that in his argument "the marginal

[44] Jacob Viner, "Some Reflections on the Concept of 'Disguised Unemployment,'" in *Contribuicoes a Analise do Desenvolvimento Economico* (Rio de Janeiro, 1957), p. 347.

[45] W. Arthur Lewis, "Reflections on Unlimited Labour," Research Project, Woodrow Wilson School, Princeton University, Discussion Paper, No. 5 (Princeton, 1968), p. 2. This essay was later published in *International Economics and Development: Essays in Honor of Raúl Prebisch*, ed. Luis Eugenio Di Marco (New York, 1972), pp. 75–96.

product of man hours was positive even while the marginal product of persons was negative."[46]

Still, he was willing to concede that he had created a firestorm for himself and had done so needlessly. He recognized that the implication for some economists, especially those who specialized in the study of peasants, was that African, Asian, and Latin American farmers were idle and that they preferred to laze about rather than work hard. But he went on to argue that a marginal productivity of zero or near zero was not essential for the functioning of his model. All that was required was for the supply of labor to exceed demand within the traditional sector.

Lewis introduced further refinements in his 1979 article. He now eschewed the phrase *surplus labor* "since it causes emotional distress."[47] He also agreed that migration of labor from the traditional to the modern sectors had not been occurring as smoothly and as automatically as he had originally thought. He even agreed that some coercive and incentive mechanisms, like taxation and housing subsidies, might be required to prime the pump of rural migration. He was by now more fully aware that many parts of the world, which while seemingly overpopulated and holding large labor reservoirs, did not seem to have abundant and cheap labor supplies. Instead they suffered from critical labor shortages. This reality caused Lewis, no doubt with the African continent very much in mind, to restate his argument. The model only worked in "countries which have . . . reached a demographic situation where, at the current level of wages in the modern sector, the supply of labor to the modern sector exceeds the demand."[48]

By 1979 Lewis was also faced with the reality that most of the poor countries had not achieved rapid economic growth. Thus, much of this essay was devoted to understanding why this was so. In his view, elaborated earlier in the UN report, the biggest barrier to economic progress was population growth. In Western Europe during the era of rapid economic progress in the nineteenth century, populations had grown at not much more than 1 percent per year. In the twentieth century, in contrast, population growth in the developing countries of the world was reaching rates of 2 and 3 percent, thus forcing economic growth rates to go at an even higher pace. If the modern sector were expected to absorb all of a country's population increase, expanding at 3 percent per year, and if this sector constituted 30 percent of the total labor force, "the

---

[46] Ibid., pp. 8–9.

[47] W. Arthur Lewis, "The Dual Economy Revisited," *Manchester School of Economic and Social Studies*, vol. 47, September 1979, p. 211.

[48] Ibid., p. 218.

modern sector would have to grow at 10 per cent per annum which it cannot do."[49] In addition, the wages in the modern sector were significantly higher than Lewis had anticipated. He had expected that a wage rate 30 percent higher than that in the traditional sector would succeed in attracting a steady labor supply. In reality, because of timorous governments, pressure from organized trade unions, and conscientious business owners, urban workforces were earning anywhere from 50 to 80 percent more than their rural counterparts. Not only did this lead industrialists to prefer machinery to workers, but it also reduced the proportion of profits and savings in the national income, the critical ingredient for economic change in the Lewis formulation.

Although Lewis had his critics, a legion of followers rallied to his defense. Gustav Ranis and John C. H. Fei gave the Lewis model a formal economic elegance in a series of important publications.[50] Amartya Sen used mathematical formulations and a logician's approach to undercut the criticisms of Theodore Schultz and especially Jacob Viner's assertion that it was impossible for the marginal productivity of labor to be zero or negligible. He argued that all the Lewis model required to work was for "the average product of labor in the subsistence sector—the sector which does not use reproducible capital—to be less than the marginal product in the incipient capitalist sector." Sen concluded: "This is the core of the model, and it remains unaltered by the many acknowledgements and refinements submitted by Lewis in later papers."[51] Writing in the 1979 twenty-fifth-anniversary issue of the *Manchester School*, two development economists, Keith Griffin and Jeffrey James, pointed out that much of what Lewis claimed would happen in developing economies had indeed happened. Wage rates in the traditional rural sector did not rise. The share of profit in the industrial sector along with investment rates did rise. Alas, what did not change was third-world poverty and underdevelopment. Lewis's optimism, in their opinion, had been misguided.[52]

At the very least, it could be said in the 1960s and part of the 1970s that the dual-sector model stood alongside the social science theory of modernization as a dominant scholarly paradigm for understanding

[49] Ibid., p. 219.
[50] Gustav Ranis and John C. H. Fei, "A Theory of Economic Development," *American Economic Review*, vol. 51, no. 4, September 1961, pp. 533–65.
[51] Amartya Sen, "Peasants and Dualism with or without Surplus Labor," *Journal of Political Economy*, vol. 74, no. 5, October 1966, pp. 425–50.
[52] Keith Griffin and Jeffrey James, "Problems of Transition to Egalitarian Development," *Manchester School of Economic and Social Studies*, vol. 47, no. 3, September 1979, pp. 248–69.

the processes of economic and social change in third-world countries.[53] In spite of deficiencies, it outperformed its rivals for explaining the experience of economic growth in much of the third world. It was the opinion of the economist Avinash Dixit, who after reviewing the debate over dual-economy models, concluded that "the dual economy has, over the last decade, proved itself to be a useful conceptual framework for analyzing several problems of economic development." Dixit added that "dual economy models provide a significantly better description and understanding of the problems of development than any aggregate model, not because two sectors are better than one . . . but because the sectoral division chosen reflects several vital social and economic distinctions in the type of economy being analyzed."[54]

THE THEORY OF ECONOMIC GROWTH

Just one year after the appearance of the article on unlimited labor supplies, Lewis published a second major work in the field of development economics, *The Theory of Economic Growth*. The volume soon became the primer for the whole field of development economics and a work that everyone interested in this emerging field, whether an economist or an interested outsider, turned to first. It achieved its high standing because, like all of Lewis's writings, it was clearly and forcefully written. It also developed the idea that all elements in a society, economic as well as noneconomic, have an impact on economic growth. Lewis, with his wide reading in history and literature, was just the right person to offer a work of synthesis, not an original statement, at this critical moment in the development of this subfield in economics.

The Theory of Economic Growth offered a comprehensive framework for viewing economic change and gave an overview of a subject that had not had a general overview, in Lewis's opinion, since John Stuart Mill published his *Principles of Political Economy* in 1848. Although the topic of political economy had engaged "world wide interest . . . no comprehensive treatment of the subject has been published."[55] Originally Lewis contemplated the inclusion of two or three case studies, but his reading of the economic histories of Egypt, Greece, Rome,

---

[53] Keith Worrell, "The Dual Economy since Lewis: A Study," *Social and Economic Studies: Special Issue in Honor of Sir William Arthur Lewis*, vol. 29, no. 4, December 1980, pp. 27–51.

[54] Avinash K. Dixit, "Models of Dual Economies," in *Models of Economic Growth: Proceedings of a Conference Held by the International Economic Association at Jerusalem*, ed. James A. Mirrlees and N. H. Stern (New York, 1973), p. 325.

[55] W. Arthur Lewis, *The Theory of Economic Growth* (Homewood, Ill., 1955), p. 5.

Islam, China, Japan, and the end of the Middle Ages persuaded him that he had "derived more pleasure than knowledge, especially of the periods before 1500 AD, partly because so little is known with certainty about early economic history."[56] In the preface he thanked P. T. Bauer, Max Gluckman, J. M. Low, J. Mars, K. Martin, the Reverend R. H. Preston, and P. Rosenstein-Rodan, an impressive list of younger and older social scientists, with diverse specializations.

The issue that Lewis chose to make the focal point of the study was economic growth, specifically the growth of output per head. He was mindful that economic change entailed much more than a general rise in output and that a fuller analysis would deal with distribution, consumption, and welfare matters. But at this stage, he felt that a detailed study focusing on goods and services, rather than welfare satisfaction and happiness, was in order. Moreover, studies of economic growth were fashionable at the time. Lewis's citations are replete with references to books on the subject, especially two studies that had become veritable classics at the time: Evsey D. Domar, *Essays on the Theory of Economic Growth*, a 1957 collection of essays that had appeared in journals before, and Ragnar Nurske, *Problems of Capital Formation in Underdeveloped Countries* (1953).[57]

In contrast to some of the other theorists of economic growth, Lewis wrote that he wished to understand not only the fundamentals of growth but also why growth was so strong in some societies and not in others. Was this because of institutional legacies, beliefs, race, or geography, or was it perhaps the consequence of historical accident? After reviewing a wide range of existing explanations, Lewis identified three proximate causes of wealth and poverty, each of which he said he would examine in detail. These were the will to economize, the accumulation of knowledge, and the accumulation of capital.

Lewis's longest chapter, slightly more than 100 pages in a book of 450 pages, dealt with capital accumulation and stands out from the others as the subject that occupied most of his thinking in this volume. As usual, Lewis stressed that economic change required elevating the saving and investment rates in societies from 5 percent to 12 percent. But this kind of a change was not purely a technical matter nor an exclusively economic issue. Raising savings and investment rates required fundamental transformations in institutions, attitudes, belief systems, the ways of acquiring and distributing knowledge, and poli-

---

[56] Ibid., p. 6.

[57] See the "Bibliographical Note" at the end of the chapter on capital on pages 302–03 of *The Theory of Economic Growth* for the articles and books that Lewis found the most helpful in writing this important chapter.

tics. Lifting the investment levels to those that economic growth demanded required "the emergence of a new class in society—the profit-making entrepreneurs—which is more thrifty than all the other classes (the landlords, the wage earners, the salaried middle classes) and whose share of the national income increases relative to that of all others."[58] Governments can be instruments of capital accumulation, as they were in Japan and the Soviet Union, and as Lewis believed they were becoming in the Gold Coast and Uganda. But the only sure route to sustained economic development was to extract savings out of business profits and to plow them back into the business sector.

"The capitalist is therefore the only person whose ambition drives in the direction of using his income to create an empire of bricks and steel. All other classes fulfill their ambitions in other ways—the salaried classes by conspicuous consumption and the agricultural classes by buying land or holding office."[59] Other than by the government squeezing the peasantry, as Stalin did in the Soviet Union, the only way to achieve 12 percent investment rates was to increase the share of profits in the national income. As Lewis had argued in his article on unlimited supplies of labor, this transformation occurred only when workers were moving from the noncapitalist sector to the capitalist sector at close to subsistence wages.

Nonetheless, governments could facilitate the transition. In discussing the place of government activity in economic development, Lewis reiterated his faith in economic planning, which he had always seen as working in tandem with private sector initiatives. Government spending on vital public works and public utilities would expand the modern sector and encourage workers to move into it. Lewis guessed that a government expenditure rate of 7 percent of national income was about right. At the same time, this man, whose name was so closely associated with development planning, cautioned that governments often failed because they tried to do too much rather than too little. In particular, "detailed centralized planning" had pitfalls too numerous to mention. In addition to being "undemocratic, bureaucratic, inflexible, and subject to error and confusion, it is also unnecessary." Greatly to be preferred was "piece-meal planning; that is to say, . . . concentrating on a few matters which it is particularly desired to influence, such as the level of exports or of capital formation, or of industrial production, or of food production, and leaving all the rest of the economy to adjust itself to demand and supply." This kind of individualized planning was most desirable for those parts of the economy

[58] Ibid., p. 226.
[59] Ibid., p. 232.

"where demand and supply are out of equilibrium at the ruling prices," especially as a result of shortages of capital, skilled labor, and foreign exchange.[60]

Glowing reviews greeted the book's publication. The well-known British development economist Dudley Seers was right to praise it as "the first book in the twentieth century to cross the accepted frontiers of the subject and to deal with the inter-relations between economic growth, social structures, political systems, scientific knowledge, and religious doctrines in the grand tradition of political economy, the tradition of Adam Smith, Ricardo, Marx, and John Stuart Mill." While Seers found the style often "ponderous . . . or supercilious," he praised Lewis for offering readers a balanced and fair-minded introduction to contentious issues. In his view, the very best part of the work was the appendix, where Lewis set forth a sober and realistic balance sheet of economic progress, comparing the positive gains from economic growth (longer and materially more comfortable lives) with the potential drawbacks (lack of guaranteed happiness and possible psychological discomfort).[61] There were many other favorable reviews, such that the book soon became a definitive work on economic development, the study that most development economists sent students to first of all.[62]

P. T. Bauer, though acknowledged in the preface, was not swept up in the crescendo of praise. His critical review of the book angered Lewis. In an exchange of letters between the two men, who had overlapped at the London School of Economics in the 1940s, Bauer apologized for not having submitted a draft of the review to Lewis so that they could "hammer out a more or less agreed version."[63] But Bauer admitted that he had been displeased with Lewis's critical review of his 1952 book, *West African Trade*, which appeared in the *Manchester Guardian*. There, Lewis took Bauer to task for not appreciating the positive role that African marketing boards were playing in channeling fi-

---

[60] Ibid., p. 384.

[61] See his review in *West Africa*, January 28, 1956, p. 85.

[62] Of the reviews in this genre, see those by A. D. Knox in *Economica*, n.s., vol. 26, no. 102, May 1959, pp. 171–72, and A. K. Cairncross in *Economic Journal*, vol. 66, no. 264, December 1956, pp. 694–97. In comparing the book with others that had appeared recently, Knox concluded that "it may safely be said that it retains a pre-eminent position" (p. 171). Cairncross concluded his long and in many ways critical review with the following summary statement: "The theory of growth is an enormous canvas on which to paint: after all, is not all economic theory about growth except when the possibility is deliberately excluded? If some of the painting is a little sketchy, the whole is still remarkable. Few economists could sustain for so long, and with such clarity and good judgment, an argument that embraces most of the major issues of economic policy" (p. 697).

[63] P. T. Bauer to W. Arthur Lewis, May 2, 1957, Lewis Papers, Box 13.

nancial resources to schools, hospitals, and roads and keeping inflation in check.

While commending the book for its comprehensive approach to the question of economic development and pointing out that Lewis "ranges even more widely than the English classical economists," Bauer claimed that Lewis's use of the concept of unlimited supplies of labor "has misled him on some fundamental issues." "Small-scale agriculture is often far from stagnant," while the process of economic growth, in Bauer's opinion, was much more gradual, less punctuated by dramatic spurts. Bauer also faulted Lewis for a lack of clarity over key terms, such as what constituted output and how output was to be measured, and whether the move from investing 5 percent of national income to 12 percent was the cause of economic development or the result. Bauer also objected to Lewis's claim that capitalists "are the only source of productive saving; other classes and groups do not save or invest significantly." To Bauer, this was a tautology, as if one were saying "that only capitalists save productively and those who save productively are capitalists." He interspersed his reservations with strong words of praise, writing that Lewis's two-sector model, however much he disagreed with parts of it, "illuminates important aspects of many underdeveloped economies, much more so than other formal models currently proposed." But his final assessment could not have pleased Lewis. "This book fails in its principal purpose, especially in its aim to serve as the basis for policy. The broad-brush technique neglects distinctions without which it is not possible to frame or assess meaningfully particular measures of policy."[64]

Lewis was stung. He penned a letter to B. F. Haley, the editor of the *American Economic Review*, which had carried the review, laying out eleven "incidents" in which he believed that Bauer had misread his book or made false assertions about it. Haley was sympathetic, offering his own opinion that the volume was "a splendid work" and adding that Lewis had a right "to be irritated by the review." But Haley, who took considerable pains assessing Lewis's complaints against Bauer's review, concluded that he did "not find them to be nearly as serious as you do." Haley was, therefore, unwilling to open the *Review* "to an interchange between you and Bauer on this matter unless I can satisfy myself that he was seriously derelict in his duty as a reviewer. This I have been unable to do."[65]

---

[64] See the review in Bauer's *Dissent on Development*, pp. 435–47. The review appeared in the *American Economic Review* in June 1956.

[65] B. F. Haley to W. Arthur Lewis, November 21, 1956, Lewis Papers, Box 10. Unfortunately, the Lewis Papers do not contain a copy of Lewis's letter of complaint to the journal editor. Hence, I do not know precisely what Lewis included in his eleven "incidents."

Conclusion

Lewis set the pace for the emerging field of development economics in the 1950s. Although he had many collaborators, even colleagues at the London School of Economics, like Nicholas Kaldor, Paul Rosenstein-Rodan, and P. T. Bauer, he was one of a small group who made the question of economic growth of poor countries the central research goal. Others, like Nicholas Kaldor and Joan Robinson at the University of Cambridge, dealt with problems of economic growth in less developed countries but only as part of larger research agendas.

Lewis worked to legitimize a field and create a consensus on development. His work yielded a surprising degree of agreement during the 1950s and 1960s among development economists. They agreed that the problems of economic development for less developed countries were solvable, even though large and difficult, that they needed a quick resolution lest the world be plunged into spasms of revolutionary violence, and that they required substantial economic assistance from the richer countries. Although many development economists were not actively engaged in Cold War politics, they were aware of the political dimensions of their work. If poverty was not overcome and economic growth did not take place, social revolutions were likely to follow. Lewis himself was a Fabian and was entirely opposed to highly coercive, nondemocratic approaches to economic development. Nor did he favor authoritarian and highly centralized economic planning. Nonetheless, like many development economists he believed that free markets left much to be desired. They were likely to be wasteful of resources, lead into unpromising avenues of economic activity, and prove too slow to eradicate poverty and generate economic growth. Although Lewis and his colleagues all valued the role of entrepreneurs as pioneers of European and North American industrialization, they were acutely aware that in most of the rest of the world entrepreneurial talents were in short supply. Fortunately, this defect could be overcome through state intervention, rigorous development planning, and programs of domestic taxation and incentives for foreign investment that would increase the levels of investment and facilitate industrialization.

Lewis developed a special niche within the general field of development economics. His writings stressed the multidimensional nature of economic growth. The outstanding contribution of *The Theory of Economic Growth* was its contention that economic growth required a supportive framework of political, cultural, and social institutions. In the purely economic sphere, he was an advocate of balanced economic growth. Hence, he argued against permitting any sector, not least the industrial sector, to progress more rapidly than the others. Nor did he disparage the market. In the view of one of his followers, Jagdish Bhagwati, he was the champion of "planning through the market."[66] He also attached importance to the role of innovators as a new breed of entrepreneurs who were the most modern members of a society and most set apart from other groups, like bureaucrats, priests, merchants, and landlords. The latter groups could not free themselves of traditional values. In contrast the new capitalist class was consumed with a passion for economic growth and devoted their newfound wealth to economic expansion.

During the 1950s, as many parts of the colonial world pressed forward toward independence, Lewis emerged as one of the most visible and accessible practitioners of development economics. His stress on industrialization through planning was what Asian and African leaders wanted to hear. In addition, he was one of a small group of world-class development economists who had grown up in the developing world. He was also a man of color, with lifelong ties to rising new nationalist elites. His sympathies for pan-Africanism dated back to childhood days when his father had taken him to hear Marcus Garvey speak. Thus, when Kwame Nkrumah, the prime minister of black Africa's first modern independent state, approached him in 1957 and asked him to act as the country's chief economic adviser, he leaped at the prospect. Lewis counted on popular leaders to galvanize the population in support of development. Nkrumah was Africa's most compelling nationalist, a man educated in the United States and Great Britain, a pan-African loyalist, and a darling of the Ghanaian electorate, whose party, the Convention People's Party, had won three straight elections in the run-up to independence (1951, 1954, and 1956). The possibilities seemed limitless, as Lewis, still a young man (forty-three years of age), embarked with his wife Gladys and his two young daughters on a new and challenging phase of his career.

---

[66] Jagdish Bhagwati, "W. Arthur Lewis: An Appreciation," in Gersovitz et al., Theory and Experience, p. 15.

CHAPTER 4

The Gold Coast

AT THE END OF 1952, shortly after returning from a tour of Asia where his intellectual breakthrough led to the article on unlimited supplies of labor, Lewis received an invitation to advise the government of the Gold Coast on industrialization. The invitation came not from British colonial offices in the Gold Coast, but the rising nationalist party, the Convention People's Party (CPP), led by its charismatic political leader, Kwame Nkrumah. In many ways, the Gold Coast was not an ideal setting for Lewis. Although he had not yet published his article on unlimited supplies of labor, he was on the verge of doing so. As he noted on many occasions, African countries, including the Gold Coast, did not have large, surplus labor forces trapped in a backward rural sector. Quite the contrary, African territories suffered from labor shortages. Their road to industrialization would need to differ from that which labor surplus countries like Egypt, India, and the British West Indies should adopt.

Yet the Gold Coast attracted Lewis. The vitality of the Gold Coast nationalists impressed him, and the opportunity to advise Africans, rather than British officials, was new and exciting. Lewis accepted the invitation—a decision that ultimately became a turning point in his career. Although he spent only several months of 1952 in the Gold Coast, preparing the report, and immediately returned to his teaching position at Manchester, his stay linked him to the Gold Coast and its leaders. From then onwards, British officials and Gold Coast nationalists alike regarded him as the top expert on their economy and turned to him to evaluate economic projects. They consulted him about the Volta River project, the budget, and changes to the ten-year plan. Not surprisingly, as soon as the country achieved its independence in March 1957, Prime Minister Nkrumah sought Lewis's services as the country's chief economic adviser and got them. In effect, the decision to advise the Gold Coast on its industrial prospects led Lewis away from purely academic endeavors and placed him squarely in the public arena.

The decision of the nationalists to seek Lewis's advice was hardly surprising. Although he had yet to publish his two classic studies on economic development (unlimited supplies of labor and *The Theory of Economic Growth*), his credentials were impeccable. His 1949 publication, *The Principles of Economic Planning*, and his central role in the writing of the United Nations report on employment in underdeveloped countries had singled him out as one of the world's leading development experts. Several of the CPP Gold Coast nationalists knew him well and admired him for those very traits that worried officials at the British Colonial Office—his independence and his suspicion of imperialist motives lying behind even the most altruistic-sounding British proposals.

Lewis had developed friendships with Africans from the moment that he arrived in London. Even when he was active with the League of Coloured Peoples and involved in publishing its journal, *The Keys*, he sought to highlight African developments and to bring Africans to the attention of Dr. Moody and other League members. As a respected and rising lecturer at the London School of Economics, Lewis was much sought after by Africans who were residing, studying, and working in London. In 1946, for instance, Kwame Nkrumah came to London and claims in his autobiography to have enrolled as a part-time student at the LSE. Even though neither noted the overlap in their tenure at the LSE, Nkrumah's invitation to be one of the featured speakers at a Fabian Bureau conference called to discuss the relations between the bureau and the British Colonial Office probably occurred because of Lewis. At the close of the war, members of the Fabian Colonial Bureau had begun to look to Lewis to expand their membership so that it included West Indians and Africans. Prior to one of the bureau's important conferences on colonial issues, Rita Hinden asked Lewis to help with the invitation list. He counseled Hinden that the bureau should invite critics as well as friends, noting that most of the Africans and West Indians on the original list were "Bureau buddies and Labour propagandists." Among those whom Lewis especially wanted to hear from were H. O. Davies of the West African Students Union, George Padmore, "whose widely publicized writings are a possible source of trouble, [and] Belfield Clarke, who is the centre of opposition among the West Indians."[1]

Rita Hinden followed Lewis's advice, sending invitations to all those whom Lewis recommended. Probably for the first time in any single gathering, the intellectual left wing of the Labour Party heard from many of Africa's future leaders. Nkrumah spoke to the audience on the reasons for the distrust that colonial peoples felt toward the British, pointing out that British colonial rulers treated educated Africans more harshly than did the other colonial powers. Peter Abrahams, the exiled

---

[1] W. Arthur Lewis to Rita Hinden, January 7, 1946, Fabian Colonial Bureau, mss. Brit. Emp. S. 365, Box 69, file 3.

South African writer, spoke about the evils of racial discrimination, soon to be hardened in South Africa into apartheid. Jomo Kenyatta discussed racism, especially condemning the missionaries for teaching Africans that white was good and black bad.[2]

Thus, it was no surprise that the Gold Coast nationalists appealed to Lewis in 1952 in their quest for an authoritative report on industrialization to guide the implementation of the first ten-year plan. Yet as Lewis knew when he accepted this assignment (and when he took on the even more demanding task as Ghana's chief economic adviser), he was entering a country with deep economic, political, regional, ethnic, and religious divisions that could easily come to a boil over economic policies. Demands for a report on industrialization had flowed out of intense debates over the allocation of resources between the major cocoa-producing areas, from which most of the Gold Coast's wealth derived, and the rest of the country. Underlying these economic divisions were intensifying political pressures, as the southern part of the colony increasingly rallied around the banner of Kwame Nkrumah and his dynamic Convention People's Party, while other parts of the Gold Coast went into opposition, notably the Northern Territories and then with the passing of time the Asante region and the other main cocoa-producing areas. These regions worried that Nkrumah and his CPP were determined to use their economic resources to promote the well-being of the southern part of the country at their expense.

The Gold Coast that Lewis entered at the end of 1952 was advancing rapidly toward independence. It appeared to have a populist nationalist party, the CPP, under dynamic leadership, but it was also clear that significant elements of opposition existed. These could easily jeopardize the political evolution of the country if the economy did not grow and if the political institutions were not responsive to people's needs. The country's monoculture and export-oriented economy, based on cocoa, was enjoying unprecedented prosperity that was unlikely to last. Ghana was, in fact, in the midst of a classic commodity boom, and although the economic planners and political leaders, British and Gold Coast alike, did not know when the boom would peter out or how rapid and hard the price downturn would be, they were all aware that the boom conditions would not last forever. Critical, then, for the country was to employ the cocoa wealth for economic diversification and in ways that would leave the country wealthier, with more taxable revenue, than when the price upturn started. A window of opportunity existed; the prospects for creating long-term and self-sustaining eco-

---

[2] Rita Hinden to W. Arthur Lewis, January 29, 1946, Fabian Colonial Bureau, mss. Brit. Emp. S. 365, Box 69, file 3.

nomic growth in the Gold Coast seemed promising. These were the background circumstances that Lewis encountered in 1952 and that he had to deal with during his involvement with the Gold Coast/Ghana.

The Political and Economic Background of the Gold Coast

The British regarded the Gold Coast as one of its most promising African colonies and looked favorably on its prospects for economic and political progress, especially in comparison with other African colonial possessions. Although, like most other African colonies, it had geographical and ethnic diversity, its small size, relative compactness, and unified history gave it advantages over other African countries where the problems of ethnic, religious, and geographical diversity were far more pronounced. The three geographical zones into which it was divided consisted of a coastal area that enjoyed a relatively temperate climate. A second region in the middle or interior of the country was largely a rainforest area and was dominated by the Asante people. This part of the Gold Coast was the heartland of the country's cocoa industry. It had an illustrious precolonial history and a proud people accustomed to ruling over others. Finally, the peoples living in the savannah lands of the northern part of the country, which contained the largest concentration of Muslims in the country, were relatively poor and less well educated compared with the communities in the south.

According to the census of 1948, the Gold Coast population was 4,111,680. That figure would soar to over 6 million in 1960. Among the countries of tropical Africa the country was undoubtedly the richest and best educated. Its per capita income of $500 (1980 dollars) in 1960 placed it among the middle-income countries of the world and was twice that of Nigeria's.[3] Economically, it looked outward, deriving 30 percent of its gross domestic product (GDP) from exports. Cocoa cultivation, which provided the Gold Coast with its primary export commodity, occupied upwards of 4 million acres, two-thirds of which were located in the Asante region. Cocoa also provided employment to half a million workers.[4] Although the Gold Coast's mineral resources were classified as a "wasting asset," in fact the country's exports of gold, diamonds, and manganese made important contributions to the local

[3] Michael Roemer, "Ghana, 1950–1980, Missed Opportunities," in *World Economic Growth*, ed. Arnold C. Harberger (San Francisco, 1984), p. 201.
[4] Tony Killick, "Cocoa," in *A Study of Contemporary Ghana*, vol. 1, *The Economy of Ghana*, ed. Walter Birmingham, I. Neustadt, and E. N. Omaboe (Evanston, Ill., 1966), p. 238.

economy and were significant to Britain's economic strength. The country was the world's fourth largest producer of manganese, after the Soviet Union, India, and South Africa. Its ore was of a high grade and was located in large deposits. Because of the Gold Coast's proximity to the markets of North America and Western Europe the manganese mines had great strategic value to the NATO alliance countries.

The Gold Coast's production of 932,452 carats of diamonds represented nearly one-quarter of the entire output of the British Commonwealth in 1950 and 6 percent of the world's output by weight. Although the country's output of 689,429 ounces of gold in 1950 was only 3 percent of the world production, excluding the Soviet Union, the country was the largest gold producer in the British colonial territories. The Gold Coast's eighteen operating mines provided employment to close to forty thousand workers, paid out nearly £3 million in wages, and yielded exports worth £23 million.

One other mineral was important to the country, bauxite, because of its great economic potential. Although the Gold Coast had only a small production at the close of World War II, the developmental possibilities were promising. If the government could build a dam over the Volta River, capable of generating cheap electricity and then entice a multinational firm to erect a factory for the manufacture of aluminum from the large bauxite deposits located in the country, the Gold Coast would have a new lucrative export industry. In addition the dam would provide ample supplies of electricity to promote local industrialization.[5]

As World War II drew to a close and British colonial officials prepared for new relationships with their African colonies, they were convinced that the Gold Coast could show the way to the rest of British Africa. In the vision of Andrew Cohen, one of the Colonial Office's architects of postwar political plans, a slow evolutionary transfer of power from British to African hands needed to be set in motion, with the Gold Coast showing the way to the other African colonies. Cohen insisted that economic progress buttress the constitutional reforms that he favored, and he believed that the Gold Coast had all of the critical ingredients for a nonviolent devolution of power. The colony possessed a good standard of living, excellent prospects for economic growth, an educated and talented African elite, with a long record of

---

[5] See the chapter on mining in Birmingham et al., *The Economy of Ghana*, as well as the following memorandums produced by the British Colonial Office: No. 9A, Colonial Office Revision of Memorandum on Mining in the Gold Coast, August 2, 1952, PRO CO 554/222: No. 20, N.J.N. Chapman, Ministry of Labour, Gold Coast, to M. G. Smith, October 20, 1953, enclosing Gold Coast *Report of the Mines Enquiry* (Accra, 1953), PRO CO 554/226: and No. 2, Government's Statistician's Office, Accra, to G. L. Unsworth, Colonial Office, May 18, 1950, PRO CO 852/1337/7.

working with British colonial officials, well-meaning British business firms, and perhaps most important of all, in light of the problems arising in settler-dominated parts of British Central and East Africa, an absence of European settlers.

It was, thus, with considerable dismay that the officials at the Colonial Office reviewed the Gold Coast's first post–World War II development plan in 1947. Cohen called the plan "a bad one" and believed that it was "especially weak on the economic side, particularly in relation to agriculture, animal health, and the use of land generally."[6] Cohen's distress was all the greater because he had such high hopes for the colony, believing that "we have greater opportunities for development than anywhere else in Africa. We have good relations between the government and the people, plenty of money, and great economic resources. But little thinking seems to have been devoted to the problem of developing the natural resources. It is a gap in what I think is an otherwise thoroughly happy picture."

Admittedly, the early ten-year plans for African colonial development were primitive documents. The colonial officials who drew them up had virtually no experience with planning and lacked much essential data, and the Colonial Office was not yet in the habit of submitting these plans for detailed criticism to outside economic experts, like Lewis. The Gold Coast officials who were responsible for the plan came mainly from the Ministry of Finance, where their expertise was finance, not development economics. Adept at preparing budgets and drafting taxation codes, these individuals had no training in laying out comprehensive schemes for promoting long-term economic growth. Perhaps, not surprisingly, given the fact that colonial officials tended to worry about satisfying the immediate material needs of the local population, the plan allocated the largest share of the country's resources to social services and communications and was short on revenue-producing economic projects—the classic problem that countries in the midst of commodity booms faced and often failed to handle effectively. To the officials at the Colonial Office a plan that earmarked no less than 59 percent of the £67 million of expenditures to roads, railways, harbors, and social services, mainly education and public health, and a mere 17 percent for industrialization and agricultural modernization was "unduly conservative."[7] It was likely to leave the

---

[6] Note by A. Cohen, on the Gold Coast Ten-Year Plan, February 27, 1947, PRO CO 96/806/1.

[7] No. 11, Colonial Office Comments on Gold Coast Draft Ten-Year Plan, n.d. but March 1947, PRO CO 96/801/1.

country with rising annual expenditures and no assured sources of revenues once the boom in the world price of cocoa had subsided.

If the ten-year plan disappointed the Colonial Office, the Gold Coast riots of 1948 stunned them. The riots that broke out in Accra in late February and spread to many other parts of the colony dealt a rude blow to the British plans for a slow transfer of power to hand-picked Gold Coast leaders. The violent outbursts were not quelled until 29 had died, another 237 had been injured, and property damages calculated at more than £2 million had occurred. The outbursts marked a true turning point in the decolonization of British Africa.[8] What the British planners had hoped would be a process unfolding over several decades was now to be telescoped into ten years.

The Gold Coast riots of 1948 occurred shortly after the creation of a new political party, the United Gold Coast Convention Party (UGCC), and were undoubtedly related to its nationalist message, though to what extent remains unclear. Founded in August 1947, under the leadership of two well-educated and powerful Akan politicians, J. B. Danquah and William Ofori Atta, both of whom were from Akyem Abuakwa, the new party attracted a large following from the coastal cities of Cape Coast, Accra, Saltpond, and Sekondi. Reflecting the aspirations of Danquah, the UGCC sought to unite the two most politically influential African constituencies of the Gold Coast: the intelligentsia and the chiefs.[9] But the party's message of greater power to the African people had a natural and obvious appeal to many others, notably frustrated primary school graduates who were experiencing difficulty finding work, ex-soldiers who had begun to organize, a burgeoning trade union movement, and a growing urban proletariat, financially pinched by increases in the prices of imported commodities and lagging wages.[10] It also expressed the resentment of many cocoa farmers, especially those in the southeast of the colony but in Asante as well, whose estates and income were being affected by the swollen shoot disease and who did not understand or approve of the government policy of destroying the trees in affected areas. Moreover, the UGCC gained immediate benefits from its appointment of a young firebrand nationalist, Kwame Nkrumah, as its secretary. Nkrumah intensified the party's appeal to the disaffected city-dwellers and primary school graduates and won many new supporters

---

[8] Robert Pearce, *The Turning Point in Africa: British Colonial Policy, 1938–48* (London, 1982). The figures on deaths and property damage come from Kwame Nkrumah, *Ghana: The Autobiography of Kwame Nkrumah* (New York, 1957), p. 77.

[9] Dennis Austin, *Politics in Ghana, 1946–60* (New York, 1964), p. 50.

[10] The literature on Gold Coast nationalism is vast. From whatever direction one approaches the topic, it is necessary to begin with Austin, *Politics in Ghana*.

to the party. But his personal ambitions meant that it was only a matter of time before he would create his own political party and overshadow the United Gold Coast Convention. Nkrumah's Convention People's Party came into being in 1949.[11]

The crucial riots of 1948 began in the capital city of Accra, when what was supposed to be a peaceful march to demand greater power-sharing and more stringent commodity price controls veered away from its route and proceeded toward the governor's house. At this moment, the police fired on the crowd, killing two and injuring another. The report of this confrontation spread throughout the city where, according to official colonial reports, a mob of fifty thousand rioted and looted. Additional riots, with looting and other forms of violence, broke out in Kumasi, Koforidua, Nsawam, Kibi, Sukum, and Sekondi. The colonial state brought military reinforcements south from Kumasi and the Northern Territories and was eventually compelled to call in a reserve battalion of the West African Frontier Force from Nigeria. As an additional show of imperial strength, the British dispatched two warships from South Africa to the waters off the Gold Coast.[12] Yet so complete and startling was the collapse of political authority that the government in Accra telegraphed the following message to London: "Police unable to protect life and property since early afternoon yesterday. Main stores, commercial centers looted, and completely emptied [of] merchandise."[13]

To the surprise and annoyance of the officials at the Colonial Office, the commission created to investigate the cause of the disturbances, the Watson Commission, which had regarded the political reforms enacted after World War II as progressive, even in some respects radical, concluded that the new Gold Coast constitution of 1946 was "outmoded at birth" and had falsely raised the hopes of the educated population by establishing an African elected majority in the Legislative Assembly that had no real legislative power.[14] Reforms would have to be effected. A second commission, known as the Coussey Committee, took up the task of reviewing the 1946 constitution and proposed significant constitutional and electoral changes. Accepting the Watson finding that the 1946 constitution was no longer viable, the Coussey Committee recom-

---

[11] Dennis Austin believes that the UGCC could not have made "a worse choice" when they made Nkrumah their secretary. He was "a very different sort of man from the members of the working committee [of the UGCC]" whose movement was "backed almost entirely by reactionaries, middle class lawyers, and merchants." Austin, *Politics in Ghana*, p. 54.

[12] No. 84, Gerald Creasey to A. Creech Jones, March 5, 1948, PRO CO 96/795/6.

[13] Telegram no. 10, Governor to Colonial Office, February 29, 1948, PRO CO 96/795/6.

[14] Alan Burns to Creech Jones, June 22, 1948, PRO CO 96/796/5.

mended a parliamentary-cabinet form of government, which would have an executive council of eleven members, of whom eight would be Africans, and an eighty-four-member Legislative Assembly, of whom seventy-five would be Africans, elected by a variety of procedures. Just over half of the seventy-five elected delegates, thirty-eight in all, would be chosen on the basis of a wide though not yet fully universal franchise and a secret ballot. Britain would still retain the upper hand, holding the key ministries of Defense, Finance, and Justice. The governor would also have reserve powers to pass laws on his own and to veto legislation.

Cocoa and Financial Surpluses

Cocoa was the great hope of the years of decolonization and early independence. By employing its wealth for projects of economic development, officials hoped to produce a greatly diversified and less dependent economy. Inevitably, then, it became the fundamental issue that roiled the political scene, for the different interest groups in the Gold Coast argued bitterly over how the cocoa wealth should be distributed. From the moment he entered the country and onwards, Lewis found himself pitched into the center of this bruising dispute. Not only was the Gold Coast the world's leading producer of cocoa, but after a decade and a half of low or controlled world cocoa prices, from the depression until the middle of World War II, the world price of cocoa had begun a sharp ascent. It was as if the world's indulgence for chocolate, so long stymied by the economic downturn and wartime rationing, now knew no restraints. The prospects before the Gold Coast were viewed as too good to be believed—an asset that at least for a while, although no one knew for how long, could moderate political animosities and promote the country's need for economic diversification. But, of course, these ever-increasing revenues were bound to arouse competing desires and political squabbles.

At the center of the wrangling was the Gold Coast's Cocoa Marketing Board, formally established in 1947. This body was the successor organization to the West African Produce Board, a buying and marketing organization that had been created at the outbreak of World War II to regulate the production and sale of British West Africa's main export items. Instead of returning to the free market arrangements that had existed before the war, the British colonial governments in West Africa chose to retain marketing boards for most of the area's major export crops. The most influential of these bodies was the Cocoa Marketing

118 • Chapter 4

Board because of the large volume being exported from the country and the high world prices for cocoa.

From the first years of its existence the board proved to be a large, unwieldy, and often contentious body. Its twelve members represented the interests of the colonial government, cocoa producers, and cocoa buyers and manufacturers. Their interests often diverged. While cocoa farmers sought the highest prices for themselves, the state was reluctant to pay farmers anything close to a constantly rising world price. Imports were still in short supply, and government officials were convinced that returning so much of the world price to farmers would produce runaway inflation. They preferred that the Cocoa Marketing Board invest the profits of the cocoa trade in gilt-edged securities in London, to be used when necessary as a buffer against a fall in world prices and for development projects. The cocoa farmers accepted the need for a stabilization fund against any future decline in world prices. They were less comfortable with proposals to use the funds for development efforts. Even when the surpluses had grown to £36 million and were known to be on their way to £50 million, cocoa producers on the board, like J. B. Danquah, opposed government requests to invest "in long-term projects having the development of the country as their object."[15] Responding to the government's repeated refrain that increasing the payout to the cocoa farmers would only produce inflation, Danquah accused the board of being "more interested in spending the Board's money on capital works such as the Takoradi Harbour extension than on the welfare of the producers of that money—the farmers." In his opinion, there was "too much emphasis on development."[16]

At the time that this heated exchange occurred (July 1950), the Cocoa Marketing Board reserves stood at £20 million, a sum that even the most developmentally inspired government officials agreed was inadequate as a buffer against a fall in world prices. The bureaucrats also agreed with the farmers that the board's first priority should be to lay away enough money to protect against harsh times. But they had little sympathy with Danquah's demand to return the funds to the farmers.

---

[15] This was the view of the chairman of the Cocoa Marketing Board, S. Macdonald Smith, as presented to the board members at the twenty-sixth meeting of the board on July 1, 1950. Copy of the Minutes in No. 3, Governor, Gold Coast, to Secretary of State, August 1, 1950, PRO CO 852/1149/7.

[16] For Danquah's arguments concerning the proper expenditures and role of the board see No. 2, Governor, Gold Coast, to Secretary of State, May 30, 1950, enclosing Minutes of the 25th meeting of the Gold Coast Cocoa Marketing Board for April 21, 1950, PRO CO 852/1149/7 and No. 3, Governor, Gold Coast, to Secretary of State, August 1, 1950, enclosing minutes of the Cocoa Marketing Board on July 1, 1950, PRO CO 852/1149/7.

British officialdom regarded Gold Coast cultivators as profligate. "What was more important in the country," officials asked themselves—increased profits to the export-import firms, "brass bands" for the farmers, or development? To them the appeal of improving the harbor at Takoradi and possibly building a dam over the Volta River far outweighed other uses for the funds.[17] It was, thus, clear that government officials were coming to the conclusion that governmental surpluses should be channeled into development schemes, even if these schemes were not of immediate benefit to the cocoa-producing areas.

As the stabilization fund grew, reaching £36 million in October 1950, several of the independent members of the board lined up behind the government's development plans. They agreed that some of these funds should be used "for the country's development scheme, due regard being paid to the maintenance of a strong liquid position."[18] Yet just as a consensus seemed to be occurring on the use of surpluses for development, changes in the world price led to renewed tensions between the government and the cocoa-producing areas. At the end of 1950, the colonial government introduced a proposal to raise the export duty on cocoa and to make it a graduated tax. Up until then the duty on cocoa exports was £3.10.0 a ton. The new law stipulated that the duty would rise as the world price of cocoa increased. The colonial government's rationale for the enhanced duty was that planters would fritter away their windfall on wedding and funeral ceremonies and needless luxuries.[19] The state was prepared to use the proceeds that would accrue from an increase in the export duty "to finance development schemes."[20] The minister of finance, R. P. Armitage, expected opposition from the producers but was prepared to resist "the claim of the cocoa farmers and their very natural indignation. . . . The Cocoa Marketing Board is not an all powerful body, dealing with an untouchable vested interest." He prayed for five years of rising world prices, by which time, to paraphrase Nkrumah's message, the economic kingdom would be won.

This legislation raising the export duty on cocoa shaped the whole of the Gold Coast's and Ghana's subsequent economic development and much of its political history. Increasingly, state officials were embracing the idea of using cocoa surpluses to promote an economic

---

[17] No. 3, Governor, Gold Coast, to Secretary of State, August 1, 1950.

[18] Note, Governor, Gold Coast, to Secretary of State, November 29, 1950, enclosing minutes of the 28th meeting of the Gold Coast Cocoa Marketing Board, October 23, 1950, PRO CO 852/1149/7.

[19] No. 14, R. P. Armitage, Minister of Finance, Gold Coast, to L. H. Gorsuch, December 9, 1950, PRO CO 96/817/5.

[20] Ibid.

transformation that would lessen the colony's dependence on a single export crop, foster economic diversification, and enhance the material standards of living at a time of rapid and potentially destabilizing political change. According to a Gold Coast Parliamentary Select Committee, "the cocoa industry is passing through a period of unprecedented prosperity and the time has come when consideration must be given to increasing taxation on cocoa so that the industry may in these times of prosperity make a larger contribution to the general development of the country."[21]

These bold economic initiatives were not the handiwork of radical nationalists or influential development economists. British officials were still in charge of the Gold Coast governance. Although Africans had a majority in the Legislative Assembly soon after these proposals had been announced, the power to enact legislation still remained with the British governor and his nominated officials in the Executive Council. No doubt the new development ideas, which economists like Lewis were just beginning to discuss in their scholarly writings, had some bearing on the thinking of Gold Coast officials and the Colonial Office. But the focus on development originated inside the Gold Coast's Ministry of Finance and was strongly shaped by a fear of inflation and political instability.

The proposed export duty produced the predictable response from the cocoa farmers. Danquah pointed out that cocoa was already the country's most heavily taxed commodity. "It is difficult to accept the argument," he added, "that because the cocoa industry is passing through a period of unprecedented prosperity therefore the cocoa farmer can be looked upon as a section of the community liable to increased taxation."[22]

In the midst of these debates, an event occurred that shifted political power in the Gold Coast. In 1951, following the recommendations of the Coussey Committee, the Gold Coast populace went to the polls. Nkrumah's Convention People's Party won a decisive victory. Critics of the CPP were quick to observe that the party's substantial majority in the Legislative Assembly was based on winning only 55 percent of votes cast, that only half of those who were eligible to register had actually registered, that only half of those who registered had actually voted, and that significant centers of opposition existed in the Northern Territories and some of the cocoa-cultivating areas of the country. Yet the reality of the election was that the CPP won thirty-four of the

[21] This report is contained in ibid.
[22] See the memorandum prepared by J. H. Chapman, Acting Financial Secretary of the Gold Coast, October 24, 1950, PRO CO 96/817/5.

thirty-eight openly contested seats. Moreover, no real opposition to the party had coalesced.

The governor, Charles Arden-Clarke, had no alternative but to designate Nkrumah as "the Leader of Government Business," releasing him from prison, where the British had placed him for creating political disorder. Africans were appointed to eight of the eleven positions in the Executive Council. The CPP did not waste time stamping its mark on the government. Although the party had objected to the Coussey constitution, its leaders accepted office under the British in spite of the fact that the British had not accepted their demand for self-government. In addition to being more forceful than the UGCC in its demands for independence, the CPP leadership was more committed to state intervention in the economy and to industrialization. It also made clear at the outset its intention to control the Gold Coast's chief economic asset—cocoa revenues. One of the first enactments by the Executive Council was a set of ordinances that placed the Gold Coast's statutory bodies more fully under the authority of the state. The new legislation further intensified the opposition that was already emerging in the cocoa regions. The law reduced the membership on the Cocoa Marketing Board from twelve to seven, placed the board under the authority of the minister of commerce and industry, who in the first CPP government was the energetic Komla Gbedemah, and required the board to direct its reports to the minister. Although three members would represent producers on the board, they were not chosen, as they had been previously, by producers' organizations but rather by the governor himself. The chairman of the board was a government official, appointed by the governor.[23]

The new streamlined and government-run Cocoa Marketing Board represented a merging of British Gold Coast officialdom and the CPP bigwigs and was strongly committed to a developmentalist vision. In describing the composition of the board to the Colonial Office, the British governor, Arden-Clarke, noted that the CPP ministers agreed with British officials that "as regards the cocoa industry, the government should keep control of all matters of policy affecting a national interest, including, of course, the vital one of fixing the price to be paid to the cocoa farmer."[24] A board composed of the minister of finance or his representatives, three cocoa farmer representatives, and three from the business community, all of whom would be appointed by the governor, was intended to ensure that the board would "get

---

[23] See the Gold Coast, Legislative Assembly, *Debates*, May 9, 1951, pp. 436ff.
[24] No. 4, Arden-Clarke to Hilton Poynton, Colonial Office, April 27, 1951, PRO CO 852/1150/2.

away from the extreme sectoral and regional representation which is the basis of the present board and substitute a board consisting of individuals chosen on their ability, integrity, and business acumen who can judge issues on a national basis." To protect the interests of the cocoa farmers or the cocoa buyers, two committees were to be established, consisting of cocoa producers and buyers, whose task it would be to "resist ... any attempt to raid them [the board's surpluses] for expenditures on objects which could not be so regarded [as for the benefit of the farmers and buyers]."

Since the surplus at the board was on its way to £80 million by this time, there was an understandable alarm regarding these government initiatives in the cocoa-growing regions. Danquah, as usual, led the opposition, his anger fueled even more than usual because the ordinance creating the new board had removed him as one of the directors. He complained that the arrangement placed vast sums of money "at the precarious mercy of politics and politicians." £80 million might seem an enormous sum, but Danquah believed that at least £100 million needed to go into the stabilization fund before any thoughts about development could be entertained. Moreover, the cocoa funds should be invested in "gilt edged securities ... and not frittered away by power-drunk politicians in their wild-cat schemes of unreal paradise for Ghana."[25] Danquah's was hardly a lone voice. The big Asante cocoa farmers held meetings all over the region to express their anxiety about government designs on their monies.[26]

The Gold Coast's first ten-year plan had lain dormant for several years as the country was enmeshed in the political outbursts of 1948, the founding of the CPP in 1949, and the election of 1951. But the growing governmental surpluses, coupled with the establishment of a predominantly African ministerial government determined to use these funds for the general well-being of the country, led to a resuscitation and revision of the ten-year plan. Ultimately, this revision, with its new emphasis on industrialization, would lead to Lewis's celebrated report, *Industrialization and the Gold Coast Economy*.

The British officials in the Gold Coast continued to believe that economic progress was an essential aspect of the transfer of power to the country's nationalists. At the Colonial Office itself, W. L. Gorell Barnes could scarcely repress his delight that the vast sums being accumulated in the Gold Coast could be employed to smooth relations between the African people and their British overlords at a time of

---

[25] J. B. Danquah, Chairman of the Parliamentary Committee of the UGCC, to Secretary of State, May 25, 1951, PRO CO 852/1150/2.

[26] Note by E.G.G. Hansott, May 16, 1951, PRO CO 852/1150/2.

heightened political awareness. "If there is increasing progress in economic development," he noted, "there seems to be a fair chance that further progress toward political independence will come in a responsible, gradual, and orderly manner." Otherwise, "unless we are prepared for a high degree of repression, we shall be forced to concede further political changes against a background of irresponsibility and disorder to the lasting harm both of the Gold Coast itself and of future relations between the United Kingdom and West Africa."[27]

Although British officials had begun to revise the original ten-year plan before the 1951 election, the electoral triumph of the CPP in that year compelled them to turn the final stages of its elaboration over to the CPP. To their delight, not only did the CPP take up the task with vigor, but the new ministry accepted the basic emphases that the British had given to the plan, even claiming it as their own work. Two ingredients were prominent in the revision. The first was that the plan allocated more funds for economic growth and development. The second was that Kwame Nkrumah himself was to be the chairman of the new development committee of the cabinet as a way to demonstrate the importance of development to the CPP. Industrialization was foregrounded, though the plan recognized that the Gold Coast required an expert report before any specific industrial plans could be put forward. It was in this regard that the CPP leaders turned to W. Arthur Lewis, asking him to draft a blueprint for the country's industrial progress.

Although the revised ten-year plan had a number of new features (industrialization, universal primary education, a national bank, to mention only a few items), on closer inspection it was not dramatically different from the scheme first developed by the British officials in 1947. The bulk of the new expenditure was still for social services—£3.5 million for primary and secondary education, £1.3 million for teacher training, and £1.2 million for the establishment of a medical facility at the University College of the Gold Coast. Hence, in spite of what was claimed to be a new stress on economic productivity, the officials at the Colonial Office found that the plan was again weighted heavily toward welfare concerns.

Lewis and Gold Coast Industrialization

Into this politically charged yet still highly optimistic economic arena strode W. Arthur Lewis. Lewis carried out his investigations in the

[27] Memorandum by W. L. Gorell Barnes, Notes on a visit to the Gold Coast, March 30-April 5, 1951, PRO CO 96/826/3.

Gold Coast in less than two months, hardly, it would seem, long enough to take the full measure of the country's economy. His report was published in 1953 and ran to less than seventy pages. Although it never gained the exposure that the article on unlimited supplies or the book on economic growth did, it is an outstanding work. Lewis was at his best—crisp, concise, not a wasted word, presenting a clear sense of priorities and leaving the reader with no uncertainty about the policies that he favored.

Lewis opened the report, as he did so often, with a bold, yet highly generalized overview of the whole process of industrialization. In his view there were three ways to industrialize: first, by processing exported primary products; second, by manufacturing for a home market; and third, by manufacturing for export. The third pathway was out of reach for the Gold Coast at this point in its development. The country lacked cheap skilled and unskilled labor and hence would not for decades be in a position to export light manufactures as a few other third-world nations had begun to do, notably some of the Asian states. Although it would seem that the Gold Coast had promising opportunities to process its major exports of cocoa and palm oil and kernels, in reality the chances were no more favorable than for the export of light manufactures. Manufacturing of this kind was possible only where large supplies of cheap labor existed and where the weight of the product to be processed and then exported would be considerably reduced. The only processing industry that seemed to hold out a strong prospect of success was the timber industry. The Gold Coast had large forests and cut and processed timber would be substantially weight-reducing.

Having cautioned against the possibilities of employing two of the three methods to industrialize, Lewis turned to the third way—manufacturing for the home market—where he was nearly as pessimistic. Here the chief problem was the relatively small size and spending power of the domestic consumer market, which, in the final analysis, depended on the overall productivity of the economy, especially agriculture. In Lewis's view—a view that must have come as a shock to the radical nationalists of the CPP—the Gold Coast's number one priority must be agricultural improvement. Although the Gold Coast was the world's leading exporter of cocoa, Lewis described the agricultural sector, including cocoa cultivation, as "stagnant." In his opinion, "the most certain way to promote industrialization in the Gold Coast is to lay the foundations it requires by taking vigorous measures to raise food production."[28] These words, coming from the man who had agitated so vigorously for the industrialization of the West Indies and was

---

[28] W. Arthur Lewis, *Report on Industrialization and the Gold Coast* (Accra, 1953), p. 4.

soon to publish an article on the extraordinary opportunities that the condition of surplus labor supplies afforded for industrialization, shocked many readers of the report.

Only after Lewis had completed these introductory remarks did he turn his attention directly to industrialization. The home market in the Gold Coast was a decidedly restricted one. The only industries that seemed to have good possibilities were salt, sugar, beer, cigarettes, textiles, cement, glass, lime, and industrial alcohol. As to how to industrialize, Lewis's advice must have been as unwelcome to the left wing of the CPP and its state planners as his cautions about industrialization in general. The investment price tag for this small spectrum of industries was a relatively modest £3 million per year. But Lewis did not recommend that the state undertake any of this investing. Its funds would be better spent in the agricultural sector. Because local savings themselves were not great and the local business elite in its infancy, Lewis recommended attracting foreign private capital. In a view that would have alarmed those among the CPP who had cut their student teeth on the writings of Marx, Lenin, Hobson, and numerous other socialist essayists, Lewis contended that there was no true financial difference between foreign and local capital since both sought high returns and would reinvest profits if local investment prospects were good.

Lewis ended his essay by reaffirming the priority of agricultural modernization. "Measures to increase the manufacture of commodities for the home market deserve support but are not of number one priority. A small program is justified but a major program in this sphere should wait until the country is better prepared to carry it out. The main obstacle is the fact that agricultural productivity per man is stagnant. After improving the agricultural sector, the government should develop public services." He concluded by observing that "very many years will have elapsed before it becomes economical for the government to transfer any large part of its resources toward industrialization.... Meanwhile it should support industries which can be established without large or continuing subsidies and whose proprietors are willing to train and employ Africans in senior posts."[29]

It is not difficult to imagine the stunned reactions that greeted the report. The Colonial Office staff could hardly believe their eyes. A. Emanuel, an old antagonist, who nonetheless had a soft spot in his heart for Lewis and great admiration for his abilities, commented, "it is certainly in refreshing contrast to his work in the West Indies."[30] One official believed that the years had mellowed Lewis. He also wondered

[29] Ibid., p. 43.
[30] A. Emanuel, October 16, 1953, PRO CO 554/202.

whether working with the Colonial Development Corporation had moderated his earlier more radical perspectives. Another noted that "his views are much more practical than they used to be."[31]

Lewis's conclusions did not represent nearly the radical departure from earlier writings that some of his critics thought they did. He had always been an advocate of balanced economic growth and had always believed that less developed parts of the world needed to increase their agricultural productivity. The Gold Coast did not have surplus laborers, as the West Indies and much of Asia did; hence it could not draw workers out of the agricultural sector at low wages. In fact, Gold Coast industrialization would need to proceed in tandem with agricultural improvement, with both sectors contributing to economic progress and spurring each other on.

Although it is hard to imagine that ardent industrializers like Gbedemah, who had been instrumental in bringing Lewis to the Gold Coast, were completely content with the report, they remained respectful of its findings in their public pronouncements. In the Legislative Assembly debates on the budget in early 1954, almost a full year after the report first appeared, Nkrumah announced that the government accepted Lewis's findings. He sounded a Lewis-like note of caution about the Gold Coast's industrial potential, observing that "it will be many years before the Gold Coast will be in a position to find from its own resources people who combine capital with the experience required in the development and management of industries. It is therefore apparent that the Gold Coast must rely to a large extent on foreign enterprise, and the government is anxious to give it every encouragement."[32] The argument was pure Lewis and would eventually stand in glaring contrast to the program of industrial development that the Nkrumah government sponsored in the 1960s. In the meantime Nkrumah was content to underscore the need for foreign firms to train and promote African personnel. The government, with its large reserve funds, would also be willing "to participate in enterprises which can be shown to be economically sound." But in order to leave no doubt of the state's intention to welcome foreign investment, Nkrumah promised to place no restrictions on the repatriation of profits. Indeed, he added that "the present government has no plans for nationalizing industry beyond the extent to which the public utilities are already nationalized, and it does not envisage any such prospects arising. If it were to do so, the government would provide fair compensation."

[31] Colonial Office Note, August 31, 1953, PRO CO 554/202.
[32] Gold Coast, Legislative Assembly, *Debates*, February 17, 1954, pp. 1082–83.

The opposition was equally impressed with Lewis's efforts. Although Danquah could not help but complain that the CPP did not know what to do about industrialization until "a West Indian Negro called Professor Lewis came here for a fortnight's visit and made a survey of the country's needs," he had no objection to the recommendations. In his opinion, they were little more than what everyone already knew. What the Gold Coast truly required was a new government that would carry out these schemes with vigor. If his own group were in office, he boasted, "we would change the face of the country."[33]

The Political and Economic Lead-Up to Gold Coast Independence

Lewis would return to the Gold Coast a mere five years after he published his report to find a radically different situation. The most obvious change was political independence and a name change. But two other developments had altered the political and economic landscape and would have an impact on Lewis's room to maneuver as the chief economic adviser. The first was the emergence of a stronger, better organized, and more vociferous opposition to the CPP, based in Asante and the cocoa-cultivating areas, which in 1954 had established a new party, the National Liberation Movement (NLM). The second was a brief but spectacular explosion in the world price of cocoa in 1954 that resulted in a series of controversial financial and development schemes. These were the products of the fertile imagination of Kenneth Tours, briefly the Gold Coast minister of finance and then an economic adviser during these years.

The economic and financial programs carried out from 1954 until the country gained its independence in 1957 took place in a radically altered political environment, one less dominated by the nationalists of the CPP. A second round of national elections took place in 1954. On the surface, they mirrored those of 1951. The CPP won an overwhelming majority of the seats in the Legislative Assembly, claiming 72 of the 104 seats and thoroughly trouncing the opposition. The Ghana Congress Party, successor to the UGCC, failed abysmally in making itself a creditable opposition party. It hardly threatened the CPP, whose members nicknamed it the "Ghost Party."[34] It was successful in only one election, and its two most formidable politicians, William Ofori Atta, son of Sir Ofori Atta and member of the ruling family in Akyem Abuakwa, along with J. B. Danquah, both lost. Once again, however,

---

[33] Gold Coast, Legislative Assembly, *Debates*, February 11, 1953, p. 83, and March 12, 1953, p. 1254.
[34] Austin, *Politics in Ghana*, p. 182.

the election statistics were deceiving. The votes were not nearly so overwhelmingly in favor of the CPP as the number of seats in the Assembly suggested. Of the 719,672 votes cast (59 percent of those who had registered to vote, which was, in turn, 57 percent of those eligible to register) 395,227 voted for the CPP and 324,445 for the other parties or independent candidates. As a number of observers noted, this result meant that the CPP had garnered the vote of a mere 15 percent of the estimated total adult population, hardly a resounding vote of confidence.[35] The opposition was centered in the north and the Asante and other cocoa-cultivating areas in the middle of the country.

The CPP did not dwell on the existence of an opposition. It took the election as proof of its mandate to rule and as support for its policies. Nkrumah, insisting that the party had passed the test of support set by the British Colonial Office, demanded that the colonial government set the date of independence. The party also took a fateful step in its cocoa policy, announcing shortly after its electoral triumph that it would freeze the price it paid to the cocoa farmers at £134 a ton for the next four years, even though the world price had recently crashed through the £500-a-ton barrier. The journal *West Africa* wondered whether the CPP had not made a major gaffe in depriving the cocoa cultivators of so much of the profit from the country's richest export.[36]

The journal did not have long to wait for an answer. Already upset by the frequent CPP interventions in local politics and an increase in the number of destoolments of local chiefs after the CPP had won its first election in 1951, younger, disaffected individuals in the cocoa areas rallied against the Nkrumah-led government and galvanized many of the traditional leaders of the region to register their dissatisfaction with the new government. One of the early signs of this heightened opposition occurred in the Asante region, where a group of dissidents took a ceremonial oath affirming "allegiance to the Golden Stool" and calling for some form of "Ashanti separatism."[37] The Asanteman Council fol-

---

[35] These statistics worried British officialdom, and they were commented on by the leading West African journal, *West Africa*. See No. 7, Governor, Gold Coast, to Secretary of State, June 28, 1954 PRO CO 554/985 and *West Africa*, July 3, 1954, p. 602. They have loomed large in the scholarly studies of the political history of the Gold Coast and Ghana during the Nkrumah years. For the rise of opposition to Nkrumah and the CPP, the reader should consult Jean Marie Allman, *The Quills of the Porcupine: Asante Nationalism in an Emergent Ghana* (Madison, 1993); John Dunn and A. F. Robertson, *Dependence and Opportunity: Political Change in Ahafo* (Cambridge, 1973); Richard Rathbone, *Nkrumah and the Chiefs: The Politics of Chieftaincy in Ghana, 1951–60* (Athens, Ohio, 2000); and Aristide R. Zolberg, *Creating Political Order: The Party-States of West Africa* (Chicago, 1966).

[36] *West Africa*, September 18, 1954, p. 866.

[37] *West Africa*, September 18, 1954.

lowed with a petition to Queen Elizabeth II, requesting a commission of inquiry to consider proposals for a federal constitution.[38] Although the opposition soon included many of the leading chiefs of the Asante people, including the Asantehene, Sir Osei Agyeman Prempeh II, most British officials in the Gold Coast and the Colonial Office sided with Nkrumah. They accepted the CPP argument that the election of 1954 had been a fair one and that the government had the legal power to enact the ordinance fixing the price of cocoa for a four-year period. They were also aware that none of the Asante MPs sitting in the Legislative Assembly supported the Asanteman Council petition.[39]

Yet, there was no gainsaying the strength of the arguments of the petition nor the likelihood that the document represented a growing mood of resentment against the government within the cocoa-growing areas. The petition argued that the cocoa farmers were losing control over the fruits of their labors "in the interest of certain removed development projects, without any guarantees for those developments, which immediately concern them and their occupation, such as improved transportation." The petition went on to object that the government pursued "a deliberate policy of insulting, vilifying, and discrediting traditional rulers and elderly folk as a means of winning and strengthening their hold on the so-called 'masses.'"[40]

Criticism revolved around the CPP's penchant for misusing funds. The critics singled out the Cocoa Purchasing Company and asserted that it operated in violation of its charter by providing funds to CPP supporters. They directed their resentment at the CPP minister of the interior, Krobo Edusei, an Asante man himself, but one who had repeatedly revealed his opposition to the Asante chiefs. According to a later scholarly account, Edusei's "ebullient, disrespectful style acquired a far more sinister and Robespierrian cast" as the opposition movement heated up.[41] The founding of the new political party, the National Liberation Movement, led several important Asante-based leaders, like Joseph Appiah, R. R. Amponsah, and Victor Owusu, who

[38] No. 18, Colonial Office Note on the Petition of the Asantehene Council to Her Majesty the Queen, n.d., but November 1954, PRO CO 554/804; and No. 29, Edward Ford of the Queen's Office to J. B. Johnston, Colonial Office, December 28, 1954, PRO CO 554/804.

[39] No. 15, Arden-Clarke to A. T. Lennox-Boyd, November 18, 1954, PRO CO 554/804.

[40] No. 29, Edward Ford of the Queen's Office to J. B. Johnston, Colonial Office, December 28, 1954, PRO CO 554/804.

[41] Rathbone, *Nkrumah and the Chiefs*, p. 105; Geoffrey Bing, *Reap the Whirlwind: An Account of Kwame Nkrumah's Ghana from 1950 to 1966* (London, 1968), pp. 121–22; and Gold Coast, Legislative Assembly, *Debates*, March 4, 1955, pp. 628ff.

had been members of the CPP during the 1954 election and two of whom had been elected to the Legislative Assembly in this election, to desert the party in favor of the NLM.[42] Although the NLM had virtually no representation in the Legislative Assembly, the fact that it drew its strength from the Asante area, one of the colony's wealthiest, most culturally advanced, and most politicized regions, meant that the CPP had to deal with a formidable foe. Moreover, the NLM's demand for a federal constitution prior to independence caused British officials to reconsider the timetable of independence and the constitutional arrangements that would best meet the needs and circumstances of the Gold Coast.

The rise of the National Liberation Movement forced the British to rethink plans for political independence. The party's existence underscored the reality of opposition to Nkrumah. Now mindful of the chaos that even a small band of rebels could cause, as the Mau Mau resistance in the highlands of Kenya had made clear, some officials expressed alarm about the prospect of a full-scale civil war or a lesser kind of opposition in the form of guerrilla warfare that could occur if even three hundred or four hundred disaffected young people from the Asante region retreated into forest areas. So concerned was the Colonial Office that the colonial secretary, Alan Lennox-Boyd, called a meeting of his top advisers and the governor, Arden-Clarke, to consider the possibility of delaying independence in order to make sure that the country was truly ready. The colonial secretary ascertained from the Gold Coast commander of the military forces that the chances of civil war were one in three and that the escort police and the army would carry out the government's order if a crisis were to occur, though the police "would probably be seriously affected in the event of an open breach with Dr. Nkrumah." Nonetheless, Lennox-Boyd listened to Arden-Clarke's contention that any delay in granting independence would increase rather than decrease the chance of violence since Nkrumah was likely to make a unilateral declaration of independence. But he also concluded that the Gold Coast would need a third election in light of the appearance of these currents of opposition to satisfy his concerns that the CPP continued to enjoy the backing of the people.[43]

---

[42] *West Africa*, February 25, 1955, p. 121; and Allman, *Quills of the Porcupine*, pp. 85–97.

[43] No. 243, Note of a meeting in the Secretary of State's room, March 22, 1956, with Alan Lennox-Boyd, Thomas Lloyd, Charles Arden-Clarke, and R. J. Vile, PRO CO 554/807.

Kenneth Tours at the Ministry of Finance

If the election of 1954 and the aggressive policies of the CPP aroused antagonism in certain regions so that Lewis would have to enter a country far more riven with factionalism than it was in 1952 and 1953, so too did the economic decisions carried out by the CPP government and forcefully articulated by Kenneth Tours, briefly minister of finance in 1954 and then, from 1954 until 1956, the government's economic adviser, precisely the same position that Lewis would occupy one year after Tours left the Gold Coast.

Scholars have held the view that the economic programs of the later Gold Coast and early Ghana years drew deeply on the emerging ideas of development economics. In reality, the architect of the Gold Coast's development scheme at the time when it was benefiting from the highest cocoa prices that it would ever enjoy and was accumulating surpluses beyond its wildest dreams was an aging government official who had joined the Gold Coast administration in 1931 and served it faithfully for twenty-three years before being asked to be its minister of finance. Kenneth Tours was unlike most colonial officials. Unflappable, slightly iconoclastic, and given to dashing off witty and irreverent letters to his superiors in the Colonial Office, he took on his new financial responsibilities with an enthusiasm and determination that was perhaps a little out of balance with his limited preparations for the position. A Cambridge-educated man, he had held numerous positions in the Gold Coast administration, many of them connected to finance. But he was hardly an expert in development economics. This background did not, however, inhibit him from devising bold ideas about how the Gold Coast should deal with its surpluses. Nor did it keep his colleagues in London from worrying about his grasp of economic affairs and the wisdom of his economic programs given the perilous political condition of the country. In one note in which he put forward what he knew to be radical financial proposals for expending the Gold Coast's newfound riches, he admitted that his overseers at the Colonial Office were liable to think him "nuts." When another one of his letters produced a large volume of skeptical replies, he said that he would require many pails of ice to be delivered to his office so that he could cool down his feverish brain. What he was not was a trained economist. Nor was he astute in recognizing the political implications of his proposals, which were certain to intensify, rather than mollify, the opposition of the cocoa-growing regions to the CPP regime.

Tours's predecessor at the Ministry of Finance, R. P. Armitage, had advised the Gold Coast government to engage a first-rate economic mind to guide the country through these boom times. In his view the Gold Coast needed an experienced, permanent secretary of finance. The country "is rapidly moving out of the extremely restricted economy of the years before the war and so the holder should be someone who has experience of financial and economic matters, at least in other parts of Africa and possibly experience from other parts of the world." What the government needed was "a financial and economic adviser to the cabinet who would be able to give to ministers the type of advice that is now expected from the Financial Secretary."[44] What he had in mind was nothing less than a figure of W. Arthur Lewis's stature. Alas, Lewis was not appointed until independence, when coincidentally the price of cocoa had already begun its sharp downward spiral. The colonial government, keeping to its customary miserliness, promoted Tours instead.

Tours entered the Ministry of Finance in 1954. Without doubt, his ideas enjoyed the backing of the CPP, particularly Gbedemah and Nkrumah, both of whom wanted to see the country transformed economically. Yet, there is no gainsaying Tours's critical influence, if only because he had more substantial economic credentials than his Gold Coast colleagues and enjoyed the confidence of the British Colonial Office. Hence his economic planning during this critical three-year period proved crucial to the country over the long run.[45]

Tours did not take long to imprint his vision of development on the government. Presenting his first budget speech (1954–55) in February 1954, before the elections of that year, he sounded a familiar note of caution. The Gold Coast must do all in its power to become more than a one-crop export economy. Tours described in graphic detail the economic distress that visited one-crop economies around the world when

---

[44] No. 1, R. P. Armitage to W. L. Gorell Barnes, April 19, 1952, PRO CO 554/371. According to Geoffrey Bing in *Reap the Whirlwind*, pp. 144ff., it was the officials in the Colonial Office in London who rejected the advice, given by Dudley Seers and C. R. Ross in their 1952 report and supported by the CPP members of the government, to bring an outside economic expert into the Gold Coast to advise the government. They did so, in his opinion, because they wanted to have as much control over these essential matters as possible.

[45] Geoffrey Bing claims that the CPP government was prepared to engage as an economic adviser either David Worswick of the Oxford Institute of Statistics or Thomas Balogh, who was later taken on as a consultant but only after independence. Whether such an adviser could have carried out some of the plans that Bing believed the Gold Coast required in these years, such as investing some of the country's large sterling balances in the Gold Coast economy, preparing the country for monetary independence, and restricting imports on consumer goods and nondurable products, is highly questionable. These matters were regularly under discussion during the Tours-Gbedemah tenure at the Ministry of Finance. See, Bing, *Reap the Whirlwind*, pp. 144ff.

the world price of their commodities plummeted, using Cuba as his example. Fortunately, the Gold Coast had an opportunity to free itself of this dependence. "This is the moment we should be bending over backwards to increase our productivity and to expand our economy. If we fail to make use of this opportunity, we shall, indeed, be leaving ourselves to 'the mercy of world trade.' . . . I do not want to see it [the Gold Coast economy] going from 'abundance to sadness, from joy to misery.' "[46] Note the language and phrases that this conventionally trained government official employed. Here there are no references to big pushes or investment rates or comparisons between developed and backward economies. This was not the mental world of Kenneth Tours. In his view, a once-in-a-lifetime window of opportunity was presenting itself to the country. The spectacular ascent of world cocoa prices provided a unique moment to achieve an economic diversification that would yield benefits for decades to come.

For Tours, the key to handling the unanticipated economic prosperity was standard commodity boom advice. The state should retain the windfall from the rise in world cocoa prices, especially keeping it out of the hands of cultivators, and use these monies to carry out the ten-year development plan as rapidly as possible. To achieve these goals, Tours first needed to demonstrate to the leadership of the CPP, even those like Nkrumah and the individual who succeeded Tours as minister of finance, Komla Gbedemah, both of whom were predisposed to favor programs of economic diversification, that this policy would work and was in the Gold Coast's best interests. He did so in his typically dramatic ways, bringing the Gold Coast prime minister into his office and showing him a graph that he kept on the wall that purported to demonstrate that whenever the government raised the price it paid to cocoa farmers, the prices of other commodities also rose. "The link is pure sympathetic magic, which makes it a bit difficult to describe in actual words, but it is easily demonstrated on the graph," he wrote to a not altogether amused Colonial Office staff member.[47] Later, he sent a copy of the graph to London, adding his own explanation of why increasing the price paid to cocoa farmers led to widespread price increases in other commodities. In his view, the small-scale market women, the so-called Gold Coast mammies, realizing that farmers and others would have more money to spend, lifted the prices of the commodities that they traded. Although British officials at the Colonial Office were skeptical of Tours's arguments and the rigid connection that he claimed existed between local cocoa prices and the prices of other

[46] Gold Coast, Legislative Council, *Debates*, February 5, 1954, p. 153.
[47] No. 4, Tours, Minister of Finance, to R. J. Vile, March 10, 1954, PRO CO 544/993.

commodities, they were delighted that Tours had won the confidence of Nkrumah and other Gold Coast politicians. They were reluctant to undermine this trust, which they hoped would extend British financial and economic influence into the postcolonial period.[48]

Tours's project for dealing with the surpluses over the next two or three years had three elements. First, as his graph seemingly magically demonstrated, permitting the funds to go back to the farmers would be counterproductive. Price inflation would wipe out the market gains. In his opinion, the local economy could not absorb more than seventy-two shillings per sixty-pound load, the equivalent of £260 a ton. Thus, he recommended that the export duty on cocoa be arranged so that the government would acquire any surplus in the world price of cocoa beyond £260 a ton. The country as a whole would become the beneficiary of the cocoa farmers, who would not have benefited in any case from any higher price.

Tours's second ingredient was that government expenditure should be earmarked for projects that had an immediate payoff and would enhance the government's taxation revenues. Already what government officials referred to as annual recurrent government expenditures were on the rise. They brought increasingly heavy budgetary expenditures for which there were no obvious revenues. If Tours's new program were not successful, these expenditures would ultimately eat up the cocoa surpluses and in time plunge the government into debt. Tours laid down the principle that the increase in annual recurrent government expenditures was to be limited to £2 million a year.

The third proposal flowed from his assumption that the world price for cocoa over the next two years would be not less than £360 a ton. In order to ensure that all of these funds were expended on development and not used to cover budgetary deficits, he proposed the creation of special funds into which these surpluses would flow and which would be used for specific development projects. The first of the special funds would finance the second development plan that was to come into being after the first plan had been completed. The second would finance the Volta River project, which Gold Coast nationalists had set their hearts on as a boon to the country's industrialization and a source of abundant and cheap electrical supplies.

Officials at the Colonial Office were skeptical. The program would remove the farmers' incentives to improve their crop and extend the area of cultivation. According to J. W. Vernon, "the Gold Coast may neglect dangerously the goose which is laying golden eggs at pres-

---

[48] Colonial Office Note by M. G. Smith, May 4, 1954, PRO CO 554/993.

ent."[49] R. J. Vile noted that Tours's proposal to increase the cocoa export duty "does represent an extremely heavy tax on a section of the community for the benefit of the territory." He enumerated the deleterious consequences that might flow from it: an overdeveloped government; an underdeveloped rural middle class; overemphasis on industrialization; and neglect of agriculture. Not the least of Vile's worries were that Tours's schemes would further alienate the cocoa-producing parts of the Gold Coast, as its residents witnessed the transfer of their wealth to other parts of the country. While studying Tours's correspondence, Vile concluded that Tours was "a good financial adviser, but . . . only an indifferent economic one."[50] He might also have added that Tours and the CPP leaders were embarking on a massive political gamble, betting their political futures that rapid economic growth would percolate into the wealthiest and most disaffected territories of the colony and persuade the residents that these development programs were indeed beneficial. Yet Tours pushed ahead, not waiting for input from the Colonial Office. Even as the London officials engaged in intense debates over the value of the program, the Gold Coast government placed the bill on cocoa duties before the Legislative Assembly. The Colonial Office offered no last-minute resistance for fear of jeopardizing Tours's influence with Nkrumah.

The best-laid plans often go awry. This one did. By late 1955, Tours had to sound a warning against rapidly rising annual recurrent expenditures lest the whole of the greatly increased cocoa duty be siphoned off to balance the budget. Thus, what proved to be the bane of the Nkrumah years—mushrooming government expenditures—was already making a lethal impact on the budget before the British ever departed. The British officials, who had first criticized the ten-year plan for its stress on social services, notably education and public health, and neglect of agriculture and industrialization, now claimed that they had been right. The development emphasis needed reorienting to "cocoa, food crops, and livestock."[51]

By the end of 1955, the government's *Development Progress Report* made clear how worrisome the Gold Coast financial situation had become. The revised ten-year plan, which the government had hoped to complete within five years, now had to be extended one or possibly two additional years. In fact, although the government had the funds, it had been able to expend only about half of the monies that had been

---

[49] Note by J. W. Vernon, August 25, 1954, PRO CO 554/993.
[50] Note by R. J. Vile, September 14, 1954, PRO CO 554/993.
[51] J. Inman, September 24, 1955, PRO CO 554/993.

set aside for the plan.⁵² Because the government believed that its resources were stretched to their maximum, the responsibility for additional development would require initiatives from the private sector. Citing Lewis's report on Gold Coast industrialization, the drafters of *The Development Progress Report* underscored how important increases in food production were if the Gold Coast was to move ahead economically.

The reference to Lewis was symptomatic of his continuing influence on Gold Coast development thinking. Not only did the main economic technocrats in the government refer back constantly to his prescriptions in *Industrialization and the Gold Coast Economy*, but the question on the minds of these individuals was, what would Lewis do? Tours seemed haunted by Lewis. On the few occasions when Lewis visited the country, prior to independence, Tours chased him from seminar room to seminar room, laying before "the professor" his schemes for development, ever anxious to win his approval. Nonetheless, Tours bristled at any objections that Lewis raised, often deriding Lewis as an ivory-towered academic out of touch with the harsh political and economic realities of the Gold Coast. On one occasion, after "chasing Lewis like a bloodhound," then catching up with him and explaining the dilemmas he faced, Tours reported to the Colonial Office, with obvious satisfaction, Lewis's remark that "he 'thanked God that he was not responsible for that [the Gold Coast finances].' "⁵³

Tours's correspondence with the Colonial Office took on a desperate tone during the 1956–57 fiscal year. Unable to moderate the growth of annual recurrent expenditures, Tours had to report that all of the country's revenue sources, including the cocoa duty, would have to be employed to balance the regular budget. In addition, the government budget was expected to go into deficit during the next fiscal year, at the very moment when the country would achieve political independence, because the price of cocoa was descending and was likely to go below £230 a ton. All of this bad news brought out the worst aspects of Tours's mercurial personality. He berated Lewis for wanting to spend money on education and to take grants-in-aid from the United Kingdom. He opposed the idea of a national bank and a national currency, fearing that radical nationalists would pull the country's funds out of London, where, Tours believed, they were managed responsibly. He mentioned his distrust of Lewis's advice to the Gold Coast nationalists, and when asked to explain why the Gold Coast was not able to put a stop to the growth in annual recurrent expenditures, he reverted to

⁵² Gold Coast, *Development Progress Report*, 1955, p. 5, PRO CO 98/100.
⁵³ No. 24, K. Tours to R. J. Vile, October 10, 1956, PRO CO 554/993.

racial stereotypes. "The African habit of mind," he claimed, "always lives beyond income."⁵⁴

By the end of 1956, the British officials concluded that the prosperous years were over. According to F. E. Cummings-Bruce at the Colonial Office, "as we come to the end of the Gold Coast's existence, British officials see development projects over; surpluses gone, except for the marketing board surplus that is £70 million but the use of which would raise serious political problems; and the Volta River project all but dead."⁵⁵

Tours departed from the Gold Coast at precisely this moment. The rise of the NLM and the increasing opposition in the Asante region prompted the British to insist on a third election before conceding independence to a CPP-led government. The elections took place between July 12 and 17, 1956, and featured 245 candidates competing for 104 seats. The CPP contested all seats, running unopposed in only 5 of them. This time, in contrast to the 1954 elections, few independents ran. The primary opposition party, the NLM, put up 39 candidates, mainly in the cocoa-growing regions of the country. Twenty-three Northern People's Party members ran in the Northern Territories. The remainder of the candidates represented splinter parties. Forty-five independents entered the race. Straight two-party contests occurred in 81 constituencies; three-cornered battles in 14; and four-cornered campaigns in 4.⁵⁶

The results were strikingly similar to the previous two elections. While the CPP claimed an overwhelming victory on the basis of winning 71 of the 104 seats in the Assembly, the opposition was able to argue a different case. The CPP's vote total of 397,938 votes provided it with a significant majority of 99,007 over all of the other candidates combined and enabled the Colonial Office to agree that the party had passed the test of achieving a "reasonable" majority, which the secretary of state for colonies had indicated was between a 10- and 20-seat control of the Legislative Assembly. Still, the concern over voter apathy and significant areas of opposition to the CPP remained.⁵⁷

A last-minute hurdle appeared. Under heavy pressure from the opposition, the government created a commission of enquiry to investigate allegations of corruption and political interference on the part of the Cocoa Purchasing Company. Created on June 27, 1952, the com-

⁵⁴ Ibid.
⁵⁵ No. 3A, F. E. Cummings-Bruce to Gilbert Laithwaite, Commonwealth Relations Office, December 15, 1956, PRO CO 554/994.
⁵⁶ *West Africa*, June 30, 1956, p. 436, and July 7, 1956, p. 471.
⁵⁷ Note by Miss M. Z. Terry, Colonial Office, July 24, 1956, PRO CO 554/807.

pany had brought forth a stream of complaints from the NLM, the NPP, and many farmers' organizations on the grounds that it operated in a close alliance with the CPP and used its reserves to finance CPP political activities. Although the Jibowu Commission found alarming mismanagement and misuse of funds in the Cocoa Purchasing Company, the consensus among Colonial Office officials was that the report did not contain "anything of sufficient magnitude—and it would have taken something of very considerable magnitude—to justify withdrawing our pledge of 11th May [to concede independence]."[58]

How many of these behind-the-scenes maneuverings Lewis was aware of when he disembarked at Accra in October 1957 is difficult to know. Probably not many. The handing-over ceremonies of March 6, which Lewis attended, glossed over the deep-seated tensions that had almost forced a postponement of independence. They also papered over the simmering antagonisms between Nkrumah and the opposition in Asante and the Northern Territories. Lewis was certainly knowledgeable about economic matters, having stayed close to the Gold Coast economy through Tours's tenure at the Ministry of Finance. He witnessed the diminution of the once large surpluses. He was regularly consulted on the Volta River project and knew that the chances of carrying out the scheme had dimmed. He was, however, unlikely to have realized the depth of regional antagonism against the CPP and the intensity of the differences over how cocoa prices should be set and what should be done with the surpluses that the cocoa exports had generated. He certainly would not have known how great had been the fear among Colonial Office officials that the country teetered on the verge of civil strife. In fact, Lewis would have been as caught up in the euphoria of independence as others inside and outside West Africa. British financial and economic experts notwithstanding, Lewis believed that the country's resources held the promise for impressive economic gains. Recurrent expenditures were, of course, a problem, but in Lewis's view ministers like Armitage and Tours had not known how to use the resources of the Gold Coast creatively and efficiently.

[58] Note by Miss M. Z. Terry, July 24, 1956, PRO CO 554/807.

The Gold Coast • 139

Figure 1. Ida Barton Lewis, Lewis's mother and probably the most powerful influence in shaping his personality

Figure 2. Lewis, graduate of the London School of Economics, 1937

Figure 3. Lewis with the League of Coloured Peoples, 1937. Lewis is in the back row, and the founder of the League, Dr. Harold Moody, is sitting in the middle in the front row.

Figure 4. Wedding of W. Arthur Lewis and Gladys Jacobs in 1947. The wedding took place on the island of Grenada, and the other adult woman in the picture is Gladys Jacobs's sister.

142 • Chapter 4

Figure 5. Lewis on a canoe ride on the Volta River with Kwame Nkrumah, prime minister of the newly independent government of Ghana in 1957. With Lewis and Nkrumah are Lewis's two daughters, Elizabeth and Barbara

Figure 6. Lewis at a cocktail party with the Ghanaian minister of finance, Komla Gbedemah, with whom Lewis worked closely during his stay in Ghana

Figure 7. Lewis, vice-chancellor of the University of the West Indies, meeting with students in 1962

The Gold Coast • 143

Figure 8. Lewis meeting with Eric Williams, the prime minister of Trinidad and Tobago, in 1962 when Lewis was traveling around the West Indies trying to save the political federation of the islands. This meeting occurred in Jamaica, and Lewis is pictured here with his wife, Gladys.

Figure 9. Lewis receiving the Nobel Prize in economics from King Carl Gustaf in Stockholm in 1979

CHAPTER 5

Ghana's Chief Economic Adviser, 1957–58

GHANA WAS TO BECOME the testing ground for Lewis's ideas on economic development. He had been a frequent consultant in the late 1940s and the early 1950s as the Gold Coast progressed toward independence, perusing the country's first development plan at the Colonial Office, advising the Colonial Development Corporation on various Gold Coast projects, and drafting a blueprint for industrialization in 1953. The excitement surrounding Ghana's independence in 1957 as tropical Africa's first decolonized territory captivated Lewis as thoroughly as it did African nationalists and Afrophiles around the world. A veritable who's who of intellectuals of African descent living in the Americas flocked to Accra, many of whom had been Lewis's friends from his days in London: George Padmore, the West Indian nationalist and pan-Africanist, St. Clair Drake, the African-American sociologist, W.E.B. DuBois, founder of the National Association for the Advancement of Colored People and a pan-African moving force, and C.L.R. James, the radical West Indian nationalist. These individuals and many others were determined to show the world that Africans could indeed govern themselves and achieve more for their people than the colonial rulers had. They were eager to make Ghana a shining example to inspire independence movements across the continent.[1]

If, then, Lewis saw Ghana as a proving ground for his ideas on economic development, later scholars have viewed the Nkrumah years—from the year that Nkrumah became Leader of Government Business in 1951 until his overthrow in February 1966—as a case study of striking failure, of economic policies gone awry and political stability destroyed. From a country that seemed on the threshold of robust economic progress, it descended into economic misery and political instability. To many, the immediate recent history of Ghana is "only a history of shattered dreams . . . [and a case study], of how not to develop."[2] When a military coup d'état removed the once-revered Nkrumah from office in 1966, few mourned his departure. Nor did they pine

[1] For the relationship of African American intellectuals to the nationalist movements in Africa and their support of the drive for political independence from Africa's colonial rulers, one should consult Von Eschen, *Race against Empire*.
[2] Roemer, "Ghana, 1950–80," p. 202.

for his recall even after successive governments proved as unsuccessful as the Nkrumah government in guiding the country's evolution.

The decade and a half of the Nkrumah years have provided scholars with no end of theorizing about third-world economic and political development. The economically inclined have given many readings to these years. Some have portrayed them as a period in which Nkrumah's efforts to rid himself of neocolonial power were stymied by a conservative military (Mary Oppenheimer and Bob Fitch and Nkrumah himself).[3] Others regard the period as demonstrating the power of the international economy and world pricing of primary products aligned against cash crop exporters (Reginald Green).[4] Still others have argued that concerns about equity were allowed to outweigh the need to promote growth (Douglas Rimmer) or that the very ideas of development economists themselves, including Lewis's, were wrong (Tony Killick and P. T. Bauer).[5] Those who prefer political answers have no shortage of explanations. Many attribute the difficulties experienced during these years to Nkrumah himself, his boundless ambitions, his quest for unchecked power, and his naïveté (Henry Bretton and many others).[6] Others regard the nature of a state-regulated economy that tempted bureaucrats to use their political offices to enhance their power and enrich themselves rather than to promote growth as the culprit (Robert Bates).[7] No matter the perspective, Ghana has become a veritable morality play, its experiences being used to illustrate one theory or another. Moreover, in many of the analyses, especially those that focus on economic factors, Lewis plays a major role.[8]

---

[3] Bob Fitch and Mary Oppenheimer, *Ghana: The End of an Illusion* (New York, 1966); and Kwame Nkrumah, *Neo-colonialism: The Last Stage of Imperialism* (New York, 1965).

[4] Reginald H. Green, "Four Development Plans: Ghana, Kenya, Nigeria, and Tanzania," *Journal of Modern African Studies*, vol. 3, no. 2, August 1965, pp. 249–79.

[5] Douglas Rimmer, *Staying Poor: Ghana's Political Economy, 1950–1990* (Oxford, 1992); Tony Killick, *Development Economics in Action: A Study of Economic Policies in Ghana* (New York, 1978); and Bauer, *Dissent on Development*.

[6] Henry L. Bretton, *Power and Politics in Africa* (Chicago, 1973); Victor T. LeVine, *Political Corruption: The Ghana Case* (Stanford, 1965); and Michael Owusu, *Uses and Abuses of Political Power* (Chicago, 1970). This is quite an inadequate list, though it does highlight some of the earliest and most influential accounts of political developments during the Nkrumah years.

[7] Robert H. Bates, *Markets and States in Tropical Africa: The Political Basis of Agricultural Policies* (Berkeley, 1981).

[8] In analyzing the Nkrumah years, commentators have failed to take seriously the cautions of Geoffrey Bing. Bing, a close adviser to Nkrumah, was the country's attorney general during much of this period, and hence severely criticized by observers and scholars for promoting the state's dictatorial actions. Yet his plea, eloquently articulated in *Reap the Whirlwind*, that Western liberals had unrealistic expectations for a small, not well-endowed West African country and were entirely too critical of the shortcomings

If, however, one looks more deeply into the history of Ghana in the postwar years (1945–66), peering behind the formal and official statements that colonial and postcolonial governments issued to argue their cases and reading instead cabinet minutes and confidential and private correspondence, a much less teleological and more nuanced picture comes to light. These investigations reveal that the British-dominated lead-up to independence after World War II imposed limitations on what Nkrumah and his party devotees as well as Lewis could accomplish once they inherited power. Lewis inherited an economic framework that had been put in place by British officials like Kenneth Tours and the CPP nationalists and that had raised expectations that the country could use its cocoa bounty to transform and industrialize the Ghanaian economy. Looking behind the scenes also demonstrates how deeply intertwined politics and economics were, yet how little the chief actors—politicians like Nkrumah and economists like Lewis—appreciated these connections and realized the need to work together, rather than at cross-purposes, to find viable and realistic formulas for promoting the dual goals of political stability and economic advancement.

Although the prospect of assisting tropical Africa's first independent country excited Lewis, he approached the Ghanaian leaders warily. He rejected Nkrumah's first offer to take up a chair in applied economics at the University of Ghana. Observing that he had been at "research institutions all his life and . . . would probably not be a good teacher," he speculated about his future. "My next move will probably be into university administration in which I am already much involved in Manchester." He had already become the dean of the Faculty of Economic and Social Studies at the University of Manchester and had been asked by the trustees of the University College of the West Indies to be a candidate for the position of principal of that institution. He had declined the latter invitation on the grounds that he still had research projects to finish. The trustees would ask again, and he thought it likely that he would accept. "I do not covet it because the Principalship of a new university college is an unenviable task, especially when it is caught between the demands of scholarship and the demands of nationalism. But if the job is offered to me, I shall probably accept and do the best I can."[9]

---

of the government, has great merit. As we shall see, Lewis shared many of these liberal Western hopes for Ghana and was himself deeply distressed when the leaders of the country fell short of the goals that he had for the country. See especially Bing's opening chapter, entitled "African Prospective."

[9] W. Arthur Lewis to Kwame Nkrumah, April 16, 1957, Lewis Papers, Box 9.

Nkrumah's next approach proved more tempting. The Ghanaian prime minister asked Lewis to join his government as its economic adviser, even proffering a lifetime contract. Lewis's earlier decisions to work with the British Colonial Office had shown his willingness, even a feeling of obligation, to accept government roles, and he must have been pleased to be approached by the leader of Africa's most advanced country. Still, Lewis knew enough of Ghana's economic and political difficulties to be cautious. Aligning himself too closely with a leader and a party that were far from being politically tested or universally liked risked a lot, not least his own academic reputation. Rather than become an employee of the Ghanaian government and be drawn directly into the Ghanaian political maelstrom as a hired supporter of the CPP, Lewis asked Nkrumah to seek his services through the United Nations.

Nkrumah's letter requesting Lewis through the UN generated only a cool response even though Lewis had alerted officials to expect a query from the Ghanaians. The main reservation had to do with the government of Ghana's failure to develop guidelines for the position. Before agreeing to send Lewis under UN auspices, UN officials insisted that the Ghanaians put in writing precisely what Lewis would do and what powers he would have. They also sought to use the appointment as a way to exercise control over the Ghanaian economy, including "such things as the consideration of sources of external capital." One UN official wondered if Lewis was "the proper one for the job," a reservation that led to searching inquires into Lewis's political opinions and personality.[10] The conclusion was that Lewis "had an outstanding reputation and that he would probably do a useful job in Ghana in spite of certain personal characteristics that might rule him out for other kinds of assignments." The note did not elaborate on what those personal characteristics were, but the author of this document is likely to have learned of Lewis's independence and his insistence on doing things his way, well known to officials in the British Colonial Office. Moreover, the UN officials believed that Lewis was "not very sympathetic to the Bank [the International Bank for Reconstruction and Development, commonly referred to as the World Bank], but we would not be in a position to rule him out on that basis."[11]

Although Henry Bloch, the UN official most critical of the appointment, proposed that the UN be entirely noncommittal in its response to Nkrumah, recommending "that we make no definitive statement in the absence of more information about the terms of reference," the

---

[10] Patterson H. French to the Central Files, July 5, 1957, International Bank for Reconstruction and Development (IBRD) Central Files, Ghana Adviser.
[11] Ibid.

other staff members did not agree.[12] They moved ahead enthusiastically, endorsing the Ghanaian request that the United Nations appoint Lewis as its economic adviser to the country. He was to be paid the top UN salary of $12,500, and the appointment was for two years.[13] At this time Lewis requested and obtained a two-year leave of absence from the University of Manchester.[14]

Prior to leaving for Ghana, Lewis met with A. W. Snelling, an official in the Commonwealth Relations Office of the British government, for a briefing on Ghana. Snelling, who had not met Lewis previously, found him "knowledgeable about Ghanaian affairs generally and not only from the economic point of view." Snelling also noted, "Lewis is a socialist, but a moderate one. I am sure he already has Nkrumah's confidence. I hope you [Ian Maclennan, the British high commissioner in Ghana] will find him to be a useful counterweight to Bing."[15] Geoffrey Bing had just recently been installed as Ghana's attorney general and was known to be quite leftist. The UN team also anticipated that Lewis could be a moderating influence in Ghana. The two leading UN officials who dealt with Ghana, David Owen and Hugh Keenleyside, "hoped that he would not confine his activities in Ghana to the giving of such external advice to Nkrumah but would exert his influence in any and every way he could."[16]

Although Lewis was remarkably well informed on Ghana and knew many Ghanaian officials personally, he was not fully prepared for the complexities of his new position or the fragility of Ghanaian economics and politics. His participation in the celebrations of independence in March left him, as it did so many others, buoyant about Ghana's prospects. In truth, independence had only intensified Ghana's internal political rivalries and raised the political temperature in the country. Nkrumah's new government, which Lewis would work with, did not lack for talent. But neither did the opposition. The three leading cabinet officials, besides Nkrumah, were Komla Gbedemah, Kojo Botsio, and Krobo Edusei. Gbedemah was an intense, industrious, and highly ambitious man who was generally regarded as the second most powerful political personage in the country. He assumed primary responsibility for financial and economic matters when Nkrumah asked him to

---

[12] Patterson H. French to Files, July 12, 1957, IBRD Central Files, Ghana Advisor.

[13] Betty K. Whitelaw, Technical Assistance Recruitment Services, United Nations, to W. Arthur Lewis, July 15, 1957, Lewis Papers, Box 13.

[14] W. Arthur Lewis to W. Mansfield Cooper, Vice-Chancellor of the University of Manchester, June 27, 1957, Lewis Papers, Box 3.

[15] No. 5, A. W. Snelling to Ian Maclennan, Office of the High Commission, October 17, 1951, PRO DO (Dominions Office), 35/9455.

[16] Ibid.

be the minister of finance. Botsio was designated the minister of commerce and industry. Although he was known to be neglectful of the details of his department, he was enormously energetic. His popularity with the electorate strengthened his standing in the government. The third leading figure in Ghana's first independent cabinet was Krobo Edusei, an Asante politician, whose "elemental and irrepressible vitality" gave him a huge public following and enhanced his visibility at public gatherings. He played a vital role in CPP party affairs because he was the leading Asante politician in the party, for which, however, many in the Asante community were resentful, regarding him "as a renegade who had gone over to the enemy."[17] Nkrumah made him minister of the interior, thus giving him responsibility for law and order. He did not shrink from the task even if it meant repressing fellow Asante leaders.

Although the opposition was small and shrinking, as a consequence of the relentless pressure from the CPP and the allurements of office, its leaders also formed an impressive team. The opposition consisted of the grand figure of Ghanaian nationalism, J. B. Danquah, who was supported by the scholarly K. Busia and the younger firebrand party orators, Joseph Appiah and Victor Owusu. Nkrumah's Convention People's Party drew its strength from the larger, mainly coastal towns, with their vast hordes of young men and women who had completed a primary school education but were often frustrated because they could not find regular employment. A center of opposition was the Asante region, which was resentful that its wealth, derived from cocoa cultivation, was being funneled elsewhere in support of development projects and educational expansion. A second disaffected area was the less politicized, less well educated, and more remote Northern Territories.

A large state with a substantial and diverse population, Asante was one of the battlegrounds between the CPP and its opposition. Nkrumah's party was deeply involved in its internal politics. The CPP leaders, after originally opposing a separate state for the Brong-Ahafo peoples, curried the favor of this community by promising to allow it to secede from Asante and have their own state. Although this appeal did not win all of the leading figures in the Brong-Ahafo area, it created followers who aligned themselves with the CPP while predictably alienating many Asante figures. In much the same fashion, many Asante leaders, aware that the CPP was the dominant political party in the country and thus the dispenser of political patronage, supported the

---

[17] This is the assessment of the British high commissioner to Ghana, Ian Maclennan, in his telegram, no. 156 to Secretary of State, Commonwealth Relations Office, June 5, 1957, PRO DO 554/824.

ruling party. These factors enabled the CPP to sustain considerable political support throughout the Asante region.[18]

As a newly independent government, inexperienced in wielding power and uncertain about maintaining its independence in a changing international world order, the CPP was uncomfortable with criticism and left little to chance. It viewed most acts of opposition as near-treason. The political disturbances surrounding the 1954 and 1956 elections had aroused great anxieties among the CPP leaders. They were followed almost immediately after independence, even while the euphoric moment still lingered in the country, by a violent outburst in eastern Ghana when a small disgruntled group of Ewes expressed in a violent fashion their determination to secede from Ghana and merge with neighboring Togoland. An even sterner challenge came from within the capital city of Accra, where the Ga community criticized the CPP leadership for preaching against "tribalism and nepotism" while "actually practicing these administrative vices as witnessed by the number of them [Fantis, Ashantis, and Ewes] who are employed in the ministries."[19] Young Ga discontents created their own ethnic union, the Ga Standfast Association, a mere four months after independence in July 1957. The CPP did not ignore these overt challenges to its authority or the coalescing of an opposition party, calling itself the United Party. The CPP charged its critics with opportunism and failing to promote true political and economic independence. Distressed CPP leaders reminded the people that the predecessor groups to the United Party had wanted to delay the country's independence and that the CPP was the true champion of Ghanaian independence.

This often irrational and deep enmity toward its opponents led the CPP to enlarge the coercive powers of the state and direct them at opposition politicians whom it was only too willing to portray as state enemies and impediments to progress. The first piece of repressive legislation was the Deportation Act, passed in late August 1957, just two months before Lewis's arrival. The law gave the state the power to deport non-Ghanaians.[20] Shortly after passing this law, the government enacted a further harsh bill entitled the Avoidance of Discrimination Bill. It prohibited parties from using racial or religious appeals. In de-

---

[18] On destoolments, see Rathbone, *Nkrumah and the Chiefs*, and on the relations of the peoples living in the Brong-Ahafo area with the Asante and the central government, see John Dunn and A. F. Robertson, *Dependence and Opportunity: Political Change in Ahafo* (Cambridge, 1973).

[19] Austin, *Politics in Ghana*, p. 373.

[20] For the government's defense of the deportations, see Bing, *Reap the Whirlwind*, pp. 218ff.

fending the law and the earlier Deportation Law, Nkrumah accused the opposition of "unfounded and unwarranted attacks upon the judiciary, police, civil service, and army."[21]

These two pieces of legislation did not satisfy the CPP's desire to fashion a Leviathan-like state. The two most repressive pieces of legislation to be enacted while Lewis was in the country were the Emergency Powers Bill, passed at the end of 1957, and the Preventive Detention Bill of 1958. The new law of 1957 permitted the state to proclaim local emergencies and to employ emergency powers in individual districts and regions. The second act allowed the state to imprison persons deemed a threat to security. The bill went before the Ghana National Assembly in July 1958 and came into effect at the end of the year. The CPP used it to jail opponents and to force many parliamentary members to join the ruling party. Others chose exile.[22]

The Lewis correspondence contains few comments on the Ghanaian turn toward repression and dictatorial rule. Perhaps this was because Lewis plunged headlong into formidable economic problems and barely had a moment to reflect on politics. Sitting on his desk at the time of his arrival was a cautionary report that the World Bank had issued following its November 1956 mission to the Gold Coast. It underscored the pessimistic views that British colonial officials had begun to form about the economy just before they left. It contained a warning that Ghana "face[d] a serious readjustment in its economy, especially in the fiscal field." The ambitious goals that the ten-year plan had espoused had resulted in rising recurrent expenditures and had compelled the government to divert a large part of the funds earmarked for development to balance the ordinary budget. Reserves while "still substantial . . . are not sufficient to maintain expenditure on anything like the current scale for very long." Officials of the bank also cautioned that the benefits of the Volta River project, which Nkrumah had set his heart on as the engine of Ghana's economic diversification and industrialization, should not be exaggerated. Nor should the project's drawbacks be ignored, since the dam was unlikely to pro-

---

[21] Ghana, National Assembly, *Debates*, August 29, 1957, p. 320.

[22] For the parliamentary discussions on the Preventive Detention Bill, see Ghana, National Assembly, *Debates*, vol. 11, July 14, 1958, pp. 407ff. Still a classic study of the move to autocratic politics during the early independence years in West Africa is Aristide Zolberg, *Creating Political Order: The Party-States of West Africa* (Chicago, 1966). Geoffrey Bing, who was attorney general at the time the bill was passed, offers an unpersuasive defense of the bill in *Reap the Whirlwind*, pp. 270ff.

vide the state with revenue, offer employment, or yield relief from rising budgetary expenditures.[23]

In addition to these fiscal problems, the price of cocoa continued on its downward trend, even more rapidly than British officials like Kenneth Tours had anticipated. The window of economic opportunity, fueled by this extraordinary commodity boom, was fast closing. To its dismay, the cabinet had been compelled to reduce the price offered to cocoa farmers from eighty shillings per sixty-pound load, which many party members had promised during the 1956 election campaign, to seventy-two shillings. They were painfully aware that this decision would be greeted with anger throughout the already disaffected Asante region. But the world price of cocoa had declined to half of what it was during the 1954–55 growing season. The price of seventy-two shillings obligated the Cocoa Marketing Board to allocate £6.5 million from its surpluses to ordinary expenditures—funds that were no longer available for development.[24]

The expectations surrounding Lewis at the time of his arrival were staggering. Since they were also highly contradictory, he could not meet all of them. The Ghanaian politicians insisted that he assert Ghana's economic independence from its former colonial rulers and from the outside world. They looked to him to design financial institutions that would free Ghana from the British economy and promote rising standards of living as well as economic strength. Lewis was supposed to make possible Nkrumah's famous slogan, "Seek ye first the political kingdom and all things will be added to it."

On the other hand, the British, the Americans, and the international financial community, powerfully represented in Ghana by the British High Commission, the American Embassy, and representatives of the World Bank and the International Monetary Fund, wanted something quite different from Lewis. They looked to him to be a moderating influence, procapitalist and pro-Western. The radical wing of the Ghanaian political elite alarmed the British and the Americans, and perhaps no one more troubled the Westerners than the Ghanaian prime minister himself, whose political and economic preferences were far from clear at this time. Interested Western observers were well aware that the Ghanaian cabinet had both a left wing, represented by Kojo Botsio, and a right wing, led by the finance minister, Komla Gbedemah. They

---

[23] IBRD, Central Files, Ghana, Box 4, Technical assistance.

[24] Memorandum from the Minister of Trade and Labour, Agenda for the Cabinet, May 7, 1957 National Archives of Ghana, Accra (hereafter GNA ADM [Administration]) 13/2/38; and No. 156, I. M. R. Maclennan, United Kingdom High Commissioner, to Ghana to Secretary of State, Commonwealth Relations Office, June 5, 1957, PRO DO 554/824.

believed that a scholarly and sensible adviser like Lewis could rein in the radical ambitions of men like Botsio and Geoffrey Bing and strengthen the position of Gbedemah.

Although Ghana was the best prepared of those tropical African countries gaining their independence in the late 1950s and early 1960s, it was still woefully lacking in administrative experience and an educated cadre. Ghana, like the other colonies in West and East Africa, had achieved independence much more rapidly than any of the imperial powers thought possible. European efforts to equip Africa's new polities for the trials of independence had been carried out with great haste after World War II and were in many respects too little and too late. The British hoped that the serious gaps in experience and training would compel the new Ghanaian rulers to continue their reliance on British officials, who, at the time, still enjoyed a powerful presence in virtually all of the country's major institutions. The Ghanaian leaders, for their part, looked to Lewis to advise them on how much of the old British legacy to retain and how much to discard. Ghana was a deeply Anglicized territory. Did this inheritance provide firm foundations for building a strong and modern society? Or was it the source of Ghana's economic backwardness and political weakness? Of course, Lewis was not the only person whom Ghana's new leaders would consult on these crucial questions. Yet given his technical credentials in the field of economics and his passionate embrace of the nationalist cause, his advice was bound to carry great weight.

Reorganizing Ghana's Sterling Balances

Lewis's arrival at the end of October 1957 filled Nkrumah with pleasure and gave him a surge of optimism about Ghana's economic future. The Ghanaian prime minister looked to his new adviser to promote Ghana's economic progress and to loosen the ties that bound his country to Britain. In a note of welcome that he dashed off to Lewis on November 4, Nkrumah spelled out what needed to be done. The most important long-range task was "stock-taking of our entire economic and financial policy." But immediate matters required attention. The Ministry of Finance was preparing the budget for 1958–59 and developing a new five-year plan, now that the original ten-year plan was winding down. Industrial projects were to be identified and supported, and the Volta River project remained a priority. Because Nkrumah expected Lewis to devote most of his time to development, he recommended that Lewis attend all meetings of the Standing Development Committee. Finally, Nkrumah hoped that Lewis would train young economists, a few of whom would be ready to take over the task of economic advising should Lewis hold to his intention to remain in Ghana for only two years.[25]

Nkrumah kept his word in the first months. The prime minister consulted his economic adviser on numerous issues, not just those that were economic, instructing Lewis to "review all of our economic and social policies." But Lewis was quick to sense Nkrumah's changeable moods and how easily outsiders got his ear. The economic adviser regretted Gbedemah's absence in late October and early November, believing that the harsh Deportation Law would not have been enacted if the minister of finance had been present for the cabinet discussions. He also worried about the growing influence of a British economic consultant, Robert Jackson, over crucial economic decisions. Lewis worried that Jackson's political ambitions outstripped his technical expertise. He believed that Jackson was exploiting Nkrumah's passion for the Volta River project as a means to aggrandize his place in government circles and to render him an indispensable adviser on this and related projects. In contrast, Lewis "considered the development of the country to be more important than the Volta River Project, which I consider to be of only marginal significance." Yet the prospect of having something like £200 million in sterling reserves overcame many of Lewis's doubts about the country's economic direction and its questionable leadership. He was confident that he could devise a workable five-year plan and that Ghana could spend up to £100 million on it "without blinking an eye-lid."[26]

Unfortunately, one of Lewis's first assignments revealed unsettling problems about those very funds that the country intended to employ for development: the sterling reserves. Questions about the true value of the funds and access to them had surfaced in May 1957, before Lewis appeared on the scene. The speed at which Ghana was going through its reserves had begun to trouble the government. Even more worrying to Gbedemah, the minister of finance, was the fact that most of the reserves had relatively low interest rates, around 2.5 percent, as a result of being invested in low-risk, long-term, gilt-edged British securities. In his opinion, the government would be in a better position to balance the budget and underwrite development if it liquidated these securities and invested the proceeds in commercial bonds yielding higher

---

[25] Nkrumah to Lewis, November 4, 1957, Lewis Papers, Box 9.
[26] Lewis to David Owen, Executive Chairman, Technical Assistance Board, United Nations, February 3, 1958, Lewis Papers, Box 9.

returns.²⁷ Gbedemah explored these possibilities during a visit to London, where he met with officials at the Bank of England.²⁸

Gbedemah was by far the most knowledgeable of the Ghanaian ministers in financial and economic matters. But he was hardly a financial sophisticate. Self-taught, he proved no match for the experts at the Bank of England on this, his first visit. His highest level of education was at Achimota, Ghana's best secondary school, which he had attended between 1929 and 1933. After achieving only moderate success running a small candy factory, he became a science teacher and then a successful timber merchant. Nkrumah coaxed him into politics by asking him to run the *Evening News* and then to become chairman of the Committee of Youth Organization of the UGCC. When Nkrumah broke with the UGCC and established the CPP, Gbedemah became vice-chairman of the party. This background as a nationalist made him suspicious of the arguments being employed by the Bank of England team to get him to drop the issue of the financial reserves. The Bank of England experts did succeed in dissuading him, however, from transferring Ghana's sterling assets on the obvious grounds that the commissions would be substantial and that the funds had declined so precipitously at the time that the Ghanaian government would lose heavily if it sold them right away.²⁹

If officials at the Bank of England and the British Treasury believed that they had silenced Gbedemah, after a single visit, they badly misjudged the man. First, Gbedemah needed to gain a better understanding of the reserves themselves if he was to talk cogently with the British financial experts. Then he needed to be supported by better advice than he had during the first visit. Lewis was to supply the latter requirement.

Ghana's reserves fell into three groups and were mostly managed by a British governmental department known as the Crown Agents. The first category consisted purely of the Ghanaian government's own reserves. They had arisen in two different ways: the sterling balances that Ghana accumulated during World War II as a consequence of its contribution to the British war effort and the budgetary surpluses real-

---

²⁷ Cabinet Memorandum, May 23, 1957, GNA ADM 13/2/28; and Memorandum from the Ministry of Finance on Cash Position, Agenda for June 18, 1957, GNA ADM 13/2/39.

²⁸ Extract from the Governor of the Bank of England Note, September 16, 1957, Bank of England Archives (hereafter BE) C40/299.

²⁹ Note from the Chief Cashier of the Bank of England, Leslie O'Brien, September 19, 1957, BE C40/299; Financial Business Carried out by the Crown Agents on behalf of the Ghana Government, n.d. but October 1957, BE C40/299; and Note by L.K.O. O'Brien, Chief Cashier of the Bank of England, October 10, 1957, BE C40/299.

ized in the immediate postwar years when tax revenues, mainly from cocoa, greatly exceeded expenditures. The Crown Agents managed all of these funds, for which Ghana had originally paid £70 million. Their value had shrunk to £61 million in 1957, so any effort to sell them at the present time would result in substantial losses from the original values for the government of Ghana. Yet the monies had maturity dates that stretched all the way out to the 1970s.

The second category was the reserves of the Cocoa Marketing Board, worth around £40 million. They, too, had been invested in far-out maturity dates and had suffered a 25 percent decline in value. Finally, the holdings of the Ghana Currency Board, which managed the reserve funds for Ghana's currency, were worth £41 million. They had been invested in short-term securities and were not subject to the increases in the United Kingdom prime interest rate that had caused such a decline in the value of long-term securities. The conclusion of A. W. Snelling at the Commonwealth Relations Office that Ghana had lost about one-seventh of the value on an original investment of well over £150 million of its reserves and surpluses was clearly an understatement.[30] Moreover, as Gbedemah had impressed on British officials during his October visit to London, the Ghanaian government was distressed with the Crown Agents' investment strategy. British investment officials in London had channeled Ghana's surpluses into long-term securities that had incurred heavy losses on their original value. In Gbedemah's opinion, the funds should have been invested in short-term securities, subject to fewer price fluctuations.

Following his return from the discussions in London, the minister of finance submitted a note to the Ghanaian cabinet in October 1957, outlining Ghana's cruel dilemma. At a time when surplus funds were desperately needed, "the value of securities in which balances are invested has been severely depressed by the recent rise in the United Kingdom Bank rate and the general lack of confidence in the pound sterling which preceded it."[31]

Gbedemah wished for one more go at the British. Nkrumah, fearing that British economists would again attempt to talk circles around his minister of finance, insisted that Gbedemah take Lewis with him to London. Lewis departed, having no prior knowledge of the issue but believing that Gbedemah had misunderstood the handling of the Ghanaian funds in London. But it did not take Lewis long to realize that the Crown Agents' decision to invest in long-term securities had not

---

[30] Note by A. W. Snelling, November 27, 1957, PRO DO 35/9426.

[31] Cabinet Agenda, October 18, 1957, The Minister Responsible for Finance, The Cash Position, GNA ADM 13/2/41.

served Ghana well. It did not help matters that the Ghanaian accountant general who made these decisions was a European who "never looked at the spread of the holdings from the point of view of the dates at which liquidity is likely to be required but has merely operated upon some archaic rules of thumb."[32]

Lewis was deeply critical of London's lack of investment oversight. According to Snelling, he "conveyed the clear impression to me that all this business had shaken the confidence a good deal of the Ghanaian government in the Crown Agents and perhaps (if it really turns out to be the case that the Accountant General had been issuing foolish instructions) in the competence of expatriates to safeguard Ghana's interest with real prudence."[33] This seemingly arcane and highly technical matter in reality had the potential for being enormously embarrassing and costly to the British government and injurious to the international standing of sterling. The Crown Agents managed upwards of one thousand different funds, totaling nearly £1,000 million in nominal value, most of which had depreciated greatly. If word began to circulate that the Crown Agents had a bad investment record and had mismanaged the large surpluses that belonged to colonial territories like Nigeria and Malaya as well as Ghana, the impact on sterling could be profound.[34]

The Bank of England and the Commonwealth Relations Office were therefore immensely relieved that the Ghanaian team had "an adviser of such unimpeachable reputation and ability as Professor Lewis."[35] Nor were they disappointed. Ever the pragmatist, Lewis saw that nothing good would come to Ghana by publicizing the failings of the Crown Agents and the Ghanaian accountant general. Better to rectify the situation by devising a gradual and relatively inexpensive program to shift the investments into securities that would be available when and as needed. The British were grateful to Lewis for being "a moderating influence" on Gbedemah, who in their view "had some wild ideas about what could and should be done."[36] Hence, they could hardly balk as Ghana began to remove funds from the Crown Agents and put them under a Ghanaian management team. They even accepted the accuracy of Lewis's final observation "that although much of the anger about the Crown Agents was due to a misunderstanding of the true position, there remained a good deal of criticism which was

[32] Note by A. W. Snelling, November 27, 1957, PRO DO 35/9426.
[33] Ibid.
[34] Financial Business Carried on by Crown Agents on Behalf of the Ghana Government, n.d. but October 1957, BE C40/299.
[35] Note by J. Loynes, Bank of England, November 28, 1957, PRO DO 35/9426.
[36] Note to Governor of Bank of England, November 27, 1957, BE C40/299.

justified. In particular, the Crown Agents had failed either to take a continuing interest in the investments made in the past for the Ghanaian government and had also accepted instructions, e. g., for long-term investments without pointing out at any time the liquidity risks."[37]

As a final resolution to this painful chapter in Ghanaian-British financial relations, Ghana established a special committee under Lord Piercy and attached it to the newly created Commercial Bank of Ghana, endowing it with the power to manage the country's reserves. This group also assumed responsibility for moving funds out of the hands of the Crown Agents and refused to make any further investments through this body. The government hired a special investment advising group, Pember and Boyle, to ensure the best return possible on its sterling reserves.[38] These investment advisers, working closely with Lewis, then gradually sold off the British securities and purchased other investments, whose maturity dates more closely matched the demands of the Ghanaian economy for capital investment.

Ghana's sharpest economic critics, then and now, have had little charitable to say about the country's fiscal policies in the Nkrumah years. Douglas Rimmer, one of the most outspoken in this regard, accused the government of practicing careless financial policies, failing to control the government budget, and borrowing profligately and unwisely from local banks.[39] Implicitly, he raises the question of whether Ghana would have been better served had it retained close ties with the Bank of England and the sterling zone. Although any policy that curbed inflation and reckless spending would have been an improvement on the fiscal record of the early 1960s, this perspective loses sight of the acute disappointment, if not to say the sense of betrayal, that Ghanaian officials, including Lewis, felt about the decline in the face value of Ghana's sterling balances. They blamed the British Crown Agents for a lack of stewardship.

The Ghanaian financial team was understandably disturbed that the country's surpluses, so welcome as a windfall and so vital in the quest to end the country's economic dependence on cocoa and for economic diversification and industrialization, had been eaten away because sterling, so vigorously championed as a rock-solid currency, consistently declined in value in the postwar years. Nor had Ghana's favorable balance of trade with the United States, so significant in strength-

---

[37] Note by J. B. Loynes, November 27, 1957, BE C40/299.

[38] Note by D. W. Spiers, April 30, 1959; Memo by J. B. Loynes, October 13, 1959; and Memo by J. B. Loynes, March 21, 1960, all in BE C40/299.

[39] See, in particular, the section of the last chapter, entitled "The Abuse of Money," Rimmer, *Staying Poor*, pp. 205–14.

ening sterling, been of much help to the country. The British had imposed rigid limits on the amount of the country's dollar earnings that it could expend on dollar imports. Indeed, Ghana had little but devaluations and restrictions against dollar imports to show for its export efforts. What Ghanaians concluded, and not unfairly, was that Britain sought first to strengthen its own economy following the devastation of the war and only later funneled resources into the colonies. Was it so surprising, then, that Ghana desperately sought to free itself from these tight financial controls? To many Ghanaian nationalists, caught up in the euphoria of political independence, it made sense to establish a currency, no longer locked into what had once been the most secure international currency but no longer was. For that matter, it was predictable that Ghanaians would want to create banks that they regarded as responsive to the needs of the state and the people rather than foreign shareholders.

Drafting the 1958–59 Budget

After dealing with the knotty question of financial reserves, Lewis turned to the 1958–59 budget. Although it is impossible to know how much of this document, when finally completed and published, represented his views, its themes and content were completely consistent with the views that he had adumbrated on development. In the first place, the budget gave priority to development, calling attention, not for the first time, to the two grave dangers to Ghana's dream of economic transformation: rising recurrent expenditures and declining cocoa prices. In addition, the budget proposed tax code incentives in order to attract foreign capital, a policy closely associated with Lewis's writings. It also endorsed a proposal to reduce military expenditures, which Nkrumah and other Ghanaian nationalists later objected to and revised.[40] In presenting the budget to the National Assembly, the minister of finance, Komla Gbedemah, stressed the importance of reducing the company tax and supporting pioneer industries as a way to signal the country's commitment to industrialization and its belief that private capital was essential in this endeavor. He also highlighted the reorganization of the Industrial Development Corporation as a signal that the state and the private sector would work together and that this body would serve as a pivotal institution in helping private

[40] Cabinet Memorandum by the Minister of Finance: The Budget, 1958–59, Agenda, August 13, 1957, GNA ADM 13/2/40.

businesspersons identify profitable industrial projects and provide start-up capital.[41]

In presenting the budget to the National Assembly, Gbedemah singled out two bodies that Lewis had reorganized as soon as he arrived in the country. To both men, the Industrial and Agricultural Development corporations were of critical importance. Lewis took them in hand, placing them under the direction of Ayeh Kumi, who was "one of two African businessmen in the town [Accra] of any standing."[42] To ensure that these organizations had as much technical expertise and political autonomy as possible, Lewis brought leading expatriate business leaders on to their boards of directors. A representative of Cadbury's was designated to serve on the board of the Industrial Development Corporation and an Elder Dempster shipping company official on the board of the Agricultural Development Corporation. To strengthen the industrial side of the economy Ghana also set up an Industrial Promotion Board to initiate new and potentially lucrative industrial ventures in league with foreign capital and local businesspersons.[43]

Lewis expected the Industrial and Agricultural Development corporations to be spearheads of economic development, linking the interests of private capital with those of the state and demonstrating the state's commitment to innovation. Unfortunately, they did not live up to expectations, in large measure because they were not insulated from politics. Within a few years they had blended into all the rest of the state's economic institutions and were being used primarily as vehicles of political patronage. A recurring complaint was that pressure from ministers forced these bodies "to take on unqualified relatives and [made them subject to] constant interference from ministers and other politicians in the operations of particular projects." A telling example was the Ghana Bottling Company, which would have succeeded financially had it not been compelled to return 75 percent of its profits to the CPP and the remaining 25 percent to the members of the Industrial

---

[41] Ghana, National Assembly, *Debates*, July 7, 1958.

[42] No. 4, R. W. B. Carter, United Kingdom Commissioner, to A. H. Reed, CRO (Commonwealth Relations Office), September 11, 1957, PRO DO 35/9299. Lewis proved to be a poor judge of character in this case. Ayeh Kumi was, indeed, a talented individual, but also highly corrupt.

[43] No. 15, G. W. Marshall, United Kingdom Trade Commission, to R. B. Dorman, CRO, July 19, 1958, PRO DO 35/9299; No. 6, G. W. Marshall, United Kingdom Trade Commission, to R. B. Dorman, July 25, 1958, in PRO DO 35/9298; Minutes of the Standing Development Committee, July 9, 1958, GNA ADM 13/2/50; and *West Africa*, July 12, 1958.

Development Corporation. Although Ayeh Kumi was recognized as a capable businessman, he was unable to resist the temptations of office. Before long, he had gained the nickname of "Mr. Ten Per Cent."[44]

THE FIVE-YEAR PLAN

By the middle of 1958 Lewis could finally devote his attention to the assignment that excited him the most: the preparation of Ghana's Second Five-Year Plan. He intended to focus on two issues: first, limiting the growth of recurrent expenditures, which many thought was the consequence of a misguided emphasis in earlier plans on social services, rather than projects that would yield immediate economic gains; and second, promoting fiscal realism. Lewis enlisted Robert Jackson in what he regarded as the more demanding of the two priorities: convincing Ghanaian politicians to be fiscally responsible by endorsing a plan that the country could afford. In his opinion, shared by Jackson, the cost of the plan should not exceed £70 to £80 million, which spread over five years meant spending £15 million a year—a sum that was well within the financial and technical capabilities of the country.[45]

Nkrumah lent his support to these early emphases, informing the Standing Development Committee in an early December 1957 meeting attended by Lewis, Jackson, and Gbedemah that "he wanted a practical plan, which would obtain quick results."[46] Further sensible comments came from a meeting of the same Standing Development Committee one month later, at the end of January, when worries about rising government expenditures and the increased use of cocoa duties to balance the regular budget were used to impress upon ministers the critical role that development was expected to play in transforming the Ghanaian economy. Moreover, the Ghanaian officials agreed with Lewis that "the general atmosphere [in the country] must be one of welcoming 'know-how' and capital overseas."[47]

[44] John Q. Blodgett, Memorandum of Conversation dealing with the Shortcomings of the Ghana Industrial Development Corporation, June 19, 1959, National Archives of the United States (hereafter USNA RG [Record Group] 59, Box 4512 845j 00/6-1959. Blodgett based his observations on a conversation he had with J. A. Harris, the general manager of the Industrial Development Corporation.

[45] No. 24, Note on talks with Sir Robert Jackson on Ghanaian Economic Questions, n.d., middle of 1958, PRO DO 35/9297.

[46] Minutes of the 4th Meeting 1957/8 of the Standing Development Committee, December 23, 1957, GNA ADM 13/2/44.

[47] Cabinet Agenda, January 28, 1958, Minister of Finance, The Financial Situation, GNA ADM 13/2/44.

The Ghanaian ministers did not, however, heed the advice of Lewis to restrain themselves when they drew up their departmental proposals for inclusion in the plan. Since Lewis and Jackson had originally balked at the figure of £100 million that some ministers suggested in early December 1957, they were hardly prepared for departmental requests that totaled £185 million.[48] Nor were the ministers willing to pare back their proposals under Lewis's and Jackson's prodding. According to Jackson, the pressure on the development planners became so intense that "even Arthur Lewis, whom he [Jackson] regarded as a remarkably equable individual, had come out of the cabinet meeting making quite startlingly profane observations."[49]

Nothing was to be done, however, except to divide the plan into two parts, or phases as they were called. Phase 1 was to consist of the high-priority items that the planners believed Ghana could achieve over five years. Phase 2 was labeled a "wish list" that would be accomplished if the money held out and time was left.[50] Many, notably Lewis and Jackson, regarded the division of the plan into two parts as purely a political ploy, so that politicians could boast to constituents that the plan included projects favored by the local electorate while knowing full well that these programs would not be realized immediately. Unfortunately, most ministers did not fully accept Lewis's division of the plan into two parts or his demands for fiscal restraint. They still championed their pet schemes even though they were not part of phase 1. They even signed contracts for the tasks that were not a part of either phase of the plan. Nor did Nkrumah dampen the enthusiasm of his ministers by stressing realism and warning against extravagance. His statement about agricultural and industrial development and electrification projects, made to the cabinet on July 8, 1958, that "we shall be justified in taking calculated risks in this matter" only intensified the pressure to encumber the development plan with expensive proposals.[51]

Lewis was still optimistic about the main lines of the plan and its priorities when he presented a draft to an IMF team. He foresaw a Ghanaian agricultural revolution and was confident that his reorganized Industrial Development Corporation would spur responsible industrial progress. He expected Ghana to spend approximately £100 million on the development effort, and though this figure was 25 percent more than he had originally projected, he believed it to be manageable. A

---

[48] No. 4, Note by A. W. Snelling on talks at the Commonwealth Relations Office with Robert Jackson, May 21, 1958, PRO DO 35/9325.

[49] No. 3, L.J.D. Wakely, High Commission, Ghana, to A. W. Snelling, CRO, July 2, 1958, PRO DO 35/9191.

[50] Cabinet Agenda, Second Development Plan, July 8, 1958, GNA ADM 13/2/40.

[51] Ibid.

full half of the total would come from abroad in the form of loans and equity capital and thus not strain Ghana's budget or exhaust its foreign reserves. Lewis expected foreign investors to favor Ghana because its plan was coherent and well constructed, stressing "rapid development under a flexible program in an open and free economy, with much emphasis on agriculture and the setting up of manufacturing industry."[52]

The five-year plan was published in early 1959. It represented a compromise, negotiated in large part by Lewis, between the radical planners (Nkrumah) and the conservatives (former British colonial officials who had stayed on in Ghana). The radicals wanted to maintain the development momentum that had been achieved in the last years of colonial rules when world cocoa prices were high. They got much of what they wanted. The plan's financing was to come overwhelmingly from public funds: £50 million from the government of Ghana's reserves and another £50 million from the reserves of the Cocoa Marketing Board. Thus, the government of Ghana would provide financing for close to 80 percent of the phase 1 projects. Lewis had no problem with this formula. He agreed with the government ministers that the surpluses should be expended. What he did not agree with was what they should be expended on, for he was fearful, and rightly so, that the politicians would look at the programs in the development plan as opportunities to engage in political patronage. As a concession to the fiscal conservatives and as a method to contain rising recurrent budgetary expenditures, the plan claimed to favor economic projects over social programs and to promote what were labeled economically productive programs. Still, the fact that 61 percent of plan expenditures were earmarked for infrastructure, public services, education, health, and housing, and another 19 percent for the central government, suggested that this plan was not radically different from the previous one. It designated only 8 percent for agriculture and 12 percent for manufacturing. These were higher percentages than in the first plan, but hardly dramatically so.[53]

The influential journal *West Africa* endorsed the plan with a headline on February 16, 1959, trumpeting it as "Jobs for All from £G (Ghana) 240 million." The journal added that the plan "will definitely mean the transformation of Ghana into the near paradise which is the goal of all our efforts."[54] Nkrumah employed similar rhetoric in a debate in the

[52] IMF Consultations with Ghana, Meeting no. 4, November 19, 1958, International Monetary Fund Archives, C/Ghana/420.1.

[53] The best analysis of the five-year plan is to be found in Andrzej Krassowski, *Development and the Debt Trap: Economic Planning and External Borrowing in Ghana* (London, 1974), pp. 33–45.

[54] *West Africa*, February 16 and 17, 1959.

National Assembly on March 4, 1959, stating that the plan would "give us a solid foundation to build the welfare state," noting that the goal is "to give us a standard of living which will abolish disease, poverty, and illiteracy, give our people ample food, and good housing, and let us advance as a nation."[55]

By the time that Nkrumah delivered his encomium on the plan its price tag had, however, skyrocketed to £343 million. The new numbers had become a source of great concern, even embarrassment, to Lewis. The first-priority items that Lewis and Jackson originally wanted to limit to £70 or £80 million and later to £100 million were now budgeted at £126 million. Another £104 million were phase 2 items that were not supposed to weigh the plan down but still had appeal to politicians and the public. Finally, the Volta River project was folded into the plan, at an estimated £103 million. Everyone realized that the last item was the scheme closest to the prime minister's heart since he believed that bountiful and cheap electrical power held the key to industrialization, economic diversification, and national prosperity.

The plan proved every bit as difficult to implement as it had been to draft. Here, too, there was an appalling lack of oversight and restraint. Much too late to make a difference, the government created an informal committee, composed of Nkrumah, Gbedemah, Botsio, Baako, Bursah, and Ayeh Kumi, to check plan expenditures, ensure that the priority items were being adhered to, and prevent bidders from inflating their bids.[56] In order to attract foreign capital, the government removed all controls over the investment of funds from outside the sterling area and permitted firms to remit all profits. The response was swift and, in many respects, gratifying, if however, largely uncontrolled and uncoordinated. Within six months of the publication of the plan, Ghana had contracted financial commitments totaling £124 billion, nearly the whole of what phase 1 had expected to spend over the full five years.[57] Of this figure, £103 billion was for projects that were part of phase 1, but no less than £21 billion had been added to the plan since its publication. Jackson worried about the signing of so many binding commitments at such an early stage in plan implementation and "urged the need for the closest financial control."[58]

[55] Ghana, National Assembly, *Debates*, March 4, 1959, pp. 189ff.
[56] Cabinet Agenda, Note of an Informal Meeting of Ministers, July 27, 1959, GNA ADM 13/2/62.
[57] Cabinet Agenda, Minister of Finance, Press Release of July 7, 1959, The Investment of Foreign Capital in Ghana, GNA ADM 13/2/62.
[58] Cabinet Agenda, December 17, 1959, Minutes of the 11th Meeting of the Standing Development Committee, December 10, 1959, GNA ADM 13/2/67.

Nkrumah worried that these huge financial obligations would result in the quick spending down of the government's reserves and would preclude doing the Volta River project, which he personally preferred to all other items.[59] Jackson agreed. He shared Nkrumah's infatuation with the Volta project. He concluded his overview of the first two years of the plan by observing that the government had gone on "a spending spree, with no true sense of priorities, with the result that it had depleted its resources which would otherwise have been available for constructive purposes, e. g. Volta."[60]

Although Lewis had left the country before the Second Five-Year Plan was published, it was widely considered to be his handiwork. Lewis did little to dispel this notion even though many insiders were aware that he had resisted the plan's final price tag and had even criticized the idea of dividing the plan into two phases. By and large the opinion of outside experts was favorable to the plan, though many commentators agreed with R. B. Dorman of the British Commonwealth Relations Office that it was "overambitious and unrealistic." It was not likely to inspire foreign investors, from whom so much was expected.[61] Still, Dorman, like most other observers, was willing to give the plan and its implementers the benefit of the doubt, agreeing with Robert Jackson that "the present development plan was intended to impress neighboring states rather than to represent a reality likely to be achieved in five years."[62]

Experts at both the Bank of England and the *Economist* were of the opinion that the second phase of the plan contained numerous nonessential projects and represented little more than "a pipe dream." J. M. Loynes at the Bank of England believed that Ghana had the funds for phase 1, but the plan would reduce Ghana's free reserves "to a small figure and might involve losses on the realization of securities beyond those anticipated by Ghana's investment advisers last year."[63]

There were, of course, more searching criticisms. The correspondent for *West Africa* found the plan wanting on the basis of those very criteria that Lewis himself had adumbrated in his 1951 book, *The Principles of Economic Planning*. According to this correspondent, the Ghanaian

---

[59] Cabinet Agenda, March 1, 1960, Minutes of a Special Meeting of the Standing Development Committee, February 25, 1960, GNA ADM 13/2/76.

[60] Record of Conversation with Robert Jackson at the Commonwealth Relations Office, May 26, 1960, PRO DO 35/9404.

[61] Note by R. B. Dorman, CRO, March 12, 1959, PRO DO 35/9303.

[62] Note by B. J. Green, CRO February 2, 1960, PRO DO 35/9303.

[63] No. 18, J. Loynes to A. W. Snelling, April 3, 1959, PRO DO 35/9303; and *Economist*, April 25, 1959.

plan failed to provide a full description of the private sector, made no forecast of the national income or the gross national product, and was sadly lacking in details—all vital ingredients of a good plan by Lewis's own reckoning.[64] Eugene Black, head of the World Bank, who had become interested in Ghana following his visit to the country in June 1960 and was involving the bank in the financing of the Volta River project, concluded that a total expenditure in the neighborhood of £300 million would put a massive strain on the local economy and that the plan, in its three phases (counting phase 3 as the Volta River project), needed to be pared back to no more than £190 million.[65] The Americans, the World Bank, and the IMF agreed that while the Second Five-Year Plan had a salutary emphasis on economic rather than social programs, "the emphasis in the Second Development Plan was considerably distorted during the first year of its creation."[66] These outsiders were particularly distressed, as was Lewis, at the addition of so many prestige projects.

Nonetheless, the observers had only high praise for the role that Lewis had played in preparing the original plan and only sympathy for the many battles that he fought to trim its overall cost. John Blodgett in the American Embassy in Accra described the plan as "the subject of constant and bitter haggling within the Ghana government for nearly a year." Lewis's laudable efforts to prune projects to an affordable level of £100 million, "which he felt was all Ghana could comfortably finance and carry out without undue strain to either the budget or the Public Works Department . . . [had] incurred the enmity of nearly every minister in the cabinet."[67] After Lewis resigned, the ministers took their revenge, raising the figure by over £100 million. British officials connected with the United Kingdom Trade Mission to Ghana came to precisely the same conclusion as Blodgett. The final figure was inflated "to enable politicians to exaggerate the scope of their policy . . . [and] to have the pet schemes of ministers included in the Plan without being driven actually to implement them."[68] Still, overall, the British found the document "a practicable Plan and there seems on the

[64] *West Africa*, May 23, 1959, p. 496.

[65] Memorandum by William Diamond, Program of Mr. Black's Visit to Ghana, June 7, 1960, IBRD Archives, Central Files, Ghana, Box 4, General Negotiations II.

[66] John Q. Blodgett to Department of State, August 4, 1960, USNA RG 59, Box 2511 845j 00.

[67] John Q. Blodgett to Department of State, March 20, 1959, USNA RG 59, Box 4512 845j 00/3-59.

[68] No. 16, R. W. B. Carter, United Kingdom Trade Commission to Ghana, to R. B. Dorman, CRO, April 4, 1959, PRO DO 35/9303.

face of it no reason why a good deal of it should not be implemented by the end of the five-year period."

Lewis was proud of his work in Ghana. When a British newspaper printed an article claiming that the Ghanaian government had largely ignored him, he dashed off a reply that he insisted the paper publish. He stated that he had left Ghana because he had completed his mission there, especially underscoring the drafting of the five-year plan, which he characterized as a realistic blueprint for development. Privately, however, he held a radically different view. In a letter to Nkrumah, during a period when Lewis had engaged in frequent disputes with the prime minister to limit expenses and eliminate prestige projects, he described the plan as "awful. It makes inadequate provision for some essential services while according the highest priority to a number of second importance." Nor did he leave Nkrumah in any doubt of who was responsible for inserting the prestige items into the plan. "Alas, the main reason for this lack of balance is that the Plan contains too many schemes on which the Prime Minister is insisting for 'political reasons.' " Lewis identified £18 million of nonessential items, including a floating dock, regional airports, an international conference center, a yacht for VIPs, and external broadcasting. "In order to give you these toys, the Development Commission has had to cut down severely on water supplies, health centers, technical schools, roads, broadcast redifusion. . . . It is not possible to make a good development plan for £100 million if the Prime Minister insists on inserting £18 million of his own pet schemes of a sort which neither develop the country nor increase the comfort of the people."

Lewis concluded this letter, the tone of which Nkrumah was unlikely to have encountered from any of his subordinates, with an appeal to the prime minster's vanity and sense of history. He begged Nkrumah to limit his projects to £5 million as "a fellow socialist to whom the idea of spending money on embassies, air forces, yachts, making Ghana's voice heard all over the world, and other such boastfulness is downright sinful so long as 80 per cent of the people still have no water and so long as one baby in every three still dies before it is five years old. You belong to the class of great leaders of small countries like Masaryk, Ben Gurion, Muñoz Marín, Cardenas, and U Nu, none of whom would for one moment consider spending £18 million on such baubles." Lewis's passion for development as an instrument for improving the lives of ordinary men and women, which leaps off the page of this document, had no impact on Ghana's prime minister.[69]

[69] Letter from Lewis to Nkrumah, August 1, 1958, enclosed in Keenleyside file, Lewis Papers, Box 7.

In addition to opposing the insertion of prestige projects into the development plan, Lewis was also dismayed at other expenditures that were being approved outside the plan and that would further erode the development capabilities of the country. Nkrumah's intention to expand the size of the military, to Africanize the officer corps, and to pursue pan-African aspirations were costly ambitions, no matter how well intentioned. They were certain to threaten the overall stability of the economy and warn off foreign investors. Robert Jackson, a retired British military officer himself, took the lead in advising the Ghanaians on military matters. He counseled moderation, even suggesting that the Ghanaians could reduce the military budget by three-quarters of a million pounds. He also advised against the rapid Africanization of the officer corps.[70] Yet Nkrumah decided to give the military a high priority and to carry out a rapid Africanization of the officer ranks and an expansion of the forces, including the creation from scratch of an air force and a navy. In justification of this new policy direction, which Nkrumah admitted would raise the military expenses at least 7 percent, and possibly 15 percent (rather than the 20 percent reduction that Jackson and others hoped for), Nkrumah argued that Ghana needed an army that could defend the country against "external aggression . . . [and] be available to restore law and order in any part of the country." With decolonization sweeping through the African continent, the prime minister wanted tropical Africa's first independent state to be able "to negotiate with neighboring states at a date when French influence will no longer hold sway." No one was in any doubt that this innocent-sounding language cloaked Nkrumah's intention to be a force in African independence movements and a promoter of African unity.[71]

Lewis also worried that Nkrumah's intention to be a major actor in West African politics would be costly and was also likely to jeopardize development projects. The first piece of evidence that this worry was legitimate occurred in 1958 when the French West African Federation first began to break up. Given an opportunity to leave the federation in 1958, only Sekou Toure's Guinea chose to vote no. The Guineans were willing to go it alone, even though they knew that a no vote would bring an end to all forms of French financial, military, and economic assistance, because the government had received a promise of a £10 million loan from Ghana in support of the economy. This decision

---

[70] Minutes of the third Meeting, 1957/8 of the Standing Development Committee, November 20, 1957, GNA ADM 13/2/42.

[71] Cabinet Agenda, Prime Minister, The Future Development of the Armed Forces of Ghana, May 27, 1958, GNA ADM 13/2/48.

troubled the more fiscally prudent members of the Ghana government, but was seen as a matter of such urgency to the prime minister that opposing it would be futile.[72]

Deteriorating Relations with Nkrumah

During the first half year of his stay in Ghana Lewis had been fully occupied. He dealt with government surpluses in London, helped to write the budget, and drafted the Second Five-Year Plan. But his differences with the prime minister over "the fluff" introduced into the five-year plan, rising military expenditures, and the bailout loan to Guinea brought him into conflict with Nkrumah and gradually led to his exclusion from the ruling circle around Nkrumah. One intensely personal dispute brought the mounting differences between the two men to a head and paved the way for Lewis's resignation at the end of 1958, just fourteen months after his arrival and a full ten months before the expiration of his contract.

On the surface, spraying cocoa trees attacked by capsid beetles was hardly the stuff of a full-blown political controversy. Yet it became so despite the fact that Lewis had demonstrated to Ghanaian government officials that spending a relatively small sum of money (£2.5 million) to treat cocoa trees infected with the capsid insects would yield anywhere from £15 to £20 million in additional cocoa exports. No one doubted the value of the program or its practicality. Only its implementation pitted Lewis against Nkrumah. Lewis insisted that the Ministry of Agriculture carry out the spraying campaign. The ministry had the equipment and trained personnel. Nkrumah, on the other hand, wanted the Cocoa Marketing Board, which in turn would contract out the work to Ghana's largest and most powerful farmers' cooperative, the United Ghana Farmers Congress.[73] Lewis saw this for precisely what it was—pure political patronage. Both the Cocoa Marketing Board and the United Ghana Farmers Congress were CPP-run and used state resources freely to build up the political strength of the party. In Lewis's opinion these two bodies would produce "ruinous corruption in the course of which we would spend more than £2.5 million a year and kill very few capsids." The Cocoa Marketing Board had no administrative machinery to do the work, and the United Ghana Farmers Council was entirely an instrument of CPP patronage. Lewis

[72] Note by D. W. Spiers, November 26, 1958, BE OV 69/5.
[73] Note of a Meeting of the Cabinet Committee on Capsid Control, December 10, 1958, GNA ADM 31/2/55.

concluded: "The sole purpose of the transfer [of the program from the Ministry of Agriculture to the Cocoa Marketing Board] was to give the party full control."[74]

The dispute came to a head just twelve months after Lewis had arrived in the country and only twenty months after the country had gained its independence. But the country's political scene had changed dramatically. The euphoria of independence had worn off, and the harsh realities of building political stability and integrating a regionally and ethnically divided population while at the same time promoting economic growth had taken their toll on the country's leadership and the rank and file of the people. Nkrumah's coercive laws had only driven the opposition under ground and had led to fear among the rulers that their days in office might be numbered. Nkrumah survived several assassination attempts during this period, and rumors were constantly swirling about of military officers and dissident political leaders plotting his overthrow. In the early months of independence, Nkrumah had traveled around the southern part of the country largely unprotected and to cheering crowds. Now he had to be carefully guarded everywhere he went. Not surprisingly, he looked at economic projects through political spectacles, calculating how vast and long-term projects like the five-year plan and smaller schemes like the capsid program could enhance the power of his party and the security of his regime and enhance the country's political stability as well as produce economic benefits.

Lewis did not see things in this fashion, and he addressed his complaints about the capsid eradication program to the Standing Development Committee, of which he was a member and whose other members included Nkrumah, Gbedemah, Botsio, and Jackson. At the Standing Development Committee meeting, predictably, Gbedemah sided with Lewis and Botsio with Nkrumah. The body agreed to refer the matter back to the cabinet, but not before Lewis unburdened himself of the frustrations of months of being marginalized in a long and passionate letter to the prime minister, of which he offered a précis in a later letter to Hugh Keenleyside, director-general of the Technical Assistance Administration at the United Nations.

In describing the note that he wrote to the prime minister, Lewis observed that he began by reminding Nkrumah of an earlier promise "not [to] allow the agencies for economic development to be used for political jobbery." If this valuable program were turned over to the Cocoa Marketing Board, he would have no alternative but to resign.

---

[74] Lewis to Hugh Keenleyside, Director-General, Technical Assistance Administration, United Nations, December 11, 1958, Lewis Papers, Box 7.

Lewis added that Nkrumah was naturally free to accept or reject the adviser's recommendations, but he insisted that the prime minister "keep your promise that the economic agencies are to be sheltered from political corruption. I had an additional reason for firing off my gun which I did not mention to the Prime Minister. In the past six months he has ignored my advice with increasing callousness. And it was becoming clear that he would soon reach the point when he did not take me seriously at all unless I dug in my heels."[75]

Lewis wrote the letter to Keenleyside prior to his resignation as Ghana's economic adviser, so it has a finality that Lewis probably did not articulate in the original letter to Nkrumah. In fact, the issue was finally settled in Lewis's favor. Nkrumah backed down and allowed the Ministry of Agriculture to implement the capsid eradication scheme. Nevertheless, given Lewis's highly principled temperament and the fact that he had always been prepared to resign from positions, no matter how exalted, when he considered that basic issues were not being dealt with correctly (as he had done when he was secretary of the Colonial Economic Advisory Committee), it was only a matter of time before he decided to leave Ghana.

As early as February 1958 Lewis had begun to prepare for his departure after his two-year contract had expired. He had tentatively agreed to become professor of economics at the University College of the West Indies, starting in October 1959. He had reason to believe that he would be offered the principalship of that institution once it became open.[76] But as he grew more discontented in Ghana, he sought a quicker escape route. He wondered if the UN would be able to find him a posting. Critics of the African independence movements, who were legion, would interpret his leaving Ghana for a professorship in the West Indies before his two-year contract had expired as nothing less than a resignation. They would exploit his departure to slow the pace of decolonization, something that Lewis did not want to see occur. Lewis did not "want to make a public issue of my departure, complete with counter statements and recriminations, which would only comfort enemies of Africans everywhere." But he admitted, "The dispute over the capsid control campaign had marked such a crisis in my position here that you should have an immediate report for future reference."[77]

[75] Ibid.
[76] I. M. R. Maclennan, Office of the High Commission, Ghana, to M. E. Allen, CRO, February 24, 1958, PRO DO 35/9455.
[77] Lewis to Keenleyside, December 11, 1958, Lewis Papers, Box 7.

Keenleyside did find the position that would camouflage Lewis's real reasons for departing. Lewis would become deputy director of a United Nations technical assistance program, called the Special Fund for Economic Development. He could, thus, write a letter to the Ghanaian prime minister stating that he had completed his primary assignment in Ghana and that the opportunity of overseeing a fund that had large amounts of investment capital for use all over the developing world was an engagement that he could not decline. He did not, of course, mention that he intended to stay in this position less than a full year and that he would be moving on to the University College of the West Indies for the beginning of the 1959–60 academic year.

In his private note to Keenleyside, however, Lewis vented his personal frustrations. "I have taken nearly as much as I can stand. In the first place, the Prime Minister has messed up the Development Plan by insisting on spending lavishly on unnecessary projects, mostly in Accra, and by pushing up the total to an unrealistic level. It is one of the worst plans ever published." He commented that the prime minister now rarely sought his advice and that funds earmarked for vital development projects were being squandered on less important items. "There is a limit to what one can take, and I get tired of sticking around just to play nursemaid to grown men. Finally, the political atmosphere gets me down. The fascist state is in full process of creation, and I find it hard to live in a country where I cannot protest against imprisonment without trial or the new legislation prohibiting strikes and destroying trade union independence. If one cannot like and respect the people one works with, smiles with, and stands to attention for, one's spirit must drop sooner or later."[78]

This letter, written a mere twenty-one months after Ghana had achieved its independence and fourteen months after Lewis had arrived in the country full of the excitement that filled the African continent at the time, is clear and moving testimony to the disillusionment that sensitive and knowledgeable figures like Lewis were beginning to have about postcolonial Africa. Yet Lewis gave Nkrumah one last chance. In a letter written on December 18, 1958, indicating that he had completed most of what he had set out to do, having reviewed Ghana's economic policies and completed the development plan, he observed, "what remains for me to do in Ghana is small compared with what we have already accomplished." He was, however, willing to stay on even though his input had been ignored over the last six months provided "my advice will be given serious consideration and not callously brushed aside, as it is at present."

[78] Ibid.

Lewis then boldly laid out the terms that Nkrumah would be required to meet if Lewis were to remain. First, he wanted to attend cabinet discussions whenever economic issues were on the agenda. Second, he wanted a promise that the government of Ghana would not invest more than £25 million of its own funds in the Volta River project, and, third, he insisted that the first phase of the five-year development plan not exceed £120 million. "If we cannot agree on these propositions, there is no point in my remaining."

Lewis used the note to Nkrumah to elaborate on all of his main worries. Overloading the development plan might please the common folk, but it would not appeal to lenders. "The chief effect of overloading the program is to make planning impossible." The note returned to one of Lewis's biggest complaints—the prestige projects, which he predicted would get done first, and then "there will be no money left for the really important ones." As for the Volta River project, this had value to Ghana, but not nearly as much as the prime minister thought. If the Ghanaians expended a lot of their own funds on it, they would exhaust their resources. "We would be ruined financially and would become such a laughingstock in the world's money markets and such an example of mismanagement that we should be unable to borrow for other purposes." If, on the other hand, Nkrumah accepted Lewis's three conditions, he would "be only too delighted to stay and to continue to serve you in every way that I can. But if we disagree on these fundamentals, it seems better that I should take on this new job and try to help the poor countries of the world to build up their productive capacities."[79]

Nkrumah responded predictably to what was nothing less than an ultimatum from a non-Ghanaian official, paid for and ultimately responsible not to the government of Ghana but to the United Nations. The boldest of Lewis's demands was his insistence that he, as economic adviser, attend all cabinet discussions on economic matters. In replying, Nkrumah did not respond to Lewis's specific requests. He understood that Lewis had an international reputation and that Ghana "cannot expect you to risk this reputation by political decisions which I consider that I must take. The advice you have given me, sound though it may be, is essentially from the economic point of view, and I have told you, on many occasions, that I cannot always follow this advice as I am a politician and must gamble on the future."[80]

Lewis was relieved to depart without a public falling-out. He recognized that "Nkrumah's pride was hurt," but he pocketed the letter

[79] Lewis to Nkrumah, December 18, 1958, Lewis Papers, Box 9.
[80] Nkrumah to Lewis, December 18, 1958, Lewis Papers, Box 9.

that praised him for having offered sound economic advice and that held out the possibility that Lewis might again consult for the Ghanaian government.[81]

This dramatic and heavily charged clash between an economic expert (Lewis) and a political leader (Nkrumah), resulting in Lewis's resignation, was repeated again and again in the late 1950s and early 1960s as African states, emerging from colonial rule, sought to buttress their political independence with economic progress. Economic advisers and ministers, some of whom were Africans and some not, regularly had to sacrifice their economic projects to the patronage-building ambitions of politicians. Rarely, however, are observers afforded the opportunity that the Lewis Papers provide to view the underlying tensions involving the political and economic elites that were so often covered up by anodyne formal announcements. The two men saw Ghana's independence from different vantage points even though they were united in wanting the country to enjoy economic progress. Nkrumah believed that the political leadership had the obligation to set the economic agenda and that economists should then design programs that would make it possible to achieve these goals. In contrast, Lewis believed that only the economists could determine what could be achieved, and only they could delineate the appropriate methods for realizing these goals. The proper role of the political leaders was to speak the truth to the people and to promote realistic views of what economic experts told them that their countries could accomplish. Lewis complained that Nkrumah regarded economists as mere technicians, whose task it was to realize the economic dreams of the public and the politicians, no matter how unrealistic. Nkrumah countered by depicting Lewis and the other economists with whom he worked as politically naive, badly misunderstanding the pressing demands that ruling over a decolonized polity placed on the political elite. Political leaders in fragile, newly independent polities had to build coalitions, use patronage to solidify their political authority, even coerce the opposition, and be responsive to the high hopes that their peoples carried about the meaning of political independence.

Even so, Lewis was hardly the dominant economic policymaker in the first two years of Ghanaian independence, as some have wanted to argue. He tried to impose his precepts on Ghana for the first eight months when Nkrumah and other ministers regularly sought him out. But he ceased to count after that, and he was distressed as he witnessed the alteration of his development plans to the point where in private

---

[81] Lewis to Keenleyside, December 20, 1958, Lewis Papers, Box 7.

correspondence he described the final document as "awful" and "one of the worst plans ever written."

Some years later, when asked to comment on a paper written by an American political scientist about Ghanaian politics during this period, Lewis noted that he had played no role in the general decolonization debates that had taken place there. Rather, he had spent his time drafting the five-year plan. As for the observation that Lewis had assisted the state takeover of many parts of the private sector, which the American political scientist considered a commendable step in ending European economic domination, Lewis demurred. His letter of reply went to the heart of what he found most destructive in Ghana and what drove him to resign: the drive of officeholders to enhance the power and size of the state for many, often contradictory, purposes. What Lewis most resented was the drive of these individuals in power to enrich themselves and solidify their hold on power at the expense of the welfare of the people. He reminded the American political scientist that the government of Ghana was not like the governments of Britain and Canada. Ghana's government "was extremely corrupt, and any enterprise that it got its hands on ran into heavy losses.... You therefore write as if every time the Ghana government or some CPP affiliate got its hands on some big business (cocoa marketing, insurance, etc.), this was a triumph for the people of Ghana. Alas, it was not so."[82]

One of the first critiques of Lewis's policies in Ghana appeared in 1966 in a book by the American political scientists Bob Fitch and Mary Oppenheimer, *Ghana: The End of an Illusion*. They claimed that Lewis had impeded Ghana's economic progress by adhering to excessively conservative fiscal policies and keeping Ghana within a capitalist orbit that benefited Western capital more than the Ghanaian people. Only after he left the country did the leadership have the courage to strike out on their own, but by then the effort was doomed to fail. The Ghanaian military, with its rigid Sandhurst training, blocked this laudable effort at establishing economic independence through a coup d'état. Unfortunately, Fitch and Oppenheimer's account ignores Lewis's strong objections to the way that the British Crown Agents had managed Ghana's surpluses and overlooks his establishment of committees and programs that moved the funds out of British hands and placed them under Ghanaian control. These Ghanaian committees established new maturity dates that finally coincided with Ghana's development needs.

[82] Lewis to John D. Esseks, Department of Political Science, Wisconsin State University, March 7, 1968, Lewis Papers, Box 4.

Lewis's economic advice to Ghana never diverged from his textbook and other writings on development. In Ghana Lewis did not do what some economists have been known to do once confronted with real political and economic conditions: trim their policies in response to political pressures and even go against their own major tenets. As he had argued in numerous publications, successful development required a blend of private and public sector initiatives, and this was the most striking feature of the five-year plan. He championed tax incentives and protective tariffs, which he insisted should be used only for nascent industries. He preferred to reserve public investment to projects in which high risk frightened the private sector. He enlarged the budget of the Industrial Development Corporation to £2 million and put in charge of it Ayeh Kumi, whom Lewis regarded as Ghana's leading businessperson, because of a belief that Ghana needed a model organization to strike a balance between private and public initiatives. Nor did he disregard the power of the free market, for he knew that the Ghanaian economic system had to be responsive to market and price incentives. But new countries, needing rapid economic development and faced with severe problems of poverty, had to overcome the inherent wastefulness and inefficiency that he believed plagued market economies. A plan that employed state intervention would ensure that resources were mobilized to the maximum and used with the least waste.

Although Lewis and Nkrumah differed on many economic programs, they were in complete agreement about one crucial policy. They both favored restraining the price paid to Ghana's cocoa farmers so that the state could accumulate surpluses and use these monies for economic development. This practice was the very essence of development economics at the time. The state endeavored to squeeze funds out of the agrarian export sector to support industrialization, education, health care, and urbanization. To be sure, there were skeptics. The British economist P. T. Bauer insisted that cultivators, if allowed to keep the profits from the trade, would themselves become the real agents of economic progress—advice that was followed in the neighboring state of the Ivory Coast, but hardly elsewhere in Africa. In Ghana, the economic and political leadership from the end of World War II onwards had seen the skyrocketing world price of cocoa as a once-in-a-century opportunity to overcome the country's dependence on a single export and a chance to bring sustained economic growth and rising standards of living to the country.

Lewis faced the question of cocoa pricing squarely in May 1958 when the cabinet debated whether it should fix the price of cocoa at eighty shillings per sixty-pound load or raise it in light of the high prices then prevailing in world cocoa markets. Lewis's response was that "unless ministers are under a strong political pressure to raise the price of cocoa, I am strongly against this being done. We are committed to spending £120 million on development in the next 5 years. Overall, government expenditure will average £65 to £70 million a year whereas revenue other than cocoa duties is now only £34 million and is likely to be reduced by proposals for incentive tax reductions. We thus face a gap of over £30 million a year, to which we shall be lucky if cocoa contributes an average of £15 million a year. It is clear to me that the Cocoa Marketing Board should not put out any more money than is absolutely essential."[83]

As Lewis made clear in all of his writings in this period, the most critical issue in achieving development was raising the investment rate from the customary 4 or 5 percent that characterized most less developed economies to something on the order of 15 to 20 percent. What better way to achieve such a breakthrough than to capture the windfall profits from the rising world prices for cocoa. Yet the chief economic adviser was aware that this policy was fraught with danger. The state was taxing the region's most dynamic and prosperous region, from which half of the country's cocoa exports and all of its timber and gold came and in which the opposition to the CPP was the most intense. It was using a large portion of this wealth in other parts of the country. In his opinion, the monies had to be spent in ways that could be seen to contribute to economic and social betterment. If not, the political anger would be irrepressible. Moreover, Lewis was much less committed to industrialization formulas than many of the CPP leaders and insisted that a large portion of state-financed programs be used to make the Ghanaian cultivators more productive, especially in the area of food production.

In identifying the keys to economic growth, Lewis always stressed the need to create a legal and political environment that would encourage the most economically dynamic element to use its energies to promote economic change. Lewis had hoped to find this energy and vision within the upper ranks of the CPP and the government bureaucracy, for the Ghanaian political economy favored them at the expense of the cocoa farmers and other businesspersons. Moreover, the Soviet Union's economic successes convinced him that state bureaucracies could be as economically dynamic as private businesspersons. In Ghana they would have to be if the five-year plan was to succeed.

[83] Cabinet Agenda, May 27, 1958, Minister of Trade and Industries, Cocoa Price, GNA ADM 13/2/48.

Yet Lewis was also aware that the pressures on Nkrumah and the CPP leadership to use these funds to solidify their political support and to build patron-client relationships were substantial. The tensions between what the CPP leaders wanted to do with the funds and what Lewis thought the monies should be used for were a constant source of conflict between Lewis and the CPP leadership. Of course, Lewis was right that Nkrumah's profligate use of political patronage was bound to be self-defeating in the long run. Equally valid was his insistence that Ghana's five-year plan needed to be fiscally sound and should be shorn of its many showy but economically wasteful programs. But believing that Nkrumah would give Lewis a free hand in economic matters, as Lewis claimed he had been promised, revealed a high degree of political insensitivity, even naïveté. His demand to be included in all cabinet discussions of economic issues was highly presumptuous, coming, as it did, from an official who was an adviser paid by the United Nations and in no way responsible to the people of Ghana.

Lewis's position from the outset was an awkward one, if not impossible. On the one hand, the Ghanaians wanted him to lead the country to economic prosperity and economic autonomy. The officials at the United Nations, who paid his salary, as well as those in Britain and the United States, who were delighted when he went to Ghana, looked to Lewis to steer Ghana in the direction of the Western capitalist world. The tensions tearing at the Ghanaian cabinet, to say nothing of the pressures that came from the growing opposition in Ghana to the policies of Nkrumah and his ruling CPP party, put Lewis under even greater pressure. The left wing in the party favored radical political and economic policies. They wanted Lewis to promote state intervention in the country's economic affairs, and they believed that Ghana should replace the old imperialist order with an autonomous set of economic and political institutions as quickly as possible. Just as adamant, however, was the right wing of the party, who believed that Ghana continued to need support from the great capitalist powers in the world. Even for an individual of the most extraordinary personal flexibility, let alone a person like Lewis, who was a rationalist through and through, believing that politicians should embrace the right economic thinking, even when the short-run political consequences were unfavorable, navigating these stormy waters would have been problematical.

CHAPTER 6

Ghana: Part 2

LEWIS LEFT GHANA IN LATE DECEMBER as a member of the Ghanaian delegation to the all-African conference meeting in Addis Ababa, Ethiopia. He did not return. In Addis, he announced his intention to take up a new post at the United Nations. He did not, however, sever his ties with Ghana, and he was to return briefly in 1963 to offer advice on the Seven-Year Development Plan. Because he had not had time to train a replacement, his departure left the Ghanaians without a full-time economic adviser. The responsibility for drafting the budget and overseeing the five-year plan devolved on a variety of outside consultants and Ghanaian ministers themselves. At first Ghana drifted in the direction of more state controls over the economy and greater suspicion of the free market; but by 1960 and 1961 the drift had become a full-scale push as the state began to replace the Lewis programs that had featured a mixed economy with ones that looked exclusively to the state. Lewis had been correct in surmising that had he not left at the end of 1958 under relatively amicable circumstances, he would have been forced to resign under much more public and antagonistic conditions later on.

As Fitch and Oppenheimer argued in *Ghana: The End of an Illusion*, soon after the departure of Lewis the Ghanaian rulers began to alter the economic programs that he had installed in the country. Lewis had wanted to use state intervention and planning mainly to supplement the activities of the private sector. He favored foreign investment and thought that the economic institutions and trading ties that bound Ghana to the United Kingdom and the United States benefited the country. His closest associates in Ghana were men like Gbedemah and Ayah-Kumi, who wanted to solidify Ghana's relationship with capitalist countries. The new young officials in the CPP, on the other hand, were attracted to radical, statist approaches to economic development and saw the Soviet experience with planning and a state-regulated economy as offering an appealing model for achieving rapid economic progress. The drive to dismantle Lewis's policies began slowly through the gradual replacement of the more conservative, pro-Western politicians in the cabinet with younger, radical individuals. It accelerated as Ghana Africanized and expanded the civil bureaucracy and armed forces and culminated with the seven-year plan, which took the place of Lewis's five-year plan and pointed Ghana firmly toward a state-controlled economy.

The early pressures to scrap the Lewis economic policies and move to the left came as much in response to problems that had haunted the Ghanaian economy throughout the late 1950s as to ideology, notably trade and budgetary deficits. The five-year plan had not stanched growing budget deficits and trade imbalances. Monetary and exchange controls and import licensing were implemented. But a cluster of political events at the end of 1960 were also responsible for even more radical political and economic departures that the British high commissioner in Ghana at the time, A. W. Snelling, colorfully described as a "lurch to the left." Some of the incentive for this leftist move came from the courtship of the Soviet Union and the argument that Soviet economic experts were making that a more state-centered economic approach, like that perfected in the Soviet Union, offered hope. Additional pressure to distance the country from the West came from annoyance at Western policies. The French decision, taken in the face of strong African opposition, to carry out atomic tests in the Sahara Desert, coupled with the turmoil of independence in the former Belgian Congo, produced a backlash against Western interests all over the continent. No less important was the fact that the British were not willing to extend critical financial support at a time of great need, while the Soviet bloc countries appeared ready. A final factor was the growing popular discontent with the CPP, leading the party moguls to enlarge the powers of the state in an effort to suppress all forms of opposition.

In Snelling's view, Ghana had become "one of the key East-West battle grounds." He strove to heighten British and American interest in the country.[1] The rise to prominence of such young politicians as Kwasi Amoaka-Atta, secretary-general of the CPP, John Tettegah, secretary-general of the Trade Union Congress, and Appiah Danquah, general secretary of the United Ghana Farmers Congress, represented a marked increase in the influence of the Left in top party positions. In addition, as unelected members of the cabinet, they owed their authority to Nkrumah and the party apparatus rather than parliament or the electorate. In turn, they ushered other left-leaning Ghanaians into key positions in the Bank of Ghana, the Commercial Bank of Ghana, and other agencies and departments as important expatriate officers were leaving the country.[2]

---

[1] No. 1, A. W. Snelling, Office of the High Commission, to Duncan Sandys, CRO, November 21/4. PRO DO 195/4.

[2] D. G. Stone, Deputy Director of the Bank of Ghana, Note on Republican Ghana, November 15, 1960, BE OV 69/6.

If the British had hoped to exercise influence in Ghana through its financial institutions, these appointments were a cause for alarm. While the governor of the Bank of Ghana continued to be an expatriate, Hubert Kessels from West Germany, chosen because of the West German experience of raising itself from a war-torn state to one of the economic powers of the world, the new deputy governor of the bank struck the British as a threat to orthodox Western central bank practices. Amoaka-Atta had gained the reputation among British observers as an "ultra left-wing," ardent party man, who had used his previous position in the Commercial Bank of Ghana to make "a large number of advances ... to party members against inadequate security." According to Komla Gbedemah, who undoubtedly saw the new appointments as a threat to his position, but who also was the most pro-Western and procapitalist individual in the cabinet, Amoaka-Atta was "a fraud and a disaster."[3]

Amoaka-Atta's appointment to Ghana's central bank signaled to many the likelihood that the Ghanaian government would use banking institutions both for political purposes and to finance development efforts through monetary inflation. The Commercial Bank of Ghana, with a mere £6.7 million in deposits, was thought likely to come under government pressure "to give accommodations [to the government] far in excess of its resources." It lacked a core of competent bankers and was headed by the thirty-two-year-old T. O. Asare, also "an ardent CPP man," who was expected to follow the already well-established practice of making funds available to party loyalists. As for the Bank of Ghana, it had not placed strict limits on the issuance of treasury bills at the very moment when the government's expenditures were increasing at a rate of £6 million per year and when the temptation simply to print more money as a way to cover government deficits was proving difficult to resist.

What Snelling described as a lurch to the left in his letter of November 21, 1960, had been prefigured in a statement ostensibly prepared in the Ministry of Finance, which Gbedemah headed, but which was clearly not his work. This memorandum laid out new economic policies that would accompany Ghana's decision to become a republic with an elected president rather than a British-style parliamentary government. The document was weighted with radical slogans, calling upon the government of Ghana to take "a revolutionary standpoint in tackling this all important phase of our struggle." The new republic, led by Kwame Nkrumah, now regularly referred to as Asagyefo, or the Redeemer, had brought Ghana's political struggle to a

[3] Ibid.

triumphal close with independence. The economic battle was just beginning, however, and would entail control of expatriate banking and insurance companies and all forms of foreign capital. In order to prevent expatriate firms from siphoning funds out of the country, the government of Ghana should impose restriction on the transfer of profits; it should also make the Commercial Bank of Ghana "the premier commercial" institution of the country by limiting the autonomy of expatriate banks.[4]

Not until Nkrumah made his famous dawn broadcast of April 8, 1961, did these policy initiatives become political and economic realities. Speaking to the people on that morning, the president asserted that business and politics had become too closely intertwined. As a way to separate them, he demanded that ministers make public their assets and their business dealings and that those officers who had a large stake in the private sector liquidate their holdings or resign their offices.[5] The dawn message was directed at the more conservative members of the government, the men with whom Lewis had been most closely associated, especially the minister of finance, Komla Gbedemah, who soon became the target of a heated press campaign in a series of articles that appeared in the CPP's major newspaper, the *Evening News*. Soon thereafter, Gbedemah moved from the Ministry of Finance to the Ministry of Health. Another of Nkrumah's early supporters and influential cabinet ministers, Kojo Botsio, was stripped of his position as leader of the National Assembly. Another battery of articles appeared in late September 1961 and characterized Gbedemah as "a man bitten with the bug of overweening ambition and self importance," adding that "of all the ministers who have held office since the party came to power in 1951 Komla Gbedemah occupies the first place as one who has relied the utmost and has stuck persistently to expatriate advisers."[6] A few days later Gbedemah was dropped from the cabinet and left the country to go into exile.

Nkrumah's policy changes resulted in sweeping alterations among the top ministers and in the major institutions. In late September, the president sacked Gbedemah, Botsio, and Ayeh-Kumi and followed this action by arresting fifty persons under the Preventive Detention Act, among whom were Joe Appiah and J. B. Danquah, leaders of the opposition.[7] He did away with the Industrial and Agricultural Development

---

[4] Cabinet Agenda, September 2, 1960, Memorandum to the Ministry of Finance on the Economic Reforms Necessary for Ghana as a Republic by the Parliamentary Secretary, E. K. Dadson, GNA ADM 13/2/75.

[5] *Evening News*, April 8, 1961.

[6] *Evening News*, September 30, 1961.

[7] See the White Paper on the subject in PRO DO 195/41.

corporations, in which Lewis had placed such great faith, on the grounds that they had "a colonial flavour."[8] The rise of Amoaka-Atta, now regarded by many as the intellectual architect of the leftist economic thrust, continued apace. Although the British and Americans thought him an economic lightweight when he first appeared on the bureaucratic scene, they now took him seriously. What he lacked in economic sophistication, he more than made up for in application. He was "a prodigious worker and reader" and was one of a few top officials completely free of corruption. Because he had the ear of the president on all economic matters, he was able to undercut the influence of Hubert Kessels, the German governor of the Bank of Ghana. In contrast to the previous economic experts in Ghana (Gbedemah, Ayeh-Kumi, and Lewis), however, he favored "a policy of development through inflation, coupled with tight exchange and private credit controls."[9] This approach impinged on the freedom of the big British trading, banking, and mining companies, heightened the economic powers of the state, and brought Ghana ever closer to the Soviet bloc through bilateral trade agreements and use of Soviet economic planners.

Although the economic and political changes stemmed in part from fiscal and economic problems, the new policies brought no relief. By 1962 the overseas surpluses, except for those that were intended for cocoa price stabilization and the backing of the Ghanaian currency, had been exhausted. Import licensing and exchange controls had not reduced the trade deficit or enabled the government to balance its budget. With the sterling balances reduced to nothing, the government could only engage in domestic borrowing from the banking system and short-term suppliers' loans if it wanted to maintain the momentum of the development plan. The state began to issue more and more treasury bills, with the result that the money supply expanded from £45.3 million in 1958 to £114 million in 1965. The rate of inflation jumped from 2 percent to 26 percent during that same seven-year period.[10]

---

[8] Cabinet Agenda, October 10, 1961, Minister Responsible for Agriculture, Proposals on the Agricultural Revolution of Ghana, GNA ADM 13/2/86.

[9] Note by J. W. Rose, Bank of Ghana, September 7, 1962, BE OV 69/8.

[10] Rimmer, *Staying Poor*, p. 81; and J. Q. Blodgett to the Department of State, December 29, 1960, USNA RG 59, Box 2513 845j 00. Blodgett reported that the uncommitted reserves at the beginning of 1961 were down to £58 million and present commitments to the Volta River project (£30 million), aircraft for Ghana Airways (£10 million), ships for the Black Star Line (£9 million), and repayment to Crown Agents of short-term money borrowed (£12 million) totaled £61 million. These were the very expenditures that Lewis had fought against, and their weighing down of the Ghana Exchequer reflected the correctness of his judgment. Blodgett also wrote that "the Ghanaian government is reported to be living on almost a hand to mouth basis at the present time and is contracting new short-term indebtedness with the Crown Agents to finance operations."

The Seven-Year Plan

Lewis had regarded his primary task and his major piece of work in Ghana, no matter how greatly spoiled by the politicians, as the Five-Year Development Plan. His records do not indicate whether he was disappointed to learn that at the end of January 1962, following all of the new major policy directions in 1961, the plan was officially suspended and would be replaced with a new seven-year plan. Although he was not involved in drafting the new seven-year plan, which was published in 1963, he did consult at a crucial state in its final preparations. Hence, this plan, though never fully implemented because of the continuing economic difficulties that Ghana faced in 1964 and 1965 and that ultimately led to Nkrumah's overthrow in early 1966, marks another stage in Lewis's connection with Ghana. Moreover, although the plan was virtually dead on arrival at government offices, it has been studied by a number of economic commentators and used as an example of the failure of the main tenets of development economics. It is worth close examination.

By 1962, the five-year plan no longer represented the thinking of the economic experts who surrounded the Ghanaian president. In response to the new team and the mounting economic difficulties that Ghana faced, the government established a National Planning Commission and charged it to formulate a new comprehensive economic plan. An Office of the Planning Commission was set up to provide expert guidance. The chief figures chosen to head up this body, H. Millar-Craig, Joseph H. Mensah, and T. T. Naer, had strong reputations for their training and expertise and were known to be favorably disposed to the West. They were expected to exercise restraint in making recommendations to the National Planning Commission.[11]

To the British and American observers, however, the most worrying element in the planning exercise was the role that Soviet-bloc economists had begun to play in Ghanaian affairs. Among the group, Josef Bognar, a forty-four-year-old former Karl Marx Professor of Trade at Budapest University and author of numerous books and articles on economic development and planning, was the most influential. In truth, he should not have worried the Western-trained economists. He had already demonstrated a streak of political independence when he served as the elected mayor of Budapest and later, from 1949 to 1956, when he was Hungary's minister of home and foreign trade. An official at the American State Department recognized that he did not toe the orthodox Marxist line. After reviewing some of the author's

---

[11] David B. Bolen, January 31, 1962, USNA RG 59, Box 2511 845j 00.

articles in professional journals, he wrote that Bognar's approach "is more closely akin to that of Western economists than that of orthodox bloc politicians of the art of central planning."[12]

The preliminary statement announcing the general goals for the Ghanaian plan reflected Bognar's thinking. The country needed a new plan because it "ha[d] outgrown the former development plans, which in their time had a great significance, and at the present time it is necessary to have a more comprehensive, many-sided and overall plan to determine the aims and to ensure the means for the realization of the latter." Because of Ghana's budgetary and balance-of-payments deficits, the state could no longer afford the luxury of a free market. Not only would it have to impose wage, price, and exchange controls, but it would have to be the dynamic force in mobilizing capital. Under firm state controls, the authors of the opening statement claimed that the economy could expand at the rate of 5 percent per year over the next seven years.[13]

Purely as a preliminary statement of goals and means, there was little to quibble with and little to differentiate this statement from Lewis's earlier plan. It was, however, in the elaboration of the details that a policy "tug of war" took place and resulted in the triumph of the more radical socialist planners like Mensah, Amoaka-Atta, and Bognar over Lewis-type planners like Ayeh-Kumi, J. B. Phillips, and Halim, the new Ghanaian governor of the Bank of Ghana, who had input into the plan.[14] In reality, the Left and the Right became so deadlocked and the need to finalize the document so intense that the executive secretary of the National Planning Commission, J. H. Mensah, wrote the entire penultimate draft at high speed so that it would be ready for review by a group of outside experts. Nkrumah and Amoaka-Atta insisted that the American-trained Mensah load the document with socialist language. Early in the deliberations, Nkrumah had criticized Mensah for lacking ideological purity and compelled the executive secretary to affirm in writing his commitment to socialism. Amoaka-Atta went paragraph by paragraph through the first draft of the plan, ensuring "the relevancy of ... particular paragraph[s] to the socialist programme for Ghana." Although Mensah put up no fight, he was apparently far from happy. According to an American observer, Mensah sat

[12] James B. Engle to Department of State, February 7, 1962, USNA RG 59, Box 1702 745j 521.
[13] An early draft of the report from February 1962 is in PRO DO 166/20.
[14] Minute by V. E. Davies, February 25, 1963, PRO DO 166/32.

"entirely poker-faced throughout the entire discussion making no remarks at all."[15]

The World Bank took a great interest in the plan, and its representatives in Accra, especially Leon Baranski, filed detailed reports as the plan began to take shape. These documents offer perceptive comments on Ghanaian decision-making in the economic sphere during the early 1960s, and they reveal that the Ghanaian political leaders disregarded sound economic advice just as stubbornly then as they had during the Lewis period.[16]

That the plan was the work of one man, J. H. Mensah, that Josef Bognar ceased to be influential after he had drafted the preliminary statement, and that Mensah worked under great time pressure from Nkrumah was clear to all the participants. Baranski was particularly critical of the way that the planning commission arrived at its conclusions. In his opinion, the body, under pressure from Nkrumah and the Ghanaian cabinet, first set the development targets that it wanted to achieve at the end of the plan. This was "putting the cart before the horse." What the planning commissioners should have done, in Baranski's opinion, was first assess Ghana's resources, including its GNP, and only then determine the goals and set the targets. Instead, in Baranski's view, Mensah had taken for granted that Ghana had the resources that it needed in order to achieve the desired outcome. Baranski worried that "what happened in India at the beginning of the Second Five-Year Plan (1956), viz. the virtual collapse of the plan due to the lack of realism in the assessment of means," would occur in Ghana.[17]

Mensah refused to budge, continuing to work entirely on his own. When World Bank consultants P. Wignaraja and K.N.R. Ramanujain submitted revised estimates of what the plan could achieve, based on what they considered more realistic assumptions of GNP and growth rates, Mensah refused to compromise. He increased "the magnitude [of these revised estimates], using the plan framework given by us but fixing the whole set of magnitudes higher than we thought feasible." The World Bank consultants had recommended £450 million for government expenditure. Mensah raised the figure to £486 million and did so without taking account of any expenditures for the Volta River

---

[15] W. B. Edmondson, United States Embassy, Ghana, to Department of State, February 7, 1963, USNA RG 59, Box 3915, pol. 1.

[16] Leon Baranski, Review of the Seven-Year Plan, to Pierre Moussa, March 13, 1963, IBRD Central Files, Ghana, Box 4, General Negotiations II.

[17] Ibid.

project or the expanded military.[18] In the opinion of the World Bank officials in Ghana, the Ghanaian planners had actually established the rate of economic growth a priori on the basis of what was required to reach the final target numbers of economic growth instead of doing so after "a careful examination of available national income figures for recent years, consumption, savings, investment patterns, and population and employment data and developing them into a reasonably consistent framework."[19]

Baranski, Wignaraja, and Ramanujain were optimistic that a conference in Accra of high-powered development experts that included Lewis would restore common sense to the Ghanaian planners. The conference, which met in March 1963, did, indeed, represent a who's who of development economics, and though not all of the invitees came, an impressive assemblage did review the plan. Nkrumah delivered the opening remarks, which were followed by a critique of the plan design, undertaken by N. C. Bos, Czeslow Bobrowski, and Osvaldo Sunkel. Lewis, Albert Hirschman, and Weekes reviewed the economic policy on which the plan was based while Kaldor and Baranski reported on the financing of the plan. K. N. Raj and P. Vuscovic submitted a document on planning in general, and Dudley Seers, Sunkel, Carney, and P. H. Ady considered whether the plan would help to expand inter-African trading. Not a single aspect of the plan escaped critical review. In order to ensure that nothing was missed and that detailed expert opinion was solicited on all aspects of the Ghanaian economy, the experts divided up as follows: Lewis, Raj, and J. G. Kiano dealt with agriculture; Bobrowski, Sunkel, and Lewis with industry; Lewis with manpower and education; Vuscovic, Raj, and deGraft Johnson with the demographic experience of Asia and Latin America; and Bhapat and Okoh with plan implementation.[20]

Baranski used the opportunity of the conference to lay out in great detail a full critique of the plan. In his view, the 5.5 percent annual rise in GNP was purely an a priori figure and unrealistic. The investment figure of £840 million was equally "arbitrary" and grossly misleading since it left out many capital expenditures like the military and was based on a period of time when Ghana had large capital reserves to draw on. These had been extinguished, and Ghana would have to get

[18] P. Wignaraja to P. L. Moussa, Monthly Report, No. 3, March 16, 1963, IBRD, Central Files, Ghana, Box 4, General Negotiations, II.
[19] Ibid..
[20] J. H. Mensah to L. Baranski, March 16, 1963, and Baranski to Moussa, March 29, 1963, both in IBRD, Central Files, Ghana, Box 4, General Negotiations, II.

by with much less. Baranski concluded by stating, "the resources available for the financing of the Plan have been seriously overrated."[21]

For once Mensah replied. The executive secretary of the planning commission took offense at the use of the words "arbitrary" and "a priori." The estimates were not drawn out of the air and arrived at because they made the final targets achievable. They were based on all of the calculations that Baranski and the others wanted, but they were not published in the report itself.[22]

Despite his many criticisms of the plan, Baranski conceded "the high level of competence and scholarship" of the conference. "Surprisingly," he commented, "there was a fair degree of consensus between the experts of the Western world, of the 'uncommitted countries,' and of the 'socialist camp.'" The overriding complaint of all of these individuals was that the plan was not "a true development plan but belongs to the category of what may be called 'pre-planning.'" The estimates were "definitely on the high side," and all of the experts agreed that the plan needed to be reworked before it was ready to be published and then implemented.[23] In light of these conclusions, the government of Ghana agreed that Mensah and others would revise the plan and submit it to a small group of experts (Bobrowski, Bognar, Lewis, and Raj), all of whom had attended the conference in Accra.

Baranski sought a private interview with Nkrumah, but was denied. Lewis met with the Ghanaian president, who "is alleged to have said that the plan presents the picture of a large and magnificent overcoat to impress Ghana and the world, but that the government would be quite satisfied if Ghana could make itself a much smaller overcoat."[24] This was not the first time Lewis had heard about "large and small coats," for the same rhetoric had been used when Lewis drew up the five-year plan in the late 1950s, so these soothing comments hardly impressed him. To Baranski's dismay, Mensah returned to his old habit of working alone, having dismissed the experts' criticisms by informing Nkrumah that the conclusions from the experts' conference were "one-sided and centered upon specific subjects."[25]

---

[21] Baranski to Moussa, March 29, 1963, IBRD, Central Files, Ghana, Box 4, General Negotiations, II.

[22] Baranski to Moussa, April 16, 1963, IBRD, Central Files, Ghana, Box 4, General Negotiations, II.

[23] Ibid.

[24] No. 35, S. J. Gross, Office of the High Commission, Ghana, to V. E. Davies, CRO, May 8, 1963, PRO DO 166/20.

[25] Baranski to Moussa, May 6, 1963, IBRD, Central Files, Ghana, Box 4, General Negotiations, II.

The hope that Mensah, E. N. Omaboe, and the other members of the National Planning Commission would take the deliberations of the experts seriously in their redraft proved forlorn. Mensah went into seclusion, and when he came out, he had not revised the total investment figure downward, which all the experts had recommended, but had increased the total to a full £1 billion.[26] This figure would require Ghana to mobilize and expend on development programs no less than £143 million per year, which no self-respecting economist, whether socialist or capitalist, considered feasible. The five-year plan had assumed that Ghana could mobilize and expend approximately £30 million per year, and this sum had been a strain on the economy. Carrying out a program that was nearly five times as large was truly "a pipe dream." The plan also assumed that the world price of cocoa would not fall below £200 per ton and the size of the crop would be 450,000 tons per year. These figures appeared to many to be grossly optimistic. As it turned out, the price of cocoa fell considerably below £200 per ton, although the country did succeed in exporting around 450,000 tons per year.[27]

Three months after the Accra conference, Mensah took the latest draft of the plan to Geneva, where he was intending to present it to K. N. Raj of the Delhi School of Economics, C. Bobrowski of the Planning Commission of Poland, Bognar, and Lewis. This proved to be an exercise in futility. Raj and Lewis declined to attend and indicated that they wanted to have nothing further to do with the plan. Only Bobrowski and Bognar attended. The Ghanaian team, consisting of Mensah, Omaboe, and Millar-Craig, had no written draft to work from, only Mensah's notes, and the effort to revise the draft on the spot with incomplete documentation proved unsatisfactory.[28]

In light of the fact that the plan, though published in 1963, was never implemented because of Ghana's growing fiscal problems, the question arises why it merits an extensive discussion. In fact, the narrative demonstrates that expert economic opinion counted for little. A. T. Killick, a member of the economics faculty of the University of Ghana at Legon and a participant at the conference of experts, has argued the opposite position, claiming in particular that the discussions surrounding the Seven-Year Development Plan proved how central the main tenets of development economics were during the Nkrumah

---

[26] Howard V. Funk to Department of State, August 8, 1963, USNA RG 59, Box 3378, E-Economic Affairs, Ghana.

[27] There is a superb précis and critique of the program in No. 35, S. J. Gross, Office of the High Commission, Ghana, to V. E. Davies, CRO, May 8, 1963, PRO DO 166/20.

[28] No. 41, S. J. Gross, Office of the High Commission, to V. E. Davies, CRO, August 20, 1963, PRO DO 166/20.

years. In his view, the country followed the main guidelines of development economics, endeavoring to promote high savings and investment rates so that the economy could experience a "big push" toward sustained economic growth and industrialization. Ghana failed economically, according to Killick and others, because it adopted the counsel of Lewis and other development economists.

In discussing the conference of experts who were assembled to review the Seven-Year Development Plan, Killick concludes as follows: "In short, constructive professional advice was offered but very little by way of fundamental criticism of the strategy. Nkrumah's planners could reasonably go away from that meeting in the belief that the principal ideas of the Plan had found general acceptance."[29] This comment, coming from an individual who attended the sessions, would seem to clinch the argument that development economics was, indeed, on trial in Ghana and that it failed. But Killick did not have access to the records of the conversations that took place behind the scenes and unpublished memorandums. He was unaware of the detailed and serious criticisms of the plan. It is undeniably true that the experts who came to Accra to debate the draft plan, including Lewis, believed that elevating investment and savings rates, engaging in planning, and promoting viable industrial projects were the critical ingredients in generating economic development, raising standards of living, and perhaps even producing a "big push" into sustained economic growth. But these were sensible and reasonable individuals, who saw no possibility of raising £1 billion in investment capital over seven years. They were skeptical about Ghana's prospects for industrialization, and, to a person, they believed that Ghana had to improve its agricultural productivity if it wanted to achieve any long-term economic success. Moreover, all believed that the setting of unreasonably high targets, however much the leading cabinet officials claimed to be aware of their unrealism, would lead only to confusion in the day-to-day planning operations.

The Seven-Year Development Plan had no opportunity to be implemented. As officials in the Bank of England observed, "The brink of bankruptcy is an unhappy position to launch a development plan which envisages capital expenditures of some £800 million over seven years."[30] By 1963 the balances of the Bank of Ghana's accounts had fallen to £2.5 million, and the government of Ghana had to liquidate United Kingdom securities and to use dollars just to replenish these accounts.

---

[29] Killick, *Development Economics in Action*, p. 53. In note 133 Killick states that he relied on notes that he took while attending the conference.
[30] G. M. Gill and A. J. Weller, Bank of Ghana, January 17, 1963, BE OV 69/7.

Ghana's sterling assets stood at a mere £74 million, of which only £15 million were uncommitted, and these assets themselves had declined in value by £5 million, leaving the country with reserves that were equivalent to only one month's worth of imports.

By 1965, unable to borrow from governments or foreign banks, the government had begun to incur massive debts to individual suppliers and contractors, in the neighborhood of £150 million.[31] At the same time, the world price of cocoa had fallen to £142 a ton, and the state concluded that it would have to reduce the price that it paid to its cocoa farmers from sixty shillings per sixty-pound load to forty shillings, the lowest price since the end of World War II and a source of grave discontent for the farmers.[32] All of the weaknesses in the Ghanaian economy came to a head in 1965 and early 1966 and served to make the military overthrow of Nkrumah an enormously popular event. The balance of payments was heavily in arrears, and the government's budget had been in deficit since the late 1950s. Although the gross domestic product had grown at a rate of 4 percent in the early 1950s and reached 6 percent in the late 1950s, this commendable performance was made possible only by using up all of Ghana's substantial sterling surpluses and reserves. Moreover, the late 1950s was the only period since the end of World War II that Ghana's economic growth had outpaced population growth and internal migration. The five- and seven-year plans notwithstanding, no significant structural economic change had occurred. Agriculture still accounted for 40 percent of the GDP and manufacturing 10 percent. Between 1960 and 1966, according to *The Economic Survey of Ghana* (1966), there was no increase in real GNP per capita. Both GNP and population had risen 17 percent during this seven-year period.[33]

The economy of Ghana failed to achieve most of the goals that the Nkrumah government had set for it. Despite a massive effort at development, based on three separate development plans, and the spending of vast sums of money on projects designed to diversify the economy and raise standards of living, the country had only a huge debt and gaping trade imbalance to show for its work. From the perspective of the economist A. T. Killick, the performance of the Ghanaian economy during this period was "appalling."[34] Douglas Rimmer believes that by making the economic decisions that they chose to make, the Ghanaians

---

[31] Cabinet Agenda, March 30, 1965, Minister of Finance, Report on the Country's Indebtedness on Suppliers' Credits, GNA ADM 13/2/17.

[32] Cabinet Agenda, July 13, 1965, The State Enterprise Secretariat, State Cocoa Marketing Board, GNA ADM 13/2/121.

[33] Ghana, *Economic Survey*, 1966, p. 12.

[34] Killick, *Development Economics on Trial*, p. 83.

had pursued a pathway of "staying poor." But was the failure due to faulty economic ideas, including those propounded by W. Arthur Lewis? Does the Ghanaian failure indict development economics?

Examining the confidential reports on the Ghanaian economy that existed in Ghana, Britain, and the United States raises doubts about the extent to which Ghana's economic failure can be attributed to development economists, including Lewis. In the first place, Lewis's influence over economic decision-making in Ghana took place within a short time frame and was confined to a small number of issues. He served in Ghana for a mere fourteen months and his primary responsibility was the preparation of the five-year plan. Moreover, the plan, when finally published, was one that he had privately repudiated and that he believed reflected the triumph of politics over economic considerations. The tendency for political considerations to outweigh economic concerns, for Nkrumah to impose his will on Ghana, and for the government to view economists as mere technicians whose task it was to achieve the goals that the politicians set for the economy, no matter how unrealistic, was apparent even during the Lewis period. This tendency became stronger after Lewis's departure.

Yet the biggest shortcoming of the practitioners of development economics of this era, and one that Lewis reflected as clearly as any of his colleagues, was precisely their belief that the economic sphere was separable from the political arena and that politicians, properly instructed by expert economic advisers, could become benevolent promoters of economic progress. Holding to this view, too many economists expected government officials to defer to them in economic matters. Witness Lewis's demand that he attend all cabinet meetings in which economic issues were to be discussed. A further, serious miscalculation of this era was the predilection of the economists to base their calculations of economic growth on the assumption that their projects could be optimally carried out. This stance assumed that politicians shared the economists' developmentalist goals when, in reality, the primary aim of most politicians in developing countries, as in the rest of the world, was to acquire office and to maximize power. Even when dealing with political leaders strongly committed to a growth agenda, and surely Nkrumah must be counted among this group, economic advisers too often ignored the coalition-building aspects of ruling and the regional and religious compromises that ruling elites had to make. Nkrumah's final note to Lewis emphasized precisely this point. Nkrumah reminded his economic adviser that he was a politician and that political leaders had to take actions that sometimes ran counter to sound economic advice.

During the latter stages of British colonial rule in the Gold Coast, British economic advisers had promoted the idea that the elevated world price of cocoa provided the country with a unique moment to diversify the economy. These officials created a sense of urgency within government circles that infected the nationalist leadership when it came to power. The prospect of attaining rapid economic growth to strengthen political independence became a high priority to the Ghanaian nationalists in spite of the fact that the world price of cocoa began to descend. The window of economic diversification seemed still to be open, and Nkrumah and his ministers were prepared to "gamble," as Nkrumah had written in a letter to Lewis explaining why he could not accept his economic adviser's recommendations, even to the extent of incurring heavy debts and running big trade deficits. These leaders believed that if Ghana stayed committed to development, the country could achieve economic growth rates, rising government revenues, and increased exports to balance the imports.

The Volta River Project

No program received Kwame Nkrumah's passionate embrace more than did the Volta River project, and no scheme better reveals the collision between economic advisers and political leaders, with the inevitable triumph of politics over economic calculations. The Ghanaian president wanted the construction of a dam across the Volta River as the signature achievement of his era and the program that would lead Ghana into a new economic age. The Volta River project was emblematic of many of the large-scale, heavily capitalized projects that nationalist leaders as well as development economists and international funding groups, like the World Bank, believed could bring about transforming economic change. It was part of the postwar development culture that produced the massive Aswan dam hydroelectric project in Egypt and the Colombo project in South Asia. Like these undertakings, it drew inspiration from the TVA program in the United States and the Soviet Union's planned and rapid industrialization and was seen as a route to a rapid industrialization in Ghana as well.

Not surprisingly, Nkrumah turned to that economist for whom he had the highest regard and whose commitment to Ghana's future he did not question, W. Arthur Lewis. Lewis responded as he had on other occasions when the country's leadership asked for his counsel. He took on the task of providing crucial advice during the 1950s at a time when the discussions were the most intense. And, like much else that Lewis was involved in, his position led to clashes with the men of power, in this case Nkrumah and his inner circle of advisers, and ultimately figured in Lewis's decision to leave Ghana at the end of 1958. Not only is an examination of this grand scheme vital to elucidating Lewis's work in Africa, but the tangled negotiations leading to its implementation cast a bright spotlight on the variety of approaches to economic development that the professional economists associated with Ghana favored and ultimately the limited influence that they exercised during the Nkrumah years.

Plans to construct a dam over the Volta River and to use the electrical power generated there to produce aluminum from deposits of bauxite of the Yenahin region went back to the end of World War I. They were revived after World War II as Cold War tensions heightened Western concerns about access to vital raw materials. The prospect of erecting an aluminum-making plant in the Gold Coast had much appeal to the British Colonial Office and the British Treasury since Britain had to pay for all of its aluminum imports in dollars. A Volta River development effort would yield two significant and desirable results. In the first place, the dam with an adjoining factory using local supplies of bauxite would promote the economic development of the Gold Coast. Second, the production of aluminum within the British empire and sterling area would reduce the drain on British sterling.

The new postwar British Labour government decided that it needed "a full survey of the contribution of the Volta River to the ecology of the Gold Coast" before it could make a decision about the feasibility of constructing a dam in the area. In April 1949, the secretary of state for colonies designated Sir William Halcrow and Partners, a prestigious British hydrological and survey firm, to carry out the preliminary study, and in July 1950, Halcrow and Partners issued its report.[35] The firm concluded that a suitable site for a dam existed on the stretch of the river between the Mem Rapids and Seuchi Rapids but conceded that further geological explorations would be required before a definite site could be determined. The company believed that a dam would be able to generate 500,000 to 545,000 kilowatt hours of continuous power at a total overall cost of £37,210,000, yielding a quite reasonable rate of 0.112 pence per unit. It also recommended the creation of a power grid, transmitting electricity from the dam to Accra, Takoradi, Sekondi, Tarkwa, and Kumasi and to the country's mining complexes, and estimated that the cost of the power would be less than existing diesel plants were charging. Nonetheless, the authors of the preliminary report came to a critical conclusion. The scheme, they pointed out, would not be practicable "without an aluminum producing industry as the

[35] No. 11, Secretary of State to Governor, April 9, 1949, PRO CO 852/846/3.

main outlet for power. [Hence], it should be developed in close collaboration with an aluminum company and with suitable guarantees on both sides."[36] On the basis of these favorable, if necessarily preliminary observations, the colonial officials in the Gold Coast made plans to establish a Volta River Authority, which was to have representatives of the Gold Coast government, the British government, and private aluminum interests, to oversee negotiations and to function as the project's controlling body.[37]

The election of Kwame Nkrumah's Convention People's Party and the creation of a transition government in 1951 brought the Gold Coast nationalists into the debate. Henceforth, no negotiations could occur and no contracts could be signed without the consent of Nkrumah and his party leaders. Indeed, the British officials were particularly distressed at what they regarded as unfortunate timing. Just when they seemed on the verge of creating a government-private consortium, they feared that the election of a nationalist government would put a chill on the plans since foreign companies were unlikely to invest "in a country where the political position offered so uncertain a future."

The arrival of the Gold Coast nationalists on the political scene was a signal that Lewis could not be far behind. Men like Nkrumah and Gbedemah had come to rely on Lewis's economic advice, and they asked him to evaluate the Volta River project in the same way that they had turned to him for guidance on industrialization. As early as 1952, even before Nkrumah and the CPP formally engaged Lewis to assess the project, they had started to inform him of the negotiations.

One of Lewis's fellow West Indians and a pan-African advocate, George Padmore, wrote to Lewis to express reservations that the British would use the Volta River project to retain their influence over the Gold Coast after they had granted the country its political independence. Lewis disagreed and used the occasion to lecture Padmore on how to judge the value of foreign capital. He pointed out that the Gold Coast suffered from two gaping economic deficiencies—investment capital and technical expertise—and that only some form of outside investment could overcome them. "What this means must be faced fully. A firm like Aluminum Ltd will not put money into this sort of enterprise unless it expects to make a profit of 25 per cent per annum; not necessarily in the first 3 or 4 years; but it expects to get all of its capital back in the first 10 years and thereafter to make 100 per cent every 4 years. . . . In my opinion, what is important is not how much a firm takes out of a

---

[36] Preliminary Report of Halcrow and Partners, July 25, 1950, PRO CO 96/828/5.
[37] No. 10, C. G. Eastwood, Colonial Office, to Charles Arden Clarke, Governor, March 16, 1951, PRO CO 96/828/7.

country but how much it puts in and how much it leaves there." He added that if a foreign company created an industry that benefited the host country and enhanced the purchasing power of the government and the people, "then, it has done the best that one could hope for." Instead of fastening one's "eyes on the size of the profits carried out, my advice would be to fasten one's eyes rather upon the size of the wealth created and left to the people of the country."[38]

This was Lewis's reasoning at its most practical and calculating level, devoid of the emotional content that made most African and Afro-Caribbean nationalists deeply suspicious of all foreign influence, especially foreign capital. Throughout the tangled debate over the Volta River project Lewis never swayed from the principle that it was possible to assess in a cold analytical way the economic benefit that foreign investment brought to a country and to weigh these benefits against the economic costs. Yet this rational economic calculus provided no way to measure the depth of anti-European, anti-imperialist sentiment and overlooked the dilemma that nationalist leaders and intellectuals, like Nkrumah and Padmore, faced when conducting negotiations with business organizations that had systematically exploited colonial countries in the past and now claimed to be ready to work for their benefit.

Whenever the political leaders of the Gold Coast/Ghana asked Lewis to advise them on whether the country should sign contracts with private firms or accept loans from foreign governments and banks, Lewis resolutely removed the political implications from his analysis. He understood the penchant that political leaders often had for grandiose megaprograms, but he believed that his role was to calculate the economic returns on these undertakings. Hence, when Nkrumah waxed eloquently about the ability of electricity to transform the Ghanaian economy, Lewis reminded the prime minister that everything turned on how cheap and abundant the electrical supplies were and the extent to which the project would foster Ghanaian employment and Ghanaian industrialization. With respect to the scheme as he knew it in 1952, he was a skeptic. Until he had a chance to review the actual figures on loan repayment charges and electricity rates, he was unwilling to offer advice. He did express to Padmore, however, grave worries that in its haste to promote a big and showy program the Gold Coast government could easily fall into the trap of failing to drive a hard bargain with foreign capital.

In marked contrast to Lewis, Nkrumah was an early and avid enthusiast of the project. Already in April 1952 he lent his backing to it, de-

---

[38] Lewis to George Padmore, April 16, 1952, Lewis Papers, Box 9.

scribing it in a Legislative Assembly debate as "a gigantic project for the industrial development of our country—a scheme which can change the face of our land and bring wealth and a higher standard of living to our people." That the scheme would require considerable foreign assistance did not dampen his enthusiasm. He assured parliamentary delegates that the government would take care that the project would not "endanger our economic independence."[39]

Nor was the mood of euphoria confined to the Gold Coast nationalist intelligentsia. A British colonial official, Norton Jones, the Gold Coast's minister of defense and external affairs, spoke lyrically about the benefits in the same debate. At a cost of a mere £130 million, a project "related more to the pages of the Arabian nights than to the economy of the Gold Coast" would transform the country. "The door stands open," he concluded, "and at our bidding prosperity will cross its threshold into this country."[40]

By 1953 the most critical question in the Volta River project was whether to go forward with negotiations with private aluminum interests by empowering a commission to arrive at a final agreement between the Gold Coast and British governments over financing. At this juncture Nkrumah looked to Lewis for formal advice. The Gold Coast Legislative Assembly pressed the government to add two members to its preparatory commission to ensure that the country's financial and political interests were protected.[41] Nkrumah asked Lewis if he would be willing to serve. In his letter to Lewis, the Gold Coast leader said that the assignment was likely to require Lewis's absence from the University of Manchester for eighteen months to two years and was certain to necessitate the permission of the university's authorities.[42] Lewis wrote back that he needed more information before agreeing to join the commission, but he also warned Nkrumah that he would not be able to get such an extended leave from his academic duties. The most that he could promise was that he would come out to the Gold Coast during Manchester's vacation periods.[43]

Eventually the Gold Coast established a national committee to oversee the work of the preparatory commission, charging it with the duty of ensuring that the country's interests were not sacrificed to foreign investment. This committee would have as its members the minister of finance and the minister of commerce and industry as well as three

[39] Gold Coast, Legislative Assembly, *Debates*, April 18, 1952, pp. 1137ff.
[40] Ibid., pp. 1141–42.
[41] Ibid., February 24, 1953, pp. 555ff.
[42] Nkrumah to Lewis, April 1, 1953, Lewis Papers, Box 9.
[43] Lewis to Nkrumah, April 8, 1953, Lewis Papers, Box 9.

individuals nominated by the Legislative Assembly. It was expected to seek the advice of outside experts among whom Dr. Arthur Morgan and Professor W. Arthur Lewis said that they would help.[44]

Two years of additional scientific investigations and intense bargaining between the Gold Coast and British governments brought the project to the verge of a final agreement.[45] The signing of the accord was set for July 1956. At this critical juncture, Nkrumah regarded Lewis's advice as vital. In the first place, Nkrumah wanted Lewis to review the findings of the preparatory commission, which Robert Jackson was heading.[46] Second, he asked Lewis to give the Ghanaian delegation "a very clear briefing on the [talking] points." Most importantly, since Nkrumah by this time was completely won over to the scheme, the Gold Coast leader wanted Lewis's approval of the preparatory report, in hopes that a public statement from an economist with impeccable credentials like Lewis's would counter any attacks that opposition groups might mount.[47]

Lewis agreed to visit the Gold Coast for seven to ten days in February 1956 and again for two months in July. He also agreed "to assist in explaining the scheme publicly in the ways you have suggested."[48] By late 1955, the Gold Coast government had decided to publish two reports on the project. Nkrumah wrote asking Lewis if he "would care to be associated with it [these reports] by writing an epilogue of say a thousand words which would appear over your signature."[49]

The year 1955 marked the apex of Lewis's enthusiasm for the scheme. By the middle of 1956 his support had waned. Not only did he distrust Jackson's advice, believing his judgment to be impaired by a desire to administer the project, but he was alarmed because the Gold Coast seemed unwilling to bargain vigorously with the foreign aluminum interests. In an April 1956 letter to Nkrumah, he advised against signing any agreement at this time, adding with finality, "I am sorry we were not able to 'bring home the bacon' on this occasion, but the price was too high."[50]

Lewis was therefore understandably distressed to read in a Gold Coast newspaper on July 30, 1956, a copy of the draft note that Nkru-

---

[44] Gold Coast, Legislative Assembly, *Debates*, July 3, 1953, p. 78.
[45] Unfortunately, for the Gold Coast advocates of the scheme, the cost of building the dam and the associated works had risen steeply and the interest of the primary aluminum company, Alcan, had declined. See James Moxon, *Volta: Man's Greatest Lake* (London, 1969), pp. 83ff.
[46] *West Africa*, October 8, 1955.
[47] Nkrumah to Lewis, November 25, 1955, Lewis Papers, Box 9.
[48] Lewis to Nkrumah, December 22, 1955, Lewis Papers, Box 9.
[49] Nkrumah to Lewis, December 31, 1955, Lewis Papers, Box 9.
[50] Lewis to Nkrumah, April 12 and April 13, 1956, Lewis Papers, Box 9.

mah had asked him to write in January to accompany Nkrumah's draft statement on Volta. He reminded Nkrumah that his essay was based on the 1952 arrangements, which assumed that the company would pay the full cost of the electrical power, that the smelter plant to be erected in the Gold Coast would use local bauxite deposits, and that the aluminum company was to put up most of the money for the smelter. Now that these conditions no longer obtained, Lewis's original approbation of the project was not relevant. As yet, unwilling to blame Nkrumah himself, Lewis concluded his note, "I am rather hurt that one of your officials should have chosen to use my name for this act of treachery to your government and to your people."[51]

The project then lay dormant until Ghana's independence, when Lewis's interest and that of the new Ghanian leaders resurfaced. Concerned that Ghana's prospects for economic development were diminishing and needed the kind of boost that a big construction project with long-term potential for industrial growth provided, Lewis suggested that the Ghanaian planners take the Volta scheme out of "cold storage."[52] It did not take long, however, for him to regret the suggestion. Over the course of 1958, as Lewis's relationship with Nkrumah deteriorated, one of the questions that roiled the understanding between the two men was Volta. Nkrumah remained committed to the program. Lewis opposed. In a sharp and didactic note to the prime minister, Lewis pointed out that cheap electricity was not the key to the country's industrialization. "In most industries," he wrote, "fuel costs less than 3 per cent of the costs of production." This was especially true in Ghana, where the industries most likely to succeed were import-substituting, had relatively small capitalizations and large labor components, and did not require large supplies of electricity. In Lewis's view the drive to build the Volta River dam was diverting time and energy away from other, more vital needs. "While Ghana resists appointing a first-class commissioner for industrial production, it is risking to pour millions into providing cheap electrical power, which will be of crucial interest only to bauxite and chemicals." These industries would not be the ones to transform the Ghanaian economy. They would promote enclave development, would be funded by multinational corporations, and would have a high capital intensity, thus offering small employment opportunities to the local population. Even if the Volta project went forward, and Lewis conceded this likelihood, given Nkrumah's ambition for it, Lewis insisted

---

[51] Lewis to Nkrumah, August 8, 1956, Lewis Papers, Box 9.
[52] Lewis to Nkrumah, March 18, 1957, Lewis Papers, Box 9.

that Ghana needed to obtain cheap as well as plentiful electricity for its internal industrial growth.[53]

Lewis's firm and challenging note had a powerful, if rather unwanted, effect on Nkrumah. The questions surrounding the scheme had finally been presented with a clarity that had been lacking previously. Nkrumah came to a fateful decision. "My mind is finally made up," he wrote back to Lewis, "and *irrespective of anybody's advice to the contrary* I am determined to see that at all cost the dams at Bui and Ajena are built in the shortest possible time."[54] Lewis was stunned by the definitiveness and frankness of the Prime Minister's note to the point of doing something that he had never done before and that was quite out of character. He removed from the government files the exchange of notes between himself and the Prime Minister and took them away when he left Ghana, wishing to retain a personal record of this historic decision in his own files. Nkrumah had crossed his own Rubicon. Sweeping aside the advice of his primary adviser on economic matters, he unwittingly advanced the day when Lewis would leave the country. Nkrumah allowed his eagerness to see Ghana achieve dramatic economic progress and his ambition to make a mark in history to prevail over any doubts that Lewis and others had about the enterprise. From this moment, he became the moving force behind Volta, and as a man of his word, at least on this matter, he did not permit the tortuous negotiations and complex financial arrangements that ensued to prevent him from achieving a final accord for a dam across the Volta River and a big hydroelectric scheme. Unfortunately, as Lewis had predicted, the terms that he accepted proved extremely lopsided, weighted heavily in favor of the aluminum interests and against the Ghanaian government and people.

The dispute between Lewis and Nkrumah was more than a clash between two strong-willed individuals or even between an economically centered view of development versus a politically centered view. It was a battle between two different approaches to development. Lewis was, and always had been, the advocate of balanced growth, of moving by stages, of promoting agricultural modernization and developing light industries for an expanding home market. He eschewed most large-scale and capital-intensive schemes, fearing that they were more showy and politically satisfying than economically beneficial. But Nkrumah's interest in Volta was not mere political showmanship and personal ambition. It, too, drew upon a body of economic writing that looked with approval on TVA-like hydroelec-

---

[53] Lewis to Nkrumah, October 31, 1958, Lewis Papers, Box 9.
[54] Nkrumah to Lewis, November 1, 1958, Lewis Papers, Box 9; emphasis added.

tric schemes and argued that large-scale hydroelectric schemes had the potential to produce far-reaching economic benefits. By generating cheap power supplies, they would spur industrial development and create economic diversification.

The remainder of the story over the Volta River project consisted of a continuing struggle between the Lewis and the Nkrumah approaches to development. Nkrumah's vision prevailed, but in the final analysis largely for political, not economic, reasons. Although Lewis played no further role in the negotiations over Volta following his departure from Ghana, his vision regarding development was on trial. In addition, the negotiations leading up to the signature to build the dam provide a crucial example of the declining influence of economic consultants on the Ghanaian economy.

Nkrumah needed help, nothing less than a deus ex machina to save the scheme, however, which seemed on the verge of extinction in 1959.[55] The Kaiser Aluminum and Chemical Corporation took on this role, entering the negotiations in 1959, and offering new, seemingly less costly terms. Kaiser Aluminum claimed that the total cost could be reduced by about £12 million, from £67 million to £55 million. What had seemed to be beyond the means of Ghana now appeared manageable.[56] Caught up in the enthusiasm of this new scheme, no one paid much attention to the fact that the agreement shifted the largest risks associated with the project from Kaiser and placed them squarely on the shoulders of the governments of Ghana and the United States and on the World Bank, who would provide most of the financing for the project. How Kaiser Aluminum was able to negotiate such a generous deal reveals more about the ambitions of an inexperienced nationalist leader and Cold War hysteria than about the shortcomings of economic planning, or misguided beliefs in big pushes into self-sustaining economic development, as some commentators have claimed.

Kaiser's appearance was as welcome to the American and British diplomats as it was to Nkrumah, for the Western powers had grown increasingly fearful that if they did not accede to Nkrumah's wishes for the Volta River project the Russians would intervene.[57] The Western diplomats and businesspersons, in fact, were acutely aware of the unwanted consequences that had followed the American decision of 1956 to withdraw funding from the Aswan dam, Gamal Abdel Nasser's big

---

[55] W. Flake, American Embassy, Ghana, to Secretary of State, June 30, 1959, USNA RG 59, Box 4515, 845j 2614.

[56] Birmingham, Neustadt, and Omaboe, *The Economy of Ghana* p. 393.

[57] No. 715, L. Bevan, High Commissioner Ghana, to M. E. Allen, CRO, December 18, 1959, PRO DO 9/323.

hydraulic project in Egypt. No one in the British or American governments wanted to see Nkrumah pursue the same pathway that Nasser had, aligning himself with the Soviet Union and expelling British and French capital. Having gained Nkrumah's confidence, the Kaiser officials moved quickly to create a consortium of aluminum interests. The new organization, which would later take the name Valco, consisted of Kaiser Aluminum and Chemical Corporation, Reynolds Metals Company, Olin Matheson Company, and Aluminum Ltd of Canada. Each company agreed to contribute a minimum of fifty thousand dollars to a maximum of seventy-five thousand in order to defray the expenses of further investigations. At the suggestion of the Ghanaian government, representatives of Valco opened discussions with the World Bank.[58]

In 1960, as additional information indicated a dimming of Ghana's economic prospects, Eugene Black, head of the World Bank, became involved, meeting personally with Nkrumah. Black cautioned Nkrumah to rein in his other expenditures if he wanted external support. "The project is a good one and bankable but not outstanding."[59] If, however, foreign financing was to be obtained, Black insisted that Ghana make alterations in its Second Development Plan. Black wanted the plan to be cut back from the £300 million that had been projected to £190 million and that this figure of £190 million include £60 million for the Volta project, of which £30 million would come from foreign borrowing and the remaining £30 million from Ghana's own resources. If the Ghanaians would agree to these stipulations, the bank would put together the external financing. Although none of the negotiators was aware of this fact, the bank's terms were precisely those guidelines that Lewis himself had wanted Ghana to insist on when he was drawing up the Second Development Plan.[60]

The Ghanaians balked at Black's terms. A Ghanaian delegation, led by the minister of finance, Gbedemah, described these obligations as a massive and entirely unwarranted interference in Ghana's internal affairs, tantamount to the reimposition of colonial rule. Black's letter to Gbedemah pointing out that the project even under the most optimistic calculations was unlikely to earn more than 6 or 7 percent on the government's investment and that this rate was "not an attractive return"

---

[58] Cabinet Agenda, January 4, 1960, Minutes of the Standing Development Committee, December 14, 1959, GNA ADM 13/2/68.
[59] R. T. Hennemeyer, Department of State, to American Embassy, Ghana, May 11, 1961, USNA RG 59, Box 2514 845j 2614.
[60] Ibid.

and that "the financial position in the first years of operation would be very poor" also fell on deaf ears.[61]

The year 1961, in which the Volta River project agreement was finally signed, was financially tumultuous for Ghana. British and American diplomats had concluded that the Ghanaian economy had entered into a crisis. Moreover, they were funneling their information about Ghana's fiscal chaos straight to the World Bank. Edward Martin, the assistant secretary of state for economic affairs at the State Department, shared an American report on the Ghanaian economy with Robert Skillings of the World Bank, who noted that the document "set forth a gloomy picture of Ghana's public finances." According to this document, the uncommitted reserves available to the government of Ghana in 1961 had declined to a trivial £15.5 million. They were projected to disappear entirely in mid-1962.

Yet, the bank failed to extract any significant concessions from a Ghanaian delegation that visited Washington in July 1961 except for a promise that Ghana would draft a "side letter" stating that it would not strive for unrealistic levels of economic development or exceed certain levels of indebtedness.[62] Black was so distressed at these vague and unenforceable promises that he wrote off the Volta River project as a thoroughly bad one from the financial and economic point of view. The bank would provide financing now only for political reasons. Nor were the American diplomats more enthusiastic. The one Ghanaian official whom the Americans had trusted, Gbedemah, had gone into exile. Although Gbedemah continued to favor Western financing of Volta, his arguments were also now entirely couched in political goals. In his view Nkrumah was a "madman," but "to withdraw at this time would only play into the hands of Nkrumah's advisers who would use the incident to go all out for socialism." He was, nonetheless, under no illusion that a dam across the Volta would transform life in Ghana.[63]

Given the uncertainties surrounding the Volta undertaking, the final decision inexorably made its way to the desk of the American president, John F. Kennedy. Cold War motives and the lessons that the British and Americans had drawn from the Aswan dam proved decisive in persuading Kennedy to endorse the agreement. When, at the last

---

[61] Black to Gbedemah, June 30, 1960, PRO DO 35/9323.

[62] Russell to Department of State, July 17, 1961, USNA RG 59, Box 2515 845j 2614.

[63] Record of Conversation with Gbedemah to Secretary of State, November 21, 1961, USNA RG 59, Box 2515 845j 2614. Earlier, when Gbedemah was still Minister of Finance and was negotiating financing of Volta with the Americans, he warned the Americans that if the Ghanaians returned with unsatisfactory terms, Nkrumah "would lose patience, press a button, call for the Soviet Ambassador, and turn the Project over to the Russians." Moxon, *Volta* p. 104.

minute, Kennedy balked at signing the accords, Black intervened, remarking to the British ambassador in Washington that a decision not to finance "could be at least as damaging as the decision not to proceed with the Aswan dam."[64]

Nonetheless, the one-sidedness of the contract was staggering. According to the journal *West Africa*, which had seen an early draft of the preliminary contract, "few companies operating in foreign countries have been treated so generously."[65] An astute observer of the negotiations, David Hart, deemed the terms to be "very generous" and commented that "they would appear to ensure that Valco [would] recoup its investment in a fairly short period of time."[66] The agreement guaranteed that Valco's tax rates would remain at their original levels for thirty years and that for the first ten years of operation the company would be treated as a pioneer company, thus exempted from all taxes, including import and export duties. The agreement was to run for thirty years, with Valco having an option to extend the contract for an additional twenty years. Valco was obligated to build a smelter at Tema, and it also agreed to purchase electrical power worth a minimum £2.5 million once the dam had been in operation for six years.

The all-important question of the electricity charges to be paid by Valco that Lewis had been so insistent about went entirely in favor of the company. Valco's rate of 2.625 mills per kilowatt hour was one of the lowest in the world. This meant that Ghana's other power consumers would have to make up the difference by paying higher rates, sometimes ten times as high as those that Valco paid.[67] In the short run, Ghana had lots of electrical power, as Nkrumah had wanted, but it was cheap only to the aluminum producers. Moreover, because of changing prices and demand for aluminum, Valco decided against exploiting the bauxite deposits in Ghana. It simply used the Ghanaian smelting plant to transform bauxite, mined in Jamaica and then transformed into alumina in Jamaican and Louisiana factories, for the manufacture of aluminum for sale elsewhere in the world.

In Nkrumah's vision the Volta River project was designed to transform the Ghanaian economy. It would promote industrialization, pro-

---

[64] No. 15, J. D. B. Shaw, British Embassy, Washington, to Algernon Rumbold, CRO, November 24, 1961, PRO DO 166/28.

[65] *West Africa*, February 25, 1961.

[66] David Hart, *The Volta River Project: A Case Study in Politics and Technology* (Edinburgh, 1980), p. 63.

[67] Ibid. In fact, although this price was supposed to remain fixed for thirty years, because the Volta River Authority did not realize its financial goals, Valco agreed to a price rise to 2.75 mills and finally to 3.25 mills in 1977. While Valco paid an average rate of 3.25 mills after 1973, the average charge that the Electricity Corporation of Ghana made to its other customers at this time was 22 mills per kilowatt hour.

vide employment, and reduce the country's dependence on a few primary product exports. It did none of these things. A study of the Volta project carried out in 1980 concluded that it had "a zero or negligible influence ... on Ghana's industrialization."[68] Valco was capital intensive, providing employment to a mere two thousand workers. The Electricity Corporation of Ghana employed another seven thousand workers, many of whom were casual laborers. Even though Ghana now exported manufactured aluminum, these aluminum exports constituted only about 5 or 6 percent of the country's total export earnings. The five major exports of cocoa, timber, manganese, gold, and diamonds still outpaced aluminum and meant that Ghana remained a primary-product-exporting country. Moreover, the earnings from the export of aluminum were almost completely offset by the payments that had to be made for imported alumina and the machinery for the Valco smelter. Indeed, aluminum manufacturing made Ghana's relationship with the world economy more vulnerable and complex, if not more dependent, than it had been before. Ghana exported bauxite to be manufactured elsewhere, imported alumina, exported finished aluminum for manufacture into specific commodities, and then turned around and imported these products.

In the Volta project, just as in the Lewis's ongoing arguments with Nkrumah, politics trumped economics. None of the economists working with the World Bank, the government of Ghana, the American Embassy, or the British High Commission favored the undertaking as a sound investment or able to yield the economic benefits that Nkrumah forecast. Each saw the project as drawing away precious investment capital that could be used more profitably elsewhere for an endeavor that would benefit a consortium of Western aluminum interests rather than the people of Ghana. Ghana's employment opportunities and the revenues that the government of Ghana could have collected if other parts of the economy had been emphasized were to be sacrificed on the altar of nationalist grandeur. From the moment Nkrumah first heard of the Volta scheme, he was smitten. He swept aside the cautions of his best economic advisers, first forcing Lewis out of the country and then insisting in the face of contrary advice from experts at the World Bank that he knew better. He was determined to have a dam across the Volta River, and the Americans, caught up in Cold War diplomacy and convinced that keeping Ghana out of the Soviet orbit had a high priority, agreed to put together the financial package.

Certainly Nkrumah bears the greatest responsibility for the one-sided arrangements relating to Volta. Indeed, the economic future of

---

[68] Ibid., p. 70.

Ghana might have looked different had he been more restrained in this matter, as in many of the other economic decisions that he made and that Lewis and other economists opposed. He was hardly unique, however, among the rulers of decolonized and developing countries in believing that large building projects, undertaken with the backing of enthusiastic populations, excited by the prospects of independence, could yield spectacular economic results and legitimize ruling elites. The new rulers of Asia and Africa wanted to be patrons and needed to create sources of patronage. They were drawn to programs that could become symbolic of the strength of their new states and around which they could rally the population. Ghana's weak control mechanisms on public expenditure and the difficulties the country had handling its fluctuating revenue sources only exacerbated these tendencies.

Lewis's *Politics in West Africa*

Although Lewis had left Africa at the end of 1958, he continued to consult with African governments. Yet with the passing of time, he cut back on his involvement in African affairs. One of the reasons that Lewis referred less frequently to Africa was his growing disillusionment with the policies of its new rulers. When he left Ghana in 1958, he wanted no one to know that he had resigned for fear that his action would impede the process of decolonization. But as one African country after another followed the Nkrumah pattern of single-party rule and glorification of the leader, using coercion against opposition groups and making impractical economic choices, he grew increasingly troubled. The result of his reflections on postcolonial Africa was a set of three lectures delivered at McMaster University in 1965 and published in that year under the title *Politics in West Africa*. Although this treatise was meant to provide a blueprint for good governance in Africa, its influence was most deeply felt as a critique of the so-called charismatic leaders and single-party states that were everywhere in existence in West Africa at the time and that a number of apologists inside and outside the continent argued suited Africa at this stage of its development.

As Lewis saw what he regarded as West Africa's political deterioration, he believed that he must move outside the comfortable realm of the economic consultant and use his experience in West Africa plus his wide reading in the works of African political scientists to offer political counsel. Obtaining financial support from the Congress for Cultural Freedom, which supported a fact-finding trip to Senegal, the Ivory Coast, and Nigeria in 1962, Lewis prepared a draft of the lectures and submitted them to approximately a dozen specialists in African politics at a three-day conference held at King's College, Cambridge. Although Lewis chose not to divulge the names of these authorities "for fear of misunderstandings and involvements," in fact the roster of persons whom Lewis considered as invitees was a veritable who's who of scholarship on West Africa.[69] The invitees represented a wide spectrum of political opinion, including those from the left and the right in political beliefs and attitudes toward Africa. The original list of potential invitees included G. D'Arbousier, French ambassador to Senegal, L. Gray Cowan, an American political scientist, Michael Crowder, a leading African historian, H. O. Davies, a Nigerian intellectual and nationalist, whom Lewis had known since his undergraduate days in London, S. E. Finer, an authority on military dictatorships, Thomas Hodgkin, author of an influential book on African nationalism, Ernest Milicent, editor of *Afrique nouvelle*, Colin Legum, an African expert and writer for the *Observer*, S. K. Panter-Brick, a British political scientist specializing on Africa, David Williams, editor of *West Africa*, Edward Shils, an American political scientist, Audrey Richards, a British anthropologist, Tom Mboya, the Kenyan nationalist, and St. Clair Drake, an African American sociologist, whom Lewis described as "an American Negro sociologist at Roosevelt university who spent three years as a visiting professor in Ghana."[70]

At the outset of *Politics in West Africa*, Lewis confided that he had "wanted to write this monograph for the past eight years for emotional reasons," adding that he had known the "chief Pan-African leaders personally for thirty years, sharing their anti-imperialism and their goal of a free Africa.... It is only the defection of some from this goal that has wrung this pamphlet from me."[71] For Lewis, the African

---

[69] W. Arthur Lewis, *Politics in West Africa* (New York, 1965), foreword.

[70] Information on this meeting and the invitees may be found in the correspondence that Lewis had with Marion Bieber of the Congress of Cultural Freedom between February 21, 1965, and May 26, 1965, in the Lewis Papers, Box 2. The correspondence contains only the tentative list. Other persons whom Lewis considered inviting later on were James Coleman, David Apter, Kenneth Robinson, and M. G. Smith, all scholars of contemporary Africa. Bieber wondered whether there ought not to be more Africans involved, but the only West African invited was H. O. Davies. Lewis did not know at the time that the Congress had been receiving financial support from the Central Intelligence Agency (CIA) of the United States government. He was deeply troubled when he learned in 1966 of the Congress's connections with the CIA, observing that "a Congress in receipt of C. I. A. funds can achieve nothing in the new states." Just prior to learning of the CIA's backing of the Congress, Lewis had agreed to serve on its board of directors. He immediately resigned from this office. There is extensive correspondence with Michael Josselson, acting director of the Congress for Cultural Freedom, in 1966 and 1967 in Box 7 of the Lewis Papers.

[71] Lewis, *Politics in West Africa*, foreword.

politicians of West Africa (and by analogy throughout the whole of the continent) had gone badly wrong in their espousal of the one-party state and the cult of the leader. Most of the responsibility for this failure came from the unchecked ambitions of politicians themselves, who, caught up in the struggle to achieve independence from colonial rulers and compelled to demonstrate mass appeal, championed themselves and their parties as the authentic voice of the people and their opponents as colonial stooges. Politicians thrust up in a time of political turmoil "have the kind of personality that it takes. They feel that they are heaven-sent and that anyone who stands in their way is a traitor to heaven's cause."[72] While conceding that many of these leaders, notably Sekou Toure in Guinea, Leopold Senghor in Senegal, and Sylvanus Olympio in Togo, were good men, inspired by the highest principles, many others were no different from aspirers to political power all over the world. They sought the comforts of office, and they wielded the power of authority with great pleasure. Acting "like Egyptian pharaohs," and finding the money "incredible," West Africa's new elite had "a life-time's chance to make a fortune." Lewis added: "It is necessary to remember that when we read in the political science books about the 'charisma' of the great men now engaged in modernizing backward societies."[73]

In addition, Lewis observed that the new rulers of West Africa had no experience of democracy. Often they came to power with only a primary school education and little acquaintance with European history. Few had traveled outside their own countries before they won elections. "For most of them independence merely means that they have succeeded to the autocracy vacated by the British and French civil servants. They model themselves on the arrogant and arbitrary patterns set by the Governors and district commissioners, if only because they know no better."[74]

If Lewis's critique had a decidedly anti-African tone, with its assumption that Africans had no viable precolonial political traditions to draw upon and its complaint that African leaders did not know *European* history and had not traveled outside the continent (as presumably their better educated, more sophisticated, and more worldly wise counselors like Lewis had), still Lewis did not spare the British and the French in his critique. Their officials had drawn up constitutions based on the class-oriented European polities of the mid–twentieth century. They were unsuited to the pluralistic nature of African societies. Euro-

[72] Ibid., p. 31.
[73] Ibid., p. 32.
[74] Ibid., pp. 32–33.

pean parties had emerged out of class antagonisms and expressed class interests. Parties sought to win elections so that they could enact programs that their class supporters favored. Losing parties went into opposition and endeavored through parliamentary and press criticism to position themselves to win the next election.

African states were not like those in Europe and the Americas; they were not divided primarily along class lines. Their basic divisions were ethnic, religious, and geographical. Hence, parties in power supported the interest of those regions, religious groups, and ethnic communities that had put them in power and impoverished and even repressed the interests of regions, religions, and ethnicities that opposed them. Africa's independence constitutions had turned politics into a zero-sum game, played in the most savage and intense fashion, so that winning brought rewards in the form of schools, filtered water supplies, electricity, and medical facilities to favored regions, ethnicities, and religious groups. Losing resulted in a denial of the basic necessities of life. It was in this setting that the single-party state took shape and the charismatic leader became all-powerful. No loyal opposition could arise. Those on the outside had two choices: join with the winner in an effort to claim some of the bounty of ruling or go underground into secret and often violent opposition.

That the single party was the necessary instrument of economic development and nation-building in the immediate postcolonial period, as its proponents claimed, was hardly the case, according to Lewis's view of West African polities. Far from promoting national unity, economic projects favored certain regions at the expense of others, thus exaggerating regional, religious, and ethnic inequalities and exacerbating rivalries and resentments. Rather than fostering national consensus and crystallizing national identities, the policy of the single-party rulers endowed certain groups with a sense that they represented the will of the people and that they were entitled to silence other groups. Citing the example of Ghana, Lewis observed that Nkrumah and his Convention People's Party favored the Fanti peoples in the south while exploiting the Ashanti cocoa farmers whose opposition became all the more determined. The single party failed because "it cannot represent all the people or maintain free discussion; or give stable government; or above all reconcile the difference between various regional groups. It is not natural to West African culture. . . . It is partly the product of the hysteria of independence when some men found it possible to seize the state and suppress their opponents. It is a sickness from which West Africa deserves to recover."[75]

---

[75] Ibid., p. 63.

There is little to fault in Lewis's critique of West African politics. The American political scientists Aristide Zolberg was making a similar argument at the same time in his equally influential book, *Creating Political Order: The Party-States of West Africa* (Chicago, 1966). Subsequent research into the careers of Africa's first generation of political rulers has, indeed, shown, as Lewis argued, that these young nationalists were novices in the art of politics and found so few checks against illicit behavior that few could resist the temptation to enrich themselves and their close followers.

While the Lewis and Zolberg books formed part of the essential reading in courses in African politics, Lewis's solution to the dilemmas of African independence—federal constitutions and proportional representation—although flowing logically from his arguments won fewer supporters among the practitioners and consultants of African politics at the time. Lewis believed that African constitutions needed to take account of the pluralistic, non-class-based nature of African communities, that they should reflect the wide regional, religious, and ethnic differences that divided people who because of the vicissitudes of the European partition of the continent found themselves obliged to live within the same nation-state. What better way, Lewis affirmed, to ensure that these diverse groups got along in a peaceful way than to diminish the powers of the central government and to have members of parliament chosen by means of proportional representation. Under these constitutional arrangements, every group would have some representation in parliament, and the government at the center could govern only by means of coalitions. Proportional representation would put an end to single-party rule since no party, however strong it might be in one or two regions, could aspire to national dominance. A parliament composed of many political parties and compelled to govern through coalitions would have to respect the interests of minority religious, ethnic, and regional communities.

Lewis's *Politics in West Africa* proved to be much more than a personally cathartic book. Like so many of his writings, it was also prescient. Ghana's chief economic expert's assertion that economic change did not operate in a vacuum needed to be heard. As he had written repeatedly and now shown through bitter personal experience, economic growth required a supportive political environment, preferably democratic institutions, and appropriate cultural beliefs. Because West Africa lacked these prerequisites, its economic programs were doomed from the outset. What later became known as the new institutional economics, with its assertions that cultural and political institutions were essential to economic growth, that historical analysis revealed the pathways to modernization, and that politics and economics could not be treated as separate from each other when analyzing a country's prospects for achieving economic betterment were imbedded in this book and, indeed, in many of the general treatises that Lewis had composed.

CHAPTER 7

The West Indies, 1959–63

THE MAJOR ASPECTS OF Lewis's public career came to a close, fittingly, in the West Indies, where he served as head of the University College of the West Indies between 1959 and 1963. Once he left the West Indies, moving on to become a professor of political economy at the Woodrow Wilson School of Princeton University, he concentrated on teaching and research, forsaking the heavy round of government consultancies and government offices that had been so characteristic of the first three decades of his career. In many respects the four-year stint in the West Indies was emblematic of his entire public career. Like the rest of the developing world, the islands of the British West Indies were in the midst of frantic decolonizing efforts. On the surface, the prospects were promising. Not only did nationalist politicians aspire to political independence, but British officials were committed to it. The British position toward the Caribbean was hardly based on altruistic or selfless motives; the islands simply no longer held strategic or economic importance to the imperial power. On the contrary, the Caribbean territories had become a burden on British taxpayers, though hardly an exorbitant one. If their independence could be secured through a viable economic and political union of member islands, most likely a federation of all of the territories, Great Britain would enhance its opportunities to realign its economy and polity toward Europe and rid itself of a financial obligation.

By the 1950s, preparing for economic decolonization had also become the guiding activity of Lewis's life. What better way, then, to put his academic training and his unique public experience to work than to promote the political and economic independence of the islands where he had grown up. Since youth, Lewis aspired to contribute to West Indian welfare. As an ardent and articulate advocate of political federation, he averred that only the union of the islands would produce economic advances and some measure of political autonomy. In his view a political merger would free the Caribbean from the grip of the vicious cycle of poverty and underdevelopment that characterized its past. Since undergraduate days, he had believed that only through industrialization and the pooling of the islands' diverse economic resources could the West Indies prosper.

It took a mere three and a half years for the West Indies to prove as unrewarding as Ghana had been and even more physically and emotionally draining. Lewis accepted the position of principal (or head) of the University College of the West Indies in 1959 with eager anticipation. After all, his writings on economic development stressed education. In his classic work, *The Theory of Economic Growth*, he had devoted a whole chapter to education, arguing that what brought economic progress was not natural resources or even high savings and investment rates, however vital these factors were, but human capital. Individuals needed to be able to identify profitable investment areas; they had to acquire the technical skills required to run factories, manufacture products, and sell their wares to consumers. Innovation relied on quality education. Although Lewis believed that mass education was vital, he also recognized the need to educate an elite of university graduates. Without scientists, doctors, lawyers, and teachers, possessing knowledge adapted to local needs, economic development would stall. Hence, Lewis was only too delighted to take on the leadership of the recently founded University College of the West Indies, which he and other West Indians regarded as the leading organization for forging bonds of unity among the island peoples of the Caribbean. As principal, Lewis aspired to assist in the creation of an educated elite that would lead the way to the long-sought-after West Indian political federation.

Lewis underscored his faith that an educated elite had the potential to transform society in remarks he made as he greeted the first group of students to enter the college under his principalship in 1960. The comments are also interesting because they reveal that Lewis was himself not immune to the racial stereotypes associated with West Indians. Admitting that his long, twenty-seven-year absence from the West Indies might render his characterization of the West Indian personality no longer valid, he proceeded to note that in many circles, especially among foreigners, the West Indian was known as a good cricketer, "a good dancer, and a wonderful companion at a picnic, irresistible to women and proud of his string of conquests. I think we took a certain pride in understanding that life was meant to be enjoyed and not meant to be taken too seriously." He confessed that he did not know whether "the foreigners' image of the West Indian" was any longer true, but if it were, he vowed that the university would play its part in creating a new more work-oriented ethos.[1]

In many ways Lewis's long absence from the area was to prove his undoing, for though he had kept abreast of West Indian affairs by read-

---

[1] University College of the West Indies, "Address by the Principal, Dr. W. Arthur Lewis," October 7, 1960, p. 5.

ing widely, the islands had changed completely from his youthful days. Not even the frequent opportunities to consult with British officials at the Colonial Office on economic, political, and educational issues involving the West Indies could have prepared him fully for the altered setting that new political parties, new charismatic political leaders (a few of whom he had come to know personally during their student days), and the rising voices of the peasant and urban workers had created.

He had, however, stayed abreast of the affairs of the University College of the West Indies. In 1951, for instance, the administration of the University College approached Lewis with a proposal to become the university's first professor of economics as part of a program for introducing the teaching of economics. He did not think that the time was propitious for the university to establish an economics faculty. Nor was he yet ready to leave Manchester. It was not long, however, before the same university officials approached Lewis with an even more flattering and challenging proposal. They asked him to become principal of the institution. Lewis's reply to Philip Sherlock, who was a member of the search committee looking for a successor to the institution's first principal, Dr. Thomas Taylor, who had announced his intention to resign at the end of the 1952 academic term, is revealing about his professional commitments and his continuing desire to return to the West Indies. "My personal inclination is for working in the West Indian sunshine with and for my fellow West Indians. . . . The point you make about the attractiveness of my present career (as professor of political economy at the University of Manchester) is not overwhelming. I became a teacher of economics rather by accident than from choice. I like the life very much but I will leave it if I can be offered a job which is more useful and which I feel I can do." The principalship of the University College of the West Indies was not, however, such a position, at least at this juncture in his career. Lewis ruled himself out on the basis of age (thirty-seven) and lack of administrative experience.[2]

One of the reasons that Lewis was unwilling to accept more than a two-year appointment as Nkrumah's chief economic adviser was that he was even then contemplating a move from Manchester to the University College of the West Indies. There is no doubt that he anticipated being asked at some point to be the college's principal, having already explored that possibility several years earlier. But the immediate cause for his willingness to move in 1959 was that the University College was preparing to expand its teaching into the social sciences and wished Lewis to join the faculty as a professor of economics and spearhead the

[2] Lewis to Philip Sherlock, February 1952, Lewis Papers, Box 11.

curricular reform. Thus, in March 1958, while things were still going well in Ghana and long before Lewis had had his falling out with Nkrumah, he agreed to become a professor at the University College once his two-year contract in Ghana had expired. As a first step in this career move, he wrote to the vice-chancellor of Manchester to resign from his chair. At the same time he sent a letter to the administration of the University College of the West Indies asking that his title be professor of political economy rather than professor of economics. "I have held this title for ten years and have grown fond of it. Besides, it describes my interests and special experience in the application of economics to policy better than does the title 'Professor of Economics.'"[3]

Lewis never did occupy the chair in political economy. In February 1959, shortly after he had left Ghana and while he was serving as deputy director of the United Nations Special Fund, the University College Board of Trustees offered him the position of principal of the college. He was to start on October 1, 1959. He was to be paid a salary of £3,500 and to receive an entertainment allowance of £1,000 per year as well as educational allowances for his two daughters, a rent-free house, a car, and a chauffeur.[4]

The University College of the West Indies had come into existence as a result of a report presented by a committee headed by James Irvine, vice-chancellor of the University of St. Andrews, and submitted to the British Parliament in 1945. The primary recommendation of the Irvine Committee was that the West Indies establish as soon as possible a residential university, centralized at a single location on the island of Jamaica and that it begin its teaching with a college of arts and sciences and a faculty of medicine.[5] Its first principal, Thomas Taylor, was appointed in October 1946, and teaching began in the medical faculty located at Mona, just outside the capital city of Kingston, Jamaica, in 1948.[6] In the following year the University College obtained its royal charter and had its degrees linked to those of the University of London. Teaching in the natural sciences began in 1949 and the arts in 1950. In 1957, by which time the college had become a vital part of the plans for the political federation of the British West Indies, its governing board contemplated the expansion of the institution geographically outside

[3] Lewis to A. K. Croston, Acting Registrar, University College of the West Indies, March 21, 1958, Lewis Papers, Box 3.

[4] A. K. Croston to Lewis, Deputy Director, United Nations Special Fund, February 13, 1959, Lewis Papers, Box 3.

[5] Great Britain, House of Commons, *Sessional Papers*, Colonial Office, *Report of the West Indies Committee of the Commission on Higher Education in the Colonies*, 1945, cmd. 6654, 1944–45, vol. 5, p. 10.

[6] No. 1 Minute by J. E. Whitelegg, August 31, 1962, PRO CO 1031/3431.

of Jamaica and educationally into the social sciences, engineering, and agriculture. It was already offering degree courses in B.A. general honors, B.Sc. general, and M.B., B.S., M.Sc., and M.A. and Ph.D.[7]

To advise on its expansion and to answer criticisms from radical West Indian nationalists that the university was costly, elitist, neocolonial, and dominated by the Jamaican elite, the Colonial Office undertook a far-reaching investigation into the operations of the university and its expansion in the mid-1950s. Its officials sought the advice of Lewis on who should be placed on the review committee from the British side. Lewis's first choice was Eric Ashby, at the time head of Queen's University in Belfast. If he were not available, as in fact he was not, Lewis recommended D. G. James, vice-chancellor of Southhampton University.[8] James agreed to serve and seemed in all respects to the officials at the Colonial Office an ideal choice. The Colonial Office required someone who had no connection with University College itself, nor with the University of London or the Inter-University Council since both bodies oversaw the administration of the University College and were regularly consulted on overseas educational matters. More to the point, James was a British educator, who had taken over Southhampton University at a time when it was detaching itself from its parent body, also the University of London, just as the University College of the West Indies was expected to achieve independent university status in the immediate future. In addition, the appointment of James would prevent American or Canadian educators from introducing American influences into West Indian higher education.[9]

The individual most critical of the University College and most responsible for the formation of this review committee was Eric Williams, an old friend of Lewis's and Trinidad's rising nationalist politician. Following his education at Oxford University and a stint as a professor of political science at Howard University, where he had gained first-hand knowledge of American higher education, Williams returned to his native Trinidad and Tobago. He founded the People's National Movement as an opposition political organ, and by the late 1950s he was in the process of becoming Trinidad's outstanding na-

[7] No. 44, S. J. Worsley, Secretary, the Inter-University Council for Higher Education Overseas, to J. S. Mordecai, Pre-Federation Organization, December 4, 1957, enclosing Memorandum on the University College of the West Indies, December 4, 1957, PRO CO 1031/2042.

[8] No. 17, J. S. Mordecai, Federal Secretariat of the British West Indian Federation, to Lewis, October 15, 1957 and No. 20, Chairman, Standing Federation Committee, Barbados, to the Colonial Office, November 2, 1957, both found in PRO CO 1031/2402.

[9] No. 29, Colonial Office to Chairman, Standing Federation Committee, Barbados, November 13, 1957, PRO CO 1031/2402.

tionalist leader. One of his targets was the University College at Mona, which Williams attacked for being elitist, expensive, pro-British, and out of touch with the needs of the West Indies. In his view the college produced a privileged cadre who identified themselves with the values and beliefs of their British overlords rather than the rank and file of the West Indian population. Williams demanded that higher education in the West Indies be more dispersed throughout the islands and more available to the people. He complained that far too many resources of the university were centralized at Mona. He insisted on cost reductions and wanted the ties to the University of London severed. His experiences in the United States had persuaded him that an American style of higher education would be better suited to the needs of this part of the world.[10]

The commission, established to look into the future of the University College, was known as the Cato Commission, taking its name from its chairman, Dr. A. S. Cato. It met between 1957 and 1958. The commission included Williams among its members, and though D. G. James regarded Williams as "quite crazy" and expounding "a lot of ideas which everybody else thought wildly impractical," the final report dealt at length with Williams's criticisms.[11] The report set forth the main guidelines that the University College of the West Indies followed over the next several decades, including those years that Lewis served as principal and then vice-chancellor. While conceding that the university needed to attract the sons and daughters of nonelite families and hence had to create schools that the less well-off could afford to attend, it favored retaining the residential college system based on the British model. It also endorsed plans that college administrators had already sketched out to strengthen the college's offerings in the arts and natural sciences and to establish new faculties in the social sciences, engineering, and agriculture. The commission supported the goal of a rapid expansion of the size of the student body to two thousand from the approximately six hundred that it was in 1957. The increase of the student-faculty ratio from five to one to more than ten to one would automatically make the university less costly and more efficient. This change, coupled with recommendations for changes in the salary structure and a more efficient management of resources, were partially in response to Williams's charge that the expenses incurred by the university were beyond the financial means of the peo-

---

[10] For a useful overview of the criticisms of the school one should consult Note by J. Whitelegg, November 6, 1857 and Note by P. J. Kitcatt, April 27, 1958. Both of them are to be found in PRO CO 1031/2042.

[11] Note by P. J. Kitcatt, April 27, 1958, PRO CO 1031/2042.

ples of the West Indies. Finally, and also in response to nationalist critiques, the commission recommended that once the expansion of faculties had taken place, the university should stand on its own academically and sever its ties with the University of London.[12]

The institution that Lewis took over was exceedingly complex and awkward administratively. It had numerous oversight groups, many of which had competing priorities. As he later observed, the principal of the University College of the West Indies had to have the fundraising skills of an American university president and the faculty negotiating talents of a British vice-chancellor. Thus, even though the University College, with its enrollment of six hundred students and 120 faculty in 1959, was no larger than a small American liberal arts college, the demands on the principal's time were massive. By the time Lewis left Jamaica he was physically worn down.

As befitted a West Indian–wide institution that had to appeal to diverse constituencies, finances were a constant worry. Funding for capital projects came mainly from the Colonial Office, through the Colonial Welfare and Development Fund. Recurrent expenditures, however, were the responsibility of the territorial governments, whose political leaders regularly complained that their territories were less favorably treated than others. The college oversight groups included representatives of all thirteen territorial governments in the British West Indies, each of which agreed to contribute a fixed percentage of the university's budget. The thirteen were Antigua, Barbados, British Guiana, British Honduras, Dominica, Grenada, Jamaica, Montserrat, St. Kitts, St. Lucia, St. Vincent, the British Virgin Islands, and Trinidad and Tobago. Each government expected to be consulted fully on budgetary issues, and each regularly complained that its island was not being treated fairly.[13]

The fact that Trinidad was one of the main financial backers of the University College only intensified Eric Williams's resentment of the centrality of Jamaica in the school's setup.[14] Williams complained that faculty and staff appointments favored men and women from Jamaica and systematically excluded those candidates who shared his brand of radical nationalism. To him the appointments system was a "racket . . . which is now becoming the vehicle for rewarding the friends and pun-

[12] The full report can be found be found in PRO CO 1031/2043 under the title Report of the Committee Appointed to Review the Policy of the University College of the West Indies, December 1957–January 1958.

[13] No. 2, Governor of British Honduras to Secretary of State for the Colonies, January 3, 1957, and T. Luke, Development and Welfare Organization, Barbados, to P. Rogers, Colonial Office, March 4, 1957, PRO CO 1031/2398.

[14] No. 1, Minute by J. E. Whitelegg, August 31, 1962, PRO CO 1031/3431.

ishing the enemies of heads of departments who are in no small minority of cases inveterate opponents of the PNM [Williams's party, the People's National Movement], having for the most part achieved their prominence by nepotism and as a result of discrimination."[15] Williams's plans to establish his own college of liberal arts and sciences in Trinidad alarmed Lewis, who pleaded with his Trinidadian friend to work within the framework of the evolving federation of the West Indies.[16]

Upon arrival, Lewis began to implement the Cato Commission's plans for expansion.[17] Lewis estimated the total cost of the plan, which entailed raising student enrollment from six hundred to two thousand, strengthening the teaching of liberal arts and sciences through the opening of branch campuses, and creating new faculties in engineering, agriculture, and the social sciences, to be $30 million. He hoped to be able to raise $6.4 million from the unit governments, with the governments of Jamaica ($2.1 million), Trinidad ($2 million), British Guiana ($1 million), and Barbados ($500,000) pledging all but $800,000.[18] These contributions were far from certain, however, since they involved substantial increases in the outlays from all of the territorial units and would require Lewis to exercise his skills of persuasion. The remaining $23 million had to come from external sources. Lewis counted on a considerable amount coming from the Colonial Development and Welfare Fund, and he had reason to expect large American foundations to be generous with the university if the territorial units provided what the plans expected from them.

The announcement of Lewis's appointment as principal occurred in 1959. He spent the entire time between the announcement and his arrival in Jamaica in mid-1960, during part of which time he was still officially deputy director of the Special Fund at the United Nations, talking with governments and private donors about funding. The territorial units, as expected, proved hard to convince. Trinidad held to its reservations about the University College, although Williams moderated his opposition to the university once he learned that Lewis would be the principal.[19] British Guiana did not, however. At the prodding of Cheddi Jagan, the country's radical nationalist politician, the government of British Guiana declared that though it would continue finan-

[15] Eric Williams to Lewis, April 25, 1957, Lewis Papers, Box 13

[16] Lewis to Eric Williams, May 8, 1957, Lewis Papers, Box 13.

[17] Philip Sherlock to N. W. Manley, n.d., but June 1959, University of the West Indies Archives, Acc. No. MA 92.1 file, F13.

[18] Lewis to Cheddi Jagan, June 8, 1959, University of the West Indies Archives, Acc. No. MA 92.1 file, F13.

[19] No. 6, W.B.L. Monsen, Colonial Office, to Jock Campbell, July 30, 1957, PRO CO 1031/2402.

cial support of the University College, since the university trained a large number of Guyanese students, it would not increase its financial contribution. Even though Lewis paid a special visit to Jagan and impressed on him that British Guiana would benefit from an expansion, Jagan refused to contribute more than the original promise of $400,000.[20]

The responses of the unit governments and also the new federal government waiting in the wings were so distressing to Lewis that he commented to the head of the newly formed West Indian political federation, Grantley Adams: "It is completely demoralizing to be given the impression that, for political reasons, your government attaches no financial priority to the University College. I reluctantly accepted the Principalship because I thought that the University College would have the full support of your government. If this is not the case, the job which has to be done, cannot be done, and there will be no point in my taking it on."[21] These were not idle words. The financial situation was dire. Not only was British Guiana unwilling to contribute the $1 million that the university needed from it, but the Jamaican government, for which $2.1 million was expected and which was widely regarded as the University College's chief beneficiary, voted a paltry $450,000. In an even more disheartening turn of events, the Colonial Office, which had turned over £9 million to the new political federation of the West Indies through the Colonial Development and Welfare Fund, had not earmarked any portion of these funds for the college. The federation was free to expend these monies as it saw fit, but preliminary discussions indicated that higher education would have a low priority. Thus, by November 1959, even before Lewis had arrived in the West Indies, he was prepared to walk away from what had earlier appeared to be the fulfillment of a lifetime ambition. Writing to Carl La Corbiniere, deputy prime minister of the West Indian Federation and the individual, along with A. S. Cato, who had persuaded Lewis to become principal, he stated: "The reason [for this decision to resign] is the federal government's refusal to support the college financially, coupled with the discourteous and almost contemptuous treatment accorded to us."[22]

Lewis did not resign. Difficulties were patched up. The territorial units increased their financial contributions, and Colonial Office's

[20] E12/b, Governor, British Guiana, Ralph Gurr, to Lord Hailes, Governor General, February 10, 1960, PRO CO 1031/3436.
[21] Lewis to Grantley Adams, October 5, 1959, University of the West Indies Archives, Acc. No. MA 92.1 file, F1.
[22] Lewis to Carl La Corbiniere, Deputy Prime Minister, Trinidad, November 2, 1959, Lewis Papers, Box 7.

funds were set aside for college use. But Lewis's start was inauspicious. He enjoyed no honeymoon period, and, as he soon discovered, he had only scratched the surface of the problems that his administration would face. Thoughts of resignation began to recur with greater and greater frequency; finally in 1962 he carried through on them.

At the core of Lewis's difficulties was the dilemma of trying to convince the unit governments that its territories got as much as the others from the college. If federal ministers of education in newly emergent countries in Africa, for instance, found it hard to resist appeals from provinces and states for their own universities, in spite of the duplication of facilities and the heavy costs, imagine the pressures on Lewis from the far-flung island units of the West Indies, some of which were one thousand to fifteen hundred miles away from the central campus of the university on the island of Jamaica. Lewis never wavered from looking at the budget with the eye of a pragmatic economist. He believed that a centralized system of education was the only feasible way for poor territories, no matter how dispersed geographically, to obtain the best return on investments in education. Faculties in highly specialized fields like medicine, engineering, agriculture, and the social sciences needed to be concentrated. A faculty of medicine required a team of sixty consulting doctors and 350 students. The West Indies could afford only one good faculty of medicine, which already existed at Mona and now needed strengthening. The same was true in engineering and agriculture. Fortunately, Trinidad already had a world-class agricultural research station, the Imperial College of Tropical Agriculture, which had been founded in 1921 and had to its credit many important research discoveries in the field of tropical agriculture. Lewis proposed to make this institute a teaching facility as well as a research center and to bring it under the jurisdiction of the University College. The West Indies also needed a school of engineering, if only because of the special engineering problems that existed in the tropics. Here, too, Lewis saw the virtue of establishing a faculty of engineering on the island of Trinidad, in part as a way of dispersing the different faculties throughout the islands and answering the charge made most insistently by Trinidadians that the college was a Jamaican preserve.[23]

Undergraduate education in the liberal arts and sciences, on the other hand, provided Lewis with further opportunities to engage in

[23] Minutes of the Meeting of the Finance and General Purposes Committee for May 16, 1962, presenting paper by W. Arthur Lewis entitled "Conference on the Common Services, the University of the West Indies," June 15, 1962, and No. 2, Interim Commission, Common Services Conference, June 20, 1962, containing Memorandum prepared by the Vice-Chancellor of the University of the West Indies for consideration by the Conference, both to be found in PRO OD (Office of the Dominion) 17/129.

geographical dispersal. Liberal arts and science colleges could be "very flexible since the number of subjects and the degree of specialization in each subject can be kept to a minimum. . . . You could get by with a dozen teachers and 50 students and so you could have such facilities in British Guiana, Trinidad and Tobago, Barbados, and Jamaica."[24]

Even though Lewis created ingenious formulas to accommodate territorial jealousies and to make the University College an institution that benefited all of the islands, his career at the university rocked from one crisis to another. Having solved the first dilemma of insufficient funding and having won the grudging support of the territorial units by implementing a fair-minded and realistic policy of dispersal of facilities, Lewis dealt with what he considered his next priority—making the university more cost efficient. Here, too, he encountered opposition that led him to proffer his resignation. Eric Williams was not the only observer to complain that the college incurred heavy expenditures and that faculty and students alike enjoyed privileges out of all proportion to the standards of life existing in the rest of West Indian society. Ever the economist, Lewis was all too aware of the folly of an institution spending upwards of £1 million to train nine hundred students when it could send this same group of students overseas at a cost of £500,000. Although Lewis often argued vigorously for home training, stressing the virtues of specialized training in medicine, agriculture, engineering, and the social sciences, tailored to meet the needs of the West Indies, he blanched at the massive educational bill that the university incurred.

As a consequence, Lewis set about to make the University College a much better value than it had been previously. The major cost-saving part of his program was an increase in student-to-faculty ratio to the level approximating that which was common in North American universities. Doubling the number of students without a corresponding increase in the size of the faculty would dramatically reduce the expenditure per student. But Lewis also decided to tackle a more sensitive and controversial problem—one that he considered to be the most intractable—the privileges of the West Indian faculty, many of whom now were West Indians themselves, but for ideological and obvious material reasons wished to be paid at the rate of the old expatriate British faculty. British staff had been paid, and indeed continued to be paid, a premium over the salary that they would have received if they had been employed in Great Britain. They were also entitled to paid

---

[24] Minutes of the Meeting of the Finance and General Purposes Committee for May 16, 1962, presenting paper by W. Arthur Lewis entitled "Conference on the Common Service, the University of the West Indies," June 15, 1962, PRO OD 17/129.

home leave and to children's educational allowances, for schools either in the West Indies or in Britain. The West Indian teaching staff demanded that they too receive these benefits and vehemently defended their interests on the grounds of equity. Lewis heartily disagreed and ran squarely into a bitter dispute.

Lewis's efforts to reduce staff salaries, to eliminate home leave, and to restrict educational allowances to schools in the West Indies produced an outpouring of faculty protest. Lewis's observation that faculty at University College were paid £900 per year more than comparable faculty in British universities and that this made the cost of a university education in the West Indies 60 percent more than it was in Britain fell on deaf ears. Just as ineffective was his argument against West Indian staff members being paid allowances to send their sons and daughters to primary and secondary schools in the United Kingdom. He also opposed the practice of providing funds to allow West Indian staff members to travel to Britain once every three years on home leave. One group of irate faculty even went so far as to leak the salaries of the faculty to the local Jamaican newspaper, the *Daily Gleaner*, in hopes that their publication would align the people on their side. In fact, the publication of the salaries had the opposite effect. Most readers were appalled at the generous faculty salaries and let the newspaper's editors know so. Readers of the press quickly fell in behind Lewis's campaign to reduce college expenses. Of the large volume of letters to the editor, nearly all were critical of the staff and supported Lewis. Yet Lewis, in spite of the great bitterness that he felt toward his opponents, prevailed on the editors of the paper not to publish the letters since he thought their appearance would only inflame the matter and make a resolution more difficult.[25]

Lewis could hardly suppress the deep sense of betrayal he felt as this issue began to unfold. Writing a year after the events to his friend and a member of the faculty who supported his views, Professor Gerrit Bras, Lewis poured out his heart. "Is there no limit to the amount of academic inferiority complex which Quashie [the West Indian people] is asked to finance. For my part I am disgusted that our West Indian staff should demand these premiums above the British salaries. If this is the moral atmosphere of the University College of the West Indies, let us close the place down and use the money to send twice as many students to older universities where they will learn something about the responsibilities of citizenship."[26] In writing to the university's chancellor, Princess Alice, one of his strongest boosters,

---

[25] Lewis to Professor G. Bras, March 15, 1962, Lewis Papers, Box 2.
[26] Ibid.

he commented that "my vision of what the college should be like is shared neither by staff nor by students." He had little sympathy for the faculty, who, he thought, should be caught up in the enthusiasm of creating something new for the West Indies but who seemed to prefer "the quiet life ... in which one confines oneself to scholarly activities with a few students. I do not feel at home in the college and the college resents my efforts to prod it into something different." He concluded by remarking how he had come to hate "making people do what they do not want to do."[27]

Philip Sherlock, over whom Lewis had been preferred as principal but who soon became Lewis's closest administrator in the university and whose admiration for Lewis knew no bounds, observed Lewis perhaps at his lowest moment.[28] The principal wrote to Sherlock that "the job has got me very angry. In the course of my life I have been angry for an hour, or a day, or even a week. But now I have been angry for two and a half months and getting angrier every day. This is an impossible way in which to live." Lewis saw only too clearly the impasses and the vested interests that stood in the way of realizing what everyone knew to be the right course. He had become irate at the students "for their selfishness" in opposing his proposal for more students. He was "mad at the staff for their lack of public responsibility ... and mad at the federal government for doing everything it can to obstruct the college."[29]

Lewis had, however, exaggerated the strength of the opposition. His opponents were vocal and energetic but a minority, especially when faced with Lewis's announcement of his intention to resign. Staff, students, alumni, businesspersons, and persons in all walks of life rallied around the principal and endorsed his vision for the college. The president of the Undergraduate Guild of Students wrote that his body had passed a resolution by a vote of 270 for, 14 against, and 13 abstentions in "support of and confidence in the principal, Dr. W. Arthur Lewis," endorsing "the general policy for the long-term development of this

---

[27] Lewis to Princess Alice, Countess of Athlone, January 30, 1961, Lewis Papers, Box 1.

[28] Sherlock's account of these years and his adulation of Lewis may be found in his general history of the university. Philip Sherlock and Rex Nettleford, *University of the West Indies: A Caribbean Response to the Challenge of Change* (London, 1990). In his chapter, "The Lewis Years: 1959–63," he writes: "I worked closely with him [Lewis], and found it an exhilarating experience to be caught up in the tidal wave of change that he generated" (p. 95).

[29] Lewis to Philip Sherlock, January 27, 1962, Lewis Papers, Box 11.

college."[30] The treasurer of the guild was Norman Girvan, who was to go on to a distinguished academic career, including a professorship at the University of the West Indies and notable scholarship on Lewis himself. The proposer of the resolution was Walter Rodney, who became a noteworthy Africanist scholar and a leader of radical causes, subsequently assassinated for his political stances.

The Executive Committee of the West Indies Group of University Teachers also distanced itself from the discontented members of the faculty and came out in support of Lewis's policies on cutting university costs. It passed a resolution, noting "with great concern the recent series of irresponsible and totally unethical actions with regard to confidential college papers taken by various persons associated with the college. These actions have culminated in the present instance in the report that the Principal of the college, Professor W. A. Lewis, proposes to resign as Principal."[31] Letters poured in from many private individuals, pleading with Lewis to stay on. Few made more of an impact than the note from a friend from student days in London, Reginald Dolly of Texaco, Trinidad, who reminded Lewis of their days as West Indian students spent together in London thinking about the future of their native land. He reminded Lewis how insular most of the students and staff of the university were and urged Lewis to remember that "those of us who have had better opportunities owe it to our new nation to stay on and help in spite of all the ingratitude to which we are subjected."[32]

Lewis bowed to this outpouring of sentiment. He withdrew his resignation, yet warned the University Council that he regarded himself as ill-suited for the tasks that lay ahead. "I still feel my talents are more appropriate to teaching than to administration, but I cannot ignore the communications that I have received from people in all walks of life inside and outside the college, urging me to remain in the post at this critical time in the history of the college and our country. In particular, I cannot resist the warm embrace extended to me by my colleagues in the college, whether teachers or students or members of the indoor or outdoor staffs."[33]

Lewis had only a little while to enjoy the resolution of the crisis of 1961. No doubt the high moment of his time in the West Indies occurred

---

[30] Amela King, President of the University College of the West Indies Guild of Graduates, to Lewis, February 7, 1961, Lewis Papers, Box 7.

[31] Brian Chapman, Professor of Government, and A. W. Sangster, Lecturer in Chemistry, to Lewis, February 10, 1961, Lewis Papers, Box 3.

[32] Reginald Dolly to Lewis, February 9, 1961, Lewis Papers, Box 4.

[33] No. 12, University Council Minute, University of the West Indies Archives, LA 87, Box 47.

when the university achieved full administrative independence. No longer attached to the University of London and now known as the University of the West Indies, the new institution celebrated its new identity with elaborate ceremonies, over which Lewis presided as the body's first vice-chancellor. Even this high moment was marred by the news that British Guiana was reevaluating its relationship with the university and was unlikely to provide the funds that the institution required from it. Its reservations were precisely those that Eric Williams had articulated before Trinidad was accommodated with schools of engineering and agriculture and a promise of a liberal arts college. C. V. Nimes, who served as the representative of British Guiana on the University Council, complained that his territory had "no real voice in its [the Council's] control and we are certainly paying too much in relation to Jamaica and Trinidad for what we get from the University College of the West Indies directly and indirectly." In the view of the British Guiana leaders, Jamaica and Trinidad got back in local taxation receipts and in-country expenditures much more than they actually contributed to the running of the university. Just as Eric Williams had complained earlier, Nimes griped that salaries were too high. In any case, even if British Guiana continued its financial contributions to the university, Nimes announced that the government of British Guiana would create its own school of arts and sciences.[34] This was a blow to Lewis, who feared that the declaration would set in motion separatist educational initiatives throughout the islands. Lewis also took the decision personally since he had made numerous visits to Cheddi Jagan in 1961, begging him to stay within the framework of a single university structure. To mollify Jagan, Lewis had promised British Guiana that he would establish a school in British Guiana for instruction in the liberal arts and sciences based "on a flexible low-cost system" that he knew Jagan favored. Moreover, as Lewis observed to Jagan, British Guiana sent some of the best students to the University of the West Indies. Their absence would be a grievous setback to the intellectual strength of the student body.[35]

THE POLITICAL FEDERATION OF THE BRITISH WEST INDIES

The supporters of the University of the West Indies expected the institution to play a leading role in promoting island unity. In his history

---

[34] Memorandum by C. V. Nimes, British Guiana Representative on the Council of the University of the West Indies, February 7, 1962, University of the West Indies Archives, file 111/6 and No. 89, Ralph Grey to K. Blackburne, February 20, 1962, PRO CO 1031/3436.

[35] No. 76, Ralph Gurl to A. R. Thomas, November 8, 1961, PRO CO 1031/3436.

of the university, Philip Sherlock wrote, "I was more than ever convinced that by starting with a centralized residential college the scattered West Indian people would develop the organic relationships, shared loyalties, and understanding of each other that would enable West Indians to show to the full the resources of character and ability that they indubitably possess."[36] If, however, the political federation faltered, as it did in the early 1960s, the prospects for a single institution of higher education with many supporting and specialized campuses on different islands would also dim. Precisely this occurred during Lewis's tenure as principal and vice-chancellor and eventually drove him to resignation.

A political federation of the islands of the British West Indies had been on the agenda of many West Indians for several decades. Lewis had argued in favor of it during his student days in London, and he was far from alone in believing that closer political and economic cooperation among the islands would be a remedy for the area's long-standing and deep-seated poverty. Virtually all of the younger West Indian nationalists and intellectuals favored some form of closer political and economic unity. This was especially the case among the younger nationalist politicians, like Norman Manley of Jamaica and Eric Williams of Trinidad, who had made political federation a fundamental tenet of their political ideologies, extolling it as a vehicle for gaining political independence from Great Britain. Largely unspoken but equally critical was their belief that a federal government would enhance their own political power and that of their parties.

To the surprise and delight of these political figures, the British Colonial Office announced its support for a political federation. With the wind of decolonizing change blowing through the old British Empire, the men and women at the Colonial Office searched for political and economic formulas that would end the islands' economic reliance on Great Britain. Since no territory by itself had a bright economic future, all of them linked together through a political and economic federation, including a customs union and free movement of peoples, might produce a stable polity capable of promoting self-sustaining economic growth.[37]

None of the interested groups was under any illusion, however, that creating a union of the British West Indies would be an easy task. The total population of the islands to be federated was slightly less than three and one-half million, and though the islands had achieved a mea-

---

[36] Sherlock and Nettleford, *University of the West Indies*, p. 27.
[37] An eyewitness account of the complicated negotiations to create a federation in the West Indies can be found in John Mordecai, *The West Indies: The Federal Negotiations* (London, 1968).

sure of economic betterment since the grim decade of the 1930s, they were still deeply mired in poverty. Nearly 85 percent of the population of the British West Indies resided on the two largest islands, Jamaica and Trinidad and Tobago, so their cooperation was essential if the federation was to succeed. Yet the two countries had glaring differences. Not only were they located at a great distant from each other, but Trinidad had a large Indian population, which Jamaica did not. Moreover, the islands had had only a brief exposure to democratic institutions, being ruled virtually autocratically by powerful governors until the rise of trade unions and nationalist leaders had forced the British Colonial Office to introduce parliamentary reforms after World War II. Then, overnight, in the decade of the 1950s, the territories moved to a voting franchise based on universal adult suffrage.

Planning to establish a closer association of the British West Indies colonies dated from the post–World War II era. In 1947, the Colonial Office established a Standing Closer Union Committee, composed of delegates from all of the unit legislatures, and charged it with the task of devising a federal scheme. Although representatives of the colonial governments of British Guiana and British Honduras opted out of the federation, the other territories accepted the idea in principle. On the basis of these positive responses, the British colonial secretary undertook to press ahead with the idea.[38] A prefederation government first came into existence in 1958 in anticipation of the day when the unit territories would accept its existence.

Discussions among the individual territories soon made apparent that there were major issues dividing the islands. In theory, the idea of a political federation was appealing. The practicalities of where to locate a federal capital, how much freedom of movement to allow to people and goods, and what tax-raising powers to authorize for the new federal parliament led to open divisions. Moreover, the rising nationalist politicians on the separate islands were wary of losing their own power to competitors on other islands.

Unfortunately, as the prospects for the creation of the federation came closer to realization, the divisions among the island leaders became more intense. Jamaica and Trinidad, the islands that had the largest populations and the greatest economic potential, had radically different stances on a federation. Separated from each other by a thousand miles, they had different population groups and looked to a federation to satisfy different needs. Trinidad, with its large East Indian population, feared being submerged in a federation dominated by the

---

[38] *Report by the Conference on the West Indian Federation*, April 1953 in *House of Commons Special Papers*, cmd. No. 8837 in PRO CO 1031/762.

black majorities that predominated elsewhere, especially in Jamaica. In addition, the political leaders of Jamaica and Trinidad had diametrically opposed views of the powers that a federation government should possess. In contrast to the Jamaican politicians, Trinidad's leading political figure, Eric Williams, wanted a strong government at the center, capable of implementing interventionist economic ideas. The federal government that Williams favored would employ rigorous economic planning to spur economic diversification and industrial development and would dramatically increase standards of living.[39]

This vision troubled the Jamaican political leadership, whose members saw Jamaica as the most advanced of the islands and, if necessary, able to go it alone. Not only did they worry about having to shoulder most of the costs of a federation, but they worried that peoples from the poorest and most heavily populated parts of the federation would take advantage of a strong federation to emigrate to Jamaica. In a tight-knit federation, Jamaica's resources would be at risk. The Jamaican politicians, whatever their ideological leanings, were willing to participate in federation conversations only if the powers of the central government were carefully circumscribed. Moreover, they were unequivocally opposed to a strong federal executive of the kind that Williams preferred.

The more that the federation issue became politicized, the less likely became its chances of success. In Jamaica the leading opposition figure, the grand old man of Jamaican politics, Alexander Bustamante, now in his seventies and, to many of his critics, a spent political force, seized on the federation question to make a remarkable political resurrection. He demanded that Jamaica stay out of the federation and announce its own political independence.[40] The excitement of immediate independence, on Jamaican terms, proved too compelling even for the immensely popular Norman Manley, whose political party was in power

[39] Trinidad, Office of the Premier and Ministry of Finance, *The Economics of Nationhood* (Port of Spain, 1959). Without any doubt, Lewis drafted the detailed economic propositions of this document, and they reflected his ideas of a federation. He wanted the federal government to have "larger and independent revenues" (p. 7) so that it would have the power to contract foreign loans. He favored "a tightly-knit federation, adequately empowered at the center, to shape and direct the future of the nation." Its overriding economic goal was "to secure the integration of the units while at the same time retaining the advantages of previous associations. For the economic integration of the area is an indispensable condition for economic development" (p. 16). Lewis proposed that the territories relinquish $103.8 million of their own revenues to the federal government, a sum that stands in glaring contrast to the miniscule $1.9 million that was agreed to in later discussions.

[40] No. 36, Memorandum on the Present Position in Regard to the Federation of Jamaica, N. W. Manley, June 2, 1962, PRO CO 1031/4269.

at the time. The British belief that Manley could easily deal with Bustamante, who, to them, seemed to have lost credibility, proved a fatal miscalculation. Manley also disappointed them. British officials expected Manley to oppose Bustamante and his go-it-alone strategy with all of the legitimacy of his office and personality; instead, without even consulting the British, he agreed to hold a referendum on the question. In a vote of 54 percent against and 46 in favor, the Jamaicans voted against remaining a member of the federation and followed this at the general election by replacing Manley's party, the People's National Party, with Bustamante's Jamaican Labour Party.[41] Jamaica then withdrew from the federation and chose to become independent on its own. The island's opting out of the federation was a defeat from which the scheme never recovered, though this was not appreciated at the time, least of all by Lewis, who had by this time become more than an interested observer.

At this juncture, when it was crucial to keep Trinidad and Barbados interested in federation, Lewis volunteered his services to Grantley Adams, the head of the prefederation government, as an emissary to salvage the project. Lewis's credentials were impeccable. He enjoyed a close personal relationship with nearly all of the West Indies' leading politicians, particularly with Eric Williams, whose stance on the federation was obviously decisive. While officials at the Colonial Office had few illusions about the likelihood of a federation without Jamaica, they believed that Lewis, and only Lewis, had the personal authority to persuade the warring and jealous factions to put aside their rivalries for the common good. A Colonial Office memo summed up their hopes. "Professor Lewis was probably the only man who could do this. He is universally respected, is known to have no political bias, and above all is liked by Dr. Williams and can gain access to him, which is not easy except for a favored few."[42]

Certainly the Colonial Office was wrong in contending that Lewis had no political biases. He was an avowed enthusiast for the political federation and had been so for all of his life. As the vice-chancellor of the University of the West Indies, he was in charge of an institution that needed a political federation behind it and that might fail if the islands of the West Indies went their separate political ways. But the Colonial Office was right about Lewis's access to Williams. The two had been friends since their interwar undergraduate days in Britain.

[41] No. 8, K. Blackburne, Jamaica, to Colonial Office, September 19, 1961, PRO CO 1031/3273.

[42] No. 3, Colonial Office Brief for Secretary of State's Visit to the West Indies, January 1962: The Lewis Report, January 8, 1962, PRO CO 1031/3374.

They had communicated with each other over the years, and Lewis had advised the government of Trinidad on its economic planning documents.[43] Moreover, as the Trinidad document, *The Economics of Nationhood,* demonstrated, both shared a belief in the efficacy of a strong federation and viewed a political union as an important element in spurring Caribbean economic growth.

Lewis had no difficulty persuading the University Council to give him a paid leave of absence from his university duties so that he could make his services available to Grantley Adams and the federation government. The federation, in turn, agreed to pay Lewis the nominal sum of one dollar to hire him as a consultant for the period that he was freed from university obligations. The university gave Lewis leave until the end of January, and the vice-chancellor quickly began his task of promoting a federation of the nine remaining territories, now that Jamaica had opted out.[44]

Lewis flew to all of the islands and met with politicians during the month of October. He also traveled to Jamaica, where he had conversations with Bustamante and Manley with a view to persuading them to delay announcing their political independence until the contours of a new federation of the remaining nine had become clear. He feared that a proclamation of Jamaican independence would stir the Trinidadians to do the same. His most important meetings were with Williams, whom Lewis knew to be a committed "federationist," but who, Lewis thought, at this stage had concluded that Trinidad would gain more if the federation collapsed and individual territories had to approach Trinidad on Trinidad's terms.[45] Although Williams's attitude sorely disappointed him, Lewis met with the Trinidad prime minister on four separate occasions and extracted from Williams a promise not to speak against the federation even though he and his party were locked in a

---

[43] The Lewis Papers contain many letters between the two men. Williams signed his letters to Lewis as "Bill." The entire correspondence can be found in Box 13 of the Lewis Papers under the name Eric Williams.

[44] University Council Minute, September 27, 1961, University of the West Indies Archives, LA 87, Box 47; University of the West Indies, Principal's Report, 1961–62, University of the West Indies Archives; and No. 56, J. S. Mordecai, Governor General, Trinidad, to A. R. Thomas, September 23, 1961, PRO CO 1031/3278.

[45] No. 66, Record of Meeting at the Colonial Office on September 26, 1961, PRO CO 1031/3278. In attendance at the meeting on the Colonial Office side were Hailes, Fraser, McPetrie, Thomas, Williams, Noakes, and Jamieson, while Lewis, Garnet, Gordon, DaCosta, D. C. Williams, and Richardson represented the West Indies Federation side. Lewis dominated the discussions of the meeting and argued that Williams could be coaxed into a federation, especially if the smaller islands were warned that they could not count on continued Colonial Office support if they did not make concessions to Trinidad.

tight battle for control of the parliament and could be made vulnerable on the federation question.⁴⁶ Williams did not keep his promise scrupulously, however. In the heat of the electoral campaign, while his political opponents were criticizing him for being soft on the political federation, he blurted out that the federation was dead since one from ten equals zero, by which he meant that without Jamaica the old federation could not survive.⁴⁷

Following his tour of the islands, Lewis wrote what officials at the Colonial Office described as "a long and masterly report in the form of a letter on the subject [of the federation] to Williams."⁴⁸ Subsequently, he submitted a more detailed report to Grantley Adams, in which he laid out an optimistic blueprint for realizing the federation.⁴⁹ Arguing that there existed for the first time a strong possibility for a centralized and powerful federal government since the primary force in the new political union would be Trinidad under Williams and since Williams was committed to a strong federation, Lewis wrote that everything would turn on the language used in the constitution. While, in fact, the political arrangements could be those of a unitary state, the document needed to employ the language of federation and appear outwardly to be a federation. Language that stressed a federal, nonunitary state, even though the reality was different, would comfort the smaller islands, worried about being dominated by Trinidad.⁵⁰

Unfortunately, as the Colonial Office feared, Lewis's efforts to paper over the differences among the unit governments and to devise formulas that said one thing and meant another did not work. The concern of one Colonial Office commentator, that "Lewis has so much persuasiveness and charm that I wonder whether some of the chief ministers have not been rather carried away and may repent at leisure," proved only too true.⁵¹ The leaders of the other eight islands grew increasingly dubious about a federation that they saw as enhancing the powers of Trinidad at their expense. By the same token, the Trinidad politicians began to clamor for a separate declaration of independence. Jamaica's buildup to its formal political independence so intensified the pressure that in January 1962 Williams's party ap-

---

⁴⁶ E 145/A (11) Lewis to Grantley Adams, November 9, 1961, PRO CO 1031/3278.
⁴⁷ *Daily Gleaner*, October 9, 1961.
⁴⁸ No. 131, Hailes to A. R. Thomas, November 4, 1961, PRO CO 1031/3278.
⁴⁹ The published report is W. Arthur Lewis, *Eastern Caribbean Federation: Report to the Prime Minister* (Port of Spain, Trinidad, 1961, second edition, with corrections, 1962).
⁵⁰ The Lewis proposals are to be found in No. 145A, Patrick Hailes to Reginald Maudling, November 10, 1961, PRO CO 1031/3278.
⁵¹ No. 131, Hailes to A. R. Thomas, November 4, 1961, PRO CO 1031/3278.

proved a resolution to proceed straight to independence without continuing the discussions on the federation.

Even this disheartening turn of events, in which the two most important British West Indies islands opted out of the federation, did not prevent Lewis from trying to keep the federation idea alive. On January 19, 1962, just five days after Trinidad declared its intention to seek its own political independence, the premier of Barbados and the chief ministers of the Leeward and Windward islands presented proposals for a federation of their eight territories.[52] In spite of the fact that this federation of eight small islands constituted a mere 800,000 people of the 21 million inhabitants living in the Caribbean and did not include any island with economic strength, Lewis rose to champion the scheme. He had no illusion that the federation of eight could produce the kind of economic progress that the British Caribbean so sorely needed, but he hoped that, supported with start-up British financial assistance, it might prove enough of a success to change the minds of the Jamaican and Trinidadian politicians.[53]

Yet, even this emasculated political federation fell apart. Grenada and Dominica, both of which had strong economic and political ties with Trinidad, were reluctant to throw their support behind the one island that had some cultural and economic weight—Barbados. Although the idea of a political federation of the eight had not died before Lewis's departure for the United States, it was well on its way to its demise. In fact, Lewis had become so discouraged by the political squabbling and fragmentation in the West Indies that he welcomed the opportunity to be away from the islands in the summer of 1962. He commented in a letter to a Colonial Office official, Patrick Hailes, that he was relieved to have commitments outside the area so that he would "not have to turn up at various celebrations [for the independence of territories] to grin and make hollow speeches."[54] So distressed was he by the failure of the politicians to seize what Lewis believed to be the only hope for the Caribbean that he recited to friends cynical remarks about the West Indian character. If you put fifty Englishmen or fifty Frenchmen down in one place, he observed, they would form a community. If you put fifty West Indians, there would still be fifty West Indians.[55]

[52] *Report of the Eastern Caribbean Federation Conference*, 1962, in *House of Commons Sessional Papers*, cmd. 1746, PRO CO 1031/3370.

[53] Lewis's account of these events may be found in *The Agony of the Eight* (Barbados, 1963).

[54] Lewis to Lord Hailey, June 21, 1962, Lewis Papers, Box 5.

[55] No. 11, John Stow, Governor, Federation of Eight, to Stephen Luke, July 7, 1962, PRO CO 1031/3308.

A year later, shortly after having taken up his professorship at Princeton University but still feeling the pain of not realizing his lifelong dream of a West Indian federation, Lewis, uncharacteristically, leveled a searing attack against the West Indian politicians for their role in the collapse of the negotiations. One needs to remember the circumstances of his departure from Jamaica, a beaten and exhausted man, who had used up his last ounce of energy to keep the University of the West Indies alive, but had failed. The year 1963 was a low point in his public career. The youngster who had sailed from the West Indies filled with idealism and ambition to serve his homeland and who obtained the best education that he could in order to better the lot of his fellow West Indians departed from Jamaica in 1963 with a deep sense of despair. No wonder, then, less than a year after leaving, he made angry, highly inflammatory, and even demeaning remarks about the political elite of the West Indies, with whom he had struggled so bitterly and whose opposition to his ambitions had worn him down. Unfortunately, the remarks that he believed to be off the record were reported in the *Sunday Guardian* of Trinidad on April 26, 1964. They led that same paper to print a critical editorial on April 30, 1964, charging Lewis with "ascribing racial motivation to the Trinidad and Tobago government to negotiate a political union of Trinidad and Tobago with Grenada."[56]

The occasion was a talk that Lewis gave to the West Indian Students Association of the City College of New York, a talk attended by Barry Auguste, a member of the Trinidad delegation to the United Nations, and Keith Johnson, consul-general in New York City, both of whom objected vigorously to Lewis's description of West Indian politicians. Although Lewis was upset that assurances not to publish his remarks had been broken and although he demanded that the *Guardian* print a retraction, in this instance, Lewis had expressed worries about what it was to grow up a West Indian. In the speech, he claimed that West Indians, including himself, suffered from an inferiority complex that results "in a very aggressive personality." The worst of these traits were to be found among the politicians, with whom Lewis had struggled and for whom "the normal diplomatic courtesies are not known."[57] Lewis believed that the unchecked ambitions of selfish poli-

---

[56] This material is taken from clippings in the University of the West Indies Archive, file 23/3. According to Professor Colin Palmer of the Princeton University history department, who is writing a biography of Eric Williams, there is much circumstantial evidence that racial motives were important in Williams's desire for a political union of Trinidad and Tobago and Grenada.

[57] The article that appeared in the *Sunday Guardian* in Trinidad was written by Lenox Raphael, who was residing in New York City at the time. Pearnel P. Charles, West Indian

ticians, concerned first and foremost to enhance their own political power, had prevented the peoples of the West Indies from enjoying the political and economic advantages that Lewis was sure would flow from a union of the islands.

This, of course, was not the first time that Lewis had jousted with politicians and had come away the loser, though it would be the last. Nor was it the first time that he had believed that aspiring nationalist politicians had failed their followers, letting their ambitions to hold office blind them to higher responsibilities. The language that he used to describe the aggressive political behavior of the West Indian political elite and his observation that these traits came to the fore in the turbulent political climate of political decolonization were more fully articulated in his later book, *Politics in West Africa*. Although he did not single out any specific West Indian politician in these remarks, he could not have overlooked Eric Williams, whose behavior surely disappointed Lewis. Lewis expected much from Williams, a fellow intellectual, a university professor and published scholar, with whom Lewis had been close over the years, so the sense of having been left in the lurch must have been intense.

In the West Indies, as in Ghana and at the Colonial Office, Lewis demonstrated little patience for decisions that were based on political rather than economic needs and calculations. But the West Indies was, if it was nothing else, a set of quite distinctive polities, having their own social and political dynamic. Lewis stressed the benefits of centralized economic planning for all of the islands and wanted to take advantage of the common cultural and educational background of the British West Indies. He was, however, insufficiently attentive to the different political trajectories of the islands—a Barbados that was dominated by its sugar-exporting economy and a political elite and a class system "so rigid to constitute a caste structure," a Trinidad with its large East Indian population and its influential multinational oil companies, a British Guiana that had a developed coastal area and a backward hinterland and a genuine socialist ideology, and a Jamaica, with its long history of violent confrontations with slaveholders and British colonial rulers.[58] No wonder that the politicians that these territories

---

Student Association, City College, New York Chapter, to Lewis, May 27, 1964, Lewis Papers, Box 3.

[58] This paragraph summarizes material found in a remarkable study of the West Indies, written in 1968, by Gordon K. Lewis, *The Growth of the Modern West Indies* (London, 1968). The quotation comes from page 229. The book provides an in-depth analysis of the islands and shows the distinctive history and personality of each one. Yet the author, like Lewis, blames the political elites for failing to use the commonalities of language and history to foster a federation and blames them for promoting narrow island nationalisms when they should have rallied behind a Caribbean-wide vision.

produced, men and women like Williams, Cheddi and Janet Jagan, Manley, Bustamante, and Adams, had disparate views of the value of a federation and looked at one another and the other islands suspiciously. For Lewis, and even more so for the British, to expect these men, who owed their prominence to the specific circumstances within their islands, to lay aside these differences, without a considerable amount of political and economic assistance from the former colonial power, was expecting the impossible.

BACK TO THE UNIVERSITY OF THE WEST INDIES

As the federation collapsed, so did the plans for the University of the West Indies as the premier Caribbean-wide institution. Lewis had to devote most of his first full year as vice-chancellor arguing for the centrality of the institution as the unit territories went their separate political ways. Although he managed to save the university as a remnant of the federation plans, he did so at a loss to his physical and emotional well-being. Suffering from ulcers and high blood pressure that resulted in dizzy spells and fainting, Lewis was told by no fewer than four physicians that he would imperil his health if he stayed on in his position.

The chief source of Lewis's anguish in his last year at the university was institutional finance. His ambitious plans for educational expansion required strong territorial financial support at the very moment that the islands were deserting the federation. Moreover, Jamaica's independence, followed by that of Trinidad, meant that these countries, since they were no longer British colonial possessions, lost their eligibility for Colonial Development and Welfare Fund assistance. In addition, unless these countries contributed their fair share to the educational budget of the university, the Colonial Office's grants that were earmarked for the university could not be released.[59]

The university's financing became even more precarious as its funding became enmeshed with a bitter set of negotiations for the independence of Trinidad. Both the British Colonial Office and the government of Trinidad used the university's continued existence to forward their own financial agendas in the days leading up to Trinidad's independence. Trinidad refused to subscribe a promised £400,000 to the university unless the British government withdrew demands that Trinidad pay to the soon-to-be-dissolved federal government of the West Indies £75,000 in defense costs and another £600,000 in housing expenses. Trinidad objected to these charges on the grounds that its government

[59] No. 100, A. A. Dudley to L. B. Walsh Atkins, February 27, 1963, PRO OD 17/30.

had never approved them. Yet in linking its financial contribution to the university to an overall financial settlement with Britain at the time of independence, it risked the financial well-being of the university.[60]

Unable to pry funds away from Trinidad and uncertain of the financial contributions that the University could count on from the Colonial Office, Lewis found himself without funds even to pay contractors who had been employed on university construction projects. Although the Colonial Office blamed Lewis for having fallen for "the lies of Eric Williams," British officials were understandably alarmed when Lewis threatened to file for bankruptcy on behalf of the university.[61] He vividly described the prospect facing the Colonial Office if the university had to file for bankruptcy, pointing out that the reputation of the university was being "ruined by being dragged as a pawn in a struggle between two governments. Please ensure that we are extracted from this mess at the earliest possible moment," he added.[62] He went on to paint a picture of imminent financial collapse that would redound in the most unflattering ways against the British as the ruling power. "What will happen to the reputation of the university with contractors and other suppliers and to our credit worthiness I do not like to think."[63]

In an age of atomic brinksmanship that featured the Cuban missile crisis, this dispute was hardly of a high order. The larger issue dividing the British government and the government of Trinidad was the amount of financial assistance Britain would offer Trinidad at the time of independence. But Lewis and the university were caught in the middle of this argument as each side tried to use the financial well-being of the university to force the other to accept its financial terms. Lewis's efforts to shame the British officials by writing relentlessly that the government "would itself be embarrassed if an institution with a royal charter were forced into the bankruptcy court because it made contracts in good faith on the strength of promises made by Her Majesty's Government" finally yielded a compromise resolution. Trinidad agreed to contribute "a reasonable share" to the capital expenditures of the university and to do so without reference to the financial discussions its officials were having with the United Kingdom over political independence.[64]

[60] No. 98, Lewis to D. M. Smith, February 21, 1963, PRO OD 17/13.
[61] No. 119, E. L. Sykes, Commonwealth Relations Office to D. M. Smith, March 8, 1963, PRO OD 17/30.
[62] No. 188/E2, Lewis to D. M. Smith, February 21, 1963, PRO CO 1031/3496.
[63] No. 98, Lewis to D. M. Smith, February 21, 1963, PRO OD 17/13.
[64] No. E207, Permanent Secretary to Prime Minister of Trinidad and Tobago to the Vice-Chancellor of the University of the West Indies, May 9, 1963, PRO OD 17/30; and

Lewis was gratified that the financing of the university had been saved and that a Caribbean-wide agreement had been struck that guaranteed the university financing for the next ten years. He could leave the office of vice-chancellor comforted by the fact that it would remain central to British Caribbean education for at least another decade. According to one of Lewis's most ardent admirers, D. G. James, who may have exaggerated Lewis's influence since James had been instrumental in securing Lewis's appointment in the first place, Lewis's achievement was monumental. He had salvaged "the only genuine federal institution which has survived the events of the last eighteen months and if the British government still cherish the long-term hope that commonwealth territories of the West Indies may one day come together again (as I suppose they do) the university is worth cherishing on those grounds alone."[65]

On this occasion, however, there were no second thoughts or last-minute interventions to prevent Lewis's resignation. Writing to the chancellor of the university, Princess Alice, Lewis described his physical situation in graphic terms. He had stomach ulcers and high blood pressure, "which causes me to fall down when I stand up." The doctors told him that these problems were caused by "excessive stress and strain on this job for which I am ill-fitted by temperament. I take things too seriously, worry too much, and cannot stand the strain. I must therefore resign." Lewis further summarized an intolerable situation. "I have had a terrible three years unsupported by a weak federal government struggling with other governments to hold the place together and trying to persuade the staff to adopt policies which would win outside support. The worst part has been not being able to rely on colleagues inside the college except for a precious few."[66]

The logic was irrefutable. Princess Alice could only agree, commenting that "it was an almost superhuman achievement to persuade all the West Indian governments to continue their support of the university for the next ten years. . . . But your second letter just filled me with despair. I am indeed distressed to hear how ill you are as a result of the great strain and many anxieties you have been put to all these months past. It really is too cruel; how rarely is virtue rewarded in life."[67]

No. 204, C. E. Diggines, High Commission, Jamaica, to E. L. Sykes, Commonwealth Relations Office, March 7, 1963, PRO CO 1031/3496.

[65] No. 137, A. Morley, British High Commission, Jamaica, to A. B. Cohen, February 1, 1963, PRO OD 17/30.

[66] Lewis to Princess Alice, July 19, 1962, Lewis Papers, Box 1.

[67] Princess Alice to Lewis, September 21, 1962, Lewis Papers, Box 1.

Lewis wrote in much the same vein to his old friend Jock Campbell, chairman of the board of the Booker business group, which dominated the sugar economy of British Guiana and who was an ardent financial backer of the university. To prevent any further discussion of his decision, he described the job in familiar terms. It is "too much for me. It combined the task of an American president who spends his full time on wrestling with governments and benefactors for support and does no administration with the tasks of a British Vice-Chancellor who spends his full time wrestling with his staff and does no public relations. It gave me stomach ulcers and a defective blood pressure and was driving me mad and four doctors advised me that I must give it up so I had no option."[68]

On August 20, 1962, Lewis submitted his formal resignation, which was to take effect no later than September 1963 when he was to take up a professorship at Princeton University.[69] How tragic, and yet how fitting, that this stint in his homeland at the head of an institution that he so loved and that he believed held the key to economic and political happiness should end in such personal despair and physical and emotional exhaustion.

Lewis's main consolation, as he departed from the West Indies for North America, was the knowledge that he had saved the university. Not only had he won significant financial backing from wealthy West Indian businesspersons and American philanthropic organizations, but he had also guided the university through a period of significant transition. He had presided over the evolution of an autonomous university, with specialized graduate and undergraduate faculties, dispersed around the West Indies. From what had been a small, precariously financed University College, he had created a university with a first-rate administrative staff and faculty. From among his top administrators, the university board of trustees selected Lewis's able deputy, Philip Sherlock, to continue the mission of making the university the leading institution of higher learning in the West Indies.

---

[68] Lewis to Jock Campbell, September 17, 1962, Lewis Papers, Box 2. Campbell's firm, Booker Bros., McConnell, and Co. Ltd. was responsible for 80 percent of the sugar output of British Guiana and "100 percent of the attacks on sugar interests." According to one critic, "their name and interests are so ubiquitous that it is said that a local man who had bought an outboard motor at Bookers' Store, was not surprised, on starting the engine, to hear it say 'booker-booker-booker.'" Although Campbell was known to be one of "the more progressive capitalists," no doubt his influence with Lewis worried nationalists like Cheddi Jagan who accused the sugar planters and Bookers of making "huge profits. . . . The workers are sweated and millions of dollars produced by them go into the pockets of sugar kings in England." These quotations come from Michael Swan, *British Guiana: The Land of Six People* (London, 1957), pp. 85 and 94.

[69] No. 38, University of the West Indies Archives, LA 87, Box 46.

CHAPTER 8

The Princeton Years, 1963-91

IN EARLY JUNE 1962, Gardner Patterson, the dean of Princeton University's Woodrow Wilson School of Public and International Affairs, was in a state of great elation. He had just received W. Arthur Lewis's letter accepting Princeton's offer to join the faculty. He and others in the Princeton community had been courting Lewis for half a year, ever since they learned that Lewis was interested in stepping down as vice-chancellor of the University of the West Indies. A luncheon gathering featuring such Princeton dignitaries as Dean of the Faculty Douglas Brown, Jerome Blum, chair of the history department, Richard Lester, chair of the economics department, and important members of the Princeton economics department, including Fritz Machlup, Oscar Morgenstern, and Richard Quandt, reflected Princeton's intention to persuade Lewis to come to Princeton. Patterson followed up the luncheon with a series of letters in which he laid out the terms of the appointment. Lewis wrote his letter of acceptance on May 31, 1962, a full six weeks after Patterson had sent the offer letter.[1]

By hiring the leading figure in the field of development economics, Princeton had enhanced its reputation in the field of economics and stolen a march on its competitors. Patterson's note to Princeton president, Robert Goheen, called the Lewis appointment "a tremendous coup. I can think of no single academic appointment which we might make which will be so widely talked about."[2] Moreover, Lewis's appointment could not have come at a more propitious time for Princeton's Woodrow Wilson School of Public and International Affairs. Just one year earlier, the university had received a major gift of $35 million from an anonymous donor, later identified as the Robertson family. Its purpose was to expand the graduate program of the school. In announcing Lewis's appointment, President Goheen emphasized that the Robertson gift was intended to make "possible the beginning of a great expansion and major advance in the post-graduate program of Princeton's Woodrow Wilson School, designed to prepare personnel for ca-

---

[1] Lewis to Gardner Patterson, May 31, 1962, Dean of the Faculty Personnel File on W. Arthur Lewis, Princeton University.
[2] Gardner Patterson to President Robert F. Goheen, June 5, 1962, Dean of the Faculty Personnel File on W. Arthur Lewis, Princeton University.

reers in public and international affairs." Just how vital the Lewis appointment was at this time became clear when Goheen identified Lewis's specialty in economics and public affairs as one of the two "pioneering ventures," in which Princeton would be able to provide training that was not available elsewhere in American public affairs graduate programs. Earlier, Dean Patterson laid out what the Woodrow Wilson School hoped that Lewis would bring to the school. "Our great need is for you to develop and to be in charge of a year-long graduate course or seminars in the wide range of problems covered by the term 'economic development.'"[3]

The appointment form from the economics department and the Woodrow Wilson School prior to the dean of the faculty's offer revealed what Princeton thought it was getting in its new economics professor. In the section devoted to teaching, the authors (Dean Patterson and Richard Lester, head of the economics department) opined that Lewis was an excellent teacher of graduate students. They made this statement despite the fact that Lewis had never taught graduate students in the way that Princeton professors did, in semester-long formal seminars in preparation for their general examinations. They commented that they had "no basis for evaluating his abilities as a teacher of undergraduates, but we have no reason to believe that he would not be other than fully satisfactory." This, too, was a curious remark since nearly all of Lewis's teaching at the London School of Economics and at the University of Manchester had been of undergraduates, where, in fact, had the Princeton authorities inquired, they would have learned of his extraordinary successes.

The evaluators of Lewis were on more solid ground when they turned to his research. They described him as "widely recognized as the world's most eminent scholar in the interdisciplinary field of economic growth and political and social change in the so-called emerging countries. He combines a superior competence in economic theory with wide experience in governmental economic and political affairs." They concluded their report by praising his book, *The Theory of Economic Growth*, labeling it a "classic."

Although Lewis may well have been ailing physically when he arrived in Princeton, he plunged into his teaching and research with unusual energy. From the outset he offered graduate seminars on economic development jointly in the Woodrow Wilson School and the economics department. The usual format that he chose was a graduate overview course on economic development followed by a team-taught

---

[3] Gardner Patterson to Lewis, April 18, 1962, Dean of the Faculty Personnel File on W. Arthur Lewis, Princeton University.

seminar dealing with economic development in selected country studies. Lewis chose the continent of Africa for his country studies, while his colleagues treated the countries of Latin America and Asia. As the custom at Princeton was for all faculty to do undergraduate teaching, Lewis experimented with various undergraduate courses, even trying his hand at one of the large introductory economics lecture courses, where he was not at his best or comfortable. He eventually developed a standard undergraduate lecture course on economic development.[4]

In attempting to strengthen the study of economic development at Princeton, as Dean Patterson and President Goheen had expected him to do at the time of his appointment, Lewis approached the Ford Foundation in early 1965 with a request for a three-year grant of three hundred thousand dollars. Lewis's proposal entailed course work and faculty appointments that would enable Princeton to expand its work on economic development. Although the foundation eventually rejected the request, the document provides a clear overview of how Lewis saw the field developing. Lewis laid out the areas in which additional research was required and where he saw his own contributions likely to occur.

He began by claiming that the study of economic development was progressing along two distinct but related lines. The first was historical. It entailed the study of the economic history of the advanced, industrialized countries, the purpose of which was to learn how the successful countries had achieved their development. Lewis confided that he had always steeped his own work in economic history and that he fully intended to return to this kind of work. The second avenue was the observation of "the current progress of less developed countries" with an eye to evaluating "the success and failure of their economic policies." In Lewis's view, research needed to take place in six critical areas in the next decade, in each of which Lewis wanted Princeton to be active. The first was analyzing and explaining the mounting urban unemployment of developing countries. Lewis had already described disguised unemployment in the rural sector, but quite perplexing to him and needing research was urban unemployment. He had not anticipated it as a problem for developing countries since according to his formula on the supply of surplus labor to capitalist sectors, such large numbers should not have drifted into the cities. In his opinion, "virtually nothing has appeared on unemployment in urban areas."

---

[4] The information on Lewis's teaching comes from the Princeton University undergraduate and graduate school *Announcement*, an annual printed catalogue that lists the courses that faculty taught and provides brief description of their contents.

The other five items were also fields that Lewis had worked in but required more careful study. They were (1) the demand for secondary and higher education, (2) development and planning, where "the time is ripe for studies of the successes and failures of planning," (3) public finance and ways to help the less developed countries raise a higher proportion of national income through taxation than they had in the past, (4) agricultural education, and (5) the development of the world economy between 1870 and 1914, which Lewis now regarded as the crucial historical era when the world economy became divided between the prosperous and advanced industrial countries and the poorer exporters of raw materials and importers of manufactures. Lewis made it clear that he intended to devote much of his research and writing in the 1970s to this last item.[5]

Although Lewis failed to persuade the Ford Foundation, he did succeed in creating a special research unit in the Woodrow Wilson School devoted to the study of economic development. Lewis used the Research Program in Economic Development to assemble a distinguished group of development economists that included over the years Frederick Harbison, the well-known manpower economist, Charles Frank Jr., an expert on the fiscal policies of African governments, and Sherman Robinson, Mark Gersovitz, and other young specialists, who like Lewis were general development economists. The program undertook to explore the questions that Lewis had outlined in his Ford proposal.[6]

So successful and contented was Lewis at Princeton that he routinely turned down requests to leave for higher pay and less teaching at other institutions. When the vice-chancellor of the University of the West Indies approached Lewis about returning to his native land, he had a reply ready at hand. Princeton had offered him a unique opportunity to do research and write, and he had found that he enjoyed this aspect of academe more than he had anticipated. In the West Indies, there were no library facilities with which to carry out demanding research projects. "In my five years here, I have published four books (highly reflective) and am about to publish two more (based on original historical research). I have also written half a dozen papers, some published and some in the mill." He was sure that he could do more good for developing countries by conducting research at Princeton and sharing his finding with scholars and students all over the world

---

[5] This material comes from Lewis to Marvin Bernstein, Dean of the Woodrow Wilson School, and Lester Chandler, Chair of the Economics Department, April 2, 1965, and a letter from Marshall A. Robinson of the Ford Foundation to Lewis, November 24, 1965, contained in the W. Arthur Lewis Personnel File in the Economics Department, Princeton University.

[6] Princeton University, Graduate School, *Announcements* for the late 1960s and 1970s.

than he could by teaching in the West Indies. His publications put him in contact with "thousands," whereas his teaching would be limited to "hundreds."[7] Similarly after turning aside offers from Stanford, Berkeley, and the Brookings Institution, Lewis wrote to Richard Lester, chair of the economics department, remarking that he enjoyed his graduate seminar and supervising dissertation students but not the other demands placed on his time. He added that "Gladys and I are very happy here among our friends and colleagues and would hate to uproot ourselves."[8]

Race in America: Black Studies and Black Power

Lewis was the first black faculty member at Princeton and, for a longer period than he would have wanted, he was the only black full professor at Princeton. At a time when civil rights was a burning issue in American society and when the recruitment of black students and faculty into what had previously been predominantly white institutions of higher education was a critical issue on the agenda of American colleges and universities, Lewis found himself drawn inexorably into the maelstrom of American ethnic politics. He could not remain silent, although his opinions caused much controversy to swirl around him.

Starting in his students days in London, Lewis had been an outspoken critic of racial discrimination. His long-standing mantra was that if individuals were judged solely on merit, race would soon cease to matter. Black power tenets had no appeal to him, and those who favored racial separation or such things as quotas for black students and faculty and set-asides for fellowships, building contracts, and the like made him uncomfortable. In his London days, even when he was protesting the British government's unwillingness to employ persons of African descent in the colonial service and to allow non-Europeans to become officers in the British armed services, his goal was the erasure of racial distinctions. Constantly describing himself as a child of the Enlightenment, he affirmed reason as his guiding principle and held matters of religion and race to be part of the private sphere of life. He was far more comfortable during his London days associating with Harold Moody's League of Coloured Peoples, with its belief in the coming together of the races, than with the more radical and often more race-conscious

---

[7] Lewis to Dr. Dudley Higgins, Pro-Vice-Chancellor, University of the West Indies, Lewis Papers, Box 6.

[8] Lewis to Lester Chandler, October 4, 1967, W. Arthur Lewis Personnel File, Woodrow Wilson School, Princeton University.

stances of West Indians who frequented Britain at this time. Men like Eric Williams, C.L.R. James, and George Padmore, with their leftist and Marxist sympathies and their greater willingness to make racial issues a significant part of their ideologies, troubled him.

America's highly charged racial politics of the 1960s was bound to discomfit Lewis. A member in good standing of the National Association for the Advancement of Colored People (NAACP) and an energetic participant in that group's economic advisory committee, he looked askance at any movement that swerved toward militant black politics. Yet this sensitivity often made it difficult for him to differentiate youthful student exuberance from deep-seated radical sentiments. His intense disillusionment with what he regarded as the radical, demagogic, and misleading policies of nationalist politicians like Nkrumah in Ghana and the West Indian politicians, who in Lewis's opinion had destroyed the political federation, made him deeply suspicious of anything that smacked of political posturing.

Lewis's worries about radical politics came to a head in the late 1960s at a time when the war in Vietnam linked with civil rights agitation to rile American campuses. The specific issue that drew Lewis most directly into campus politics was the creation of a black studies program at Princeton University. Having already served on a committee to establish an African studies program at Princeton, Lewis was an obvious choice to participate in a parallel committee to found an African American studies program. Here, the stakes were high. The African studies committee had been entirely faculty-composed and had drafted its report without student input. The same was not possible in the African American studies committee. This body had faculty, staff, and student members, and when it submitted its report, which called for the establishment of an African American studies program, the matter was closely debated in the faculty before being adopted.

The big question that Princeton, and other like-minded colleges and universities, had to resolve was whether African American studies should be a full-fledged, freestanding degree-granting department, like history or English, having its own faculty and resources, or, rather, a program whose faculty held their appointments in other departments and that offered a certificate of proficiency rather than an A.B. degree. Lewis and committee chair William Baumol, also of the economics department, were of one mind: Princeton should not establish an African American studies department. Rather, it should have a program, with a strong research component, capable of attracting the leading researchers in the field. They reasoned that faculty members, whether they were historians, economists, political scientists, or sociologists, if they were at the top of their professions, would insist on being in mainline research-oriented departments and would regard being appointed in a freestanding department that lacked a clear scholarly disciplinary agenda as an inferior appointment. Creating a separate department could have the undesirable effect of bringing scholars to the university who lacked standing in their formal disciplines and would ultimately render the African American studies field one of lesser scholarly standards.

Lewis spelled out these concerns in a memorandum that he drafted on May 28, 1969, and sent to McGeorge Bundy, head of the Ford Foundation. Entitled "Notes on Black Studies" and based on his experiences on the Princeton African American studies committee and his knowledge of black studies programs and departments elsewhere in the United States, the memo was an answer to a request from Bundy "to know the reaction of a few men like yourselves—scholars who are themselves able to speak with authority about the stake of black men in these subjects."[9] Much of the Lewis memo dealt aggressively with his chief worry that black studies programs and departments would be taken over by "black militants who want to show that individual blacks did this or that and do so for its therapeutic value to bolster black pride. This is history as taught in grade school. History as studied in colleges deals with groups. It has no therapeutic value since it mainly reveals human folly and weakness. The Foundation should surely steer clear of programs desiring to teach inspirational history at the college level."

In the memo, Lewis also developed another theme relating to black studies. In his view, white students needed to be involved. "The white students sharpen the discussion since they are not dominated by black militants who discourage awkward questions and frank answers." Lewis was adamantly opposed to establishing a major in black studies, regarding the field as a fad. "Fads come and go. Within five years agitation re black studies will have died away. Colleges which have hastily put on undergraduate inspirational courses will be caught with faculty programs and students who are generally despised and black studies will be just one more source of black shame and inferiority in such institutions."[10]

This would not be the last time that Lewis would invoke the muse of history to buttress his arguments. Nor would it be the last time that he would bend history to serve these purposes. His notion that history, even supposedly serious historical inquiry, had not been used in the past for "therapeutic" and "inspirational" ends was hardly an accurate

[9] McGeorge Bundy to Lewis, May 21, 1969, Lewis Papers, Box 2.
[10] Lewis to McGeorge Bundy, May 28, 1969, Lewis Papers, Box 2.

assessment of much historical work. Nor was it a fair complaint against the purposes lying behind the formation of black studies programs. The sponsors of these programs at the time were committed to uncovering an authentic historical record, though their suspicion that white scholars had ignored black initiatives and underplayed the degree to which white culture had dominated and exploited "black" populations surely was a valid charge against the historical profession at the time.

In the memo to Bundy, Lewis was only warming to the task. Lewis had already published a highly publicized and controversial article in the *Princeton Alumni Weekly* in March 1969, which was then given national circulation in the *New York Times Sunday Magazine*. Lewis could be an intellectual contrarian and take delight in questioning academic enthusiasms at the moment when they were generating their greatest acceptance. He was in just such a mood when he wrote this essay. In the first place, Lewis feared that African American studies programs and departments might deflect black students from what he regarded as their best opportunity to claim a place for themselves in the American establishment. Lewis introduced his essay for the *Alumni Weekly* by observing that the key to black economic advancement was entry into the fifty or sixty elite schools among the more than two thousand American degree-granting institutions of higher education. Admission to these elite colleges was "absolutely fundamental to the larger economic strategy of black power."[11] Lewis added an even more combative statement to the previous remark. "Those black power advocates who favored the separation of blacks from whites in higher education through separate housing and eating facilities and the creation of black courses taught by black faculty almost exclusively for black students were doing a serious disservice to the interests of a rising black middle class." As for black studies, which Lewis regarded as an important ingredient of the separatist black power agenda, Lewis contended that African American studies should be for white students, not for blacks. The black student should study "engineering, medicine, chemistry, economics, law, agriculture, and other subjects, which are going to be of value to him and his people. And let the clever whites go to college to read black novels, to learn Swahili, and to record the exploits of Negro heroes of the past. They are the ones to whom this will come as an eye-opener."[12]

---

[11] W. Arthur Lewis, "Black Power and the American University," *Princeton Alumni Weekly*, vol. 69, no. 21, March 18, 1969, p. 14.
[12] Ibid., p. 15.

No doubt there was an element of irony and exaggeration in Lewis's essay. He was made acutely uncomfortable when right-wing intellectuals began to cite the essay in opposing this academic initiative. He was certainly aware that black American students, by taking courses in African American studies, would derive emotional and intellectual energy from them. But he wanted black students to master science and technology and claim their share of the top positions in American society.[13]

Lewis returned to the theme of blacks and higher education the next year when he published an article entitled "The Economic Profile of the American Black," in the *Journal of Religion and Health*. He opened the essay by remarking that if the economic status of blacks were set right, three-quarters of the problem of social status would be solved. "The central economic strategy of the black community has to be to get its fair share of the jobs all the way through the [occupational] hierarchy." At present American blacks congregated at the lower end of the occupational and income ladder, and their goal must be to get the 11 percent of the top paying jobs and not more than 11 percent at the bottom. "Until this happens, the black community is neither making its full contribution to the American economy nor getting its share of the outcome." The barrier to economic advancement was educational deficits, many of which stemmed from discrimination. Two-thirds of the persons in *Who's Who* came from fifty elite colleges, most of which did not take black students until recently, so that blacks had not been able to get the best jobs, or for that matter, the middle level jobs. No wonder Lewis wanted the African American population to take full advantage of the educational opportunities that were suddenly opened up to them in the elite schools. Although he saw "a bitter struggle" between the races as likely in the American future and believed that "the two races would still be separate and would still, for the most part, live their own social lives, but without class tension, cultural tension would be much reduced."[14]

The heated discussions at this time forced Lewis to clarify his views on race. Lewis rejected the widely held notion that America was a melting pot where peoples from different parts of the world came together and merged their cultural and racial heritages into a singular American way of life. At least at this stage of American development, the United States was better described as a welding shop, not a melting pot. The races, especially whites and blacks, came together primarily

---

[13] Lewis was one of the founding members of Princeton University's Program in African Studies and was always a strong supporter of this initiative.

[14] W. Arthur Lewis, "The Economic Profile of the American Black, *Journal of Religion and Health*, vol. 9, no. 4, October 1970, pp. 323–30.

in the workplace, only rarely outside of it. In Lewis's opinion, peoples of different ethnic, cultural, and historical traditions preferred to associate and live side by side with like-minded individuals. Thus, integration occurred in the workplace and produced the extraordinary American economic efficiency that was the world's envy. But not for many years did Lewis believe that integration was likely to spread beyond the floor shop and the business firm into social and family relations.[15]

Other, smaller, almost seemingly inconsequential episodes spurred Lewis to think through the issues of race and to lay out his own views about the historical trajectory of humankind. At the core of his thinking was surely his own experience in the West Indies and elsewhere where racial discrimination had severely restricted his career choices. He viewed the changes in civil rights in America as opening opportunities to people of color that had not been available before and that might not be available in the future. He feared that radical politics might deprive the black community of what was a significant opportunity, perhaps even a unique opportunity, the opening of the window of education and occupation that the civil rights movement had brought about. Nor did he agree with radical, and not-so-radical black, groups that these new opportunities existed because of energetic black protest movements. In 1970, as a trustee of the University of Rochester, Lewis responded to the request of its president, W. Allen Wallis, to meet with thirty African American students and to report back to the president on the mood of the black students. His note to President Wallis makes for interesting reading given the fact that the war in Vietnam was riling the campus and at some institutions, including his own, students had begun to mount protests in favor of South African divestiture. Lewis's note asserted that "politically the situation among the students is extremely healthy." What he meant by "healthy" would have surprised many campus observers though it undoubtedly cheered the president. He noted, "I heard nothing about South African divestment and very little about the university's obligations to the black community in Rochester or the slowness of starting black studies, or the desirability of separate accommodations or any of the other issues which have proved so inflammatory on other campuses."[16]

---

[15] I am indebted to William Baumol for these insights, especially for bringing to my attention the terms *melting pot* and *welding shop* that Lewis employed frequently at the time. Baumol was the chairperson of the African American studies committee at Princeton University, of which Lewis was a member, and thus had many opportunities to discuss questions of race with Lewis. Interview with William Baumol, September 1, 2004.

[16] Lewis to W. Allen Wallis, president of the University of Rochester, April 13, 1970, Lewis Papers, Box 12.

One of the issues that Lewis referred to in the note, specifically the obligations to the black community of Rochester, must have struck a sensitive chord in him. He had been deeply involved with West Indian seamen living in the ports of western England during his London days and then had carried this social concern to Manchester, where he helped to establish a community center to ameliorate the deplorable social and educational conditions of the black community living in the run-down district of Moss Side. But, of course, he regarded these matters as private concerns, not institutional university problems. Lewis returned to his bedrock belief that students had one reason to be attending universities, and that was to equip themselves with the knowledge and skills that would enable them to go forth and make the world a better place. Colleges and universities were not altruistic institutions.

Lewis's stature as a distinguished black social scientist with relatively moderate stances on racial questions gave him an appeal to many foundations and private organizations. He served on the board of the National Humanities Center in the late 1960s at a time when it had acquired the reputation as "not a place where black scholars would be welcome" under the direction of William Bennett.[17] Bennett dispatched Lewis to the Ford Foundation to counter these views. Lewis endeavored to defend the Humanities Center by describing Bennett's position on offering fellowships to minority applicants in the following terms. They were "neo-conservative, that there be no special criteria for any candidates and that all be judged fairly. He [Lewis] did not personally agree with Dr. Bennett's line of reasoning but he said, followed to its logical conclusion it is more just and more beneficial to minorities."[18] The Ford Foundation did not relent in its demand that the center increase the number of minority and women fellowship recipients if it wished to receive Ford support, and Lewis worked with Bennett to find a formula by which Ford could offer money to the center for minority fellowships without interfering with the council's right to make the final choices.[19]

Discussions that revolved around the place of race in higher education occasionally provoked Lewis to write at length about deeper questions of history and human evolution. One such occasion occurred during the highly charged year of 1969. Lewis received a draft chapter of a book that later was published under the title *Beyond Black or White:*

---

[17] This was the view of some influential members of the Ford Foundation, as expressed in a letter from Phyllis Zagano of the Ford Foundation to William T. Bennett, January 10, 1980. Lewis Papers, Box 2.

[18] Ibid.

[19] Lewis to William Bennett, January 14, 1980, Lewis Papers, Box 2.

An Alternate America. The author of the essay, Vernon Dixon, was a black graduate student in the economics department at Princeton, somewhat older than most graduate students at the time. Dixon went on to become a professor of economics at Haverford College.

Dixon wished to try out his main argument on Lewis and get the older scholar's feedback before seeking a publisher. His primary point was that because blacks and whites in America tended to deny the validity of each other's experiences, the future of race relations in the United States was not promising for either group and would not improve until each was willing to accept the other's points of view. The essay provoked a passionate response from Lewis. While admitting he liked some aspects of Dixon's theory, he claimed to being put off by "the Talcott Parsons jargon." What Lewis most disapproved of, however, were the notions of white and black experiences and values. He claimed to have no idea what Dixon meant by white and black culture and believed that these terms were pure stereotypes. "Since stereotypes contribute little to scientific discussion, I am alienated every time I see the phrase [*modal white*]."

Next, Lewis offered Dixon a lesson in history that would have raised the eyebrows of many professional historians. He reminded Dixon that Europe had not entered into "the march of civilization" until 1500 and asserted "that white America contributed nothing to any branch of civilization before 1933." He saw black Americans grappling with the problem of "how to relate to the great river of human civilization" and wondered why the American population, whites as well as blacks, did not "read some non-American books for a change instead of trying to invent every thing anew." In his opinion the leaders of the third world were having an easier time than African Americans in relating to this river of civilization. They were able to separate out the universals of modernity, like science, technology, and the modern business organization from superficialities, like dress, hairstyle, food preferences and the like, which "American blacks are making so much fuss about at this particular phase of their liberation struggle."

Lewis went on to identify the fundamentals of advanced Western civilization, which he regarded as "the nuclear family (which is gaining everywhere at the expense of the extended family), the permissive childhood, and the universal drift towards atheism. The trivial parts, which each nation tends to hold on to, include its own food, style of dress, and language." The Japanese had been "the most graceful in coming to terms with modernity," while the American blacks were in "ferment now on what is or is not appropriate to their culture. One can only hope that as *their* feelings of rejection subside, *they* will have a less adolescent approach to matters of this kind" (emphasis added).

What blacks were expressing, in Lewis's opinion, was hardly a modular black culture, which did not exist, but "a reaction to persecution—a negative, not a positive concept. . . . It is that having grown up in a hostile world, as underdogs, subject to rejection, *we* have a set of reactions in common" (emphasis added), consisting of "skepticism, cynicism, some willingness to stand by each other (combined with fierce hatred of those we think of as traitors), a desire to show that we are as good as our persecutors, which takes two opposite forms of (1) showing that anything that they can do, we can do better or (2) denying that what they do is worth doing."[20]

Of all of the Lewis papers and writings, the note to Dixon is, in many respects, the most introspective and revealing. It begins, unexceptionally, except for its emotional language, as a standard critique of radical black thinking and a restatement of modernization theory, in which Lewis described the West as the latest in a long evolutionary process leading inexorably to a reason-based modernity. In this presentation, those populations that have been exposed to a heavy, often coercive, and highly discriminatory form of Western civilization, like the assimilated populations in Africa and the West Indies and especially the minority African American community in the United States, had the greatest difficulty coming to grips with the universals of modernity. But toward the end of the long missive, Lewis substituted the pronoun "we" for "they," which he had employed throughout when talking about African Americans. Here, when describing blacks as underdogs, aspiring to outperform whites, linked in a battle against white power, Lewis was no longer the dispassionate and distant intellectual. He was recounting his own upbringing and life experiences.

The Lewis critique of Dixon's draft chapter ran to six full pages, typed and single-spaced. Despite its highly critical comments, it was entirely in keeping with the attention that Lewis gave to his students. He read dissertation drafts with great care and wrote lengthy and detailed comments. Lewis approached his responsibilities as a teacher as virtually a religious calling, for he believed that the pursuit of truth was what set modern men and women off from their early forebears.

Lewis developed many of these same themes, though in more temperate language, in a letter to the economist Carlos Diaz-Alejandro,

---

[20] This very long critique of the essay that Dixon submitted is in Lewis to Vernon Dixon, October 1, 1969, Lewis Papers, Box 4. Lewis did not keep the essay among his papers, but Dixon and a fellow graduate student from Rutgers University, Badi Foster, published their work under the title *Beyond Black or White: An Alternate America* (Boston, 1971). Although Dixon gracefully acknowledges Lewis's help in the preface, remarking that Lewis "gave an invaluable critique of an early draft," the book contains most of the ideas that Lewis objected to. Dixon and Foster, *Beyond Black or White*, p. ix.

who was at the Yale Economic Growth Center at the time. Praising Diaz Alejandro's "splendid chapter in the Kenen book," he used the opportunity to lay out his opposition to a school of economic thinking gaining popularity in the social sciences. This school, which Lewis labeled the "de-linkers," others would have called dependency theory. The central tenet of dependency theory was that the poverty and lack of development in the third world were direct results of colonial and semicolonial dependence on the Western world. According to dependency theorists, the less developed parts of the world could begin to develop economically only if they severed their ties with the capitalist West. Lewis wrote that he opposed the de-linkers not for political or economic reasons but "because of a different view of human evolution. As a child of the French Enlightenment, I think that all mankind will gain from, and will come to be steeped in, the scientific outlook, egalitarian vision, the civil freedom of the common man, and the restricted, pluralist state. The things which separate mankind—cultural patterns, religion, language, racial and regional affiliations—emerged before the great revolutions in transportation and communications and to the extent that they survive in the future, they will be of small importance. In my experience most 'de-linkers' are separatists, who want to defend their local way of life against the consequences of the French Enlightenment."[21]

Public Service and a Return to the West Indies

For all of his engagement in teaching and research and increasing involvement in questions of race in American higher education, Lewis could not resist the siren calls of public service. They beckoned him once again in 1969 when he agreed to serve on the Pearson Commission. This international body was created under United Nations auspices and headed up by Lester Pearson, former prime minister of Canada, to examine the slowing down of economic assistance to less developed countries of the world. In the opinion of John P. Lewis, the dean of the Woodrow Wilson School at the time, the Pearson Commission was "the most important international panel on problems of development and foreign assistance in at least a decade." Lewis was its only "practicing academic," and, true to form, he proved to be "the most stimulating commissioner, contributing not only analytical rigor

---

[21] Lewis to Carlos Diaz Alejandro, September 2, 1977, Lewis Papers, Box 1.

but operational focus to the commission's study, of which he drafted the key chapters."[22]

Nor could Lewis stay away from the West Indies for long. When a non-Marxist government came to power in British Guiana, having ousted Cheddi Jagan's administration in 1964, Lewis agreed to provide the new leaders with a five-year development plan. Shortly after drafting the plan, Lewis became chancellor of the University of Guyana. Lewis took on the task because he wanted to ensure that the new university got off to a good start. The trustees were delighted to have Lewis as their chancellor, looking to him to spearhead a fund-raising effort through his connections with American philanthropic institutions. Lewis remained as the chancellor into the 1970s, leading the fund-raising efforts, selecting a new vice-chancellor, and regularly attending graduation exercises, where he routinely offered advice to the graduates. Finally, recognizing that the university had grown substantially since its inception, he stepped down, believing that the institution now required a chancellor who resided in the country and would be on call.

By 1970, Lewis had already spent seven years at Princeton, nearly as long as he had been on the faculty of the University of Manchester. Hence, when a group of West Indian political and business leaders approached him with a proposal to become head of the new Caribbean Development Bank, he agreed to take on this task. He asked for and obtained a leave of absence from Princeton, believing that the bank could play a role in promoting the future political integration of the islands and that his expertise in project evaluation and economic development would enable him to advance the Caribbean's economic development.

The Caribbean Development Bank was officially founded in 1969, but it did not complete its first full year of activities until 1971. It began with an authorized capital of $50 million, of which just a little less than half was paid in. By the time Lewis left in mid-1973 the amount of paid in capital had tripled to nearly $70 million. Although the British and the Canadian governments provided a substantial portion of the start-up capital and were soon joined by the French, German, and Italian governments, the Bank's charter restricted to 40 percent the amount of equity capital that non-Caribbean governments could contribute. All of the islands, except Cuba, were members, with the biggest and

---

[22] Salary recommendation for W. Arthur Lewis, signed by John P. Lewis, Dean of the Woodrow Wilson School, and Richard Quandt, Chair of the Economics Department, January 14, 1970, W. Arthur Lewis Personnel File, Woodrow Wilson School, Princeton University.

wealthiest islands, Jamaica and Trinidad and Tobago, holding the largest amount of equity capital at 16.6 percent.[23]

Lewis did not arrive in Bridgetown, Barbados, the bank's headquarters, until February 1971. He had intended to combine directing the bank with other, more research-oriented assignments like drafting reports on industrial and agricultural development for the Caribbean. But he had to devote all of his time to administering the banks because "three of the six division heads were weaklings so I had to think out for them what they should be doing, check out their activities, and do what they could not do. . . . It became a fifteen-hour a day job." His first year was nightmarish. He observed that had he known at the time how time-consuming the job would be, he would never have taken it. The bank's treasurer could not keep his books in the ten different currencies that were in use in the Caribbean. The secretary was "ignorant and lazy," and not a single person on the bank's staff had experience in project evaluation," so I had to train people in project evaluation and the first two years to check on every project personally."[24]

In addition to having to recruit new staff, Lewis had to preside over a bank that was ringed about by many restrictions. Unlike most development banks, the Caribbean Development Bank had no government underwriting. No governments would bail it out if it made bad loans, and hence it had to scrutinize with the utmost care all of the project applications that were submitted to it. Moreover, its lending capability of $20 million a year was miniscule compared with the Caribbean's annual gross capital formation of $400 million. The bank could support only forty new projects each year. Thus, each project that it endorsed had to promote innovative kinds of economic development from which private entrepreneurs could learn.[25]

Although Lewis was eventually able to hire a good treasurer and secretary, project evaluation remained a problem. "The future of the Bank hangs on this," he pointed out. When John Lewis, dean of the Woodrow Wilson School, approached Lewis about returning to Princeton after his first year, Lewis wrote that his return was out of the question. He had "set in motion in this Bank studies of development possibilities, agricultural and industrial, which will not be complete until

---

[23] Chandra Hardy, *The Caribbean Development Bank* (North-South Institute, 2003).
[24] Lewis to Horace Barber, Financial Secretary, Jamaica, November 19, 1973, Lewis Papers, Box 1.
[25] Lewis provides a useful and succinct overview of his first two years at the Bank in W. Arthur Lewis, "The Caribbean Development Bank," in *Proceedings of the Seventh West Indian Agricultural Economics Conference* (St. Augustine, Trinidad, 1972).

about Easter of next year, and I must stay on to give practical effect to anything that comes out of these studies."[26]

Lewis thought that his biggest challenge would be finding money. While admitting that fund-raising was enormously time-consuming, he never found funds to be a restraint on the bank's projects. In fact, what became the largest barrier for the bank was its own restriction on using soft money exclusively in the smaller islands. Although intended to prevent the larger islands from monopolizing the bank's resources, the restriction left the bank with unexpended funds. Lewis noted that "although the leaders [in these small islands] were full of talk, they were already receiving as much money as they could receive from Britain and Canada." As a consequence, "the Bank was forced to manufacture additional programs for them without much cooperation on their part."[27]

Lewis regarded the restriction on soft money as a gross misallocation of resources. It made the choice of whether to stay on at the bank or to return to Princeton beginning in September 1973 "easy." The one salutary effect of his decision to leave was the board of governors' agreement to use soft money wherever it saw fit. Lewis believed that this change in the charter would make the Caribbean Development Bank "the main financial institution in the region, playing a vital role in the MDC [more developed countries] financing though the LDCs [less developed countries] will have to sink into the background."[28]

The Turn to Economic History

In Lewis's outline of the most pressing research concerns in the field of economic development, he gave high priority to economic history. Lewis's belief in the importance of economic history was well known. His famous article on unlimited supplies of labor had drawn heavily on the social and economic history of Britain. Some of his earliest and most widely appreciated publications dealt with the evolution of the European economy in the period between the two world wars. Finally, and most importantly, Lewis had come to believe that the underlying explanation of why the rich countries continued to outpace the poor countries economically was rooted in the evolution of the world economic system during the second half of the nineteenth century.

[26] Lewis to John P. Lewis, Dean of the Woodrow Wilson School, Princeton University, May 28, 1971, Dean of the Faculty W. Arthur Lewis Personnel File, Princeton University.
[27] Lewis to Prime Minister, Minister of Finance, Financial Secretary of Jamaica, and Arthur Brown, November 19, 1973, Lewis Papers, Box 1.
[28] Ibid.

In citing Lewis's achievements, the Nobel Prize committee singled out four publications: his 1954 article in the *Manchester School* on unlimited supplies of labor; *The Theory of Economic Growth*; *Aspects of Tropical Trade*; and *Growth and Fluctuations, 1870–1913*.[29] Lewis wrote the last two books while at Princeton, and they were squarely in the field of economic history, although they drew heavily on insights originally put forward in the 1954 article. Both were based on extensive work in European and North American trade statistics, most of which were included in the statistical tables of the book *Growth and Fluctuations*.

Lewis provided a preview of his research in the Wicksell Lectures, which he delivered in Stockholm in 1969 and which were published under the title *Aspects of Tropical Trade, 1883–1965*. What intrigued Lewis in this study, which was focused on the tropics, was "how rapidly tropical trade was growing in the period before the First World War." Even more perplexing was why these areas, which had entered into the world economy so quickly and seemingly so successfully, remained poor compared with the advanced, industrial states. His conclusion, which he had offered but had not elaborated in his 1954 article, was that the income of a man growing cocoa and earning one-tenth of the wage of a man making steel ingots was determined by the relative productivity in food production in their respective economies. Both the steelworker and the cocoa farmer had to be paid wages that would attract them away from the food-producing sector. In developed, industrial economies where an agricultural revolution had already occurred, this would be a high wage. Elsewhere, it would be a low wage.[30]

Lewis posed the same question of the causes of wealth and poverty even more sharply in his three Janeway lectures, delivered at Princeton University and published in 1978 under the title *The Evolution of the International Economic Order*. Although he regarded his next book, *Growth and Fluctuations, 1870–1913*, as his most important scholarly work, the Janeway Lectures, which drew upon all of the historical and statistical materials that *Growth and Fluctuations* highlighted, was unquestionably one of Lewis's most powerful and influential publications. The arguments were clear, often highly provocative; the reasoning was impeccable; and the supporting material kept to the bare minimum. Critics of Lewis who occasionally snipe that his only truly groundbreaking publication was his 1954 article on labor surpluses need to reread this short classic.

---

[29] "The Nobel Memorial Prize in Economics, 1979," *Scandinavian Journal of Economics*, vol. 82, no 1, 1980, pp. 59–61.

[30] W. Arthur Lewis, *Aspects of Tropical Trade, 1870–1965* (Stockholm, 1969), pp. 8ff.

Lewis's trolling through historical statistics had by now convinced him that the decisive moment in the evolution of the world economy had not occurred at the time of the Great Depression, as he had been led to believe during his undergraduate days. By letting his interest in economic history extend beyond Western Europe and North America, Lewis concluded that the moment when the world divided between the rich and poor took place roughly between 1870 and the outbreak of World War I.

While conceding that the British economy had surged ahead of other economies in the first half of the nineteenth century as a result of its industrial revolution, he noted that Britain's industrial successes were almost entirely self-generated and self-contained. British industrialization was based on local raw materials and a local market. Its worldwide impact was small because the volume of its foreign trade was still small. All of this changed, however, during what Lewis described as the second industrial revolution. The new industrializing states in Western Europe and North America (Britain, France, Germany, and the United States) now looked abroad for raw materials and markets. As a result, the whole of the world economy was confronted with a challenge. Countries could imitate the industrialization already underway in the economically advanced countries or they could trade with them. The choices that they made created the great historical divide, separating the industrial states from the raw material exporters.

Lewis's assertion that countries had a choice of whether to industrialize or trade with the industrial countries was provocative and problematical. In his view imitation was still relatively easy. The industrial machines of the period were simple, and the capital requirements small. Nor was colonization the reason that many did not industrialize, as some historians had argued, for the great era of colonialism followed, rather than preceded, decisions to industrialize or trade.

The crucial variable in Lewis's opinion was a prior or simultaneous agricultural revolution since in closed economies the size of the industrial sector was limited by agricultural productivity. Agriculture had to produce the surplus food and raw materials consumed in the industrial sectors, and it was only "the affluent state of the farmers that enables them to be a market for industrial products."[31] Here, Europe had the decisive advantage since it "had been creating a capitalist environment for at least a whole century. Thus, a whole new set of peoples, ideas, and institutions was established that did not exist in Asia or Africa or even, for the most part, in Latin America despite the close cul-

---

[31] W. Arthur Lewis, *The Evolution of the International Economic Order* (Princeton, 1978), pp. 9–10.

tural heritage."[32] In Europe, the prime movers were entrepreneurs. In Asia, they were landed classes, who with the opportunity to imitate Europe's industrial development "saw no reason to support the exigencies of a new industrial class."[33] They chose instead to grow wealthy through exporting raw materials and linking their economies to the developed economies by buying their manufactured products.

A second critical development took place in the late nineteenth century when nearly 50 million Europeans migrated to the temperate regions of the world and an equal number of East Asians and South Asians moved to the tropics. These massive streams of population took with them their differing levels of productivity, thus establishing the different terms of trade between the tropics and the temperate areas of the world. The major difference between the two areas was their divergent rates of agricultural productivity. Whereas in Britain the yield of wheat was sixteen hundred pounds per acre in 1900, in the tropics its equivalent in grain production was only seven hundred pounds. Areas that wished to attract European migrants had to offer income levels that exceeded those in Europe. In contrast, in the tropics, the income levels only had to exceed seven hundred pounds of grain per acre. The result was that the average wage in the tropics was one shilling per day in the 1880s compared with nine shillings in temperate regions.

Anyone familiar with Lewis's articles on unlimited supplies of labor would easily recognize the outlines of the 1954 essay. Lewis drew out the parallels by noting that "this analysis turns on the long-run infinite elasticity of the supply of labor to any one activity at prices determined by farmer productivity in Europe and Asia." Lewis was back to the old conundrum—why farmers in the tropics had to work so many hours to purchase the products made by factory workers. Coffee and steel exchanged at the prices that they did because European and North American food production was so much more efficient than Asian and African food production.

In his 1954 and 1958 articles on unlimited supplies of labor, Lewis had dealt at great length with closed domestic economies. His forays into economic history had convinced him that the closed economy did not hold the real key to wealth and poverty. In reality, at the end of the nineteenth century the world became an open economy and was likely to remain so, however hard the "de-linkers" tried to wall off their countries from world trade. The only solution to the economic problems of the tropics was a dramatic increase in the productivity of farmers in the food producing sectors. Alas, no matter, how hard and effi-

[32] Ibid., pp. 10–11.
[33] Ibid., p. 11.

ciently a Nigerian peanut farmer worked, he would receive no more than the value of seven hundred pounds of grain for his export until the Indian and Chinese reservoirs of labor had been exhausted. Lewis observed that "the factoral terms offered to the tropics . . . the opportunity to stay poor—at any rate until such time as the labor reservoirs of India and China might be exhausted."[34]

RETURNING TO ECONOMIC DEVELOPMENT

Although Lewis had devoted most of his research and writing to economic history in the 1970s, he was regularly pulled back to make observations on the area of research where he had made his first mark—economic development. Beginning in 1979, when he wrote an article on the occasion of the twenty-fifth anniversary of the publication of his essay on unlimited supplies of labor, he wrote a series of short pieces on the state of the field. The most important of these was his 1982 presidential address to the American Economic Association, later published in the profession's journal, the *American Economic Review*.

Commenting on the many developments in the rapidly evolving field of economic development proved to be no easy task, especially because it had borne the brunt of much criticism since its heyday. In the 1982 address, Lewis had to concede that the field of economic development was "in the doldrums after a couple of spirited decades, having been deserted by most American Ph.D. candidates though still of great interest to foreign students."[35] Nor did he succeed in quelling the storm of criticism, some of which was directed at his labor supply theory, let alone dispose of the more threatening complaint that development economics itself had led the less developed countries in the wrong directions.

The critics abounded, coming at the development economists from the left and the right. Lewis had little patience with the leftist assault. Its main advocates were dependency theorists, whose main prescription, the rupture of relations with the developed world, Lewis saw as nothing short of an invitation to economic disaster. To be sure, many

---

[34] Ibid., p. 19.

[35] W. Arthur Lewis, "The State of Development Theory," *American Economic Review*, vol. 74, no. 1, March 1984, p. 1. Lewis's other writings on development in this period, in addition to the 1979 article published in *The Manchester School* and discussed in chapter 3, were "What Have We Learned from Development?" published by the Caribbean Development Bank as a mimeograph in 1985 and reprinted in Patrick A. M. Emmanuel, ed., *Sir William Arthur Lewis Collected Papers, 1941–1988* (Barbados, 1994), vol. 3, pp. 2073–81, and "The Roots of Development Theory," in *The Handbook of Development Economics*, ed. H. Chenery and T. N. Srinivasan (Amsterdam, 1988), vol. 1, pp. 28–37.

dependency theorists held Lewis personally responsible for having promoted what they called "industrialization by invitation," thereby they believed producing greater dependence of third-world countries on the developed parts of the world. Lewis did not deny that many newly independent countries had saddled themselves with heavy foreign debts and had launched development programs that heightened their dependence on the outside world. But these failures had nothing to do with his advice. They came about because politicians like Nkrumah in Ghana and the West Indian nationalist elites had spurned sound economic formulas, preferring showy projects that promised short-run political gains.

Lewis took more seriously the attacks from the right, many of which came from respected professional economists. The nub of their complaints was that Lewis and the first generation of development economists had gone too far in unmooring development economics from the mainstream. The British economist P. T. Bauer had been the earliest to mount this criticism, and with the passage of time and the seeming failure of third-world development projects Bauer had won many other economists over to his views. Bauer and the other critics asserted that these first practitioners of development economics had exaggerated the beneficial role of governments and failed to understand the power of free markets and prices.

Much of the criticism came, not unexpectedly, from the economics department of the University of Chicago, a bastion of free market economics. From there, Theodore Schultz continued to carp at Lewis's ideas on the zero marginal productivity of labor. The Chicago economist, however, who wrote the most passionately and critically about the field of development economics from a free market and monetarist point of view was Lewis's former colleague at the University of Manchester, Harry Johnson. Johnson had moved to Chicago in the early 1960s and had steadily sought to counter the influence of Keynesian thought among professional economists. Arguing that Keynes was an "opportunist," really not much more than "a brilliant applied theorist," whose great work, *The General Theory*, was the very "apotheosis of opportunism," Johnson believed that Keynes's greatest sin was his influence on development economists. Keynes had encouraged this group of analysts to believe that increasing the rate of fixed capital through governmental interventions in the economy was the essential ingredient in economic growth.[36]

Although Johnson made no references to Lewis in his book, *The Shadow of Keynes*, it is hard to believe that Johnson's strictures against

---

[36] Elizabeth S. Johnson and Harry G. Johnson, *The Shadow of Keynes: Understanding Keynes, Cambridge, and Keynesian Economics* (Oxford, 1978), pp. 211–12.

the developmentalists were not directed straight at Lewis. In highly evocative language, Johnson dismissed the notion of disguised unemployment. "The notion that there exist masses of 'disguised unemployed' people leads easily into the idea that 'development' involves merely the mobilization and transfer of these presumably costless productive resources into economic activities, primarily investment or industrial production, at an obvious and virtually costless economic gain. What is required to realize this gain, gratifyingly enough, is merely cleverness on the part of the economist in outwitting the stupidity of the competitive system and determination by the political leaders in generating the social will needed to implement the appropriate economic policies."[37] These theories led development economists to "the faith that capital accumulation in the form of planned industrialization would quickly result in the closing of the gap between the poor or less developed countries and the rich or advanced countries."[38]

Other critics raised more specific questions about certain aspects of the Lewis model. Bent Hansen of the economics department at the University of California, Berkeley, reported that his studies of rural Egypt did not reveal surplus labor and disguised unemployment. If Egypt, with its huge population, did not fit the model, what countries did?[39] Dale Jorgenson, also of the economics department at Berkeley, accepted the underlying notions of unlimited supplies of labor but upbraided Lewis for claiming that this idea was "inconsistent with standard economic theory." Jorgenson regarded Lewis's statement about zero and negative labor productivity as "a red herring, for which I am afraid you must bear some responsibility."[40] Nearly everyone was skeptical of Lewis's claim that economic growth would follow nearly automatically once countries got their savings and investment rates up to 15 or even 20 percent. Nor were they convinced by Lewis's assertion that he was not arguing that "investment is the sole contributor to growth but [that] it is highly correlated with growth and may serve as a proxy for the forces propelling the economy."[41]

By the 1970s and 1980s, much of the work being done on economic growth and developing economies no longer cited Lewis's earlier contributions. In part because his earlier studies were not rigorously math-

---

[37] Ibid., p. 229.

[38] Ibid., p. 233.

[39] Bent Hansen, Department of Economics, University of California, Berkeley, to Lewis, January 27, 1969, Lewis Papers, Box 5.

[40] Dale Jorgenson, Department of Economics, University of California, Berkeley, to Lewis, January 23, 1969, Lewis Papers, Box 7.

[41] W. Arthur Lewis, "The State of Development Theory," *American Economic Review*, vol. 74, no. 1, March 1984, p. 7.

ematical, he suffered the fate of many of the scholars of this generation. Their contributions were ignored. Yet even so, a great deal of the work being done on economic growth, often though not exclusively, within the developed parts of the world, implicitly challenged Lewis's understanding of the crucial factors for attaining economic progress. Robert Barro claimed that economic growth rates did not correlate with cheap labor. On the contrary, poor countries did not have faster economic growth rates than rich countries and did not attract the substantial amounts of capital and technology that the Lewis model predicted. Barro, Robert Lucas, and Paul Romer all came to an identical conclusion that contradicted some of the formulas of economic development that had prevailed in the 1950s and 1960s. Economic growth depended on high levels of human capital formation, which "makes it easier for a country to absorb the new products or the new ideas that have been discovered elsewhere."[42]

An attack on the field of development economics, though not directly on Lewis, came from a different corner. The theorists of the new institutional economics, drawing inspiration from the writings of Ronald Coase and Douglass North, argued that development economists had failed to pay sufficient attention to the institutional components essential to economic growth. In the words of Robert Bates, a political scientist, new institutional economics "seeks to apply to non-market institutions the same forms of reasoning that neo-classical economics has applied to the analysis of markets."[43] To these political scientists and economists sustained economic development required the establishment of rights to private property and the creation of a society governed by laws rather than the whims of ruling elites.

Lewis was entirely comfortable with the notion that economic growth must occur in a supportive institutional context. His book *The Theory of Economic Growth* devoted many pages to institutions. In addition, *Politics in West Africa* was an indictment of the West African political institutions, which the political elites had used not to promote economic progress but to enhance their power and wealth at the expense of the rank and file of the population.

Lewis had at least an indirect connection with the new institutional economics through Ronald Coase. Both Lewis and Coase had been stu-

---

[42] Robert J. Barro, "Economic Growth in a Cross Section of Countries," *Quarterly Journal of Economics*, vol. 106, no. 2, May 1991, p. 406. For more on this line of reasoning, see also Robert E. Lucas, "On the Mechanics of Economic Development," *Journal of Monetary Economics*, vol. 22, July 1988, pp. 3–42.

[43] Robert H. Bates, "Social Dilemmas and Rational Individuals: An Assessment of the New Institutionalism," in *The New Institutional Economics and Third World Development*, ed. John Harriss, Jane Hunter, and Colin M. Lewis (London, 1995), p. 27.

dents of Arnold Plant, and though both men had the utmost respect for Plant as a teacher, both reacted critically to his stress on the virtues of a laissez-faire and free market economy. Lewis took his reservations in the direction of economic planning and state intervention. Coase pursued the place of noneconomic institutions, like legal systems and private property arrangements, in his research and writings. In his 1991 acceptance speech for the Nobel Prize in economics, Coase said that he found his way to institutional economics when he began to question the free market emphasis that Arnold Plant had stressed in his teaching of economics and that was drawn from one of the standard tenets of laissez-faire economics. This principle, that "the normal economic system works itself," had also worried Lewis.[44] If this were the case, Coase wondered, why did business firms exist? He concluded that markets were not free but had their own costs, which institutions like the business firm, the legal system, and the monetary system discharged. Economies, especially developing economies, did not fail because their economic plans were misconceived. They faltered because countries lacked the appropriate institutional infrastructure of well-run business firms and legal systems based on private property rights, without which private sector and business communities could not function effectively.

Lewis's reflections during the 1980s on the field of development economics did not truly deal with the new institutional economics, nor did they grapple with the rush of criticisms that now surrounded the subject in general and his writings specifically. In his 1982 address as president of the American Economic Association, he reasserted the validity of two-sector models, insisting that development economics was a distinct subfield in the discipline of economics, thus disputing the contention of many that standard neoclassical analytical tools and a one-sector model sufficed for understanding all economic systems. The poorer countries of the world, by which he meant those with less than 1980 U.S.$2,000 per head, "differ in structure or behavior in ways that require different concepts or tools to understand their functioning." These differences did not amount, however, to an "unbridgeable gap between development economics and the economies of the developed any more than a pediatrician would claim that geriatrics is an unrelated body of knowledge." The basic tools in any economist's tool kit, namely supply and demand and the quantity theory of money, "will carry you a long ways in any economic analysis." But the two fields had their own methods, and in this respect "development analysis can-

---

[44] R. H. Coase, "The Institutional Structure of Production," *American Economic Review*, vol. 82, no. 4, September 1992, p. 715.

not leave out of their calculation ... the government's behavior." Hence development economists must arm themselves with a knowledge of political science and anthropology if they hope to succeed.[45]

As for the other more specific criticism of his original model and its later elaborations—an overemphasis on savings and investment, inattention to bottlenecks between the subsistence and capitalist sectors, and disregard for the place of education and human capital in growth—he could easily reply that a careful reading of the full corpus of his writings showed that he was fully aware of these factors. More importantly, he claimed that the evolution of the world economy from World War II to the mid-1970s had been an exceptional period of economic growth for the less developed countries. This was so because these nations had received ample foreign financial and technical assistance and had adopted the economic policies that he and other development economists had favored. He reminded the critics that the economic growth rates and the quality of living indices for less developed countries had been at record levels for the three decades after World War II, despite population growth rates of 3 percent per year in most of these countries. Never before had these countries experienced such rapid economic growth.[46]

In 1979 Lewis shared the Nobel Prize in economics with Theodore Schultz. In nominating Lewis for the award, his supporters used the opportunity to reflect on his stature and accomplishments. John P. Lewis, the dean of the Woodrow Wilson School. and one of his chief advocates, initiated the campaign in 1974, asserting in a letter to the Nobel committee that "in the field of development economics, no one has made such seminal contributions to the central theory of the subject as Sir Arthur." He concluded by observing that "his naming would be doubly appropriate since he is clearly the greatest of the first generation of modern development economists who remains a

[45] W. Arthur Lewis, "The State of Development Theory," *American Economic Review*, vol. 74, no. 1, March 1984, pp 1–10.

[46] A brief but useful statement of this perspective can be found in Lewis's article "What Have We Learned from Development?" I have found especially helpful for understanding the criticisms of the ideas of development economics the following books: William Easterly, *The Elusive Quest for Modernity: Economists' Adventures and Misadventures in the Tropics* (Cambridge, Mass., 2001); William Easterly, "*The Ghost of the Financing Gap: How the Harrod-Domar Growth Model Still Haunts Development Economics*," Policy Research Paper Working Paper 1807 (The World Bank, Washington, D.C., 1997); John Toye, *Dilemmas of Development: Revolutions on the Counter-revolution in Development Theory and Policy* (Oxford, 1987); and Arturo Escobar, *Encountering Development: The Making and Unmaking of the Third World* (Princeton, 1995).

citizen of a developing country."[47] He also sent a letter to Jan Tinbergen hoping to get "the endorsement of the first laureate in economics."[48] Dean Donald Stokes continued the campaign, remarking in a follow-up letter to the Nobel committee that "Sir Arthur Lewis is quite simply the founder of economic development as a serious subdiscipline of economics."[49]

Lewis retired from the faculty of Princeton University at the end of the academic year 1982–83, at the age of sixty-eight. He had spent almost the entirety of his adult life working in universities, during which he had acquired almost a reverence for the role that higher education played in promoting progressive social change and preserving and extending knowledge. Even when Lewis served as Ghana's chief economic adviser or when he became deputy director of the United Nations Special Fund or when he served as president of the Caribbean Development Bank, he was either on leave of absence from a university or committed to moving to a new university. It is hardly a surprise, then, that his writings and especially his speeches about the place of higher education in creating more humane and civilized societies revealed the best of Lewis's thinking and displayed his underlying humanity. The most eloquent of these speeches was undeniably the one that he made in 1967 when he was installed as the new the chancellor of the University of Guyana.

Lewis began his remarks by stressing the economic gains from education, asserting that the most recent studies on economic development had identified knowledge as the single most important factor in raising human productivity. "Poverty is not primarily due to people not working hard enough, or to inadequate land, or even to inadequate capital. It is primarily due to inadequate knowledge and primitive techniques which keep output per head low." But it did not take long for the Princeton professor to become rhapsodic about the place of colleges and universities in social transformation. "The university recognizes only excellence.... But excellence is achieved not only from intellect; it derives even more from character. As the old saying goes,

---

[47] John P. Lewis, Dean of the Woodrow Wilson School, Princeton University, to the Prize Committee for Economic Sciences, Royal Academy of Sciences, Stockholm, January 3, 1974, W. Arthur Lewis Personnel File, Woodrow Wilson School, Princeton University.

[48] John P. Lewis, Dean of the Woodrow Wilson School, Princeton University to Jan Tinbergen, January 3, 1974, W. Arthur Lewis Personnel File, Woodrow Wilson School, Princeton University.

[49] This formed an attachment to the salary recommendation form submitted by Donald Stokes, Dean of the Woodrow Wilson School, Princeton University, to the Dean of the Faculty, February 5, 1976, W. Arthur Lewis Personnel File, Woodrow Wilson School, Princeton University.

'genius is an infinite capacity for taking pains.' To achieve excellence, one must have self-discipline; to practice the same thing over and over again, while others are enjoying themselves; to push oneself from the easy part to the hard part; to listen to criticism and use it; to reject one's own work and try again. Only the humble achieve excellence, since only the humble can learn. . . . In the university we build character, no less than brain, since brain without character achieves nothing."

Lewis went on, asserting that the universities were not just the repositories of knowledge. They were civilization's most liberal institution since here commitment to excellence superseded concerns about class, race, and language. The lives of early men and women, living in caves, "were dominated by fear—fear of the elements, of drought and flood and fire; fear of other animals; and fear of other men, who wandered around in families, or tribes ready to exterminate each other." What brought beings out of this primitive state was the "handing down from generation to generation knowledge of two sets of principles, those relating to controlling nature, which we call science, and principles relating to controlling human behavior, which we call ethics." Those who have preserved this knowledge and added to it were the men and women associated with learning and ultimately with universities and colleges, who "are like a thin veneer, easily rubbed off by mass hatreds and ignorance."[50]

---

[50] Lewis originally delivered the speech at his installation ceremony at the University of Guyana on January 25, 1967, but I have quoted from a fuller version of these remarks that he wrote for *University: A Princeton Quarterly*, vol. 35, Winter 1967–68, pp. 20–23.

CONCLUSION

W. ARTHUR LEWIS DIED ON June 15, 1991, at his summer home in Barbados and was laid to rest in a state funeral on the island of St. Lucia, where he had been born some seventy-six years earlier. Lewis's death led to an outpouring of obituary notices and eulogies in newspapers and magazines all over the world. Most lacked an intimate knowledge of this intensely private man and merely recited his many accomplishments. These were, of course, extraordinary. Even so, not many singled out one of the most important set of attainments: the racial breakthroughs that he achieved in his lifetime and that in hindsight appear to be among his most significant accomplishments, neglected presumably because writers were uncomfortable calling attention to issues of race. But Lewis was, in fact, the first person of African descent to teach at the London School of Economics, the first to hold a named professorship in a British university, the first vice-chancellor of the University of the West Indies, the first black faculty member at Princeton University, and the first individual of African descent, other than those who won the award for contributions to literature and world peace, to win a Nobel Prize. Perhaps the authors of the obituary notices were not aware of these facts. More likely, they preferred to ignore the obvious implications of long-standing racial discrimination that existed in British and American institutions.

Some obituaries, however, written by individuals who knew Lewis as a friend and a colleague, offered telling insights into the man. Those that were written by colleagues from London and Manchester days described a young man of exceptional talent who challenged powerful authorities and was not afraid to express his anger. The anonymous author of the obituary notice in the *Times* wrote that Lewis took an "unpretentious, sensible, and cool approach to a contentious, highly politicised, and often needlessly obscure discipline [that] was widely admired. Lewis was a man like his writing, though sometimes prickly and awkward as well."[1] In another unsigned obituary, the writer noted that Lewis was "short-tempered and impatient in his personal relations; he had no time for fools or for pretentious dogmatists. But he was a kindly and sympathetic teacher to responsive students, a lucid

---

[1] *The Times*, June 17, 1991.

exponent of his economic views, and a sharp debater who did not hesitate to face squarely up to his critics."[2]

His Princeton colleagues seemed to have known a different Lewis. They extolled his gentleness and equipoise. President William Bowen, who had known Lewis for many years, first as a colleague in the economics department and the Woodrow Wilson School and then as president of Princeton, wrote movingly of his friend. While admitting to having been in awe of Lewis when the West Indian economist first arrived in Princeton, even suffering from a slight case of hero worship, Bowen soon learned to admire Lewis as a caring human being. What impressed Bowen was Lewis's decency and dignity, his respect for others, his sense of fair play, and his constant good cheer. Bowen concluded his remarks, observing that "Arthur was a supremely civilized man, quietly, thoughtfully passionate."[3] Bowen and others on the American side of the Atlantic stressed Lewis's kindliness and underscored the support that he provided to friends, colleagues, and students.

If, perchance, one might have thought that Lewis had undergone a personality change or perhaps that the experiences in Ghana and the West Indies had changed Lewis from a young firebrand to a deeply conservative, even perhaps politically disillusioned, individual, a perusal of the obituaries from West Indian friends, who had known him longest and through all of his experiences, would have dispelled this notion. Neville Nicholls, one of Lewis's successors as president of the Caribbean Development Bank, collected the tributes paid to Lewis from friends and colleagues in the West Indies to present them to his widow, Gladys, on the occasion of the bank's celebration of its founder's life. The comments highlighted Lewis's lifelong commitment to a single goal. His life's purpose was to overcome the marginalization of human beings wherever it appeared, whether in racial, political, cultural, or economic spheres. If in London, he railed against the conservatism of the Colonial Office and objected to professional and day-to-day forms of racial discrimination, while later he spoke against American black power advocates, this was not because he had changed his mind. He was, in truth, continuing to pursue his lifetime goal of combating racial prejudice and in ways that were entirely consistent. Since his days growing up on the island of St. Lucia and studying at the London School of Economics, he had focused his writings, research, teaching, and public service on three critical issues: racial justice, end of empire, and improved standards of living for the less

---

[2] *The Annual Obituary*, 1991, p. 352.

[3] I am indebted to former Princeton president William G. Bowen for supplying me with a copy of his remarks on that occasion.

well off. The instrumentality to accomplish these goals became the field of economics, in large part, as he so often reminded people, because he was unable to pursue what had once seemed to him more attractive occupations.

Lewis would never have suggested that his life should be measured by the successes that he had in advancing these goals, but there is much to be said for concluding this study by considering the methods that Lewis favored and the achievements that he realized in the three arenas that he held so high: eradicating racial injustice, bringing empires to a close, and promoting worldwide economic progress.

As Karl Marx observed, human beings make history, but not always in ways that they intended. They also observe history, and their observations, especially when made by men and women caught up in the historical processes of change, seeking both to direct these developments and to understand them, are the grist of historical research. William Arthur Lewis tried to bring about change, but as his personal papers make eminently clear, he was also an astute witness to the historical transformations of this epoch.

Writing in 1900, W.E.B. DuBois famously predicted that race would be the decisive issue of the twentieth century. Lewis might well have agreed, but he was certain that racial prejudice did not exist in a vacuum; it was buttressed by imperial subjugation and economic backwardness. There could be no enduring racial justice for the colonized and impoverished peoples of Africa, Asia, and Latin America if they did not succeed in ending colonial rule and achieving economic development. Indeed, virtually all of Lewis's writings and actions were intended to find solutions to the problems that race and poverty posed to the colonized parts of the world. Naturally, Lewis had personal reasons for his sensitivity to the linkage between racial discrimination and economic opportunity. At critical moments in his early career, racial and other barriers had closed off desirable occupational opportunities for him. When he left the West Indies to study in Britain, he intended to return in a capacity that would enable him to serve the islands. Even when the Colonial Office rejected his application to become a West Indian colonial administrator and he returned to the London School of Economics to work for a Ph.D. in economics, he did not set aside his eagerness to find practical solutions to the problems of race and poverty or suppress his ambition to return to the West Indies in a useful capacity. These goals were integral to his growing up on the island of St. Lucia.

Judging by his later writings and correspondence, however, he became less outraged by issues of race than he was during the early years in Britain. Lewis sometimes expressed amusement later in his life at how radical he had been on social and political issues in his youth and how time had modified his positions. He certainly had the question of race in mind when he made this remark. This is not to suggest that Lewis left the issues of race behind once he had made his mark as a respected economist and a consultant, for he did not. Nor is it surprising that he when he spoke and wrote about race and racial discrimination, later as well as earlier in his life, he did so with passion. As his account of his travels on the European continent revealed, his first exposure to the underlying racism of British society was deeply traumatic. Coping with the racial undertones of British society, however, did not keep Lewis from succeeding in his studies or deter him from making his mark academically or advising those very same individuals who had chosen not to offer him a position in the British colonial service. He also challenged what seemed to be the accepted premise of the British elite that the world should be dominated by people of European descent. Yet, although he fought with the British establishment, he was proud to accept a knighthood for his contributions as vice-chancellor of the University of the West Indies. He migrated to the United States and spent more of his life in America than anywhere else. But when asked why he had not chosen to become an American citizen, he asked his questioner why he would want to accept the fate of black Americans.[4]

Lewis's chief racial concern throughout his life was insuring equal employment opportunities for blacks and combating what he regarded as the widespread racial intolerance in the white world. He was especially vigilant about employment prospects for blacks after he moved to the United States in 1963, when he became a professor of economics at Princeton University. He was an active member of the NAACP. He did not hesitate to write about race and economics, claiming that the real key to economic betterment for the black community in America was not equal pay for equal work (though this was clearly essential) but a proportionate number of elite jobs for black Americans. The great disadvantage that black Americans suffered was that the African American community had a lower percentage of the high-paying, skilled, and powerful jobs in America and a disproportionately high number of the low-paying, unskilled positions. Believing that access to the best education was critical to economic advancement, Lewis strove to identify black talent and to bring young and talented African Americans to the attention of fellowship-granting foundations. He served with enthusiasm on the board of the National Humanities Cen-

[4] I am indebted to Lawrence Stone, late of the Princeton University history department, and his wife, Jeanne, for this observation. They were close friends of the Lewises and greatly encouraged me to undertake this study.

ter of North Carolina and made special efforts to ensure that young black scholars gained fellowships there.

Lewis found himself much less sympathetic, however, to the efforts in higher education to advance blacks through racial quotas and to create what he feared were likely to become separatist-leaning black studies programs. He believed that positions should be open to persons of talent and assumed that race should play no role in hiring and teaching decisions. This stance sometimes put him at variance with more radical black academics and was a prime reason for his comment on how radical he had been in his youth in comparison with later life. In fact, he had not changed his point of view on race at all. He rejected discrimination in any form, but was uncomfortable with the more radical perspectives that favored quotas and set-asides, even if employed temporarily and justified on the basis of past discrimination.

Over a lifetime of great scholarly productivity, Lewis ventured into print on issues of race only occasionally. In his early years, when discrimination blocked his career prospects, he was quite outspoken in complaint of the attitudes of many whites, especially the British ruling classes. Later, however, as race became a more politicized issue and arguments raged over the best ways to eradicate race prejudice and promote the economic, political, and social advancement of blacks, Lewis's views took on a more conservative tinge. Throughout his life, Lewis preferred to work from within. At no time was this preference more clearly revealed than during the radical decade of the 1960s. Certainly, Lewis never tolerated the denial of civil and political rights to the black population, but his emphasis on the mastery of the hard scientific and social science subjects in the university and elsewhere and his rejection of black power separatism and what he regarded as its companion, black studies programs, demonstrated his preference for gradualism and reform over radical change.

Development economics was the academic interest in which Lewis made his most lasting contributions, and it was as a development economist that he came to prominence after World War II. Not surprisingly, since the field focused on promoting economic development in the poorer, often formerly colonized regions of the world, this subdiscipline of economics attracted a remarkable cadre of scholars of diverse nationalities and backgrounds. Its founders included an Argentine scholar (Raúl Prebisch), a Swede (Gunnar Myrdal), several Eastern Europeans (Paul Rosenstein-Rodan and Albert Hirschman), many Indians, as well as numerous Americans and Western Europeans. Among the top tier of development economists, Lewis was the only individual of African descent—a fact that undoubtedly made him attractive to official organizations like the British Colonial Office and the United Nations who were sensitive to geographical and racial representation when selecting consultants.

Development economics built upon the writings of John Maynard Keynes, who had argued that economies, even highly developed ones, could settle into a state of low-level economic equilibrium, characterized by high unemployment and low investment rates. Like Keynes, the development economists also believed that only an activist state, using employment-generating state programs, could jolt such an economy into sustained growth. They, too, latched on to Keynes's faith in the powers of the state to stimulate economic progress and promote the efficient use of economic resources.

Lewis's most significant contributions to this new field were his 1954 article on unlimited supplies of labor and his 1955 book, *The Theory of Economic Growth*. They epitomized the optimism of this period and reflected a faith in newly independent countries. In Lewis's view, developing economies, rightly guided, could achieve dramatic economic progress. His own maxims for how to achieve economic development were consistently cited, if often improperly practiced, in the policies that rulers of decolonizing territories in Asia and Africa adopted in their programs. For example, Lewis's article on unlimited supplies of labor suggested that a seeming disadvantage of less developed societies—the presence of large numbers of unskilled workers in the agricultural sector—could become an advantage if this very same unskilled, largely redundant agrarian workforce were put to work in an expanding industrial sector. *The Theory of Economic Growth* went even further, providing a full blueprint of the diverse prerequisites for increasing per capita output. It cautioned that economic growth demanded societal-wide transformations in cultural values, family organization, and commitment to a work ethos as well as the standard economic prerequisites of high levels of savings and investment and precise government planning.

Nonetheless, by 1979, when Lewis received the Nobel Prize in economics, the field of development economics had already begun to lose its luster. The high point had surely been the decade of the 1960s, when the development economists had joined with officials from the decolonizing empires, international organizations like the World Bank and the International Monetary Fund, and nationalist politicians to chart out economic programs for the newly independent countries of Asia and Africa. Yet, by the 1970s, much of this had changed. The economic miracles that some had hoped for were few and far between. None had occurred in Africa. Most of the economic successes were to be found in East and Southeast Asia, where much more highly capitalist and outwardly oriented programs had proved more effective than had the protectionist, centrally planned, import-substitution industrialization approaches favored by many development economists. The economic results of five-year plans, "big pushes," and enforced high savings and investment rates had not produced rapid economic growth. In many parts of Africa large segments of the population were materially no better off than they had been at the time of independence. Disillusionment was widespread; many blamed the failings on the economists.

No doubt, there is a considerable degree of justification in these criticisms. Development economics had embraced unreasonable aspirations. Its practitioners often failed to realize that economic plans could not be drawn up in a social and political vacuum. This failure was most visible in the dealings that development experts had with political elites, whom the economists, including Lewis in Ghana, expected to defer to them on economic matters. Lewis even sought to extract (and believed that he had extracted) a promise from Nkrumah not to permit political considerations to interfere with economic decisions. Nor were most development economists prepared to pay much attention to public opinion or the short-run desires of the common people.

To an extent, Lewis was an exception in this area. He had opposed some of the development schemes that the Colonial Office favored in tropical Africa, arguing that the funds should be expended on mass education, including the training of adult men and women for agricultural and industrial projects, rather than used to pay the salaries of high-powered foreign technicians. But in Ghana, he endorsed the government's program to fix the local price offered to cocoa farmers well below the world market price so that these funds could be set aside for development projects. His only reservation was a political one. As long as the politicians were comfortable that the population would not balk at these low prices, he favored them. Of course, he opposed Nkrumah's showy building projects, believing that the monies saved through paying cocoa farmers prices that were lower than the world price should be plowed back into the Ghanaian economy in the form of filtered water, more schools, and better roads so as to ameliorate the lives of the ordinary people.

In spite of mounting criticisms, Lewis remained committed to the ideas that he had first enunciated in the mid-1950s in his unlimited labor supplies article and *The Theory of Economic Growth*. In the 1960s and 1970s, he turned to economic history and found additional proofs for his labor surplus arguments. His researches into the history of the world economy convinced him that the labor surpluses of the third world and the high agricultural productivity in Western Europe and North America explained why some nations became rich and others stayed poor. To the criticism that his theory of economic growth had placed too great an emphasis on high savings and investment rates and that he had not paid enough attention to human capital, he responded with a request that his critics reread *The Theory of Economic Growth*. Of one aspect in his theory he was certain, that developing economies required economic tools of analysis different from developed economies. He had elaborated this idea when he propounded the notion that many economies were best analyzed as if they had two sectors. This dual-sector model of economies stressed that there were developed and less developed sectors in all economies, but that this feature was particularly true of underdeveloped economies. While conceding that he may have overstated his case for the big differences that separated developed and less developed economies and also agreeing that standard tools of economic analysis applied in both, his analogy between doctors who specialize in treating the illnesses of aging and those who deal with infants was persuasive. Many professional economists still associate the dual-sector model with Lewis and regard it as his most significant contribution to economic analysis.

Ghana was to be the proving ground for Lewis's ideas on development. His fourteen-month stint there as Nkrumah's chief economic adviser hardly turned out as he had hoped. He went to West Africa fired with enthusiasm about the country's economic prospects and confident in his knowledge of the country and its economic needs and potential. He had drafted the country's blueprint for industrialization in 1953 and was well known to its nationalist leadership. He viewed Nkrumah as just the right kind of populist nationalist leader who could inspire his followers to transform their lives and the country. Yet in less than a year, the Ghanaian prime minister had shunted his chief economic adviser aside, and Lewis was preparing an unpublicized exit from the country.

Since then, scholars have been far from kind to Lewis in his role as economic adviser to the Ghanaian government. Although only a few have held him primarily responsible for Ghana's economic failures, most have lumped him together with other economic consultants and Ghanaian government officials as the individuals responsible for leading a country with sound economic foundations to the edge of bankruptcy within the first decade of its independent political existence. Hardly a critic, however, has spared Kwame Nkrumah himself, and the Lewis Papers, along with copious records from the Ghanaian national archives, the British Commonwealth Office, the United States State Department, the World Bank and the International Monetary Fund make clear that the young Ghanaian nationalist leadership, at all times spurred onward by the ambitions of its preeminent figure, opted for grandiose economic projects in the face of the more restrained advice of their chief economic advisers.

Nkrumah's tendency to override economic advice grew bolder and bolder even as Ghana's economic situation became more precarious. The first evidence of his penchant for challenging expert economic opinion occurred over the First Five-Year Plan when he balked at Lewis's pleas to remove the showy parts of the plan from the final scheme. Nkrumah reminded Lewis that the decisions that political leaders made had political as well as economic consequences and that in this case he could not accept Lewis's proposals. By the time that the Ghanaians had substituted the seven-year plan for Lewis's five-year plan the opinions of economists of every political persuasion, including those from the Communist world, were being subordinated to the wishes of the Ghanaian president. Perhaps, by then, Nkrumah was more interested in political patronage than in promoting economic growth, though the documents are silent on this matter. Finally, the Volta River project, so deeply embedded in the psyche of Nkrumah and so closely associated with his sense of how economic transformations were to be achieved, took precedence over other projects. Alas, only the politics of the Cold War allowed Nkrumah to negotiate an agreement with the Americans and the World Bank to finance a scheme that virtually every single economist of any standing regarded as financially dubious.

The last phase of Lewis's public career should have been triumphant. Lewis had always wanted to return to the West Indies, and what better arrangement could he hope to have than to be the principal and then the vice-chancellor of the University of the West Indies. Although Lewis worried that he did not have the temperament to be an administrator, he had been heavily and successfully involved in academic administration while on the faculty at the University of Manchester. His commitment to higher education and to strengthening the University of the West Indies was well known. Here, too, however, he ran afoul of politics and politicians. The University of the West Indies was the premier institution of the British West Indies. Its future was closely connected to plans for the political and economic federation of the islands of the West Indies, a goal that Lewis had espoused from his student days in London. Not only did the University of the West Indies attract its students from all over the islands, but the island governments contributed to its finances.

Lewis strengthened and expanded the university. But try as he did, he could not preserve the political federation of the British West Indies, which was on the political horizon when he became principal of University College in 1959 but was in tatters when he left for the United States in 1963. Lewis blamed the West Indian politicians, believing that they, like Nkrumah, placed their own careers and the narrow interests of their island populations above the common good.

The West Indies was a microcosm of Lewis's life and a fitting climax to the public part of his career. As he so often reminded his readers and friends, he saw himself as a child of the Enlightenment. By this he meant that he believed in the power of reason and rational discourse, enabling men and women to fathom the laws of the universe, including those that dictated the operations of an economic system, and to use this understanding to improve their lives. Armed with this knowledge, expert advisers, like himself, could lay out projects for promoting economic development, build modern universities, create useful political federations, and persuade political leaders to use their influence with the population to implement these schemes. Lewis chose to work with political elites, from within, not merely because he saw little virtue in radical political and economic proposals, like Marxism or right-wing authoritarianism, but because he was confident that people in power would listen to reason and strive to implement programs that would yield economic obvious benefits. Often, this trait led him to underestimate political pressures and to demand too much of the politicians. It inevitably put him at odds with powerful individuals. In the 1940s and early 1950s, he collided with officials at the British Colonial Office. After that, he battled with Kwame Nkrumah, and finally he struggled with West Indian politicians. In all three of these cases, he ended his relationship with the powerful by resigning. His resignation in 1963 left him physically exhausted, but eager to resume an academic career, in which he expected to make further scholarly contributions. Princeton proved an ideal setting, and his ultimate accolade, the award of the Nobel Prize in economics, was a fitting tribute to a life of scholarship and public service.

Bibliography

PRIMARY SOURCES

Archives and Papers

Records of the British Colonial Office at the Public Record Office in London, especially those pertaining to the Gold Coast, the West Indies, the Colonial Economic Advisory Committee, the Colonial Economic and Development Council, the Colonial Development Corporation, the Colonial Research Council, the Colonial Advisory Committee on Education, and the League of Coloured Peoples.

Records of the Dominions Office and the Foreign Office mainly relating to Ghana at the Public Record Office in London.

Records of the Treasury and the Board of Trade at the Public Record Office in London.

Records of the Bank of England in London, relating to Ghana.

Records of the United States Department of State at the United States Archives in Maryland pertaining to the Gold Coast/Ghana and the West Indies.

Records of the International Bank for Reconstruction and Development in Washington, D.C., pertaining to the Gold Coast/Ghana.

Records of the International Monetary Fund pertaining to Ghana.

Records of the National Archives of Ghana in Accra, Ghana, especially discussions of the Council of Ministers during the Nkrumah years.

Records of the University College of the West Indies and the University of the West Indies covering the years 1959 to 1963, when Lewis was principal and then vice-chancellor, housed at the university campus in Mona, Jamaica.

Papers at the Colonial Research Project at Rhodes House Library, Oxford University, especially the papers of Arthur Creech Jones and the papers of the Fabian Colonial Bureau.

Papers of W. Arthur Lewis at the Mudd Library, Princeton University.

Archives of the London School of Economics at the Library of the London School of Economics, London.

Archives of the government of St. Lucia on the island of St. Lucia.

Archives and personnel files at Princeton University, relating to Lewis's activities in the Department of Economics and the Woodrow Wilson School.

Archives of the University of Manchester, relating to Lewis's career there in the Faculty of Economics and Social Studies.

The Writings of W. Arthur Lewis

There are excellent bibliographies of the writings of W. Arthur Lewis in Mark Gersovitz, editor, *Selected Economic Writings of W. Arthur Lewis* (New York, 1983) and in the special edition of *Social and Economic Studies* devoted to the life and writings of Lewis, vol. 29, no. 4, 1980, compiled by Audine Wilkinson, pp. 5–15.

The most comprehensive bibliographies of the works by and about Lewis are those compiled by Audine Wilkinson, "Sir William Arthur Lewis: A Bibliographical Portrait," and the bibliographies in the three volumes of Lewis's collected papers, edited by Patrick A. M. Emmanuel, *Sir William Arthur Lewis, Collected Papers, 1941–1988* (Barbados, 1994). This collection is quite comprehensive and includes many essays written by Lewis but difficult to locate. I am indebted to Andrew Downes, Professor of Economics at the University of the West Indies, Cave Hill campus, Barbados, who sent me the typescript of the Audine Wilkinson manuscript, which was a 1996 updated version.

BOOKS AND PAMPHLETS, ARRANGED BY DATE OF PUBLICATION

The Evolution of the Peasantry in the British West Indies, typescript of a 1936 manuscript in the library of the University of the West Indies.

Labour in the West Indies: The Birth of a Workers' Movement with an Afterword, "Germs of an Idea" by Susan Craig (London, 1977, but first published by the Fabian Society with a preface by A. Creech Jones, MP as Research Series, no. 44).

Economic Problems of To-Day (London, 1940).

Monopoly in British Industry: Fabian Research Series No. 92 (Wiesbaden, Germany, 1945), vol. 8.

Economic Survey, 1919–1949 (London, 1949).

Overhead Costs: Some Essays in Economic Analysis (New York, 1949).

The Principles of Economic Planning: A Study Prepared for the Fabian Society (London, 1949).

Industrial Development in the Caribbean (Port of Spain, Trinidad, 1950).

The Industrialization of the British West Indies (Barbados, 1950).

Attitude to Africa, written with Michael Scott, Martin Wight, and Colin Legum (Harmondsworth, England, 1951).

Measures for the Economic Development of Under-developed Countries: Report by a Group of Experts Appointed by the Secretary-General of the United Nations (United Nations, Department of Economic Affairs, New York, 1951).

Principles of Economic Planning: A Study Prepared for the Fabian Society. Rev. ed. (London, 1952).

Aspects of Industrialization: National Bank of Egypt: Fiftieth Anniversary Commemoration Lecture (Cairo, 1953).

Report on Industrialization and the Gold Coast Economy (Accra, 1953).

The Theory of Economic Growth (Homewood, Ill., 1955).

Prospects for International Investment: Fourteenth Montagu Burton Lecture on International Relations (Leeds, England, 1956).

Address to the University College of the West Indies by the Principal, Dr. W. A. Lewis at Mona on the Occasion of the Matriculation of New Students (Mona, Jamaica, 1960).

Merger of the Imperial College of Tropical Agriculture with the University College of the West Indies (Mona, Jamaica, 1960).

Eastern Caribbean Federation: Report to the Prime Minister (Port of Spain, Trinidad, 1961 and second edition, with corrections, 1962).

The Agony of the Eight (Barbados, 1963).
Education and Economic Development (Saskatoon, 1965).
Politics in West Africa: The Whidden Lectures for 1965 (Toronto, 1965).
Development Planning: The Essentials of Economic Policy (New York, 1966).
Installation Address by the Chancellor of the University of Guyana, Sir Arthur Lewis (Guyana, 1967).
Reflections on Nigeria's Economic Growth (Paris, 1967).
Reflections on Unlimited Supplies of Labour: Development Research Project, Woodrow Wilson School, Princeton University, Discussion Paper no. 5 (Princeton, 1968).
Aspects of Tropic Trade, 1883-1965: The Wicksell Lectures (Stockholm, 1969).
Some Aspects of Economic Development (Accra, 1969).
Tropical Development, 1880-1913: Studies in Economic Progress (London, 1970).
The Evolution of Foreign Aid: The Inaugural David Owen Memorial Lecture (Cardiff, Wales, 1971).
Socialism and Economic Growth (London, 1971).
Speeches by Sir W. Arthur Lewis at the 1971 Graduation Ceremonies of the University of the West Indies at St. Augustine, Mona, and Cave Hill (Mona, Jamaica, 1971).
Development Economics: An Outline (Moorestown, N.J., 1974).
Dynamic Factors in Economic Growth (Bombay, 1974).
The University in Less Developed Countries (New York, 1974).
The Evolution of the International Economic Order (Princeton, 1977).
The International Monetary System in Operation: The 1977 Per Jacobsson Lecture, with Wilfried Guth (Washington, D.C., 1977).
Growth and Fluctuations, 1870–1913 (London, 1978).
Economic Inequality in the United States: An Analysis of Racial Differences in Earnings and Employment (New York, 1981).
Black Bourgeoisie: The Franklin Frazier Lecture (1982).
Some Trends in World Trade: The Fifth Leverhulme Memorial Lecture (Liverpool, 1984).
Racial Conflict and Economic Development: The W. E. B. DuBois Lecture, 1982 (Cambridge, Mass., 1985).
The Economics of Racial Inequality: The Whitney M. Young Jr. Distinguished Lecture, 1985 (New York, 1985).
What Have We Learned from Development? (Caribbean Development Bank, Bridgetown, 1985), mimeograph.
Collected Papers, 1941–1988, edited by Patrick A. M. Emmanuel, 3 vols. (Cave Hill, Barbados, 1994).

ARTICLES, ARRANGED BY DATE OF PUBLICATION

"The Inter-relations of Shipping Freights," *Economica*, n.s., vol. 8, no. 29, February 1941, pp. 52–76.
"The Two-Part Tariff," *Economica*, n.s., vol. 8, no. 31, August 1941, pp. 240–70.
"The Two-Part Tariff: A Reply," *Economica*, n.s., vol. 8, no. 32, November 1941, pp. 399–408.
"Notes on the Economics of Loyalty," *Economica*, n.s., vol. 9, no. 36, November 1942, pp. 333-48.
"Monopoly and the Law: An Economist's Reflections on the Crofter Case," *Modern Law Review*, vol. 6, no. 3, April 1943, pp. 97–111.

"An Economic Plan for Jamaica," *Agenda: A Quarterly Journal of Reconstruction*, vol. 5, no. 4, November 1944, pp. 154–63.

"Competition in Retail Trade," *Economica*, n.s., vol. 12, no. 48, November 1945, pp. 202–34.

"Spare Time Activities of Employees," *Modern Law Review*, vol. 9, no. 3, October 1946, pp. 280-83.

"Fixed Costs," *Economica*, n.s., vol. 13, no. 52, November 1946, pp. 231–58.

"The Colonial Development Corporation," *Jamaica Arise*, vol. 1, no. 6, August 1947, pp. 6–7.

"The Prospect Before Us," *Manchester School*, vol. 16, no. 2, 1948, pp. 129–64.

"Colonial Development," *Transactions of the Manchester Statistical Society*, Session 1948–49, January 12, 1949, pp. 1–30.

"Developing Colonial Agriculture," *Three Banks Review*, June 1949, pp. 3–21.

"The Effects of an Overseas Slump on the British Economy," with F. V. Meyer, *Manchester School*, vol. 17, no. 3, 1949, pp. 233–65.

"The British Monopolies Act," *Manchester School*, vol. 17, no. 2, 1949, pp. 208–17.

"Industrial Development in Puerto Rico," *Caribbean Economic Review*, vol. 1, nos. 1 and 2, 1949, pp. 153–76.

"Sur quelques tendances séculaires," *Economie appliquée*, vol. 2, nos. 3–4, 1949, pp. 374–91.

"The Price Policy of Public Corporations," *Political Quarterly*, vol. 21, no. 2, April–June 1950, pp. 184–96.

"Issues in Land Settlement Policy," *Caribbean Economic Review*, vol. 3, nos. 1 and 2, 1951, pp. 58–92.

"Food and Raw Materials," *District Bank Review*, no. 99, September 1951, pp. 1–11.

"World Production Prices and Trade, 1870–1960," *Manchester School*, vol. 20, no. 2, 1952, pp. 105–38.

"Reflections on South-East Asia," *District Bank Review*, no. 104, December 1952, pp. 3–20.

"United Nations Primer for Development: Comment," *Quarterly Journal of Economics*, vol. 67, no. 2, May 1953, pp. 267–75.

"Thoughts on Land Settlement," *Journal of Agricultural Economics*, vol. 11, no. 1, 1954, pp. 3-11.

"Trade Drives," *District Bank Review*, no. 112, December 1954, pp. 1–15.

"Economic Development with Unlimited Supplies of Labour," *Manchester School*, vol. 22, no. 2, 1954, pp. 139–91.

"India's Economic Prospects for 1980: The Need to Develop Export of Manufactures," supplement to *Capital*, December 16, 1954, pp. 7–11.

"Recent British Experience in Nationalization," in *Monopoly and Competition and Their Regulation: Papers and Proceedings of a Conference Held by the International Economic Association*, edited by Edward H. Chamberlain (London, 1954), pp. 459–70.

"Secular Swings in Production and Trade, 1870–1913," with P. J. Leary, *Manchester School*, vol. 23, no. 2, 1955, pp. 113-52.

"The Economic Development of Africa," in *Africa in the Modern World*, edited by Calvin W. Stillman (Chicago, 1955), pp. 97–112.

"Investment Policy," *Bulletin of the Oxford Institute of Statistics*, vol. 17, no. 1, 1955, pp. 57–58.

"A Socialist Economic Policy," *Socialist Commentary*, vol. 19, June 1955, pp. 171–74.

"Patterns of Public Revenue and Expenditure," with Alison Martin, *Manchester School*, vol. 24, no. 3, 1956, pp. 203–44.

"The Economic and Social Council," in *The United Nations*, edited by Calvin W. Stillman (Chicago, 1957), pp. 97–112.

"International Competition in Manufacturers," *American Economic Review*, vol. 47, no. 2, May 1957, pp. 578–87.

"Recent Controversies over Economic Policy in the British Labour Party," *World Politics*, vol. 10, no. 2, January 1958, pp. 171–81.

"Unlimited Labour: Further Notes," *Manchester School*, vol. 26, no. 1, 1958, pp. 1-32.

"Employment Policy in an Underdeveloped Area," *Social and Economic Studies*, vol. 7, no. 3, September 1958, pp. 42–54.

"On Assessing a Development Plan," *Economic Bulletin of Ghana*, vol. 3, nos. 6 and 7, 1959, pp. 2–11.

"The Economic Commission for Africa," *United Nations News*, vol. 15, April–June 1959, pp. 3–5.

"Sponsored Growth: Challenge to Democracy," in *Problems of Economic Growth*, edited by M. K. Haldar and E. Ghosh (Delhi, 1960), pp. 107–20.

"The Shifting Fortunes of Agriculture: The General Setting," in *Proceedings of the Tenth International Conference of Agricultural Economists* (London, 1960), pp. 27–34.

"Sources of Tension in West Africa," *Africa Special Report*, vol. 5, no. 9, September 1960, pp. 5–6.

"Education and Economic Development," *Social and Economic Studies*, vol. 10, no. 2, June 1961, pp. 113–27.

"Depreciation and Obsolescence as Factors in Costing," in *Depreciation and Replacement Policy*, edited by J. L. Meij (Amsterdam, 1961), pp. 15–45.

"The Emergence of West Africa," in *The Promise of World Tensions*, edited by H. Cleveland (New York, 1961), pp. 87–100.

"The Growing Pains of African Democracy," *The Reporter* (New York), vol. 25, no. 7, 1961, pp. 35–38.

"Science, Man, and Money," in *Science and the New Nations*, edited by R. Gruber (New York, 1961), pp. 24–33.

"Competition and Regulation in the West Indies," in *Economic Systems of the Commonwealth*, edited by C. B. Hoover (Durham, N.C., 1962), pp. 501–18.

"Tensions in Economic Development," in *Restless Nations*, edited by Lester B. Pearson (New York, 1962), pp. 68–98.

"Education for Scientific Professions in the Poor Countries," *Daedalus*, vol. 91, no. 2, 1962, pp. 310–18.

"Economic Problems of Development," in *A Study of World Tensions and Development, Sponsored by the Council on World Tensions and Development* (Westport, Conn., 1974, reprint of a 1962 edition), pp. 68–91.

"Industrialisation and Social Peace," in *Conference across a Continent: Report of HRH The Duke of Edinburgh's Study Conference* (Macmillan of Canada, 1963), pp. 46–60.

"Social Services in Development Planning," in *Planning for Economic Development in the Caribbean* (Caribbean Organization Conference Report, Puerto Rico, 1963), pp. 156–67.

"Closing Remarks," in *Inflation and Growth in Latin America*, edited by W. Baer and I. Kerstenetzky (New Haven, 1964), pp. 21–33.

"Jamaica's Economic Problems: A Series of Seven Articles," *Daily Gleaner* (Kingston, 1964).

"Secondary Education and Economic Structure," *Social and Economic Studies*, vol. 13, no. 2, June 1964, pp. 219–32.

"Unemployment in Developing Areas," in *A Reappraisal of Economic Development: Perspectives for Cooperative Research*, edited by Andrew H. Whiteford (Chicago, 1964).

"A Review of Economic Development," *American Economic Review*, vol. 55, nos. 1 and 2, March 1965, pp. 1–16.

"Economic Development and World Trade," in *Problems in Economic Development: Proceedings of a Conference held by the International Economic Association*, edited by E.A.G. Robinson (London, 1965), pp. 483–97.

"Education and Economic Development," in *Education and Nation-Building in Africa*, edited by L. Gray Cowan, James O'Connell, and David G. Scanlon (New York, 1965), pp. 200–211.

"Aspects of Economic Development," in *Africa: Progress through Cooperation*, edited by John Karefa-Smart (New York, 1966), pp. 115–30.

"Opening Address," in *A Reappraisal of Economic Development: Perspectives for Cooperative Research*, edited by Andrew H. Whiteford (Chicago, 1967), pp. 1–16.

"Planning Public Expenditure," in *National Economic Planning: A Conference of the Universities—National Committee for Economic Research*, edited by Max F. Milliken (New York, 1967), pp. 201–27.

"International Trade and Economic Growth," in *Fiscal and Monetary Problems in Developing States*, edited by D. Krivine (New York, 1967), pp. 350–58.

"Unemployment in Developing Countries," Stephenson Memorial Lecture, *World Today*, vol. 23, no. 1, 1967, pp. 13–22.

"On Hating the Sin, not the Sinner," *University: A Princeton Quarterly* vol. 35, Winter, 1967–68, pp. 20–23.

"Development Planning," in *International Encyclopedia of the Social Sciences*, edited by David L. Sills, vol. 12 (New York, 1968), pp. 118–25.

"World Trade since the War," *Proceedings of the American Philosophical Society*, vol. 112, 1968, pp. 362–66.

"Economic Aspects of Quality in Education," in *Qualitative Aspects of Educational Planning*, edited by C. E. Beeby (Paris, 1969), pp. 71–88.

"Black Power and the American Universities," *Princeton Alumni Magazine*, vol. 67, no. 21, March 18, 1969, pp. 12–16.

"The Economic Profile of the American Black," *Journal of Religion and Health*, vol. 9, no. 4, October 1970, pp. 323–30.

"The Export Stimulus," in *Tropical Development, 1880–1913: Studies in Economic Progress*, edited by W. Arthur Lewis (London, 1970), pp. 13–45.

"Government," in *Taxation for Economic Development*, edited by Milton C. Taylor (New York, 1970), pp. 4–24.

"Summary: The Causes of Unemployment in Less Developed Countries," *International Labour Review*, vol. 101, no. 5, 1970, pp. 547–54.

"On Being Different," Graduation Address Delivered at the University of the West Indies, Cave Hill, Barbados, 1971, *Bim*, vol. 14, no. 53, 1971, pp. 3–9.

"Presidential Address to the Board of Governors of the Caribbean Development Bank at the First Annual General Meeting, 1971," Bridgetown, Barbados, Caribbean Development Bank, 1971.

"The Purposes of the Pearson Report," in *The Widening Gap: Development in the 1970s*, edited by Barbara Ward, J. D. Runnals, and Lenore d'Anjou (New York, 1971), pp. 4–8.

"The Caribbean Development Bank," in *Proceedings of the Seventh West Indian Agricultural Economics Conference* (St. Augustine, Trinidad, 1972), pp. 3–7.

"Presidential Address to the Board of Governors of the Caribbean Development Bank at the Second Annual General Meeting, 1972," Bridgetown, Barbados, Caribbean Development Bank, 1972.

"Objectives and Prognostications," in *The Gap between Rich and Poor Nations*, edited by G. Ranis (London, 1972), pp. 411–20.

"Reflections on Unlimited Labour," in *International Economics and Development: Essays in Honor of Raúl Prebisch*, edited by L. E. Di Marco (New York, 1972), pp. 75–96, distributed originally in 1968 by the Woodrow Wilson School as Discussion Paper No. 5.

"The Development Process," in *The Case for Development: Six Studies* (New York, 1973), pp. 52–84.

"Growth and Income Distribution," *Eastern Economist* (New Delhi), vol. 61, no. 21, 1973, pp. 968–73.

"Presidential Address to the Board of Governors of the Caribbean Development Bank at the Third Annual Meeting," Jamaica, 1973.

"Development and Distribution," in *Employment, Income Distribution, and Development Strategy: Problems of the Developing Countries: Essays in Honour of H. W. Singer*, edited by Alec Cairncross and Mohinder Pari (New York, 1976), pp. 26–42.

"The Diffusion of Development," in *The Market and the State: Essays in Honour of Adam Smith*, edited by Thomas Wilson and Andrew S. Skinner (Oxford, 1976), pp. 135–56.

"The Dual Economy Revisited," *Manchester School of Economic and Social Studies*, vol. 47, no. 3, September 1979, pp. 211–29.

"Development Strategy in a Limping World Economy," Elmhurst Lecture, in International Conference of Agricultural Economics, 1979, reprinted in *Lead-

ing Issues in Economic Development, edited by Gerald M. Meier (New York, 1989), pp. 320–23.

"The Less Developed Countries and Stable Exchange Rates," *Third World Quarterly*, vol. 1, no. 1, 1979, pp. 18–29.

"The Slowing Down of the Engine of Growth," *American Economic Review*, vol. 70, no. 4, September 1980, pp. 555–64.

"Rising Prices: 1899–1913 and 1950–1979," *Scandinavian Journal of Economics*, vol. 82, no. 4, 1980, pp. 425–36.

"Autobiographical Note," *Social and Economic Studies*, vol. 29, no. 4, December 1980, pp. 1–4.

"The Rate of Growth in World Trade, 1830–1973," in *The World Economic Order: Past and Prospects*, edited by Sven Grassman and Erik Lundberg (New York, 1981), pp. 1–74.

"Eliminate Both Unemployment and Inflation," *Crisis*, vol. 90, no. 1, 1983, p. 40.

"The State of Development Theory," *American Economic Review*, vol. 74, no. 1, March 1984, pp. 1–10.

"The Rate of Growth of the World Economy," Ching-Hua Series of Lectures by Invited Eminent Economists, No. 6 (Nankang, Taipei, Taiwan, 1984).

"The Roots of Development Theory," in *Handbook of Development Economics*, edited by H. Chenery and T. N. Srinivasan, vol. 1 (Amsterdam, 1988), pp. 28–37.

"W. Arthur Lewis," in *Lives of the Laureates: Seven Nobel Economists*, edited by William Breit and Robert W. Spencer (Cambridge, Mass., 1986), pp. 1–20.

Newspapers and Journals

Daily Gleaner, Kingston, Jamaica.
Economic Bulletin, The Economic Society of Ghana.
Evening News, Accra, Gold Coast/Ghana.
Jamaica Arise: Official Organ of the People's National Party, Kingston, Jamaica.
The Keys, Journal of the League of Coloured Peoples.
Newsletter, publication of the League of Coloured Peoples.
West Africa, London.

Government Publications

GOLD COAST

The Development Plan, 1951.
The Development Plan, Development Progress Report, 1955.
Estimates of Expenditure from Development Funds, 1956–57 to 1963–64.
The Financial Situation, 1954–55+.
Government Proposals in Regard to the Future Constitution and Control of Statutory Boards and Corporations in the Gold Coast, Part I, and *Report of the Commission of Enquiry into the Affairs of the Cocoa Purchasing Company Ltd*, Part II, 1956.
The Government's Proposals for Constitutional Reform, 1953.
The Government's Revised Constitutional Proposals for Gold Coast Independence, 1956.

Progress Report on Development and Welfare for the Period January 1950 to March 1951, 1952.
Progress Report for the Financial Year, 1 April, 1952–31 March, 1953, 1955.
Report by Sir Cecil Trevor on Banking Conditions in the Gold Coast, 1957.
Report of the Constitution Adviser, 1955, The Bourne Report.
Report on the Gold Coast for the Year 1946+.
Statement of the Gold Coast Government on the Report of the Commission of Enquiry into Representational and Electoral Reform, 1953.
Statement of the Gold Coast Government on the Report of the Commission on the Civil Service of the Gold Coast, 1951.
Statement on the Programme of the Africanisation of the Public Service, 1954.
The Volta River Project, 1956, 3 vols.
Legislative Assembly, *Debates*, 1951–57.
Legislative Assembly, Finance Committee, *Report*, 1956.
Legislative Council, Select Committee on the Africanisation of the Public Service, *Report*, 1950.
Legislative Council, *Report on the Commission of Enquiry into Disturbances in the Gold Coast*, 1948.
———, *Report of the Commission of Enquiry into Mr. Braimah's Resignation*, 1954.
———, *Plan for Mass Literacy and Mass Education*, 1952.
Marketing Board, *Annual Report and Accounts*, 1948+.
Ministry of Education, *Gold Coast Education*, 1955.
———, *Progress in Education in the Gold Coast*, 1953.
Ministry of Finance, *Economic Survey*, 1952+.
———, *A Survey of Some Economic Matters*, 1952.
Office of the Government Statistician, *Economic and Statistical Bulletin of the Gold Coast*, 1952–53, continued as *Digest of Statistics*, 1953+.
Office of the Government Statistician, *Educational Statistics*, 1954.
———, *Statistical Abstracts*, 1956+.
———, *Statistical and Economic Papers*, 1953+.
———, *Statistical Reports*, nos. 1 and 2, 1954 and 1955.
Treasury, *Report on the Finances and Accounts of the Gold Coast for the Year, 1939–40*, 1940+.
Seers, Dudley, and C. R. Ross, *Report on Financial and Physical Problems of Development in the Gold Coast* (Accra, 1952).

GHANA

Second Development Plan, 1959–64, 1959.
Parliamentary Debates, *Official Report*, 1957+.
Population Census of Ghana, 1960, 1962.
Central Revenue Department, *Annual Report*, 1961–62+.
———, *Report of the Commission of Enquiry into Irregularities with the Issued Import Licenses*, 1964.
White Paper on the Report of the Commission of Enquiry into Concessions, 1961.
Commission of Enquiry into the Final Administration of the University of Ghana, 1970.

Final Report of the Commission of Enquiry into the Working and Administration of the Present Company Law of Ghana, 1961.
Report of the Committee on Agricultural Indebtedness, 1968.
Revised Report on the Delimitation Commission, 1964, 1965.
Department of Social Welfare and Community Development, *Community Development in Ghana*, 1959.
Cocoa Marketing Board, *Annual Report*, 1957+.
Report of the Commissioners Appointed to Inquire into the Insolvency Law of Ghana, 1961.
Report of the Jiagge Commission of Enquiry into the Assets of Specific Persons, 1969.
Ministry of Education, *Education Report*, 1957.
Ministry of Finance, *The Consolidation Development Plan*, 1957.
———, *Economic Survey*, 1957+.
———, *Overseas Capital and Investment in Ghana: Speech by Kwame Nkrumah*, 1962.
Ministry of Finance, Port of Tema, *Official Handbook*, 1962.
Ministry of Finance, *Survey of High Level Manpower in Ghana, 1960*, 1961.
Ministry of Trade and Industries, Commission of Enquiry into Concessions, *Report*, 1961
Ministry of Trade and Industries, *Report on the Labour Division*, 1957+.
National Liberation Council, Commission of Enquiry on the Commercial Activities of the Erstwhile Publicity Secretary, *Report*, 1967.
National Research Council, *Record and Accounts for the Period, 1959–60*, 1961+.
Office of the Auditor-General, Director of Enterprises, *Ghana*, 1960.
Office of the Auditor-General, *Educational Statistics*, 1956+.
———, *Industrial Statistics*, 1965–66.
———, *Labour Statistics*, 1956+.
———, *Statistical and Economic Papers*, 1958+.
———, *Statistical Handbook of Ghana*, 1968+.
———, *Statistical Reports*, 1957+.
———, *Statistical Yearbook*, 1962+.
———, *Survey of Cocoa Producing Families in Ashanti*, 1957.
———, *Survey of Population and Budgets of Cocoa Producing Families in the Oda-Swedru-Asamanhese Area*, 1957.
Office of the Planning Commission, *Seven-Year Development Plan*, 1963.
Office of the President, *Statement by the Government on the Recent Conspiracy*, 1961.
State Farms Corporation, *First Bi-annual Progress Report*, 1962–63+.
Convention People's Party, *The Party*, 1962.
———, *Programme of the Convention People's Party for Work and Happiness*, 1962.

GREAT BRITAIN

Board of Trade, *Report of the United Kingdom Trade and Industrial Mission to Ghana* (London, 1959).
Colonial Office, *Report of the Commission of Enquiry into Disturbances in the Gold Coast* (London, 1948).

House of Commons Sessional Papers, *Recommendations of the West India Royal Commission*, vol. 5, 1939–40, cmd. 6174.

House of Commons Sessional Papers, *West India Royal Commission, 1938–39: Statement of Actions Taken on the Recommendations*, vol. 10, 1944–45, cmd. 6656.

House of Commons Sessional Papers, Colonial Office, *Report of the West Indies Committee of the Commission on Higher Education in the Colonies*, 1945, vol. 5, 1944–45, cmd. 6654.

House of Commons Sessional Papers, Treaty Series No. 36 (1970), *Agreement Establishing the Caribbean Development Bank*, no. 1, 1970, cmd, 4358.

WEST INDIES

Trinidad, Office of the Premier and Ministry of Finance, *The Economics of Nationhood*, 1959.

Caribbean Development Bank, Board of Governors, Annual Meetings of the Board of Governors, *Summary of Proceedings* (Bridgetown, Barbados, 1971, 1972, 1973).

Caribbean Development Bank, *Special Development Fund Rules* (Barbados, 1970).

Caribbean Development Bank, *The First Ten Years* (Bridgetown, Barbados, 1980).

Caribbean Development Bank, *The First Twenty Years, 1970–1990* (Bridgetown, Barbados, 1990).

UNITED NATIONS

United Nations, United Nations Development Programme, *Caribbean Development Bank: Report of the Preparatory Mission* (New York, 1967).

Books by Other Authors

Afrifa, A. A., *The Ghana Coup: 24th February 1966* (New York, 1966).

Alexander, H. T., *African Tightrope: My Two Years as Nkrumah's Chief of Staff* (London, 1965).

Appiah, Joseph, *Joe Appiah: The Autobiography of an African Patriot* (New York, 1990).

Ashton, T. S., *The Industrial Revolution, 1760–1830* (1948; Oxford, 1997).

Bauer, P. T., *Dissent on Development: Studies and Debates in Development Economics* (Cambridge, Mass., 1972).

———, *West African Trade: A Study of Competition, Oligarchy, and Monopoly in a Changing Economy* (Cambridge, 1954).

Bing, Geoffrey, *Reap the Whirlwind: An Account of Kwame Nkrumah's Ghana from 1950 to 1966* (London, 1968).

Burns, Alan, *Colonial Civil Servant* (London, 1949).

———, *History of the British West Indies* (London, 1965).

Busia, K. A., *The Position of the Chief in the Modern Political System of Ashanti* (New York, 1958).

Cardoso, F. Henrique, *The Originality of the Copy: ECLA and the Idea of Development* (Cambridge, 1977).

Cudjoe, Selwyn R., editor, *Eric Williams Speaks: Essays on Colonialism and Independence* (Wellesley, Mass., 1993).
Deane, Phyllis, and W. A. Cole, *British Economic Growth, 1688–1959: Trends and Structure* (Cambridge, 1962).
Dixon, Vernon J., and Badi Foster, editors, *Beyond Black or White: An Alternate America* (Boston, 1971).
Hall, Douglas, *A Quinquagenary Calendar, 1948–1998* (Kingston, 1998).
Hammond, Barbara, and J. L Hammond, *The Village Labourer, 1760–1832: A Study of the Government of England before the Reform Bill* (London, 1911); *The Town Labourer, 1760–1832* (London, 1917); and *The Skilled Labourer, 1760–1832* (London, 1919).
Hare, Paul, and Herbert H. Blumberg, editors, *A Search for Peace and Justice: Reflections of Michael Scott* (London, 1980).
Harrod, R. F., *The Life of John Maynard Keynes* (New York, 1954).
———, *Towards a Dynamic Economics: Some Recent Developments of Economic Theory and their Application to Policy* (London, 1948).
Hirschman, Albert O., *Essays in Trespassing: Economics to Politics and Beyond* (Cambridge, 1981).
———, *The Strategy of Economic Development* (New Haven, 1968).
James, C.L.R., *Nkrumah and the Ghana Revolution*, (London, 1962 and 1977).
———, *Party Politics in the West Indies* (San Juan, Trinidad, 1962).
Johnson, Elizabeth S., and Harry G. Johnson, *The Shadow of Keynes: Understanding Keynes, Cambridge, and Keynesian Economics* (Oxford, 1978).
Johnson, Harry G., *The Two Sector Model of General Equilibrium* (Chicago, 1971).
Krueger, Anne O., *Economic Policy Reform in Developing Countries: The Kuznets Memorial Lectures at the Economic Growth Center, Yale University* (Oxford, 1992).
Lal, Deepak, *The Poverty of 'Development Economics'* (Cambridge, Mass., 1985).
Little, Ian M. D., *Economic Development: Theory, Policy, and International Relations* (New York, 1982).
Lucas, Robert E., Jr., *Lectures on Economic Growth* (Cambridge, Mass., 2002).
Mandelbaum (later Martin), Kurt, *The Industrialization of Backward Areas* (Oxford, 1955).
Meier, Gerald M., *Leading Issues in Economic Development* (New York, 1970, 1989, 1995, and 2000 editions consulted).
Mordecai, John, *The West Indies: The Federal Negotiations* (London, 1968).
National Liberation Movement, *Statement of the National Liberation Movement and Its Allies on the Gold Coast Government's Constitutional Proposals for Gold Coast Independence* (Kumasi, 1956).
Nkrumah, Kwame, *Ghana: The Autobiography of Kwame Nkrumah* (London, 1957).
———, *I speak of Freedom* (London, 1961).
Nurske, Ragnar, *Problems of Capital Formation in Underdeveloped Countries and Patterns of Trade and Development* (New York, 1967).
Padmore, George, *The Gold Coast Revolution* (London, 1952).

Pearson, Lester B., *Partners in Development: Report of the Commission on International Development* (Washington, 1969).
Plant, Arnold, editor, *Some Modern Business Problems* (Freeport, N.Y., 1937, reprinted in 1967).
Robbins, Lionel, *Autobiography of an Economist* (London, 1971).
———, *An Essay on the Nature and Significance of Economic Science* (London, 1935).
———, *The Great Depression* (London, 1935).
———, *A History of Economic Thought: The LSE Lectures*, edited by Steven G. Medema and W. J. Samuels (Princeton, 1998), with a foreword by William J. Baumol.
———, *The Theory of Economic Policy in English Classical Political Economy* (1952; London, 1978).
Schultz, Theodore W., *Transforming Traditional Agriculture* (New Haven, 1969).
Scott, Michael, *A Time to Speak* (New York, 1958).
———, *Shadow over Africa* (London, 1949).
Sen, Amartya, editor, *Growth Economics: Selected Readings* (Middlesex, England, 1970).
Solow, R. M., *Growth Theory: An Exposition* (New York, 1970).
University of the West Indies, *Special Awards Ceremony, July 23, 1998* (Jamaica, 1998).
Williams, Eric, *Forged from the Love of Liberty: Selected Speeches of Eric Williams*, compiled by Paul K. Sutton (Trinidad, 1981).
———, *Inward Hunger: The Education of a Prime Minster* (London, 1969).
———, *The Negro in the Caribbean* (Washington, D.C., 1942).

Articles by Other Authors
Barro, Robert J., "Economic Growth in a Cross Section of Countries," *Quarterly Journal of Economics*, vol. 106, no. 2, May 1991, pp. 407–43.
Coase, R. H., "The Institutional Structure of Production," *American Economic Review*, vol. 82, no. 4, September 1992, pp. 713–19.
———, "The Nature of the Firm," *Economica*, vol. 4, no. 16, November 1937, pp. 386–405.
Debreu, Gerard, "Economic Theory in the Mathematical Model, *American Economic Review*, vol. 74, no. 3, June 1984, pp. 267–78.
———, "The Mathematization of Economic Theory," *American Economic Review*, vol. 81, no. 1, March 1993, pp. 1–7.
Diaz Alejandro, Carlos F., "Trade Politics and Economic Development," in *International Trade and Finance: Frontiers for Research*, edited by Peter B. Kenen (Cambridge, 1975), pp. 95–150.
Dixit, Avinash K., "Models of Dual Economies" in *Models of Economic Growth: Proceedings of a Conference Held by the International Economic Association at Jerusalem*, edited by James A. Mirrlees and N. H. Stein (New York, 1973).
Dixon, Vernon J., and M. Reginald Lewis, "Black Consciousness, Societal Values, and Educational Institutions, *Journal of Conflict Resolution*, vol. 12, no. 3, September 1968, pp. 402–7.

Domar, Evsey, "Capital Expansion, Rate of Growth, and Employment," *Econometrica*, vol. 14, no. 2, April 1946, pp. 137–47.

Frankel, S. Herbert, "Reply," *Quarterly Journal of Economics*, vol. 67, no. 2, May 1953, pp. 280–85.

———, "United Nations Primer for Development," *Quarterly Journal of Economics*, vol. 66, no. 3, August 1952, pp. 301–26.

Hansen, Bent, "Employment and Wages in Rural Egypt," *American Economic Review*, vol. 59, no. 3, June 1969, pp. 298–313.

———, "The Distributive Shares in Egyptian Agriculture, 1897–1961," *International Economic Review*, vol. 9, no. 2, June 1968, pp. 175–94.

———, "Marginal Productivity, Wage Theory, and Subsistence Wage Theory in Egyptian Agriculture," *Journal of Development Studies*, vol. 2, no. 4, July 1966, pp. 367–407.

Harrod, R. F., "An Essay in Dynamic Theory," *Economic Journal*, vol. 49, no. 193, March 1939, pp. 14–33.

Hayek, F. A., "The London School of Economics, 1895-1945," *Economica*, n.s., vol. 13, no. 49, February 1946, pp. 1–31.

Johnson, Harry G., "The Keynesian Revolution and the Monetarist Counter-Revolution," *American Economic Review*, vol. 61, no. 2, *Papers and Proceedings of the Eighty-Third Annual Meeting of the American Economic Association*, May 1971, pp. 1–14.

Johnston, Bruce F., and John W. Mellor, "The Role of Agriculture in Economic Development," *American Economic Review*, vol. 51, no. 4, September 1961, pp. 566–93.

Jorgenson, Dale W., "The Role of Agriculture in Economic Development: Classical versus Neoclassical Models of Growth," in *Subsistence Agriculture and Economic Development*, edited by Clifton R. Wharton, Jr. (Chicago, 1969), pp. 320–47.

Kaldor, Nicholas, "Alternative Theories of Distribution," *Review of Economic Studies*, vol. 23, no. 2, 1955–56, pp. 83–100.

Krueger, Anne O., "The Political Economy of the Rent-Seeking Society," *American Economic Review*, vol. 64, no. 3, June 1974, pp. 291–303.

Krugman, Paul, "Towards a Counter-Counter-revolution in Development Theory," *Proceedings of the World Bank Annual Conference on Development Economics*, 1992, pp. 15–38.

Lesson, P. F., "The Lewis Model and Development Theory," *Manchester School of Economic and Social Studies*, vol. 47, no. 3, September 1979, pp. 196–210.

Lewis, John P., "William Arthur Lewis," in *Luminaries: Princeton Faculty Remembered*, edited by Patricia H. Marks (Princeton, 1996), pp. 157–65.

Lucas, Robert E. Jr., "On the Mechanics of Economic Development, *Journal of Monetary Economics*, vol. 22, no. 1, 1988, pp. 3–42.

Mabro, Robert, "Industrial Growth, Agricultural Under-employment, and the Lewis Model: The Egyptian Case, 1937–1965," *Journal of Development*, vol. 3, no. 4, July 1967, pp. 322–51.

Millar-Craig, H., "Financing the Second Development Plan," *Economic Bulletin*, vol. 4, no. 6, June 1960, pp. 1–8.

Mokyr, Joel, "The Industrial Revolution in the Low Countries in the First Half of the Nineteenth Century: A Comparative Case Study," *Journal of Economic History*, vol. 34, no. 2, June 1974, pp. 365–91.

Nobel Memorial Prize in Economics, 1979, "The Official Announcement of the Royal Academy of Sciences," *Scandinavian Journal of Economics*, vol. 82, 1980.

North, Douglass C., "Institutions and Economic Growth: An Historical Introduction," *World Development*, vol. 17, no. 9, 1989, pp. 1319–32.

North, Douglass C., and Barry Weingast, "Constitutions and Commitment: The Evolution of Institutional Governing Public Choice in Seventeenth-Century England," *Journal of Economic History*, vol. 49, no. 4, December 1989, pp. 803–32.

Ranis, Gustav, and John C. H. Fei, "A Theory of Economic Development," *American Economic Review*, vol. 51, no. 4, September 1961, pp. 533–65.

Rosenstein-Rodan, P. N., "Problems of Industrialisation of Eastern and South-Eastern Europe," *Economic Journal*, vol. 53, nos. 210–11, June–September 1943, pp. 202–11.

Rostow, W. W., "The Take-off into Self-Sustained Economic Growth," *Economic Journal*, vol. 66, no. 261, March 1956, pp. 25–48.

Seers, Dudley, "The Birth, Life, and Death of Development Economics," *Development and Change*, October 1979, pp. 707–19.

Sen, Amartya K., "Peasants and Dualism with or without Surplus Labor," *Journal of Political Economy*, vol. 74, no. 5, October 1966, pp. 425–50.

Stiglitz, Joseph E., "Comment on 'Toward a Counter Counter-revolution in Development Theory' by Krugman," *Proceedings of the World Bank Conference on Development Economics*, 1992, pp. 39–49.

Viner, Jacob, "Some Reflections on the Concept of 'Disguised Unemployment,'" *Contribuicoes a analise do desenvolvimento economico* (Rio Janeiro, 1957), pp. 345–54.

Williamson, Jeffrey G., "The Historical Content of the Classical Labor Surplus Model," *Population and Development Review*, vol. 11, No. 2, June 1985, pp. 171–91.

———, "Why Was British Growth So Slow During the Industrial Revolution?" *Journal of Economic History*, vol. 44, no. 3, September 1984, pp. 687–712.

Interviews

P. T. (Lord) Bauer, London, distinguished economist, colleague of Lewis's during Lewis's London days, and critic of the development economists, July 24, 1998.

William Baumol, Princeton, colleague of Lewis's from London and Princeton University, September 15, 1998, and again on September 2, 2004, at which time Hilda Baumol, his wife and a longtime friend of the Lewises, was present.

Erica Williams Connell, née Erica Williams, daughter of Eric Williams, by telephone, June 16, 2003.

Vernon Dixon, graduate student in economics at Princeton in the late 1960s and participant on the committee that created the Afro-American Studies Program at Princeton in 1969. At present he is a professor of Economics at Haverford College. The interview took place July 13, 2004.

294 • Bibliography

Joseph Keyes, Washington, D.C., official of the International Monetary Fund and member of the fund's team involved in Ghanaian negotiations in the 1960s, October 31, 2000.

Winville King, St. Lucia, knowledgeable personage about the West Indies and St. Lucia, February 1, 2002.

Gladys Lady Lewis, Princeton, wife of Sir W. Arthur Lewis, and Elizabeth Lewis, daughter of Arthur and Gladys Lewis, August 11, 2003, and September 2, 2004.

John P. Lewis, Princeton, Dean of the Woodrow Wilson School and colleague of Lewis, December 17, 1997.

Vaughan Lewis, St. Lucia, nephew of Lewis, February 2, 2002.

Charles Merwin, Washington, D.C., official of the International Monetary Fund and member of the fund's team involved in Ghanaian negotiations in the 1960s, October 31, 2000.

Richard Quandt, Princeton, colleague of Lewis on the economics faculty of Princeton University, September 17, 1998.

Douglas Rimmer, development economist, who taught at the University of Ghana at Legon in the 1960s and has written extensively about the Ghanaian economy, London, July 20, 1998.

Deidre Williams, St. Lucia, historian of St. Lucia, February 1, 2002.

SECONDARY SOURCES

Books

Allman, Jean Marie, *The Quills of the Porcupine: Asante Nationalism in Emergent Ghana* (Madison, Wisc., 1993).

Apter, David, *Ghana in Transition* (New York, 1963).

Arndt, H. W., *Economic Development: The History of an Idea* (Chicago, 1987).

———, *The Rise and Fall of Economic Growth: A Study in Contemporary Thought* (London, 1978).

Austin, Dennis, *Politics in Ghana, 1944–1960* (London, 1964).

Austin, Dennis, and Robin Luckham, editors, *Politicians and Soldiers in Ghana, 1966–1972* (London, 1975).

Bates, Robert H., *Markets and States in Tropical Africa* (Berkeley, 1981).

———, *Prosperity and Violence: The Political Economy of Development* (New York, 2001).

———, editor, *Toward a Political Economy of Employment: A Rational Choice Perspective* (Berkeley, 1988).

Bates, Robert H., and Anne O. Krueger, editors, *Political and Economic Interactions in Economic Policy Reform: Evidence from Eight Countries* (Cambridge, Mass., 1993).

Benn, Denis, *The Caribbean: An Intellectual History* (Kingston, Jamaica, 2004).

Bhagwati, Jagdish, and Richard S. Eckhaus, editors, *Development and Planning: Essays in Honour of Paul Rosenstein-Rodan* (London, 1972).

Bing, Geoffrey, *Reap the Whirlwind: An Account of Kwame Nkrumah's Ghana from 1950 to 1966* (London, 1968).

Birmingham, Walter, I. Neustadt, and E. N. Omaboe, editors, *A Study of Contemporary Ghana*, vol. 1, *The Economy of Ghana* (Evanston, Ill., 1966).
Bourret, F. M., *Ghana: The Road to Independence, 1919-1957* (London, 1960).
Breen, Harry H., *St. Lucia: Historical, Statistical, Descriptive* (London, 1844).
Buhle, Paul, editor, *C.L.R. James: His Life and Work*, (London, 1986).
Butler, L. J., *Industrialization and the British Colonial State: West Africa, 1939–1951* (London, 1997).
Cell, John W., *Hailey: A Study in British Imperialism, 1872–1969* (Cambridge, 1992).
Chazan, Naomi, *An Anatomy of Ghanaian Politics: Managing Political Recession, 1969–1982* (Boulder, Colo., 1983).
Cooper, Frederick, *Decolonization and African Society: The Labor Question in French and British Africa* (Cambridge, 1996).
Crofts, N.F.R., *British Economic Growth during the Industrial Revolution* (Oxford, 1985).
Dahrendorf, Ralf, *LSE: A History of the London School of Economics and Political Science, 1895–1995* (London, 1995).
Danso-Boafa, Kwaku, *The Political Biography of Dr. Kofi Abrefa* (Accra, 1996).
Daunton, M. J., *Progress and Poverty: An Economic and Social History of Britain, 1700–1850* (Oxford, 1995).
Dunn, John, and A. F. Robertson, *Dependence and Opportunity: Political Change in Ahafo* (Cambridge, 1973).
Dzorgbo, Sarah-Bright, *Ghana in Search of Development: The Challenge of Governance, Economic Management, and Institution Building* (Aldershot, England, 2001).
Easterly, William, *The Elusive Quest for Modernity: Economists' Adventures and Misadventures in the Tropics* (Cambridge, Mass., 2001).
Eatwell, John, Murray Milgate, and Peter Newman, editors, *The New Palgrave: A Dictionary of Economics* (New York, 1987), 4 vols.
Ebenstein, Alan, *Friedrich Hayek: A Biography* (New York, 2001).
Escobar, Arturo, *Encountering Development: The Making and Unmaking of the Third World* (Princeton, 1995).
Fitch, Bob, and Mary Oppenheimer, *Ghana: The End of an Illusion* (New York, 1966).
Foster, Philip, *Education and Social Change in Ghana* (London, 1965).
Foster, Philip, and Aristide R. Zolberg, editors, *Ghana and the Ivory Coast: Perspectives on Modernization* (Chicago, 1971).
Frimpong-Ansah, J. H., *Professor Sir W. Arthur Lewis: A Patriarch of Development Economics: Paper Presented at the Annual Conference of the Development Studies Association, University of Manchester* (Manchester, 1987).
———, *The Vampire State in Africa: The Political Economy of Decline in Ghana* (London, 1992).
Garlick, Peter C., *African Traders and Economic Development in Ghana* (Oxford, 1971).
Geiss, Immanuel, *The Pan-African Movement*, translated by Ann Keep (London, 1974).

Genoud, Roger, *Nationalism and Economic Development in Ghana* (New York, 1969).
Gochet, Charles, *A History of the Roman Catholic Church in St. Lucia* (Port of Spain, Trinidad, 1975).
Goldsworthy, David, *Colonial Issues in British Politics, 1945–1961: From Colonial Development to the Wind of Change* (Oxford, 1971).
Hardy, Chandra, *The Caribbean Development Bank* (The North-South Institute, 2003).
Harriss, John, Janet Hunter, and Colin M. Lewis, editors, *The New Institutional Economics and Third World Development* (London, 1995).
Hart, David, *The Volta River Project: A Case Study in Politics and Technology* (Edinburgh, 1980).
Havinden, Michael, and David Meredith, *Colonialism and Development: Britain and Its Tropical Colonies, 1850–1960* (London, 1993).
Hinds, Allister, *Britain's Sterling Colonial Policy and Decolonization, 1939–1958* (London, 2001).
Holt, Thomas C., *The Problem of Freedom: Race, Labor, and Politics in Jamaica and Britain, 1832–1938* (Baltimore, 1992).
Hooker, James R., *Black Revolutionary: George Padmore's Path from Communism to Pan-Africanism* (New York, 1967).
Hoyos, F. A., *Grantley Adams and the Social Revolution* (London, 1974).
———, *The Rise of West Indian Democracy: The Life and Times of Sir Grantley Adams* (no place of publication indicated, 1963).
Institute of Social and Economic Research, University of the West Indies, *Sir Arthur Lewis: The Simplicity of Genius* (Cave Hill, Barbados, 1989).
James, Harold, *The End of Globalization: Lessons from the Great Depression* (Cambridge, Mass., 2001).
James, Winston, *Holding Aloft the Banner of Ethiopia: Caribbean Radicalism in Early Twentieth-Century America* (London, 1998).
James, Winston, and Clive Harris, editors, *Inside Babylon: The Caribbean Diaspora in Britain* (London, 1993).
Jesse, C., *The Amerindians in St. Lucia* (Castries, St. Lucia, 1968).
Jones, Trevor, *Ghana's First Republic, 1960–1966: The Pursuit of the Political Kingdom* (London, 1976).
Kay, G. B., *Development and Underdevelopment: A Marxist Analysis* (London, 1975).
———, *The Political Economy of Colonialism in Ghana: A Collection of Documents and Statistics, 1900–1960* (Cambridge, 1972).
Killick, Tony, *Development Economics in Action: A Study of Economic Policies in Ghana* (New York, 1978).
Kimble, David, *A Political History of Ghana: The Rise of Gold Coast Nationalism, 1850–1928* (Oxford, 1963).
Kindleberger, Charles, *The World in Depression, 1929–1939* (London, 1975).
King, Bruce, *Derek Walcott: A Caribbean Life* (Oxford, 2000).
Knight, Franklin W., *The Caribbean: The Genesis of a Fragmented Nationalism* (New York, 1990).

Krueger, Anne O., *Economic Policy Reform in Developing Countries* (Cambridge, Mass., 1991).
Lal, Deepak, and H. Myint, *The Political Economy of Poverty, Equity, and Growth: A Comparative Study* (Oxford, 1996).
Lalljie, Robert, *Sir Arthur Lewis, Nobel Laureate: A Biographical Profile* (Castries, St. Lucia, 1996).
Lee, J. M., *Colonial Development and Good Government: A Study of the Ideas Expressed by the British Official Classes in Planning Decolonization, 1939–1964* (Oxford, 1967).
Lee, J. M., and Martin Petter, *The Colonial Office, War, and Development Policy: Organization and the Planning of a Metropolitan Initiative, 1939–1945* (London, 1982).
LeVine, Victor T., *Political Corruption: The Ghana Case* (Stanford, 1978).
Lewis, David Levering, *W.E.B. DuBois: The Fight for Equality and the American Century, 1919–1963* (New York, 2000).
Lewis, Gordon K., *The Growth of the Modern West Indies* (London, 1968).
Little, Kenneth, *Negroes in Britain: A Study of Racial Relations in English Society* (London, 1947 and revised edition with a new introduction, London, 1972).
Macey, David, *Frantz Fanon: A Biography* (New York, 2000).
Marable, Manning, *C.L.R. James and Nkrumah* (Black Praxis Series, Occasional Paper, No. 14, Dayton, Ohio, no date).
———, *African and Caribbean Politics: From Kwame Nkrumah to the Grenada Revolution* (London, 1987).
Marglin, Frederique Apffel, and Stephen A. Marglin, editors, *Dominating Knowledge: Development, Culture, and Resistance* (Oxford, 1999).
McCormick, Brian, *Hayek and the Keynesian Avalanche* (New York, 1992).
McWilliam, Michael, *The Development Business: A History of the Commonwealth Development Corporation* (New York, 2001).
Meier, Gerald M., *Emerging from Poverty: The Economics That Really Matters* (Oxford, 1984).
Meier, Gerald M., and Dudley Seers, editors, *Pioneers in Development: A World Bank Publication* (New York, 1984).
Mikell, Gwendolyn, *Cocoa and Chaos in Ghana* (New York, 1989).
Milburn, Josephine F., *British Business and Ghanaian Independence* (London, 1977).
Mintz, Sidney W., *Caribbean Transformations* (Chicago, 1974).
Mintz, Sidney W., and Sally Price, editors, *Caribbean Contours* (Baltimore, 1985).
Moggridge, Donald E., *Keynes* (London, 1993).
Mokyr, Joel, editor, *The British Industrial Revolution: An Economic Perspective* (Boulder, Colo.).
Morgan, D. J., *The Official History of Colonial Development*: vol. 1, *The Origins of British Aid Policy, 1924–1945* (London, 1980); vol. 2, *Developing British Colonial Resources, 1945–1951* (London, 1980); vol. 3, *A Reassessment of British Aid Policy, 1951–1965* (London, 1980); vol. 4, *Change in British Aid Policy, 1951–1970* (London, 1980); and *Guidance Towards Self-Government in British Colonies, 1941–1971* (London, 1980).

Moxon, James, *Volta: Man's Greatest Lake* (London, 1969).
Nettleford, Rex, *Manley and the Politics of Jamaica: Towards an Analysis of Political Change in Jamaica, 1938–1968* (Mona, Jamaica, 1971).
Nugent, Paul, *Big Men, Small Boys, and Politics in Ghana: Power, Ideology, and the Burden of History, 1982–1994* (London, 1995).
O'Brien, D. P., and John R. Presley, editors, *Pioneers of Modern Economics in Britain* (Totowa, N.J., 1981).
O'Shaughnessy, Andrew Jackson, *An Empire Divided: The American Revolution and the British Caribbean* (Philadelphia, 2000).
Owusu, Michael, *Uses and Abuses of Political Power* (Chicago, 1970).
Oxaal, Ivar, *Black Intellectuals and the Dilemmas of Race and Class in Trinidad* (Cambridge, Mass., 1982).
Palmer, Colin, *Eric Williams and the Making of the Modern Caribbean* (forthcoming).
Parry, J. H., and Philip Sherlock, *A Short History of the West Indies* (Hong Kong, 1971).
Pearce, Robert D., *The Turning Point in Africa: British Colonial Policy, 1938–48* (London, 1982).
Rathbone, Richard, *Murder and Politics in Colonial Ghana* (New Haven, 1993).
———, *Nkrumah and the Chiefs: The Politics of Chieftaincy in Ghana, 1951–60* (Athens, Ohio, 2000).
Ratheford, Donald, *Dictionary of Economics* (New York, 1992).
Rendell, William, *The Historiography of the Commonwealth Development Corporation, 1948–1972* (London, 1976).
Rimmer, Douglas, *Staying Poor: Ghana's Political Economy, 1950–1990* (Oxford, 1992).
Rooney, David, *Kwame Nkrumah: The Political Kingdom in the Third World* (London, 1988).
———, *Sir Charles Arden-Clarke* (London, 1982).
Ryan, Selwyn D., *Race and Nationalism in Trinidad and Tobago: A Study of Decolonization in a Multiracial Society* (Toronto, 1972).
Sachs, Wolfgang, editor, *The Development Dictionary: A Guide to Knowledge and Power* (London, 1992).
Seidman, A. W., *Ghana's Development Experience, 1951–65* (Nairobi, 1978).
Sherlock, Philip, and Rex Nettleford, *The University of the West Indies: A Caribbean Response to the Challenge of Change* (London, 1990).
Skidelsky, Robert, *John Maynard Keynes*; vol. 2, *The Economist as Saviour, 1920–1937* (London, 1992).
———, *Keynes* (New York, 1996).
Smith, M. G., *The Plural Society in the British West Indies* (Berkeley, 1965).
Stockwell, Sarah, *The Business of Decolonization: British Business Strategies in the Gold Coast* (Oxford, 2000).
Swan, Michael, *British Guiana: The Land of Six Peoples* (London, 1957).
Tabili, Laura, *"We Ask for British Justice": Workers and Racial Difference in Late Imperial Britain* (Ithaca, 1994).
Targetti, Fernando, *Nicholas Kaldor: The Economics and Politics of Capitalism as a Dynamic System* (Oxford, 1992).
Thirwall, Anthony P., *Nicholas Kaldor* (Brighton, 1987).

———, editor, *Keynes and Economic Development: The Seventh Keynes Seminar Held at the University of Kent at Canterbury, 1985* (London, 1987).

———, editor, *Keynes and Laissez-Faire: The Third Keynes Seminar Held at the University of Kent at Canterbury, 1976* (London, 1978).

Thompson, W. Scott, *Ghana's Foreign Policy, 1957–1966: Diplomacy, Ideology, and the New State* (Princeton, 1969).

Timothy, Bankole, *Kwame Nkrumah* (London, 1955).

Toye, John, *Dilemmas of Development: Reflections on the Counter-revolution in Development Theory and Policy* (Oxford, 1987).

Tullberg, Rita McWilliams, editor, *Alfred Marshall in Retrospect* (Aldershot, Eng., 1990).

Turner, Marjorie S., *Nicholas Kaldor and the Real World* (London, 1993).

Von Eschen, Penny, *Race against Empire: Black Americans and Anticolonialism, 1937–1957* (Ithaca, 1997).

Wallerstein, Immanuel, *The Road to Independence: Ghana and the Ivory Coast* (The Hague, 1964).

Waters, Mary C., *Black Identities: Indian Immigrants' Dreams and American Realities* (Cambridge, Mass., 1999).

Waterston, Albert, *Development Planning: Lessons of Experience* (Baltimore, 1965).

Whitaker, John K., editor, *Centenary Essays on Alfred Marshall* (Cambridge, 1990).

Wrigley, E. A., *Continuity, Chance, and Change: The Character of the Industrial Revolution in England* (New York, 1988).

Articles and Dissertations

Agyemang, Solomon, "The Early Education of a Nobel Laureate in the West Indies," *Bulletin of Eastern Caribbean Affairs*, vol. 18, no. 1, 1993, pp. 49–57.

Ahene, Rexford, "William Arthur Lewis," in *Nobel Laureates in Economic Sciences: A Biographical Dictionary*, edited by Bernard S. Katz (New York, 1989), pp. 173–89.

Arhin, Kwame, "The Ghana Cocoa Marketing Board and the Farmer," in *Marketing Boards in Tropical Africa*, edited by Kwame Arhin, Paul Hesp, and Laurens van der Laan (London, 1985), pp. 37–52.

Ariga, Fusao, "The Politics of Development Policy and Planning during the Nkrumah Years, 1951–1966," Ph.D. diss. in history at the School of Oriental and African Studies, University of London, 2001.

Austin, Gareth, "The Emergence of Capitalist Relations in South Asante Cocoa-Farming, c. 1916–33, *Journal of African History*, vol. 28, no. 2, 1987, pp. 259–79.

Bernal, Richard, Mark Figueroa, and Michael Witter, "Caribbean Economic Thought: The Critical Tradition," *Social and Economic Studies*, vol. 33, no. 2, 1984, pp. 5–96.

Bhagwati, Jagdish N., "W. Arthur Lewis: An Appreciation" in *The Theory and Experience of Economic Development: Essays in Honor of Sir W. Arthur Lewis*, edited by Mark Gersovitz, Carlos F. Diaz-Alejandro, Gustav Ranis, and Mark R. Rosenzweig (London, 1982).

Callaway, Barbara, and Emily Card, "Political Constraints on Economic Development in Ghana," in *The State of the Nations: Constraints on Development in Independent Africa*, edited by Michael F. Lofchie (Los Angeles, 1971).

Cell, John W., "On the Eve of Decolonization: The Colonial Office's Plans for the Transfer of Power in Africa, 1947," *Journal of Imperial and Commonwealth History*, vol. 8, no. 3, May 1980, pp. 235–57.

Collier, Paul, and Jan Willem Gunning, "Explaining African Economic Performance," *Journal of Economic Literature*, vol. 37, March 1999, pp. 64–111.

Cooper, Frederick, "Modernizing Bureaucrats, Backward Africans, and the Development Concept," in *International Development and the Social Sciences: Essays on the History and Politics of Knowledge*, edited by Frederick Cooper and Randall Packard (Los Angeles, 1997).

Cowen, Mike, "The Early Years of the Colonial Development Corporation: British State Enterprise Overseas during Late Colonialism," *African Affairs*, vol. 83, no. 330, January 1984, pp. 63–75.

Cowen, Michael and Robert Shenton, "The Origin and Growth of Fabian Colonialism," *Journal of Historical Sociology*, vol. 4, no. 2, June 1991, pp. 143–74.

Crook, Richard, "Decolonization, the Colonial State, and Chieftaincy in the Gold Coast," *African Affairs*, vol. 85, no. 338, January 1986, pp. 75–106.

Easterly, William, "The Ghost of the Financing Gap: How the Harrod-Domar Growth Model Still Haunts Development Economics," Policy Research Working Paper, no. 1807 (World Bank, Washington, D.C., 1997).

Easterly, William, and Ross Levine, "Africa's Growth Tragedy: A Retrospective, 1960–89," Policy Research Working Paper, no. 1503 (World Bank, Washington, D.C., 1995).

Figueroa, Mark, "Class Issues in Industrialization Policy: Lewis's Ideas and the Case of Jamaica, 1945–1956," University of Salford, *Salford Papers in Economics*, no. 1, 1991.

———, "The Formation of the Middle Strata National Leadership in Jamaica: The Crisis of the Seventies and Beyond," *Caribbean Studies*, vol. 21, nos. 1 and 2, January–June 1988, pp. 44-66.

———, "W. Arthur Lewis' Socio-economic Analysis and the Development of Industrialization Policy in Jamaica, 1945–1960," Ph.D. diss. at the University of Manchester, 1993.

Findlay, Ronald, "On W. Arthur Lewis's Contributions to Economics," in *The Theory and Experience of Economic Development: Essays in Honor of Sir W. Arthur Lewis*, edited by Mark Gersovitz, Carlos F. Diaz-Alejandro, Gustav Ranis, and Mark R. Rosenzweig (London, 1982).

Fitzgerald, E.V.K., "Kurt Mandelbaum and the Classical Tradition in Development Theory," in *Strategies of Economic Development: Readings in the Political Economy of Industrialization*, edited by Kurt Martin (London, 1991), pp. 3–27.

Girvan, Norman, "Sir Arthur Lewis: A Personal Appreciation," in *Sir Arthur Lewis: The Simplicity of Genius* (Cave Hill, Barbados, 1989), pp. 19–26.

Green, Reginald H., "Four African Development Plans: Ghana, Kenya, Nigeria, and Tanzania," *Journal of Modern African Studies*, vol. 3, no. 2, 1965, pp. 249–79.

Hill, Robert A., "In England, 1932–1938," in *C.L.R. James, His Life and Work*, edited by Paul Buhle (London, 1986).
Hymer, Stephen H., "The Political Economy of the Gold Coast and Ghana," in *Government and Economic Development*, edited by Gustav Ranis (New Haven, 1971), pp. 129–80.
Ingham, Barbara, "Colonialism and the Economy of the Gold Coast, 1919–1945," in *Development Studies and Colonial Policy*, edited by Barbara Ingham and Colin Simmons (London, 1987), pp. 229–62.
———, "The Manchester Years, 1947–1958: A Tribute to the Work of Arthur Lewis," University of Salford, *Salford Papers in Economics*, Paper no. 10 of 1991.
———, "Shaping Opinion on Development Policy: The Lewis and Seers and Ross Reports of the Early 1950s," University of Salford, *Salford Papers in Economics*, Paper no. 8 of 1987.
Killingray, David, "Race and Rank in the British Army in the Twentieth Century," *Ethnic and Racial Studies*, vol. 10, no. 3, July 1987, pp. 276–90.
———, "Soldiers, Ex-servicemen, and Politics in the Gold Coast, 1939–50," *Journal of Modern African Studies*, vol. 21, no. 3, 1983, pp. 523–34.
Meredith, David, "The British Government and Colonial Economic Policy, 1919–39," *Economic History Review*, second series, vol. 28, no. 3, 1975, pp. 484–98.
Petter, Martin, "Sir Sydney Caine and the Colonial Office in the Second World War: A Career in the Making," *Canadian Journal of History*, vol. 16, no. 1, April 1981, pp. 67–85.
Rathbone, Richard, "Businessmen in Politics: Party Struggle in Ghana, 1944–57," *Journal of Development Studies*, vol. 9, no. 3, April 1973, pp. 391–402.
———, "Some Aspects of the Prehistory of the Ghanaian Economy," *Journal of Commonwealth and Comparative Politics*, vol. 31, no. 1, March 1993, pp. 7–19.
Rimmer, Douglas, "The Crisis in the Ghana Economy," *Journal of Modern African Studies*, vol. 4, no. 1, 1966, pp. 17–32.
———, "Learning about Economic Development from Africa," *African Affairs*, vol. 102, 2003, pp. 469–91
Roemer, Michael, "Ghana, 1950–80: Missed Opportunities," in *World Economic Growth*, edited by Arnold C. Harberger (San Francisco, 1984), pp. 201–25.
Rothchild, Donald, and E. Gyimah-Boadi, "Ghana's Economic Decline and Development Strategies," in *Africa in Economic Crisis*, edited by John Ravenhill (London, 1986), pp. 254–85.
Social and Economic Studies, vol. 29, no. 4, December 1980: *Special Issue in Honor of Sir William Arthur Lewis: 1979 Nobel Laureate*, Institute of Social and Economic Research, University of the West Indies.
St. Clair Drake, J. G., "Vale Systems, Social Structure, and Race Relations in the British Isles," Ph.D. diss., Department of Anthropology, University of Chicago, 1954.
Sunkel, Osvaldo, "The Development of Development Thinking," in *Transnational Capitalism and National Development: New Perspectives on Dependence*, edited by Jose J. Villamil (Hassocks, Sussex, 1979), pp. 19–30.

Wisman, Jon D., "The Methodology of W. Arthur Lewis's Development Economics: Economics as Pedagogy," *World Development*, vol. 14, no. 2, 1986, pp. 165–80.

Worrell, Keith, "The Dual Economy since Lewis: A Study," *Social and Economic Studies: Special Issue in Honor of Sir William Arthur Lewis*, vol. 29, no. 4, December 1980, pp. 27–51.

Index

Abrahams, Peter, 110–11
Accra, 115–16, 150, 160, 172
Adams, Grantley, 13, 231–32, 236
Ady, P. H., 187
Africa, ix-x, 4, 6, 26, 108; Colonial Economic Development Council and, 68–70; decolonization and, 42; free market and, 63–64; pan-Africanism and, 3, 14, 33–35, 144, 168, 206–11; *Politics in West Africa* and, 206–11; ten-year plans and, 114–15. *See also* Ghana
"African Economic Problems" (Lewis), 35, 91–92
Africans and British Rule (Perham), 35–36
Afrique nouvelle, 207
Aggrey, J., 35
agrarian excess, 96–97
Agricultural Development Corporations, 160, 182–83
agriculture, 11, 13, 72–73, 98, 243; cocoa and, 112, 114–15, 117–23, 127, 133–34, 137–38, 152, 156, 163, 169–71, 176–77, 183, 189, 193, 209; Egypt and, 86–87; Gold Coast and, 112, 114–25; industrialization and, 86–87; (*see also* industrialization) small-scale, 106; "Unlimited Supplies of Labour" article and, 82, 98–99; West Indian Welfare Fund and, 46
alcohol, 11
Alice, Princess of West Indies, 223–24, 38
Allen, Ray, 18
all-in planning, 60
aluminum, 194–97, 202, 204
Aluminum Ltd. of Canada, 202
American Economic Association, 264
American Economic Review, 106
Amoaka-Atta, Kwasi, 180–81, 183, 185
Amponsah, R. R., 129
Anglicans, 7–8
Anstey, Vera, 19
Antigua, 6–7, 32–33, 218
Apartheid, 1
Appiah, Joseph, 129, 149
Apter, David, 93
Archbishop of York, 52

Arden-Clarke, Charles, 121, 130
Armitage, R. P., 131–32, 138
Arndt, H. W., 80n3
Asagyefo. *See* Nkrumah, Kwame
Asante region, 112, 128–30, 149–50
Asare, T. O., 181
Ashanti farmers, 128, 209
Ashby, Eric, 216
Ashton, T. S., 19, 90–91
Aspects of Tropical Trade (Lewis), 257
Atta, William Ofori, 127
Auguste, Barry, 234
Austrian school of economics, 17–18
Avoidance of Discrimination Bill, 150–51

Baako, 164
Bank of England: Ghanaian sterling reserves and, 155–58; Second Five-Year Development Plan and, 165
Bank of Ghana, 180–81, 183, 185
Banquah, J. B., 127
Baranski, Leon, 186–88
Barbados, 13, 45–46, 218–19, 222, 235; Caribbean Development Bank and, 255; Lewis' death and, 268. *See also* West Indies
Barnes, W. L. Gorell, 122–23
Bates, Robert, 145, 263
Bauer, P. T., 19, 98, 103, 105–7, 145, 176, 261
Baumol, William, 9, 249n15
bauxite, 204
Beales, 19
Belgian Congo, 180
Ben Gurion, 167
Bennett, William, 250
Berkeley, 244
Beveridge, William, 16–17
Beyond Black or White: An Alternate America (Dixon), 250–51
Bhagwati, Jagdish, 108
Bhapat, 187
Bible, 8
Bing, Geoffrey, 132n45, 145n8, 152
Black, Cyril, 93

Black, Eugene, 166, 202–3
Black Jacobins, The (James), 14, 34
Black Power. *See* racial issues
Bloch, Henry, 147–8
Blodgett, John, 167, 183n10
Blum, Jerome, 240
Board of Trade, 56
Bobrowski, Czeslow, 187–89
Bognar, Josef, 184–89
Botsio, Kojo, 148–49, 152–53, 164, 170, 182
Bourdillon, 60
Bowen, William, 267
Box, N. C., 187
Bras, Gerrit, 223
Brazil, 26
Bretton, Henry, 145
Britain, 1–2, 6, 175; Bank of England and, 155–58, 165; Conservative Party and, 73–74; Coussey Committee and, 116–17; decolonization and, 42; Great Depression and, 15, 17–18, 22, 26; imperial system of, 77; Labour Party and, 73–74; London School of Economics and, 15–24 (*see also* London School of Economics); racial issues and, 3–4, 15–16, 33, 48, 53–54; Seven-Year Development Plan and, 184–85; United Kingdom Trade Mission and, 166; Volta River project and, 194–95; West Indies and, 212, 226–36(*see also* West Indies); World War II era and, 43–44
British Colonial Office, ix-x, 2–3, 8, 19, 41, 81, 144, 269, 272, 275; arrogance of, 43; Barnes and, 122–23; Boyd and, 130; Colonial Development Corporation (CDC) and, 71–78; Colonial Economic Advisory Committee (CEAC) and, 56–67; Colonial Economic Development Council and, 67–71; Colonial Note No. 206 and, 55; Coussey Committee and, 116–17; education and, 214; Gold Coast and, 114, 120, 122–26, 130; Hailes and, 233; Hailey and, 52–54; information access and, 43; Keynesianism and, 20; League of Coloured Peoples and, 47–52; Lewis's early contacts with, 43, 52–55; military enlistment and, 47–49; Moyne Commission and, 44–47; Nkrumah and, 110; rejection of Lewis by, 19–20; St. Lucia and, 10; Standing Closer Union Committee and, 228; University College of the West Indies and, 216, 220; Volta River project and, 198; Watson Commission and, 116–17; West Indian federation and, 227–36
British Commonwealth Relations Office, 165
British Guiana, 13, 45, 218–22, 226, 235, 254
British High Commission, 152
British Honduras, 218
British Medical Journal, 51
British Public Record Office, ix
British Virgin Islands, 218
Brookings Institution, 244
Brown, Douglas, 240
Brown, Phelps, 19
Budapest University, 184
Bulletin and Scots Pictorial, 52
Bundy, McGeorge, 246–47
Burma, 87
Bursah, 164
Busia, K., 149
Bustamante, 230–31, 236

Caine, Sydney, 47, 56–61, 64–67, 75
Cairncross, A. K., 105n62
Campbell, Jock, 239
Canada, 175
capital flows, 54–55
capitalism, 104
Capitalism and Slavery (Williams), 14
Capital (Marx), 83
capsid beetle, 169, 171
Cardenas, 167
Caribbean Development Bank, 254–56, 266, 269
Carl Gustaf, King of Sweden, 143
Carney, 187
Carr-Saunders, A. H., 21, 37–38, 64
Cato, A. S., 217, 220
Cato Commission, 217, 219
Central African Federation, 74–75
Ceylon, 87
Chaddock Chair of Economics, 37–38
Chaucer, 12
China, 26, 103
Church of England, 7–8
City College of New York, 234
civil rights. *See* racial issues
Clark, Colin, 40
Clauson, Gerard, 54–61, 65–66
Coase, Ronald, 18, 263–64
Cobden Lecturer, 39

cocoa, 112, 114–15; Asante farmers and, 122, 127; capsid beetle and, 169, 171; CPP and, 120–23; Crown Agents and, 156; Ghana and, 152; *Politics in West Africa* and, 209; price issues and, 152, 176–77, 183, 189, 193; Second Five-Year Development Plan and, 163; Tours and, 133–34, 137–38
Cocoa Marketing Board, 117–22, 152, 156, 163, 169–70
Cocoa Purchasing Company, 129–30, 137–38
Codrington College, 46
Cohen, A., 114
Cold War, 81, 107, 194, 203–4
Cole, G.D.H., 90–91
Colombia, 26
Colonial Development Corporation (CDC), ix–x, 78, 144; Central African Federation and, 74–75; Conservative Party and, 73–74; industrial model of, 71–72; Labour Party and, 73–74; laissez-faire policy and, 76–77; Lewis dismissal and, 75–76; Reith and, 74; Trefgarne and, 73, 75
"Colonial Development: The Defect of the Plans" (Lewis), 70, 83–84
Colonial Economic Advisory Committee (CEAC), 56–67
Colonial Economic Development Council, 67–71, 75
"Colonial Economic Development" (Lewis), 62–63
colonialism, 28–30; British Colonial Office and, 43–44; Caine and, 56–67; Clauson and, 56–66; Colonial Development Corporation (CDC) and, ix–x, 71–78, 144; Colonial Economic Advisory Committee (CEAC) and, 56–67; Colonial Economic Development Council and, 67–71, 75; education and, 69–71; free market and, 63–64; Gold Coast and, 112; industrialization and, 62–63; laissez-faire policy and, 76–77; Nkrumah and, 144–45 (*see also* Nkrumah, Kwame); propaganda and, 42–43; ten-year plans and, 114–15; "Unlimited Supplies of Labour" article and, 82–102
Colonial Service Recruitment Manual, 51
Commercial Bank of Ghana, 158, 180, 182
Committee of Youth Organization, 155
communism, 14, 81

Conditions of Economic Progress (Clark), 40
Congress for Cultural Freedom, 206
Conservative Party, 73–74
Convention People's Party (CPP), 108–11, 120, 123, 146–47; Asante region and, 128–29, 149–50; Avoidance of Discrimination Bill and, 150–51; Cocoa Marketing Board and, 121–22; criticism of, 150; Emergency Powers Bill and, 151; *Evening News* and, 182; Gbedemah and, 155; Ghana Bottling Company and, 160; Gold Coast independence and, 127–30; Lewis and, 125, 127; misuse of funds by, 129–30; NLM and, 127, 130, 137; political patronage and, 167–69, 178; *Politics in West Africa* and, 209; popular discontent with, 180; Tours and, 131–38; United Party and, 150; Volta River project and, 195
Cooper, Frederick, 80n3
Coussey Committee, 116–17, 120–21
Cowan, L. Gray, 207
Creating Political Order: The Party-States of West Africa (Zolberg), 210
Creole, 7
Crowder, Michael, 207
Crown Agents, 155–56, 183n10
Cuba, 46
Cumming-Bruce, F. E., 137

Daily Gleaner, 223
Dalgleish, 60
Danquah, J. B., 118, 122, 149
D'Arbousier, G., 207
Davies, H. O., 110, 207
Dean, Phyllis, 90
Deane, 91
decolonization, 1, 4; Africa and, 42; dating beginning of, 42; growth and, 81; Trefgarne and, 75; West Indies and, 212
de Graft Johnson, 187
Delhi School of Economics, 189
Denmark, 36–37
Deportation Law, 151, 154
development economics, 272–73; Caribbean Development Bank and, 254–56, 266; critics and, 260–65; ECLA and, 79; Ghanaian sterling reserves and, 154–59 (*see also* Ghana); industrialization and, 79–80; institutionalism and, 263–64; Keynesianism and, 261–62; Pearson Commission and, 253–54; poverty and,

development economics (cont'd)
  266–67; Princeton University and, 241–44, 260–67; Rosenstein-Rodan and, 79–80; "Unlimited Supplies of Labour" article and, 82–102; West Indies and, 261 (see also West Indies); worldwide growth and, 80–81
"Development of Manufacturing Industries, The" (Lewis), 62
Development Progress Report, 135–36
Devons, Ely, 39
Diaz-Alejandro, Carlos, 252–53
District Bank Review, 87
Dixon, Vernon, 250–52
Dolly, Reginald, 225
Domar, Evsey, 97, 103
Dominica, 218, 233
Dorman, R. B., 165
Drake, St. Clair, 207
Du Bois, W.E.B., 34n81, 144, 270
Durbin, Evan F. M., 57, 60–61

Economic Commission for Latin America (ECLA), 79
"Economic Development with Unlimited Supplies of Labour" (Lewis), 79, 84; agriculture and, 98–99; clarity of, 82–83; criticism of, 97–100; disguised unemployment and, 85–86, 97; Hammonds' study and, 90–93; impact of, 88–89, 93–102; investment and, 91, 95–96; modernization theory and, 93–95; neoclassical economics and, 88–89, 91; prices and, 88–90; wages and, 88
economic issues: African ten-year plans and, 114–15; all-in planning and, 60; Austrian school and, 17–18; business firms and, 27; capital flow, 54–55; Caribbean Development Bank and, 254–56, 266, 269; Colonial Economic Development Council and, 67–71; colonial territories and, 22–23; development economics and, 261 (see also development economics); economic planning and, 28–32; Five-Year Development plans and, 59, 96, 153–54, 161–69, 176–77, 184, 186, 276; Ford Foundation and, 242–43; free market and, 57, 63–64, 76; Ghanaian sterling reserves and, 154–59 (see also Ghana); Great Depression and, 15, 17–18, 22, 26, 258; historical studies on, 256–60; human capital and, 4; industrialization and, 62–63 (see also industrialization); international pricing and, 26; Keynesianism and, 17–20, 97, 261–62; laissez-faire policy and, 76–77, 264; London School of Economics and, 15–24 (see also London School of Economics); modernization theory and, 93–95; Moyne Commission and, 44–47; neoclassical economics and, 88–91; North American Trade Organization (NATO) and, 113; outline planning and, 60; population growth and, 100–101; Seven-Year Development Plan and, 179, 184–93; University College of the West Indies and, 218–26, 236–38; "Unlimited Supplies of Labour" article and, 82–102; Volta River project and, 151–54, 164–65, 173, 193–206; West Indian federation and, 226–36; West Indian Welfare Fund and, 45–46; World War II effects on, 1–4
Economic Journal, 97
Economic Plan for Jamaica, An (Lewis), 29
Economic Problems of To-Day (Lewis), 25–26, 29
"Economic Profile of the American Black, The" (Lewis), 248
Economics of Nationhood, The, 231
Economic Survey, 1919–1939 (Lewis), 25
Economic Survey of Ghana, The, 191
Economist magazine, 19, 165
education, 4; agricultural, 243; British Colonial Office and, 214; class distinctions and, 11–12; Colonial Economic Development Council and, 69–71; competition and, 11–12; English, 7, 11–12; Gold Coast and, 112–14, 123; importance of, 213–14; industrialization and, 72–73; labor and, 213; mass, 69–71, 213; Moyne Commission and, 46–47; racial issues and, 5, 10–15, 213; University College of the West Indies and, 212–26; West Indian Welfare Fund and, 45–46
Edusei, Krobo, 129, 148–49
Egypt, 26, 53, 86–87, 94, 102, 202, 262
Egyptian Society of Political Economy, Statistics, and Legislation, 86–87
Electricity Corporation of Ghana, 205
Elizabeth II, Queen of England, 129
Emanuel, A., 125
Emergency Powers Bill, 151
engineering, 46

Enlightenment, 244, 253, 277
entrepreneurship, 77, 82
equilibrium theory, 84
"Essay in Dynamic Theory, An" (Harrod), 97
Essay on the Nature and Significance of Economic Science, An (Robbins), 23
Essays on the Theory of Economic Growth (Domar), 103
Ethiopia, 34, 179
Evening News (CPP newspaper), 182
Evolution of the International Economic Order, The (Lewis), 257
"Evolution of the Peasantry in the British West Indies, The" (Lewis), 17

Fabians, 2, 32, 44, 107; British Colonial Office and, 53, 55; Bureau conferences of, 28–29, 110; Colonial Economic Development Council and, 67; Hammonds and, 92; Tories and, 75; Trefgarne and, 73, 75
Fanon, Frantz, 14, 16
Fanti people, 209
Fascism, 1–4
Fei, John C. H., 101
Figueroa, Mark, 14
Finer, S. E., 207
Fitch, Bob, 145, 175, 179
Five-Year Development Plan, 153–54, 276; Bank of England and, 165; Second, 161–69, 176–77, 184, 186; Soviet Union and, 59, 96
food, 87–88
Ford Foundation, 242–23, 246–47, 250
France, 6–7, 26, 36, 180
free market, 57, 63–64, 76

Gambia Poultry Scheme, 73
Garvey, Amy Jacques, 33
Garvey, Marcus, 14, 33, 108
Ga Standfast Association, 150
Gbedemah, Komla, 121, 126, 133, 142, 170, 179, 181; background of, 155; Bank of England and, 155; as conservative, 152–53; CPP and, 155; Crown Agents and, 155–58; firing of, 182; Ghanaian sterling reserves and, 154–59; press campaign against, 182; UGCC and, 155; Volta River project and, 164, 195, 202–3
Geiss, Immanuel, 34n83
General Theory, The (Keynes), 261
Germany, 1, 26, 48, 51, 181

Gersovitz, Mark, 28n64
Ghana, ix-x, 2–3, 8–9, 111, 131, 213, 215, 235, 266, 169, 275–76; Accra and, 115–16, 150, 160, 172; Africanization of, 179–80; aluminum and, 194–97, 202; American Embassy and, 152; Amoaka-Atta and, 180–83; Asante region and, 112, 128–30, 149–50; Avoidance of Discrimination Bill and, 150–51; banking issues and, 180–85, 190–91; Bognar and, 184–89; British High Commission and, 152; budget of 1958–59 and, 159–61; cabinet of, 148–49, 152–53; cocoa and, 152, 156; CPP and, 149, 177; Crown Agents and, 155–58, 183n10; deficits in, 180; Deportation Law and, 151, 154; dictatorial rule and, 151–52; as East-West battleground, 180; economic boom in, 78; Emergency Powers Bill and, 151; Five-Year Development Plan and, 153–54, 161–69, 177, 184, 276; fragile economics of, 148; as Gold Coast, 4 (see also Gold Coast); Guineans and, 168–69; IMF and, 152, 162, 166; independence for, 144, 174–78, 182, 199; Industrial Development Corporation and, 159–63, 176; investment and, 179; labor and, 163–64; National Planning Commission and, 184–86, 189; Nkrumah and, 144–48 (see also Nkrumah, Kwame); postwar years and, 146, 153; Preventive Detention Bill and, 151, 182–83; private sector and, 179; Seven-Year Development Plan and, x, 179–80, 184–93; Standing Development Committee and, 153–54; sterling reserves issues and, 154–59; Tours and, 146; United Kingdom Trade Mission and, 166; U.S. trade and, 158–59; Volta River project and, 151–54, 164–65, 173, 193–206; wild-cat schemes in, 122; World Bank and, 151–52, 166, 186–87, 202–5; young radicals and, 179–80
Ghana Bottling Company, 160
Ghana: The End of an Illusion (Fitch & Oppenheimer), 175, 179
Girvan, Norman, 225
Gluckman, Max, 103
Goheen, Robert, 240–52
Gold Coast, 4, 104, 144; Accra riots and, 115–16; agriculture and, 114–15; Asante region and, 128–30; Ashanti separatism and, 128; British Colonial Office and,

Gold Coast (cont'd)
114, 120, 122–26, 130; cocoa and, 112, 114–23; colonialism and, 112; conditions in, 111–12; Coussey Committee and, 116–17, 120–21; CPP and, 120–38; decolonization and, 42; economic background of, 112–17; education and, 112–14, 123; geographical zones of, 112; home market manufacturing and, 124–25; independence for, 127–30; industrialization and, 111, 123–27; labor and, 109; Lewis and, 123–27, 132, 136; NLM and, 127, 130, 137; Parliamentary Select Committee and, 120; politics in, 111–17, 127–38; population of, 112; precious metals and, 112–13; Tours and, 131–38; UGCC and, 115–16; Volta River project an, 109; Watson Commission and, 116–17; World War II era and, 113–14. *See also* Ghana

Great Depression, 15, 17–18, 22, 26, 258
Great Powers, 19
Greece, 102
Green, M. M., 36n86
Green, Reginald, 145
Grenada, 32, 218, 233
Griffin, Keith, 101
growth: Cold War and, 81; development economics and, 80–81 (*see also* development economics); disguised unemployment and, 85–86; education and, 213; industrialization and, 91 (*see also* industrialization); "Unlimited Supplies of Labour" article and, 82–102
Growth and Fluctuations, 1870–1913 (Lewis), 257
Growth and Fluctuations, 1870–1914 (Lewis), 25–26
Guiana, 13
Guinea, 168–69

Hailes, Patrick, 233
Hailey, Lord, 52, 54, 57, 75
Haiti, 14, 46
Halevy, Daniel, 3
Haley, B. F., 106
Halim, 185
Hammonds, Barbara & John, 90–93
Hancock, Keith, 56
Harrod, R. F., 97
Hart, David, 204
Haverford College, 251
Hayek, Friedrich, 17–25

Henderson, Hubert, 56, 60–61
Hicks, John, 18, 38
Hinden, Rita, 110
hiring discrepancies, 49–51, 68
Hirschman, Albert, 97, 187, 272
Hobhouse, Leonard, 92
Hobson, J. A., 92, 125
Hodgkin, Thomas, 207
Howard University, 216
Hungary, 184

Imperial College of Tropical Agriculture, 46, 221
imperialism, 14–15
India, 1, 87–88, 94, 113
Industrial Development Corporation, 159–63, 176, 182–83
industrialization, 62–63, 273–74; Ashton and, 90–91; Botsio and, 149; cocoa and, 112, 114–23; Colonial Development Corporation (CDC) and, 71–78; development economics and, 79–80 (*see also* development economics); education and, 72–73; Egypt and, 86–87; Gold Coast and, 109–38; Hammonds's study and, 90–93; import-substitution and, 87; modernization theory and, 93–95; neoclassical economics and, 88–89; population growth and, 100–101; revolution of, 90–92; Rosenstein-Rodan and, 79–80; "Unlimited Supplies of Labour" article and, 82–102; Volta River project and, 151–54, 164–65, 173, 193–206
Industrialization and the Gold Coast Economy (Lewis), 122, 136
Industrialization of Backward Areas, The (Martin), 39
Industrial Revolution, 1760–1830, The (Ashton), 90
institutionalism, 263–64
International Monetary Fund (IMF), 152, 162, 166, 273, 275
Inter-University Council, 216
investment, 91, 95–96; Caribbean Development Bank and, 254–56, 266, 269; Crown Agents and, 155–58; Ghanaian sterling reserves and, 154–59; Gold Coast cocoa and, 112, 114–23; government and, 103–5; Industrial Development Corporation and, 159–60; savings and, 103–4; Volta River project and, 193–206
Iran, 87

Irvine, James, 215
Islam, 103
Ivory Coast, 176

Jackson, Robert, 154, 161–65, 168, 170, 198
Jagan, Cheddi, 13, 219–20, 226, 236, 254
Jagan, Janet, 236
Jamaica, 13, 44, 94, 204, 227; Bustamante and, 230–31; Caribbean Development Bank and, 254–56; University College of the West Indies and, 215–23; West Indian federation and, 226–36 (*see also* West Indies)
Jamaica Arise journal, 72
Jamaican Labour Party, 230
James, C.L.R., 14, 33–34, 144, 245
James, D. G., 216–17, 238
James, Jeffrey, 101
Japan, 1, 26, 103
Jewkes, John, 19, 39
Johnson, Harry, 261–62
Johnson, Keith, 234
Jones, Arthur Creech, 67, 71–72
Jones, Norton, 197
Jorgensen, Dale, 262
Journal of Religion and Health, 248
Judaism, 8

Kaiser Aluminum and Chemical Corporation, 201–2
Kaldor, Nicholas, 18–19, 107, 187
Keenleyside, Hugh, 148, 170–72
Kennedy, John F., 203–4
Kenya, 35, 64, 130
Kenyatta, Jomo, 111
Kerr, L. J., 52
Kessels, Hubert, 181, 183
Keynes, John Maynard, 17–18, 40, 273
Keynesianism, 17–20, 97, 261–62
Keys, The (League of Coloured Peoples), 3, 35–37, 91, 110
Kiano, J. G., 187
Killick, A. T., 80n3, 145, 189–91
King, Bruce, 12n16
King's College, Cambridge, 207
Knox, A. D., 105n62
Krugman, Paul, 82n5
Kumi, Ayeh, 160–61, 164, 176, 179, 182, 185

labor, 13, 55; agrarian excess and, 96–97; agriculture and, 86–87, 106 (*see also* agriculture); disguised unemployment and, 85–86, 97; economic history and, 256–60; education and, 213 (*see also* education); food and, 87–88; Gold Coast and, 109, 112–26; Hammonds study and, 90–93; hiring discrepancies and, 49–51, 68; London School of Economics and, 84; modernization theory and, 93–95; Moyne Commission and, 44–47; negative productivity and, 93–94, 99–101; neoclassical economics and, 88–89, 91; population growth and, 100–1; shortages and, 109; surplus population and, 96–100; unemployment categories and, 85; "Unlimited Supplies of Labour" article and, 82–102; wages and, 88, 94
Labour Party, 73–74
La Corbiniere, Carl, 220
laissez-faire policy, 76–77, 264
Laski, Harold, 19, 24
Latin America, 79
Leading Issues in Economic Development (Meier), 96
League of Coloured Peoples, 3, 34–35, 75, 110, 140, 244–45; British Colonial Office and, 47–52; Colonial Economic Development Council and, 68; hiring discrepancies and, 49–51; Lewis and, 212–226; military enlistment and, 47–49; publication issues and, 51–52
Leeward Islands, 45
Legum, Colin, 207
Lenin, 125
Lennox-Boyd, Alan, 130
Lerner, Daniel, 93
Lester, Richard, 240–41, 244
Levy, Marion, 93
Lewis, Barbara, 33, 142
Lewis, Elizabeth, 33, 142
Lewis, George, 6–7
Lewis, Gladys née Jacobs, ix-x, 32–33, 108, 141, 143, 269
Lewis, Gordon K., 235n58
Lewis, Ida Barton, 6–8, 139
Lewis, John, 96, 253–56, 265–66
Lewis, William Arthur, ix; accomplishments of, 2–5, 17, 79, 85, 109–10, 143, 212, 257, 265–66, 268, 273–77; African American studies program and, 245–48; attacks West Indian politicians, 234–35; background of, 1–2, 6–10, 40; Black Power and, 244; British Colonial Office and, 43 (*see also* British Colonial Office); business firms and, 27; Caine and, 56–

Lewis, William Arthur (cont'd)
66, 67; capital flow studies of, 54–55; Caribbean Development Bank and, 254–56, 266, 169; Central African Federation and, 74–75; Clauson and, 56–66; Colonial Development Corporation (CDC) and, 71–78; Colonial Economic Advisory Committee (CEAC) and, 56–67; Colonial Economic Development Council and, 67–71; colonial economics and, 28–30; CPP and, 125, 127; credentials of, 109–10; Crown Agents and, 156–58; death of, 268; decolonization and, 42, 212; development economics and, 260–67 (*see also* development economics); Director's Prize and, 17; duodenal ulcer and, 66–67; economic history and, 256–60; economic planning and, 28–32; education and, 213 (*see also* education); Enlightenment and, 244, 253, 277; Ford Foundation and, 242–43; Ghana and, 144–78 (*see also* Ghana); Great Depression and, 158; health of, 236, 241–42; hiring discrepancies and, 49–51; idealism of, 59–60; Industrial Development Corporation and, 159–61; international pricing and, 26; Keynesianism and, 19–20; League of Coloured Peoples and, 47–52, 140; London School of Economics and, 15–24 (*see also* London School of Economics); Moyne Commission and, 44–47; NAACP and, 144, 271; National Humanities Center and, 250, 271–72; Nkrumah and, 169–78 (*see also* Nkurmah, Kwame); Nobel Prize and, 2, 79, 85, 143, 257, 264–66, 268, 273, 277; Pearson Commission and, 253–54; personality of, 8–10, 162, 268–70; pictures of, 140–43; politics and, 9, 13–14; Princeton University and, 240–67; publications/papers of, 20, 24–33, 40–41, 53–54, 62–63, 68, 76, 79, 82–102, 109–10, 122, 124–26, 136, 167, 206–11, 246–48, 256–60, 273–75; racial issues and, 33–40, 270–72 (*see also* racial issues); radicalism and, 249, 272; religion and, 7–8, 244; retirement of, 266; St. Lucia and, 10–15, 268; Second Five-Year Development Plan and, 161–69; Seven-Year Development Plan and, 179–80, 184, 187–88; Special Fund for Economic Development and, 172; sterling reserves and, 154–59; student abilities of, 8–13; as teacher, 21; thesis of, 20–21; University College of the West Indies and, 212–26; University of Guyana and, 254; "Unlimited Supplies of Labour" article and, 79, 82–102; Vietnam War era and, 245; Volta River project and, 151–54, 164–65, 173, 193–206; wedding of, 141; West Indian federation and, 229–236; West Indian Students Association talk and, 234; Wicksell Lectures and, 257; World War II and, 1–4

Lewis Papers, 174, 207n70, 275
liberalism, 10, 15, 38, 43
Liverpool Daily Mail, 52
London School of Economics, 3, 52–53, 56, 62, 66, 268–69; Ashton and, 90; Beveridge and, 16–17; colonial economics and, 29–33; Director's Prize and, 17; faculty of, 17–19; Great Depression and, 17–18; Hayek and, 17–19; intellectual environment of, 17–18; Keynesianism and, 17–20; labor and, 84; Nkrumah and, 110; racial issues and, 2, 20–21, 37–40; Robbins and, 17–24, 83; University of Cambridge and, 17; World War II era and, 21–22
Low, J. M., 103
Loynes, J. M., 165
Lugard, Lord, 50

McFadyen, 60
"Machinery for Economic Planning" (Lewis), 62
Machlup, Fritz, 240
McKay, Claude, 14–15
Magee, Brian, 17
Mair, Lucy, 18–19
Malaya, 87, 157
Malinowski, Bronislaw, 18–19, 24
Malta, 62
Malthus, Thomas, 24, 83
Manchester Guardian, 52, 70
Manchester School journal, 3, 79, 82, 98, 101
Manchuria, 26
manganese, 112–13
Manley, Norman, 13, 227, 229–30, 236
markets: agriculture and, 86–87 (*see also* agriculture); food and, 87–88 (*see also* cocoa); free 57, 63–64, 76; North Ameri-

can Trade Organization (NATO) and, 113; "Unlimited Supplies of Labour" article and, 82–102. *See also* labor
Mars, J., 103
Martin, Kurt, 39, 103
Marx, Karl, 33–34, 83, 105, 125, 184–85, 269
Masaryk, 167
Mass Education Sub-Committee, 70
Mboya, Tom, 207
medicine, 46
Meier, Gerald M., 96
Mensah, Joseph H., 184–89
Milicent, Ernest, 207
military enlistment, 47–49
Mill, James, 24
Mill, John Stuart, 24, 102, 105
Millar-Craig, H., 184
Mining Policy in Africa" (British Colonial Office), 55
Mintz, Sidney, 13
modernization theory, 93–95
Montserrat, 218
Moody, Harold, 34–35, 47–48, 51, 110, 140, 244
Moravians, 7
Morgenstern, Oscar, 240
Mountford, J. F., 38
Moyne, Lord, 44, 51
Moyne Commission, 44–47, 52
Mudd Library, ix-x
Munoz Marin, 167
Muslims, 112
Myrdal, Gunnar, 272

Naer, T. T., 184
Nasser, Gamal Abdel, 201–2
National Association for the Advancement of Colored Peoples (NAACP), 144, 245, 271
National Humanities Center, 250, 271–72
nationalism, 33, 42; CPP and, 109–10; Gold Coast and, 109–38; UGCC and, 115–16
National Liberation Movement (NLM), 127, 130, 137
National Planning Commission, 184–86, 189
Nazism, 1, 42, 48
Negro in the Caribbean, The (Williams), 10–11

Newsletter (League of Coloured Peoples), 52–53
News Notes (League of Coloured Peoples), 50–51
New Statesman and Nation, 52
New York Times Sunday Magazine, 251
Nigeria, 64, 69, 112, 157
Nimes, C. V., 226
Nkrumah, Kwame, x, 4, 8, 60, 78, 108, 142, 146, 214–15, 275, 277; April 8, 1961, broadcast of, 182; as Asagyefo, 181–82; Avoidance of Discrimination Bill and, 150–51; British Colonial Office and, 110; cabinet of, 148–49; CPP and, 109, 120–21, 178; Deportation Law and, 154; dictatorial rule and, 151–52; failures of, 144–45, 154; Gbedemah and, 155; as Leader of Government Business, 121; lectures of, 110–11; Lewis report and, 126; London School of Economics and, 110; 1958–59 budget and, 159–60; NLM and, 130; overthrow of, 184, 191; policy changes of, 182–83; political patronage and, 167–69, 178; *Politics in West Africa* and, 209; Preventive Detention Act and, 182–83; racial issues and, 245; Second Five-Year Plan and, 161–69; Seven-Year Development Plan and, 190–92; Standing Development Committee and, 153–54; Tours and, 132–33; Volta River project and, 193–206
Nobel Prize, 2, 18, 79, 85, 143, 257, 265–66, 268, 273, 277
North, Douglass, 263
North American Trade Organization (NATO), 113
"Notes on Black Studies" (Lewis), 246–48
nuclear weapons, 180
Nurske, Ragnar, 103

Observer, 207
Okoh, 187
Oldham, J. H., 52
Olin Matheson Company, 202
Olympio, Sylvanus, 208
"On Planning in Backward Countries" (Lewis), 30–31
Oppenheimer, Mary, 145, 175, 179
outline planning, 60
Overhead Costs (Lewis), 20, 27–28
Owen, David, 148
Owen, Frank, 52

Owusu, Victor, 129–30, 149
Oxford University, 22, 33, 38, 216

Padmore, George, 9–10, 14, 144; ideologies of, 245; racial issues and, 33–34, 110; Volta River project and, 195–96
pan-Africanism, 14, 33, 144; League of Coloured Peoples and, 3, 34–35; NAACP and, 144; Nkrumah and, 168 (*see also* Nkrumah, Kwame); *Politics in West Africa* and, 206–11
Panter-Brick, S. K., 207
Parsons, Talcott, 93, 251
Passing of Traditional Society, The (Lerner), 93
Patterson, Gardner, 240–42
Pearce, Robert, 42
Pearson Commission, 253–54
Pember and Boyle, 158
People's National Movement, 216, 219
Perham, Margery, 35–36
Phillips, J. B., 185
Piercy, Lord, 158
Planning Commission of Poland, 189
Plant, Arnold, 17–25, 56, 66, 264
Polanyi, Michael, 39
Politics in West Africa (Lewis), 206–11, 235, 263–64
poverty, 1, 67, 266–67; food and, 87–88; free market and, 63–64; government and, 104; growth and, 81; Moyne Commission and, 44–47; population and, 87–88; "Unlimited Supplies of Labour" article and, 82–102; vicious cycles of, 81; West Indian federation and, 226–36
Prebisch, Raúl, 32, 79, 88n16, 272
Prempeh, Osei Agyeman, II, 129
Preston, R. H., 103
Preventive Detention Act, 151, 182–83
Princeton Alumni Magazine, 247
Princeton University, 234; academic atmosphere of, 243–44; African American studies program and, 245–48; Bowen and, 269; development economics and, 241–44; economic history studies and, 256–60; Ford Foundation and, 242–43; Goheen and, 240–42; Mudd Library and, ix–x; Patterson and, 240–42; racial issues and, 244–53; Robertson donation and, 240–41; undergraduate teaching methods of, 242; Vietnam War era and, 245; Woodrow Wilson School of Public and International Affairs and, 212, 240–44, 253, 255, 265–66, 269
"Principles of Developmental Planning, The" (Lewis), 68
Principles of Economic Planning, The: A Study Prepared for the Fabian Society (Lewis), 28–30, 43, 110, 165–66
Principles of Political Economy (Mill), 102
Problems of Capital Formation in Underdeveloped Countries (Nurske), 103
propaganda, 42–43, 48
Protestantism, 7–8, 91
Puerto Rico, 46

Quandt, Richard, 239
Queen's Royal College, 12
Queens University, 216

rabbis, 8
racial issues, 8–9, 19, 270–72; African American studies program and, 245–48; Avoidance of Discrimination Bill and, 150–51; Britain and, 3–4, 15–16, 33, 48, 53–54; careers and, 248–50; Central African Federation and, 74–75; Denmark and, 36–37; Dixon and, 250–52; education and, 5, 10–15, 213, 247; elitism and, 216–17; enlistment and, 47–49; hiring discrepancies and, 49–51, 68; imperialism and, 14–15; integration and, 1; Kenyatta and, 111; League of Coloured Peoples and, 3, 34–35, 47–52, 68, 75, 110, 140, 212–26, 244–45; Lewis's early career and, 33–40; London School of Economics and, 2, 20–21, 37–40; merit judgment and, 244; Moody and, 34–35; NAACP and, 144, 245, 271; pan-Africanism and, 3, 14, 33–35, 144, 168, 206–11; Paris and, 36; Princeton University and, 244–53; propaganda and, 48; radicalism and, 249, 272; religion and, 111; riots, 2; St. Lucia and, 10–15; slavery and, 11, 45; stereotyping and, 251; two-tiered system and, 11; United States and, 10, 14–15; Vietnam War era and, 245
Raj, K. N., 187–88
Raj, K. R., 189
Ramanujain, K.N.R., 186–87
Ranis, Gustav, 101
Read, Margaret, 52
real democrats, 84

Reith, Lord, 74
religion, 7, 18, 91, 244; Avoidance of Discrimination Bill and, 150–51; racial issues and, 111
Reynolds Metals Company, 202
Rhodesia, 35, 48
Ricardo, David, 24, 83, 105
Richards, Audrey, 207
Rimmer, Douglas, 145, 158, 191–92
riots, 2
Robbins, Lionel, 83; British Colonial Office and, 56, 61, 66; free trade and, 57; racial issues and, 17–25; right-wing policies of, 57
Robeson, Paul, 33–34
Robinson, E.A.G., 56
Robinson, Joan, 107
Rodney, Walter, 225
Roman Catholicism, 7–8
Rome, 102
Rosenstein-Rodan, Paul, 19, 79–80, 83, 96–97, 103, 107, 272
Rostow, W. W., 39

Sahara Desert, 180
St. Kitts, 13, 218
St. Lucia, 6, 10–15, 218, 268, 270
St. Mary's College, 12
St. Vincent, 218
Santo Domingo, 46
scholarships, 12–13
Schultz, Theodore, W., 85–86, 98, 101, 261, 265
Schumpeter, Joseph, 39
secretaries of government, 56–57
Seers, Douglas, 187
Seers, Dudley, 105
Sen, Amartya, 80–81, 101
Senegal, 207
Senghor, Leopold, 208
Seven-Year Development Plan, x, 179–80; Accra conference and, 187–89; Bank of England and, 190; Bognar and, 184–89; Britain and, 184–85; cocoa prices and, 189, 193; Five-Year Development Plan and, 184; Killick and, 189–91; Lewis and, 184, 187–88; Mensah and, 185–89; National Planning Commission and, 184–86, 189; Nkrumah and, 190–92; Rimmer and, 191–92; United States and, 184–85
Shadow of Keynes, The (Jackson), 262

Shakespeare, 12
Shaw, George Bernard, 51
Sherlock, Philip, 214, 225, 227
Shils, Edward, 207
Singer, H. W., 88n16
Skilled Labourer, The (Hammonds & Hammonds), 92
Skillings, Robert, 203
slavery, 11, 45
Smith, Adam, 24, 83, 105
Snelling, A. W., 148, 156, 180–81
"Social and Economic Planning in the Empire" (Caine & Clauson), 60
socialism, 2, 28–32
Somaliland, 62
"Some Aspects of the Flow of Capital in the British Colonies" (Lewis), 54
South Africa, 26, 35, 113
Southampton University, 216
Soviet Union, 26, 104; economic planning methods of, 179–80, 193; Five-Year Development plans of, 59, 96; manganese production and, 113; Volta River project and, 193
Stalin, 96, 104
Stamp, Lord, 21
Standing Development Committee, 153–54, 161, 170
Stanford University, 244
Stanley, Oliver, 57–61
Stanley Jevons Professor of Political Economy, 39
sterling reserves, 154–59
Stiglitz, Joseph, 28n63
Stone, Lawrence and Jeanne, 271n4
Stopford, John S. B., 38
subsidies, 100
Sunday Guardian, 234
Sunkel, Osvaldo, 191

Tanganyika, 64, 73
tariffs, 55
Tawney, R. H., 19, 24
taxes, 55, 100
Taylor, Thomas, 214–15
Thailand, 87
"Theory of Economic Development, The" (Lewis), 39
Theory of Economic Growth, The (Lewis), 24, 76, 80, 98, 273–75; as classic, 241; education and, 213; governmental role and, 103–5; impact of, 102–8; institu-

314 • Index

Theory of Economic Growth, The (Lewis) (*cont'd*)
  tionalism and, 263–64; investment and, 103–4; Nobel Prize committee and, 257; savings and, 103–4; West Indies and, 24
Tinbergen, Jan, 266
Tobago, 45, 146, 216, 218, 222, 234, 255. *See also* West Indies
Togoland, 150
Tories, 75
Toure, Sekou, 168, 208
Tours, Kenneth, 131–38, 146, 152
Toussaint-Louverture, 14, 33, 34
Town Labourer, The (Hammonds & Hammonds), 92
Toynbee, Arnold, 19, 24
Transforming Traditional Agriculture (Schultz), 98
Trefgarne, Lord, 73, 75
Trinidad, 12–13, 19, 45–46, 143; Caribbean Development Bank and, 255; University College of the West Indies and, 216, 218–19, 221–22, 225, 227, 234, 236–37. *See also* West Indies
Truman Harry, 1
Turkey, 26
TVA project, 59, 193, 200–201

Uganda, 64, 104
Undergraduate Guild of Students, 224–25
unemployment. *See* labor
United Ghana Farmers Congress, 169
United Gold Coast Convention Party (UGCC), 115–16, 155
United Nations, 3, 81, 98, 272–73; Auguste and, 234; ECLA and, 79; labor issues and, 84–85; Nkrumah and, 147–48, 170–71; Special Fund for Economic Development and, 172, 215, 219, 266
United Party, 150
United States, 4, 6; Ghana and, 152, 158–59; Great Depression and, 17, 22, 26; Kennedy and, 203–4; Moyne Report and, 45; racial issues and, 10, 14–15; Seven-Year Development Plan and, 184–85; State Department, 275; TVA program and, 59, 193, 200–201
University College of the West Indies, 2–4, 142, 171, 212, 214, 243; administrative structure of, 218, 226; available degrees at, 216; British Colonial Office and, 216, 220; Cato Commission and, 217, 219; economic issues of, 218–26, 236–38; educational methods and, 221–22; elitism and, 216–17; enrollment of, 218; founding of, 215–16; Lewis's resignation and, 238–39; People's National Movement and, 219; social sciences and, 214–15; staff salaries and, 215, 222–23; territorial issues and, 218–20, 226; Undergraduate Guild of Students and, 224–25; West Indies Group of University Teachers and, 225; Williams and, 216–22, 226, 237
University of Cambridge, 17, 23, 107
University of Ghana, 146
University of Guyana, 254
University of Liverpool, 37–38
University of London, 216, 226
University of Manchester, 4, 38–39, 72, 146, 214, 254
University of Rochester, 249–50
University of St. Andrews, 215
University of the West Indies, 2–4, 141
U Nu, 167

Valco, 202, 204–5
Venezuela, 26
Vernon, J. W., 134–35
Vietnam War era, 245
Vile, R. J., 135
Village Labourer, The (Hammonds & Hammonds), 92
Viner, Jacob, 98–99, 101
Volta River project, x, 151–54, 164–65, 173; aluminum and, 194–97, 201–2; Black and, 202–3; British Labour government and, 194–95; CPP and, 195; final agreement on, 198; Gbedemah and, 195, 202–3; Kaiser Aluminum and Chemical Corporation and, 201–2; Kennedy and, 203–4; Lewis's methods and, 195–206; national committee for, 197–98; other financial needs and, 199–200; Padmore and, 195–96; plan of, 194; TVA program and, 193, 200–201; World Bank and, 202–3, 205
Vuscovic, P., 187

Walcott, Derek, 12n16
Wallace-Johnson, I.T.A., 34
Wallis, W. Allen, 249

War Office, 48
Watson Commission, 116–17
Wealth of Nations (Smith), 83
Weekes, 187
West Africa journal, 20, 52, 128, 163, 165, 204, 207
West African Students Union, 110
West African Trade (Bauer), 105–6
Western Mail, 52
West Indian Welfare Fund, 45–46
West Indies, ix-x, 2–10, 40, 268, 272, 276–77; Caribbean Development Bank and, 254–56, 266, 269; decolonization and, 212; disappointment of, 213; educational environment of, 10–13; export prices and, 45; free market and, 63–64; Ghanaian sterling reserves and, 155–56; independence for, 212; intellectuals of, 33–34; Irvine Commission and, 215; League of Coloured Peoples and, 3, 34–35, 47–52, 68, 75, 110, 140, 212–26, 244–45; Moyne Commission and, 44–47; nationalism and, 33; political federation of, 226–36; "precocious modernity" of, 13; slavery and, 45; Standing Closer Union Committee and, 228; University College of, 212–26 (*see also* University College of the West Indies); University of Guyana and, 254
West Indies Group of University Teachers, 225

West Indies Royal Commission, 44–47
Whale, P. B., 53
"When the Trustee Becomes a Partner" (Lewis), 74–75
Who's Who, 248
Wicksell Lectures, 257
Wignaraja, P., 186–87
Williams, David, 207
Williams, Eric, 10–14, 33, 143, 235; ideologies of, 245; University College of the West Indies and, 216–22, 226, 237; West Indian federation and, 227, 229–33
Windward Islands, 45
Woodrow Wilson School of Public and International Affairs, 212, 240–44, 253, 255, 265–66, 269
World Bank, 3, 151–52, 273, 275–76; Ghana and, 166, 186–87, 202–3, 205; Volta River project and, 202–3, 205
World War II era, 1–4, 12, 14, 77; British Colonial Office and, 43–44; cocoa prices and, 117; Colonial Economic Development Council and, 67; Gold Coast and, 113–14; imperial relations and, 42–43
Wretched of the Earth, The (Fanon), 14

Yale Economic Growth Center, 253
Yorkshire Post, 52

Zolberg, Aristide, 210